MW01628126

Power, Image, and Memory

Power, Image, and Memory

Historical Subjects in Art

PETER J. HOLLIDAY

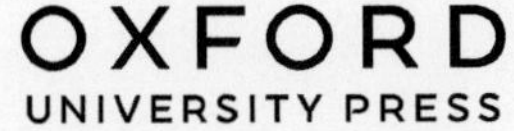
OXFORD UNIVERSITY PRESS

OXFORD
UNIVERSITY PRESS

Oxford University Press is a department of the University of Oxford. It furthers the University's objective of excellence in research, scholarship, and education by publishing worldwide. Oxford is a registered trade mark of Oxford University Press in the UK and certain other countries.

Published in the United States of America by Oxford University Press
198 Madison Avenue, New York, NY 10016, United States of America.

CIP data is on file at the Library of Congress

ISBN 978–0–19–090108–0

DOI: 10.1093/oso/9780190901080.001.0001

Printed by Integrated Books International, United States of America

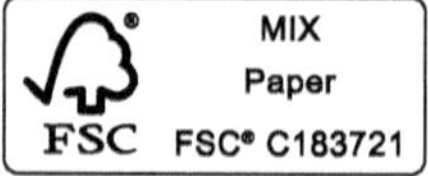

the smallest one was Madeline
Ludwig Bemelmans

Contents

Acknowledgments

In *American Arcadia: California and the Classical Tradition* I explored how Californians as diverse as Spanish conquistadors, Yankee settlers, and postwar suburbanites deployed the classical tradition to fashion their private and public identities. Tradition becomes a matter of dispute when it becomes exclusive, but the "classical" is expansive enough to be construed as a radical challenge to one's contemporary milieu as much as a conservative embracing of it. Those identities were sometimes conflated with the proverbial California Dream, and when those dreamers—as individuals or members of a demographic or social group—jockeyed for power, their dreams collided. The resulting discontent found expression in the bitterness of Raymond Chandler's Philip Marlowe, who in *The Little Sister* grumbled, "I used to like this town" to Joan Didion's acknowledgment in *Where I Was From* that "A good deal about California does not, on its own preferred terms, add up."

This study also explores the shaping of identity. More specifically, it examines the way those holding the power to commission works of art, primarily but not exclusively public monuments, employ historical subject matter to persuade viewers to accept a particular construct of recent events. Those constructs become the stuff of individual and collective memory and play a role in the formation of individual and collective identities. It is a practice with a very long and widespread history—I examine the process in artistic traditions from the earliest civilizations to the modern West—and with consequences that affect contemporary discourse.

During the recent pandemic, closed libraries led me to reach for books on my own shelves I had not read in years. Among them was Millard Meiss's *Painting in Florence and Siena after the Black Death*, a study of Italian art in the aftermath of the plague that arrived in Europe in 1347 (having already devastated Egypt, Syria, Persia, India, and parts of China), which seemed unnervingly appropriate. Meiss incorporated social and political history with close observation and the traditional art history based in methodology learned from the German exiles with whom he studied (whose work also remains vital); knowing that it was written with the memory of his wartime experiences still fresh adds to its substance. A colleague questioned wasting my time on something so outdated and not "engaged with current critical discourse." This is not, I should note, a colleague whose opinion I have sought on this or any other subject. Certainly theory is essential for contemporary practice in art history; I examine some of the critical systems that are important to my subject in the introduction, and bring theory forward in subsequent chapters to the extent that it helps explain the significance of artworks in their diverse social and cultural contexts. And although I employ recent research throughout this study, I also purposely draw on older texts that I believe still have much to offer.

My greatest debt is to my teachers, both undergraduate and graduate, who used some of those texts in opening my eyes to the multiple levels of meaning works of visual art encompass; my memories of those courses continue to affect my current work. It was also first in those classes and then in subsequent years I have been fortunate to develop friendships with art historians, classicists, and colleagues specializing in other areas in the humanities. Many of them generously shared their time and expertise to answer specific questions, point the way to improving the bibliography, and read drafts of the following chapters through their various iterations. For their valuable contributions, I want to thank especially Christopher Baswell, Lawrence L. Berman, Kendall Brown, Eve D'Ambra, Diana Depardo-Minsky, Diane Favro, Karen Kleinfelder, Thomas Michie, Andrew Munro, Mariah Proctor-Tiffany, Patricia Lee Rubin, Fronia W. Simpson, Marc Simpson, Kevin Stayton, and Fikret Yegül. Specific debts to them are indicated throughout the text and notes. The conversations engendered by this project have driven home the privilege of those friendships: those friends sometimes questioned what they read, and I amended my work accordingly, while on other occasions they came to reconsider their views. In addition, through the years I have benefited from provocative questions asked by my students and the challenges they raised when customary explanations failed to satisfy them. Finally, the anonymous readers for Oxford University Press challenged me to expand the scope of this study, both to cast wider and go deeper. Such challenges are rarely fun, but in this case the criticisms and suggestions of those perceptive reviewers enriched my approach to the material, which has certainly enhanced the final study; its readers will certainly profit from them, too.

Open access to works in the public domain has facilitated art historical research and publication immensely. For other works, Lisa Marine expedited my ability to acquire images and permission from the Wisconsin Historical Society, Jenny Greiner facilitated acquiring images from the Chester Beatty Library at Dublin Castle, Susan Allison similarly assisted at the Oriental Institute of the University of Chicago, as did Mark R. Dickerson at the Pitt Rivers Museum, and Esra Müyesseroğlu helped secure images from the Topkapi Palace Museum and permission to publish them from the Republic of Turkey's Directorate of National Palaces Administration. Jeffrey Ryan worked his magic to refine some of my own images that were less than satisfactory. As always, the librarians and exceptional staff at the Getty Research Institute and the Huntington Library, Art Museum, and Botanical Gardens have been enormously helpful, especially during this extraordinary time of pandemic lockdowns. Finally, my editors at Oxford University Press, initially Sarah Humphreville and now Alodie Larson, have offered support and valuable guidance throughout the project; members of their team, including Zara Cannon-Mohammed, Nirenjena Joseph, Thomas Kiefer, Rachel Perkins, and Anne Sanow have helped see this project to completion.

Introduction

History into Art

As America reckons with its legacy of racial injustice, monuments commemorating the Civil War remain a particularly contentious sphere of discourse.[1] The *Cyclorama of the Battle of Atlanta* presents an instructive case. Originally intended as a lucrative attraction, 140 years of promotion, mythmaking, revisionism, distortion, and misinterpretation, largely determined by where the painting was displayed, turned it into what Jack Hitt describes as "a palimpsest of Civil War memory."[2] Cycloramas—massive panorama paintings designed for exhibition in large rotundas—thrilled nineteenth-century audiences with immersive experiences that transported them to other worlds.[3] Several American companies produced panoramas that traveled across the country, just like the carnivals and theatrical troupes of the era. By the 1880s, savvy entrepreneurs recognized that the generation that had fought the Civil War was ready to tell its stories, and audiences wanted to hear them.[4] More crucially, as Caroline E. Janney observes, "the veterans and civilians who survived the four bloody years of war were acutely aware that people were actively shaping who should be remembered—and omitted—from the historical record . . . What individuals and communities elected to tell of the war held enormous potential for staking claims of authority and power."[5]

At Milwaukee's American Panorama Company (APC), William Wehner hired Friedrich Heine to lead seventeen German and Austrian painters in rendering the fateful battle (Fig. I.1). In preparation, the artists (using translators) spoke with Union veterans, traveled to Atlanta to make field studies of the battle site, and there also spoke with Confederate combatants. Back in the studio, Theodore Davis, a war illustrator for *Harper's Weekly* who witnessed the battle, assisted.[6] They settled on a precise time and place to depict: 4:45 p.m. on July 22, 1864, on the railway line just outside Atlanta near the Troup Hurt House, where Union forces had established a battery line. Four Confederate brigades broke through the line and took control of the Union artillery. Almost immediately General John Logan led Union reinforcements in a counterattack and beat back the rebel forces. It was pivotal moment when the battle—and perhaps the war itself—could have gone either way. In the end, however, it was a decisive Union victory that boosted Northern morale, secured Lincoln's reelection that November, and led to the collapse of the Confederacy. It was worthy of commemoration.

Power, Image, and Memory. Peter J. Holliday, Oxford University Press. © Oxford University Press 2024.
DOI: 10.1093/oso/9780190901080.003.0001

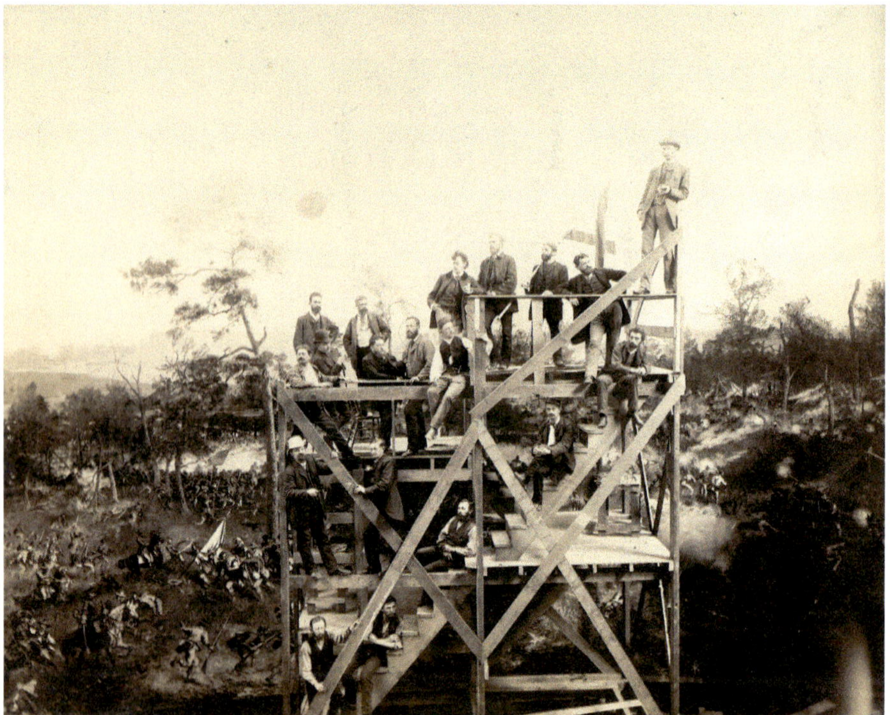

Fig. I.1 Artists of the American Panorama Company, including Friedrich Heine (in pith helmet at far left, second level) in front of the nearly finished *Battle of Atlanta* in their Milwaukee studio on June 6, 1886. Photo: Wisconsin Historical Society, WHS-26071

With portrayals of celebrated Union officers but no recognizable Confederates,[7] the cyclorama was originally designed to appeal to Northern audiences. It opened in Minneapolis in 1886, and successive audiences in Detroit, Indianapolis, and Baltimore marveled at its massive scale: originally 49 by 382 feet in circumference (now 49 × by 371.2 feet, or 13 × by 109 m); they delighted in the accuracy of its detailed uniforms, weaponry, and topography (Fig. I.2). General Sherman claimed it was "the best picture of a battle on exhibition in this country."[8] Nevertheless, facing competition from the new magic lantern shows and other mass entertainments, the owners declared bankruptcy in 1890.

Victory usually confers the power to shape how a conflict is remembered, but at this time the South was attempting to rewrite the war's history. When national cemeteries established by the Union after the Civil War excluded the burial of Confederate soldiers, Ladies' Memorial Associations (LMA) were formed to retrieve the remains of Confederate soldiers and establish Confederate cemeteries, often solemnized with simple markers or cornerstones for future monuments. The Ladies were the elite women of their community, the wives of doctors, lawyers, prominent businessmen, and property owners. Ostensibly interested exclusively in domestic matters, these matriarchs exerted immense influence over customarily

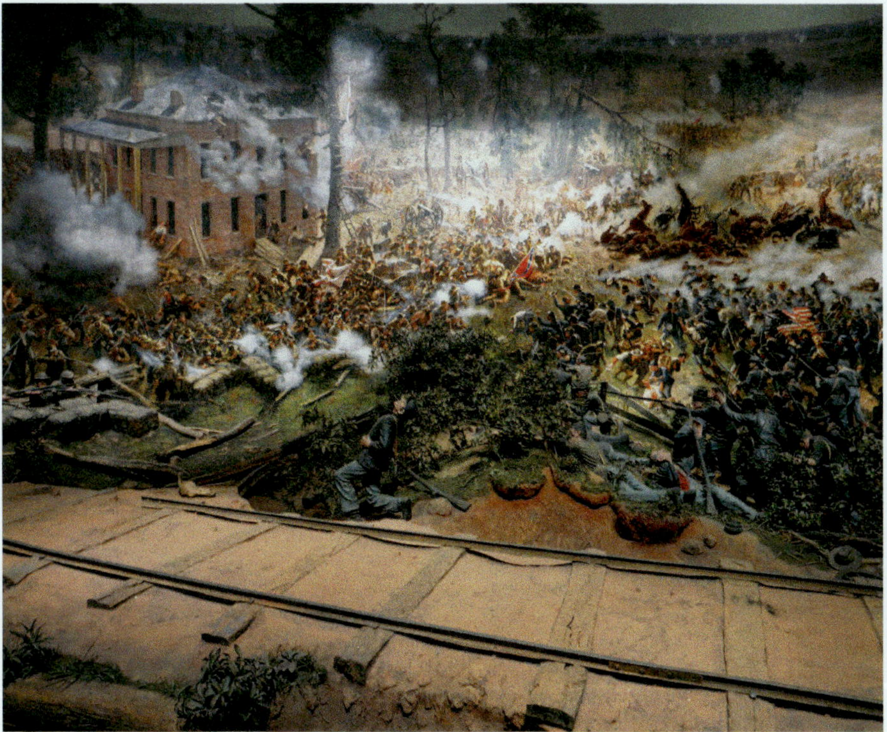

Fig. I.2 *Cyclorama of the Battle of Atlanta*, detail. Atlanta, Atlanta History Center. Photo: Carol M. Highsmith Archive, Library of Congress, Prints and Photographs Division)

male civic prerogatives.[9] In 1894, the newly established United Daughters of the Confederacy (UDC) became the central administering organization for regional LMAs. Its members understood that how people remembered the Civil War would profoundly affect the ability of their families to maintain their inherited entitlement. Consequently, they became instrumental in promoting the "Lost Cause," a conscious effort to substitute slavery's primary causal role with disingenuous Constitutional disagreements over state and federal authority.[10] They helped fabricate the tradition of a gracious white antebellum culture, in which the slave-labor camp of cotton production was reshaped into the magnolia-scented arcadia of the plantation manor, a construct designed to represent the past as self-evident, an ideological strategy to determine not only which past is sanctioned but also how the present finds its own lineage in that past. The UDC successfully secured public and private funding to erect hundreds of Confederate memorials in public spaces from the 1890s through the 1920s—notably the period coinciding with the implementation of Jim Crow laws and the resurgence of the Klan—since "monuments would speak more quickly, impressively, and lastingly to the eye than the written or printed word . . . ([and]) attract more attention."[11] Rather than simply honoring the Southern war dead, these memorials substituted alternative memories in order to sever those "mystic chords of memory" that Lincoln had trusted would bind the wounded nation together.

In 1891, Georgia promoter Paul Atkinson saw fresh potential in the way the cyclorama did not depict the actual outcome of the battle. He purchased and removed it to Atlanta where he recast the impending Northern victory as a Southern triumph by having artisans add nearly a dozen Confederate soldiers, overpaint Union flags with that of the Confederate States, and renovate a cowering group of surrendering Confederate soldiers to portray Yankees fleeing the battle, their fallen Union flag trampled in the mud. When it opened in 1892, Atlanta newspapers hailed the painting as "wonderful, from the mere fact that it is the only one where the Confederates get best of things."[12] By depicting a victory that never happened, the cyclorama was altered to provide propaganda for the Lost Cause narrative and consequently become Atlanta's Confederate monument, a symbol to uphold white supremacy under the pretense of commemorating history.

After Atkinson took a financial hit, the cyclorama passed among several owners, was moved to Grant Park, and was finally donated to the city. In 1922, it was given a new stone building in the park befitting its role as the city's Confederate shrine but had to be cut down to fit. The renovation was marked with Lost Cause celebrations coordinated by the UDC, Sons of Confederate Veterans, and veterans themselves.[13] Nevertheless, the cyclorama suffered from neglect until the Works Progress Administration funded a restoration under the direction of Atlanta painter Wilbur G. Kurtz, which included new lighting and the addition of 128 plaster figures to a three-dimensional diorama in front of the painting, heightening its illusionism for audiences now used to the spectacle of Hollywood movies (Fig. I.3); a display of additional pictures and artifacts underscored its Lost Cause message.[14] In 1937, Mayor William B. Hartsfield led a group that sought to divorce the cyclorama from the Lost Cause to fit their progressive vision of a new city driven by commerce: "It must be remembered that this picture is not a shrine or a memorial. It was painted purely for exhibition purposes, not to be worshipped or venerated as a relic, but as a vivid portrayal of the Battle of Atlanta."[15] The hoopla attending the 1939 Atlanta premier of "Gone with the Wind" upended their efforts, however, ensuring the cyclorama remained a monument to the Confederacy.

In the 1970s, white suburbanites pushed to have the cyclorama moved again to become part of a neo-Confederate mega-shrine at Stone Mountain. Maynard Jackson, the first African-American mayor of Atlanta, intervened to free the cyclorama from Confederate myths and reclaim it for an Atlanta reshaped by the civil rights movement: "The Cyclorama depicts the Battle of Atlanta, a battle that the right side won, a battle that helped free my ancestors . . . I'm going to make sure that that depiction of the battle is saved."[16] Finally in 2019, a newly restored cyclorama opened with a New South perspective at the Atlanta History Center in suburban Buckhead. Using documentation for the original APC project, Lincoln Stone and half a dozen other artists recreated missing sections of the painting, restored the fleeing Yankees to Confederate prisoners, and repaired the diorama foreground.

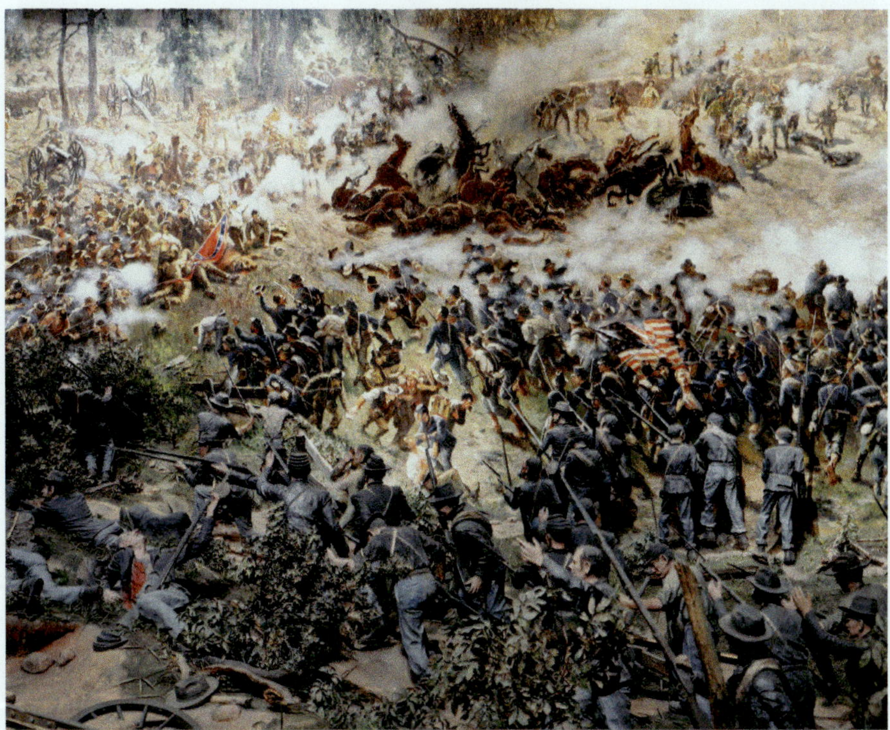

Fig. I.3 *Cyclorama of the Battle of Atlanta*, detail showing foreground diorama figures. Atlanta, Atlanta History Center. Photo: Carol M. Highsmith Archive, Library of Congress, Prints and Photographs Division)

The new installation transforms the cyclorama from an attraction to an artifact—no longer a monument effecting Atlantans' collective memory, but rather a meticulous explanation of how this work was revised to reflect fluctuating understandings of the past, a changing history of Southern identity.[17]

Collective Memory

The story of the Atlanta Cyclorama—even as condensed here—demonstrates how divisive the process of historical reckoning can be, particularly when provoked by shifts in power and the conflicting collective memories of diverse communities. The French sociologist Maurice Halbwachs first developed the concept of collective memory (also sometimes called social memory) as "a reconstruction of the past in light of the present."[18] Although only individuals remember, Halbwachs argued that when individuals call up thoughts about past events, their understanding of them conforms to the customs, tastes, beliefs, and interests of the social groups and institutions (families, organizations, and nation-states) to which they belong: the network of their social and cultural conditions. Consequently, while intrinsically private, memory is also collective in that its frame of reference is the larger social context.

Crucially, Halbwachs's construct assumes an instrumental presentism, that is, it asserts that present issues and understandings influence social interpretations of the past.[19] In this way groups—families, organizations, nations—select different memories to explain current problems and justify courses of action. Halbwachs further argued that collective memories acquire a prestige and sense of certainty seemingly steeped in reality; they hold the power to unite communities over space and time, to create and stabilize political power structures, and to cement identities. When group leaders reconstruct a past in order to explain the present, they determine which events are remembered, which are eliminated, and rearrange them to conform to the required social narrative. David Rieff argues that history derives its meaning from the way individuals "order their experience of it and their aspirations for how it might be ordered in the present and in the future, thus infusing it with significance and passing it along to posterity."[20] Collective memory thereby becomes an essential vehicle for constructing and affirming a group's cohesive collective identity.

Aby Warburg's interdisciplinary study of culture laid the foundations for examining the role material objects play in shaping cultural memory. His treatment of images ("cultural objectivations") as carriers of memory suggest how monuments like the cyclorama are implicit forms of collective memory that put forward a particular narrative of the past to reflect the perspectives of those in power during the commemorative process.[21] Their display in open, shared spaces provides visible manifestations of collective memories. More than merely passive reflections, these monuments reinforce those memories and, by conferring them prestige, impact even those who do not share those memories. Monuments even have the potential to become the memory themselves,[22] which helps explain why calls for their removal can be so threatening: such calls can be understood as an attack on one's identity itself.

Historical Subjects as Propaganda

Patrick Geary asserts that "the study of historical memory is a study of propaganda, of the decisions about what should be remembered and how it should be remembered."[23] In its strictest sense, forms of propaganda are officially devised and centrally controlled to disseminate messages that celebrate and advertise power. Throughout this study I use the term more conventionally, mindful that although of Latin derivation, it is actually of relatively modern origin.[24] It would be anachronistic to consider some artworks with historical subjects examined here as centrally conceived by some ministry of information; rather, they are propagandistic in that they foster a supremely favorable conception of those responsible for their creation, publicizing them in the most conspicuous manner, testimonials in themselves to their power or authority; they are material signs of their wealth and pervasive influence, and sometimes demonstrations of their utter capacity for shaping the physical environment at will.

This book examines how those holding power over commemorative decisions engaged artists to represent historical subjects to communicate, reinforce, or sometimes even subvert authority. The artworks were used as instruments operating within society to achieve particular ends: specifically, to embody and reinforce ideological assumptions about that society. A characteristic shared by historical representations is the emphasis they purport to give to the veracity of their narratives; as will be seen, makers employ numerous techniques to assure the viewer of their authenticity. Nevertheless, the primary purpose of representations of historical subjects is not to document events, but to commemorate them. As demonstrated by the cyclorama's various adaptations, that commemorative function can skew the narrative by celebrating the achievement of certain figures at the expense of others. Partisan viewers will applaud the results, while opponents will respond very differently.

I explore here how artworks functioned as propaganda to shape memories of specific events, and how those memories were sometimes deployed to affirm collective identities to mold social groups and even nations. Because victory in war cements pride in national identity and images of triumph underscore regime legitimacy by demonstrating effective leadership, battle scenes come forward as a central theme. Such commemorations helped engender what Michel Foucault called a "politics of truth": the construction and attempted control of reality. How were such works produced and displayed to ensure they would affect audiences in the desired way? Is it possible to reconstruct and interpret the meaning works had for their makers and viewers? In order to begin answering these questions, it is necessary to clarify additional terms and set boundaries.

What Constitutes Historical Subjects?

Trained as an historian of classical art and archaeology, I work regularly with monuments designated "Roman historical relief sculpture."[25] According to the conventions defining that category, a work is called historical by reason of its subject matter, that is, by the content of its visual imagery and how that imagery is interpreted. Historical subjects draw inspiration from and celebrate past and present events important to the community; representations, therefore, are usually distinctive and clearly recognizable to contemporary viewers. Toward that end, historical subjects generally feature identifiable protagonists, sometimes distinguished by portraiture, carefully rendered details, and inscriptions, and often placed in specific landscape settings. Specificity, combined with commemorative intent, differentiates historical subjects from scenes conceived generically or drawn from daily life. Finally, in celebrating happenings meaningful to those holding power, historical works often feature a narrative character to describe dynastic, civil, military, and other events through recurring compositional types, such as victories and scenes of sacred ritual. Although these criteria, largely drawn from the study of ancient Roman art, provide a starting point for discussion and have guided the initial selection of artworks for examination here, the desire to find works from a variety of other cultures that also employed historical subjects obliges that these delineations will be modified and expanded.

Distinguishing Historical Subjects from History Painting

Historical subjects and history painting are not synonymous, although for several centuries in the West they overlapped and intersected. History painting is a genre in painting that is also classified by its subject matter (rather than artistic style) and comprises large works produced between the Renaissance and the late nineteenth century. Both "history" and "historical" are derived from the Latin word *historia* (inquiry) through the wider senses of the Italian *istoria* (story or narrative), emphasizing the genre's narrative quality. Narrative is a more inclusive category than history as we generally understand it, however, embracing stories from mythology, legend and folklore, religious accounts, and allegorical and genre scenes. In fact, most scenes portrayed in history painting are not historical subjects, that is, they do not represent events from history.

The divergence was present from the start. In his 1564 treatise *Dialogue on the Errors and Abuses of Painters*, Giovanni Andrea Giglio da Fabriano argued that Michelangelo's *Last Judgment* could not be considered history painting—an *istoria*—since it takes place in the future, not in the past.[26] Some writers sought to distinguish between *istoria* (which included biblical and religious incidents), and *fabula*, comprising pagan myth, allegory, and incidents from fiction, which could not be viewed as factual. These problems in classification remained unsettled two centuries later when Sir Joshua Reynolds, in his *Discourses on Art*, a series of lectures presented at the English Royal Academy of Arts from 1769 to 1790, proposed clarifying the division by introducing the term "poetical painting" (*poesia*).[27]

In his 1435 treatise, *De pictura* (On Painting), Leon Battista Alberti defined *istoria* as paintings based on classical or religious texts, but not necessarily history.[28] Their purpose was to instruct people through the moral lessons to be drawn from what happened, a Renaissance echo of Livy's use of didactic *exempla* in his history of early Rome. This emphasis rendered history painting subject to rules of *decorum* or appropriateness; artists idealized their figures, elevating them from the everyday in costume and posture. Alberti stressed the depiction of the interactions between the figures through gesture and expression.[29] He maintained that its very difficulty rendered multifigure history painting the noblest form of art and that with the greatest ability to affect the viewer. Many of these ideas had a wide circulation and were complicated in their development; nevertheless, Alberti's treatise, even if more symptom than cause, provides a convenient point of reference.

In subsequent generations, this notion of history painting was promoted by European art academies. Charles Le Brun, court painter to Louis XIV and driving force behind the establishment of the French *Académie Royale de Peinture et de Sculpture* (Royal Academy of Painting and Sculpture), advocated images that relayed complex stories.[30] Academic promotion of history painting corresponded with a formalized hierarchy of genres that ranked different subjects in terms of their esteem and edifying value, distinguishing, in descending order, between history painting (including religious, mythological, and allegorical subjects), portraiture, scenes of everyday life, landscape, animal painting, and still life.

The rise of nationalism in the modern era generated an interest in depicting dramatic moments from recent or contemporary history in the form of history painting (with a corresponding decline in religious and mythological subjects).[31] The promotion of nationalist ideology through the academic genre facilitated the confusion of history painting with historical subjects. (This phenomenon will be examined in later chapters.) As the nineteenth century progressed, however, tastes changed, driven largely by shifts in patronage and audience preferences. As artistic movements began to defy the authority of academic art, the previous moral and ethical purposes of art gave way to pleasure, and history painting lost its place in the increasingly obsolete hierarchies. By the late nineteenth century, adherents of avant-garde movements often explicitly rejected history painting.

Finally, another development in the nineteenth century was the popularity of "historical painting" as a distinct subgenre of history painting, in which subjects taken from secular history, whether specific incidents or generalized events, were treated as scenes of everyday life (genre scenes). The Troubadour style, for example, depicted anecdotal scenes from the lives of the great or unnamed figures participating in historical (particularly medieval) events. Modern writers tend to avoid the phrase "historical painting" to avoid potential confusion. This muddled terminology rarely affects discussions of artworks produced in other periods and by non-Western cultures, hence my use here of "historical subjects" or "historical subject matter" to refer to the depiction of historical events.

Narrative Structures and Emplotment

Historical subjects in the visual arts carry with them from the etymological origins of the term *istoria* not only the sense of history but also of a story or narrative, which Alberti associated with the persuasive powers of classical rhetoric to "move the soul of the beholder,"[32] an important strategy to lend visual representations prestige and a sense of reality. Hayden White argues that all history writing requires a narrative structure or "emplotment." He suggests that, like a novelist, the historian employs literary devices to order events so that they make sense and persuade the reader that the narrative being told is plausible and coherent. "The very distinction between real and imaginary events, basic to modern discussions of both history and fiction, presupposes a notion of reality in which 'the true' is identified with 'the real' only insofar as it can be shown to possess the character of narrativity."[33] As Halbwachs argued, it is that sense of reality that bestows collective memory with its authority. A visual representation's ability to mold effectively a community's memory of an historical event depends on the ability of viewers to apprehend clearly the story depicted. Its narrative has to make sense. Therefore, visual artists deploy compositional techniques analogous to the literary devices used by word-based historians.

Narrative—story, *istoria*—occurs in space and unfolds in time. A work may represent a moment drawn from a continuing account or a sequence of actions occurring over time. Some works therefore show a climactic moment or turning point in the story that reveals the character of the protagonist, while others portray the story with multiple episodes. Narrative art can be categorized by distinct compositional or structural types, which constitute its emploting devices.[34] Monoscenic narrative represents an action in a single scene. In contrast, continuous narrative represents multiple scenes from a story against a unified background but within a single frame, and synoptic narrative shows a single scene in which a protagonist or protagonists are portrayed several times within a frame to establish that several distinct episodes are being depicted.[35] A sequential narrative differs from a continuous narrative through its use of enframement to describe the passage of time; each scene and action is depicted as a particular moment within its own frame as a unit. (Many illuminated manuscripts use sequential narrative, as do modern comics.) Panoptic narrative shows multiple scenes and actions without protagonists reappearing; those actions may occur either sequentially or simultaneously during an event (as in the cyclorama). Finally, a progressive narrative depicts a single scene in which protagonists do not recur; however, multiple actions take place in order to establish temporal progression. A progressive narrative should not be construed as a group of simultaneous events but rather a sequence that is contingent on its setting.

An artwork may have one type of narrative as a whole or employ other types of narrative as well in different places. In this manner the front panels of Duccio's *Maestà* make up a large Madonna and Child adored by saints and angels; the predella panels and forty-three panels on the rear employ diverse narrative types to depict the lives of the Virgin and Christ, which when combined can be read as a sequential narrative (Fig. I.4).[36] One criterion for choosing the historical subjects examined in this study, then, has been to feature works that use different compositional strategies to emplot their visual narratives; some of them represent notable innovations, which sometimes endured to become conventional.

Although establishing the precise meaning of specific figures or scenes in works from the remote past can present difficulties, given the distance in time from their original cultural contexts, the narratives examined here all purport to

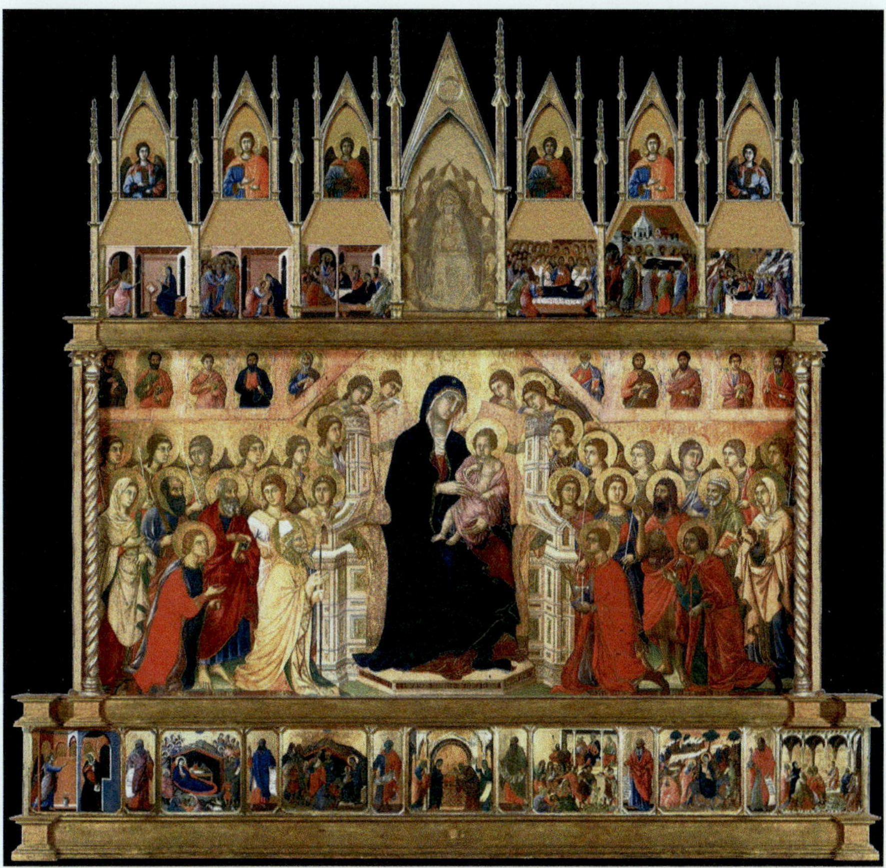

Fig. I.4 Duccio di Buoninsegna, *Maestà* (1308–1311). Siena, Museo dell'Opera Metropolitana del Duomo. Photo: Wikimedia Commons

represent actual (that is, historical) events, not religious or mythological stories. Even though there can be slippage between the representation of historical and nonhistorical events in visual artworks (as is also found in the various literary forms of history and fiction), this does not detract from the ability of historical narratives to provide some kind of knowledge about the past. The question becomes "what kind of knowledge?" Every representation of the past carries specific ideological implications. Again, Hayden White: "The issue of ideology points to the fact that there is no value-neutral mode of emplotment, explanation, or even description of any field of events, whether imaginary or real, and suggests that the very use of language itself implies or entails a specific position before the world which is ethical, ideological or more generally political."[37] Correspondingly, when those holding power over commemorative decisions erect monuments representing historical subjects, those subjects are invariably rendered to promote an ideology, to sway public opinion, and sometimes to suppress dissenting voices and consolidate power, especially when displayed in public spaces.

The Production and Reception of Historical Subjects

Who is responsible for how an artwork represents a historical subject—how it comes to demonstrate a concise expression of its action and meaning that transforms it into a strong and memorable image—is not always transparent. At first glance, the artist of a visual narrative appears to be both playwright and director. As in theater, the scene in the story must be carefully staged, with the setting, scenery, props, and lighting composed for effect and coherence; the actors must be placed within the set for visibility, choreographed to advance the action cogently, and coached in their expressive body language. There is no dialogue, however: the actors remain mute (works with inscriptions or accompanying texts examined in this study provide important exceptions). Artists seem to choose how to portray the story *visually* in narrative art, to choose which narrative structure to represent space and shape time. Their vantage point becomes our vantage point and profoundly conditions our experience.

Artists, however, rarely work in isolation, especially when works are created for commemorative purposes: commissioning patrons frequently intervene to ensure that the vantage point conveys the story in a way that corresponds with their requirements. Although Friedrich Heine and his crew painted the original cyclorama canvas, they did so for Wehner and APC; they were further assisted by carpenters, crane operators, plasterers, and other fabricators. The various artists who recast the work for Atkinson and those who restored it under Kurtz and later Stone—again assisted by numerous technicians—are also responsible for its appearance. "Authorship" is thus shared between the artist(s) and the patron(s); the role is no longer conceived of as an autonomous creator but as a mediator in a communicative chain between collective cultural concepts and anticipated audiences.[38]

The sociologist Howard Becker suggests a model in which art production is understood as a "collective action." He proposes that a work of art is made through the coordination of many individuals and distinct social groups: "art worlds" that attend "complex cooperative networks" of production and consumption.[39] An artwork comes about when these different groups undertake specific sets of responsibilities to negotiate its form, materials, and abstractions: what he terms conventions. Conventions in the sense of the material composition of an artwork will be discussed below; here I want to emphasize Becker's insight into convention designating the social meeting that brings together different groups sharing a common interest in effecting the artwork. Conventions in this sense "regulate the relations between artists and audiences, specifying the rights and obligations of both,"[40] and along these lines relate to the agreements or rules establishing the place and meaning of art in society. The primary referent of the image, however, is the viewer, for it is only through the act of viewing that the artwork is engendered with meaning. The viewer is not a passive observer; instead, the work must arouse an active response. Ideally, from the perspective of the producers, this response will cause the viewer to endorse their agenda and engage additional participants, for the meanings of artworks are not only visually perceived by viewers in isolation but also interpreted and discussed with others.

Consequently, Becker stresses the role shared meaning plays in attributing significance to art; it is nearly impossible for a work to have any social resonance without a common understanding of a work's significance. By using the language and the visual customs and practices of their society and period, communities of makers display their individual intentions within a structure of inherited collective modes of perception, thought, and expression. Alfred Gell states that "the nature of the art object is a function of the social-relational matrix in which it is embedded,"[41] that is, a consequence and a purpose of the social and political context that gave rise to it. As noted, patrons—which following the expansive definition here also includes those who act as agents on behalf of ruling elites—produce commemorative works featuring historical subjects to shape what is remembered and how it is remembered. These works represent "systems of action, intended to change the world."[42] They do not merely mirror society, they are implicated in it.

According to Becker's model, the cyclorama is the product of a community of makers that collaborated to determine its appearance and positioning: these included not only designers, painters, and other fabricators but also the diverse entrepreneurs and promoters who exploited its commercial power, the philanthropists and bureaucrats who oversaw its relocation first to Grant Park and then the Atlanta History Center, and all the politicians and propagandists who manipulated its meaning. When groups deploy artworks representing historical subjects in public spaces, the commemorative imperative is such that the portrayed person or event embodies an essential component in an authoritative or official narrative. Public monuments transform private and internalized responses into a collective moral purpose, insofar as they are shared communally. The absence of events that cause a community shame, such as loss in war, demonstrates society's attempt to eliminate them from the collective memory, or as with the cyclorama, rectify them in the narrative. When power shifts occur that allow the expression of differing experiences and perspectives, then social ruptures allow heterogeneous, conflicting memory communities the opportunity to express themselves. This is what has happened with Confederate monuments.

The Sources for Visual Representations of Historical Subjects

The makers of visual representations of historical subjects control their intention and significance. They select from certain sources to communicate a particular political meaning, to indicate who, both politically and culturally, is in charge, and to legitimize or convey other messages about the elite's rule. Those sources are of two kinds: texts and artistic traditions. A text might be just that, a memoir written by a participant in the event, the account of a writer who recorded the memories of others, or the testimony of contemporary witnesses (perhaps even the artist).

Artists may sift through conflicting oral accounts including soldiers' stories, and even rumor and gossip. Materials like court proceedings, contracts, and treaties constitute different kinds of texts, as do preserved relics and artefacts, and maps, drawings, and other artworks, reference to which can help a visual representation establish the sense of reality that heightens its authority. How the information drawn from these accounts is conveyed visually—what form the representation takes—is a crucial component in the negotiation put forward by Becker.

Artistic tradition takes into consideration conventions in the more specialized art historical sense, that is, the practices governing the material composition of artworks, such as the choice of medium, the handling of materials, and visual references to other works of art; these are generally referred to as aesthetic or stylistic conventions, which also extend to established ways of representing things, generally recognized by artists and patrons at a specific time and place. Aesthetic conventions, contemporary with a work's production, represent the tradition by which the groups involved in that production authoritatively locate themselves in their present by determining that such authority comes from an historically privileged continuity. A classic study of representational conventions (emphasizing the psychology of perception) is Ernst Gombrich's *Art and Illusion*.[43] Visual artists play with the ambiguities of vision perception and establish conventions differing from everyday perception to resolve them through composition, three-dimensional layout and spatial scale, light and color, shape, and movement. By framing them as inherited schemata—formal motifs—Gombrich emphasized representational conventions as an emergent process in his art history.[44] Although aspects of his model have been rightly challenged, his identification of representational conventions as a method to make visual imagery comprehensible to contemporary viewers, and his research into how their implementation can take precedence over accuracy, complement Becker's social dynamic and remain highly useful to the topic at hand.[45]

Artistic tradition is not something simply copied from its models, but is transformed by its use in a new context. It is a rhetoric of identity shared by the parties that negotiate the production of an artwork, an expressive construct that presents the past as self-evident and regulates claims about meaning and belonging. It is a factor contributing to the cultural context, what Pierre Bourdieu terms the cultural *habitus*—the way individuals and societies perceive and react to the world based on their particular background—an interesting way to think about traditions, history, and identity. Bourdieu describes this ethos or *mentalité* as an artifact of history that "produces individual and collective practices—more history—in accordance with the schemes generated by history. It ensures the active presence of past experiences, which deposited in each organism in the form of schemes of perception, thought and action, tend to guarantee the 'correctness' of practices and their constancy over time more reliably than all formal rules and explicit norms."[46]

Art historians also work within traditions when they construct histories that locate an artwork in some temporal and geographic continuity (such as early Italian

Renaissance or Nigeria's Edo period), further refined by medium and other criteria, in order to evaluate it, to reconstruct the conventions contemporary with its production, and understand its system of signs. The exercise is therefore somewhat reflexive (as with the characteristics attributed to Roman historical relief sculpture above). When art historians write their narratives they contribute to an academic tradition that is complex and sometimes contentious, for each narrative, including this one, is conditioned by contemporary priorities and is the expression, conscious or not, of a cultural ideology writing its own history. It is provisional and can only tell a partial story.

Structure and Scope of this Study

The following chapters, proceeding generally chronologically, provide a series of case studies, the aim of which is to shed light on a broad range of cultural formations from throughout the history of art.[47] Uniquely among various modes of communication, visual images—especially those operating within figurative traditions, as is the case with the works examined in this study—concretely embody what they mean. (The cultural context in which some works once operated was such that they can also be said to *be*, in a sense, what they mean.) Figural art is basically mimetic and for historical subjects is understood to reproduce some experienced reality.

Many readers will be familiar already with the monuments in this study from standard art history survey texts where they are put forward as exemplary products of their cultures. The historical events they commemorate usually play only a minor role in those accounts, but here they are of crucial importance. The event is the artwork's subject matter—the experienced reality it reproduces—that was chosen to affirm ideas of power relationships and social hierarchy, while exercising power itself over the minds of receptive viewers. Since it is essential that their factual subject matter be identified precisely in order to construe how these images functioned within their originating cultures, I will pay particular attention first to the historical event the work commemorates and then examine the figures, actions, and other details it represents.[48] When the evidence permits, I also examine the reasons patrons and makers might have chosen a particular event for commemoration.[49]

Contemporary viewers' interpretation of a work's meaning is realized in keeping with their collective cultural concepts, with dominant social structures and values, political circumstances, religious and cultural premises, and collective mentalities. The makers convey, through a system of contemporary visual signs and cultural codes (which often have an abstract relationship to their meaning), a meaning particular to the subject for those viewers, which when construed influence how that subject is apprehended and remembered. When the viewer comes from a different time and place and does not share those cultural concepts, it is necessary to reconstruct them and to decipher the signs and codes within the work; this is a task for the art historian. The reconstruction of factual meaning and what a work meant within its own cultural sphere depends on the well-established three-stage theoretical system developed by Aby Warburg and Erwin Panofsky, by which analysis follows from the identification of subjects to the recognition of culturally marked meanings, and finally to understanding an artwork as the expression of perceptions and attitudes of societies and historical periods.[50]

That approach, however, has also been criticized for its positivism and for singling out one essential, dominant meaning embedded in a work recognized by some ideal contemporary viewer; nor does it recognize different, unfixed meanings.[51] After its making, the act of viewing by all its viewers throughout time—a chain of reception that also includes art historians and their narratives about the work—engender an artwork with fresh meaning. I therefore also draw upon semiotic approaches to open up the system and allow for diverging interpretations by viewers of different cultural frameworks.[52] In addition, comparisons here with other, related works from the same period provide a broader footing for analysis that demonstrates how these monuments not only characterize their cultures, but also facilitate our understanding of what was added, borrowed, or altered to the artistic traditions then current to enhance a work's commemorative function.

Finally, particular historical subjects were chosen in their cultural contexts not merely as reflections of social values but as agents in social interaction. The question is not only what images mean but how they are used, and what they do. This requires investigating not only the images as such but also the social practices of erecting and using them. Historical commemorations play a role in the negotiation of political and social power. I therefore explore viewing as a response to the formal effects of these works as a practice of social relevance. The makers of Confederate monuments may have sought to stir pride in a (contrived) shared past with viewers in their community, but we can no longer deny the very real experience of other viewers who interpreted the monuments quite differently: as admonitions to "remember your place," as memorials to oppression, fear, and hatred through a cultural ideology that was rarely voiced more than a century ago when the monuments were erected.

This is the first work that undertakes a broad examination of historical commemorations across temporal and geographic boundaries.[53] A global scope comparing and contrasting different cultural practices helps demonstrate how particular decisions operated within a range of diverse synchronic and diachronic possibilities, and may help redress a surging backlash found in some circles against globalization and opposition to openness and connection. A close reading of these artworks, which are rhetorical constructs of their contemporary worlds, demonstrates how their imagery helped individuals and groups shape their apprehension of those worlds. The choice of monuments may strike some readers as idiosyncratic, but it is hardly arbitrary. My goal is not to privilege one set of monuments or artistic practices over others. As scholarship grows increasingly narrow, it is my hope that an investigation like this one, which is necessarily synthetic, will suggest to specialists what can be done when they use what they know about their own areas of expertise to ask questions about others. This process encourages what Joan Didion calls "taking a long view," here of an artwork's place in history, a practice that promises a more profound comprehension of the work's layered significance.

1

The Victory Stele of Naram-Sîn

The Genesis of a Commemorative Tradition

Between 4000 and 3000 BCE, the first known cities were established on the expansive plains between the Tigris and Euphrates rivers, called by ancient Greeks Mesopotamia ("the land between the two rivers"), now in Iraq. Within these walled enclaves the sacred sites and rituals of institutionalized religion facilitated social organization under dominant elites, of which the officiating priesthoods were a fundamental component. The alluvial plains that generated Mesopotamia's agricultural wealth also left the country with few natural defenses and thus vulnerable to political upheaval. Over the centuries, regional dominance passed successively to cultures that amassed ever-larger empires, including the Sumerians, Akkadians, Babylonians, Assyrians, and ultimately Achaemenid Persians.[1]

Here writing was invented, initially for record-keeping, but this system of two-dimensional symbols representing both physical reality and abstract concepts eventually came to alter peoples' perceptions of the world and their position in it.[2] The Mesopotamians developed architecture as another representational medium, one altering peoples' relationship to space,[3] and that ultimately inspired them to identify as citizens.[4] Artists explored new conceptions of representational processes and monumentality in sculpture and refined craftsmanship along aesthetic lines when fashioning both cult statues representing gods and votives offered to them.[5] Mesopotamian elites celebrated their achievements with the invention of the public monument; some featured standardized pictorial compositions showing religious rituals or royal ceremonies, whereas others were intended to commemorate actual events. These iconographies, with the image of the ruler depicted as a hunter, warrior, or priest, were adapted to diverse media, sculpted in the round and in relief, larger than life, and in seal images.[6] The most common form was the stele, a freestanding slab of stone (usually limestone, basalt, or diorite) displayed in a temple court, an urban public space, and even at a significant rural site. Artists first introduced narrative images to steles, whose inscriptions made clear that they were meant to stand for eternity.

Power, Image, and Memory. Peter J. Holliday, Oxford University Press. © Oxford University Press 2024.
DOI: 10.1093/oso/9780190901080.003.0002

The First Historical Commemorations

The commemorative stele first appears in the history of art with a carved relief dated to ca. 3200 BCE (Fig. 1.1). Found in the Eanna sanctuary at Warka (ancient Uruk), it represents a lion hunt. A male figure wears a long skirt with a vertical crease at the center secured by a wide belt (or girdle); his torso and feet remain bare. His distinctive hairstyle—drawn back into a chignon or twisted knot—and long beard characterize him as a priest-king. He is shown twice on the relief: smaller at the top of the stele where he impales a lion with a long spear, and slightly larger below, aiming his arrow at one of two threatening lions. The depiction of the same figure in two

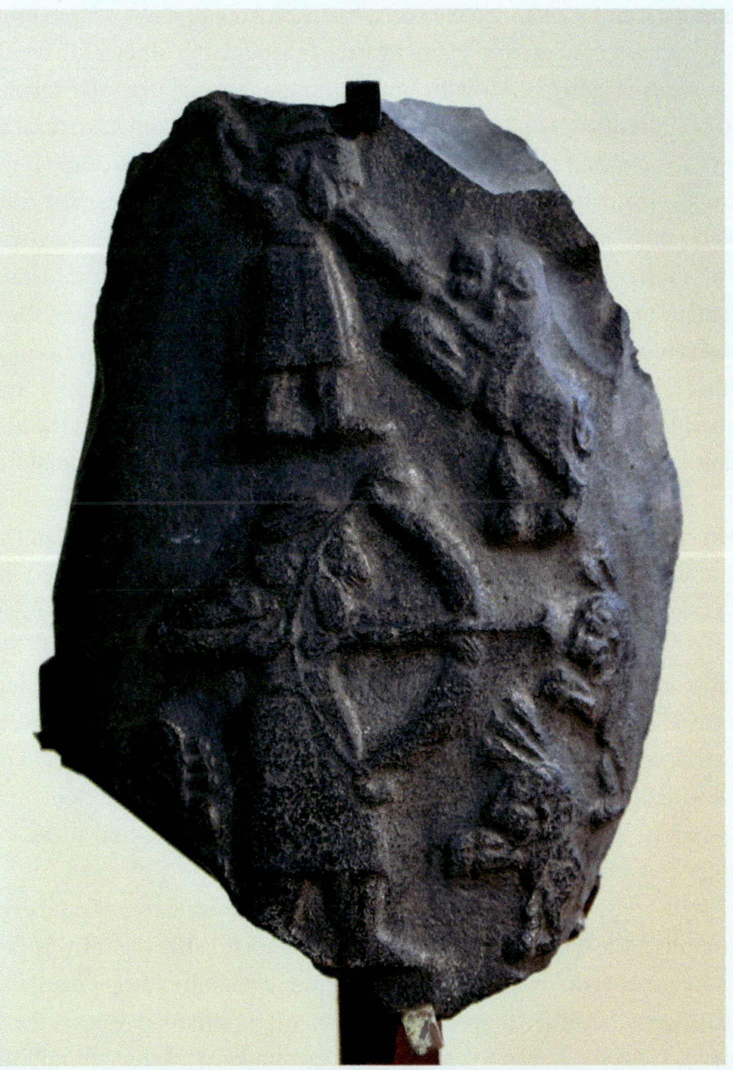

Fig. 1.1 Stele of a Lion Hunt from Warka (ca. 3200 BCE). Baghdad, Iraq Museum. Photo: Osama Shukir Muhammed Amin for Wikimedia Commons

separate episodes on the same pictorial field, indicating two separate activities in two successive moments in time, makes this one of the earliest attempts at continuous or sequential pictorial narrative representation, a Mesopotamian innovation that will be fully developed in the Neo-Assyrian period.[7]

To modern eyes a lion hunt hardly seems deserving of monumental commemoration. Henri Frankfort suggested that in early Mesopotamia the encounter with wild beasts represented a phase in the reclamation of untamed marsh and wasteland indispensable to the development of the city-state, so that the valor of this leader deserved to be celebrated.[8] In pre- and early modern societies the theme of the successful hunt also provided a metonym for military victory: the weapons the hunter brandishes are the same as those of war and are thus emblems of authority. Hunting scenes from the palaces of Nineveh and Nimrud represent the prowess of later Neo-Assyrian kings, and Alexander the Great and Roman emperors adapted the theme in works that were emulated still later by rulers through the nineteenth century. The Warka stone is roughly hewn with no attempt at shaping a regular form. Zainab Bahrani proposes that it operated as a living rock removed from its natural environment into the city, but transformed by having been carved with graphic imagery.[9] By taking the stone from its rural setting and bringing it into an urban context the material becomes a vital part of the message: the priest-king brings the city security and civilization by subduing the anarchic forces of the outside world. Although we know that in later times similar monuments were placed in public view, the original location for this stele remains uncertain.

Urnanshe, the "divine bailiff of Lagash," commemorated a ritual associated temple building with a limestone plaque (Fig. 1.2).[10] At the upper left the king bears a workbasket of mud on his head to mould and then lay the ceremonial first brick for a new temple for the god Ningirsu at Girsu. His children, each identified by an inscribed name, stand before him in a row to witness the ceremony. In the right-hand bottom corner Urnanshe celebrates the completed temple. Seated, he raises a cup in celebration; a cupbearer, snake charmer, and three more sons (again each with identifying inscription) attend him. The scenes recall the *Epic of Gilgamesh*, Mesopotamia's great contribution to world literature.[11] Gilgamesh, a legendary king of Uruk, sought immortality and ultimately found it through architecture and the construction of cities. He learned that monumental structures made of bricks stamped with his name—"where the names of famous men are written"—provided the passport to immortality, a guarantee that a king's name and memory of his achievements would live forever.[12]

The plaque comprises a visual narrative commemorating two related events: the inauguration of the temple and its dedication. The artist has inventively fashioned both a monument and a tablet, recounting the events in complementary image and text. As will become the practice in later Mesopotamian works, the inscription spreads from the image to cover all background spaces that are not otherwise sculpted with a representation. Denise Schmandt-Besserat has demonstrated the impact the conventions of writing, including its linear organization and semantic

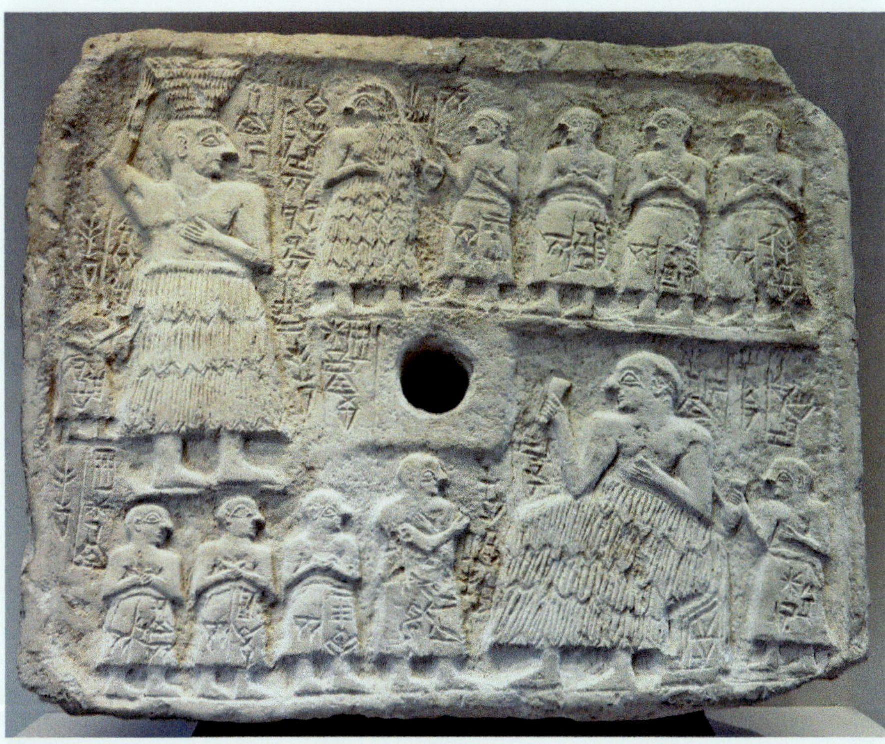

Fig. 1.2 Relief of Urnanshe (2550–2500 BCE). Paris, Musée du Louvre. Photo: Marie-Lan Nguyen for Wikimedia Commons

application of form, size, and order had on the making of artworks enabling the presentation of complex visual narratives in place of the recurring motifs found in preliterate art.[13] Art historians call this type of artwork an image-text dialectic, in which both image and text construct its meaning.[14] The plaque also demonstrates Mesopotamian advances in carving, with the details of the figures now modeled, rather than merely engraved. The perforation in the center allowed it to be attached to the interior wall of a temple by means of a stone or clay peg, perhaps finished with an ornamental head.[15]

Frequent wars between city-states ensured that military success developed into the dominant commemorative theme on public monuments. None has survived complete, but conservators have assembled several fragments found in the 1880s to reconstruct a flat stele with semicircular top, totally carved on both sides (Fig. 1.3). Popularly known as the Stele of the Vultures, it once stood six feet high and is the earliest surviving monument commemorating a known historical event.[16] It was erected by Eannatum of Lagash to commemorate his victory over the neighboring city-state of Umma. During a long-standing border dispute, the people of Umma wrecked a boundary stone ritually set up by a previous king and occupied fields belonging to Lagash. One side of the stele chronicles the ensuing historical events. The upper register of the stele shows Eannatum as a warrior king, wielding a

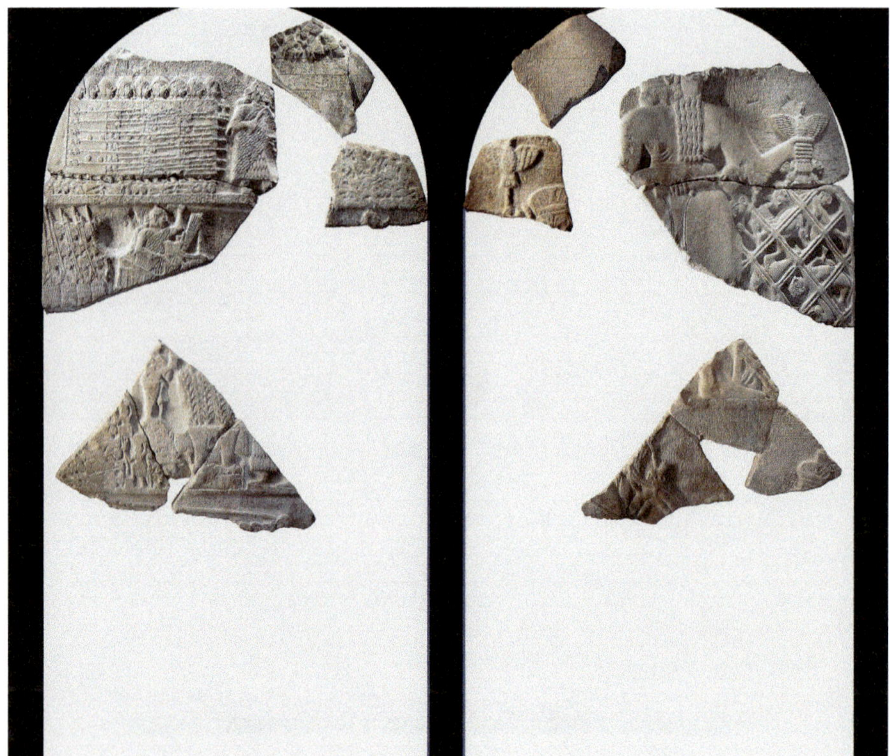

Fig. 1.3 Stele of the Vultures, historical side (left) and "mythological" side (right) (ca. 2450 BCE). Paris, Musée du Louvre. Photo: author

battle-axe and leading a phalanx of his spearmen into battle. A wall of shield-bearers protects the spearmen, who advance directly over the prostrate bodies of dead enemy soldiers, while at the right vultures and lions feast on the naked corpses. In the second register Eannatum reappears, this time driving a war-chariot at the head of his light infantry. He raises his spear, perhaps against the enemy king. (A similar scene recurs in the bottom register, where the spear of a now-lost figure strikes the head of his victim, who looks back over the heads of his retreating troops.) The lowest surviving register depicts Eannatum (of whom only the feet remain) presiding over the burial of his dead. The king pours a libation over two vases filled with branches, and an ox secured to the ground is sacrificed to the god Ningirsu. To the left men carry on their heads baskets of earth to cover the bodies laid out side by side in a common grave. Clarity of the pictorial narrative appears paramount in the composition of victory steles, with decorative matters playing only a minor role.

The opposite "mythological" side reveals the divine forces that direct these events. A large bearded male figure, representing the god Ningirsu, occupies two-thirds of the stele's height. In his right hand he carries a mace; in his left hand he grasps the handle of the mythical Sushgal net deployed in battle by Mesopotamian gods to catch and destroy their enemies. The handle takes the shape of the god's emblem: a lion-headed eagle over two lions. The dominant figure of Ningirsu is followed by a smaller divinity beneath the lion-headed eagle, while below it stands the god's chariot. Before the small head of the divinity are visible the chariot's front, with the bowed end of the pole, the rein-ring capped by the figure of a lion, and the wings of the lion-headed eagle.

Inscriptions envelop the relief wherever there is any space not covered with imagery. As on the Urnanshe relief, counterbalanced image and text recount the same narrative in different ways. A major portion of the inscription relates the oaths taken by the king of Umma on the battle nets of the gods that he will not breach the border, alluding to its violation by the people of Umma that precipitated the war. By declaring an end to the battle and marking the geographical frontiers, it provides the contractual agreement its termination.[17] The stele commemorates more than just a particular war: it venerates two faces of power, military and divine, thereby celebrating a victory that occurred on both heaven and earth. Both the stele's imagery and inscriptions confirm Eannatum's claims that this war was just and validated by the gods.

In addition to public monuments, military victories were also celebrated with smaller-scale objects that could be displayed indoors. Early Dynastic craftsmen excelled at inlaid ornament in colored stone and other materials for uses varying from pictorial friezes embellishing the façades of buildings to the fine decoration of valued articles such as gaming-boards, toilet boxes, and the sound-boxes of harps. Excavations by the British archaeologist Sir Leonard Woolley of what were identified as royal tombs at Ur (present-day Muqaiyir in Iraq) south of Uruk during the 1920s uncovered delicately carved pieces of shell or mother of pearl and inlaid with bitumen.[18] We are uncertain what the use was of two inlaid panels known as the Standard of Ur (Fig. 1.4); the absence of inscriptions suggests that they may have decorated furniture or a wooden box. The two trapezoidal-shaped side panels are ornamented with mythological subjects, but the two rectangular main panels depict the complementary subjects of Sumerian success in battle and the subsequent celebratory feast.[19] In contrast to the floating figures on the lion hunt from Warka, the artist of the Standard of Ur divided the face of each panel into three horizontal registers to depict linear movement across each register from left to right and vertically from the bottom register to the main scene at the top. One panel depicts the battle itself. In the bottom register chariots, each with a driver and a spearman with javelins projecting from their quivers, advance over the strewn bodies of the enemy dead. In the middle register infantrymen dispatch some adversaries and capture others. At the top the king, half a head taller than his men and carrying spear as an attribute of command, has descended from his chariot to inspect the prisoners brought before him. They are naked, bound, and some of them are wounded. The lower registers on the second panel represent the spoils of war, with livestock and porters carrying portable goods on their backs on wooden packs held by straps passing round their foreheads. In the topmost register the king, again hierarchically larger than his companions and now further distinguished by wearing an elaborate tasseled kilt, sits facing his officers at a victory banquet. At the right a musician plays a harp, followed by a female singer, perhaps acclaiming the achievements of the

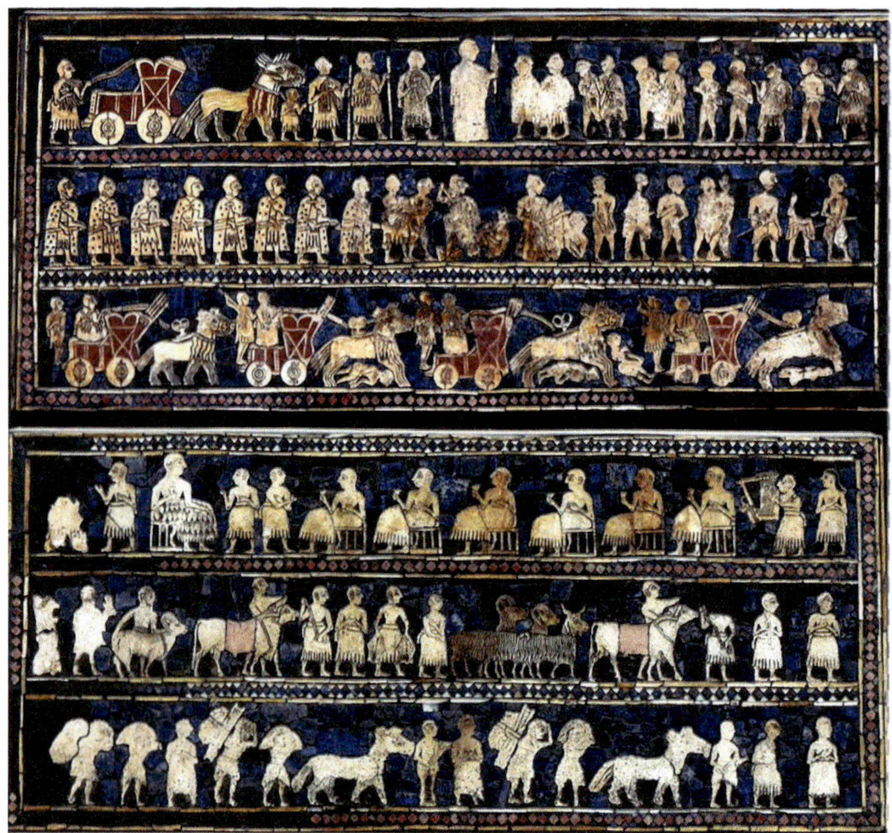

Fig. 1.4 Standard of Ur (ca. 2600 BCE). London, British Museum. Photo: Wikimedia Commons

king or his legendary predecessors. The registers are the best surviving examples of pictorial narrative from this period of Mesopotamian art.

In early Mesopotamian art the monarch appeared as the earthly representative of the god of the city-state; the activities of rulers made manifest the will of those gods. Representational art remained a part of sacred history, and peaceful activities were shown within the framework of religious belief, initially rarely linked to narratives of specific events. Eventually images commemorating specific victories in war gained emphasis. A king's activity was recorded in relatively monumental work only after a progressive exaltation that finally endowed him, if only temporarily, with divine powers.

The Rise of Akkad

According to later ancient tradition, the creator of the vast Akkadian empire, Sargon of Akkad (r. 2334–2279 BCE), was found in a basket in the river when he was an infant but grew to consolidate all the sovereign Sumerian city-states under his authority and conquer what ancient texts entitle the "four quarters of the universe," establishing the first empire, stretching beyond Mesopotamia to Asia Minor, Arabia, Iran, and as far west as Cyprus in the Mediterranean Sea. Akkadian kings fashioned a new form of royal authority and commissioned official monuments to disseminate it throughout their domain. In addition to the traditional separation of imagery into registers, Akkadian artists devised a new narrative strategy using successive episodes that advance across the field; and whereas earlier Sumerian works tended to evoke a pious ruler ensuring peace and prosperity, Sargon deployed a series of large steles to emphasize a new royal persona: the warrior king. The preferred material was diorite, a hard, dark volcanic stone imported from distant Oman on the Persian Gulf, whose splendid, gleaming surface heightened the prestige and value of these monuments.[20] None remain intact today, but three fragments found in Susa of two different monuments depicting scenes from the triumphant aftermath of Sargon's victories over anonymous enemies suggest their form and effect.[21]

The first two fragments belonged to a stele, perhaps dedicated to Ishtar (Fig. 1.5). One depicts an Akkadian soldier driving before him two bound prisoners, nude

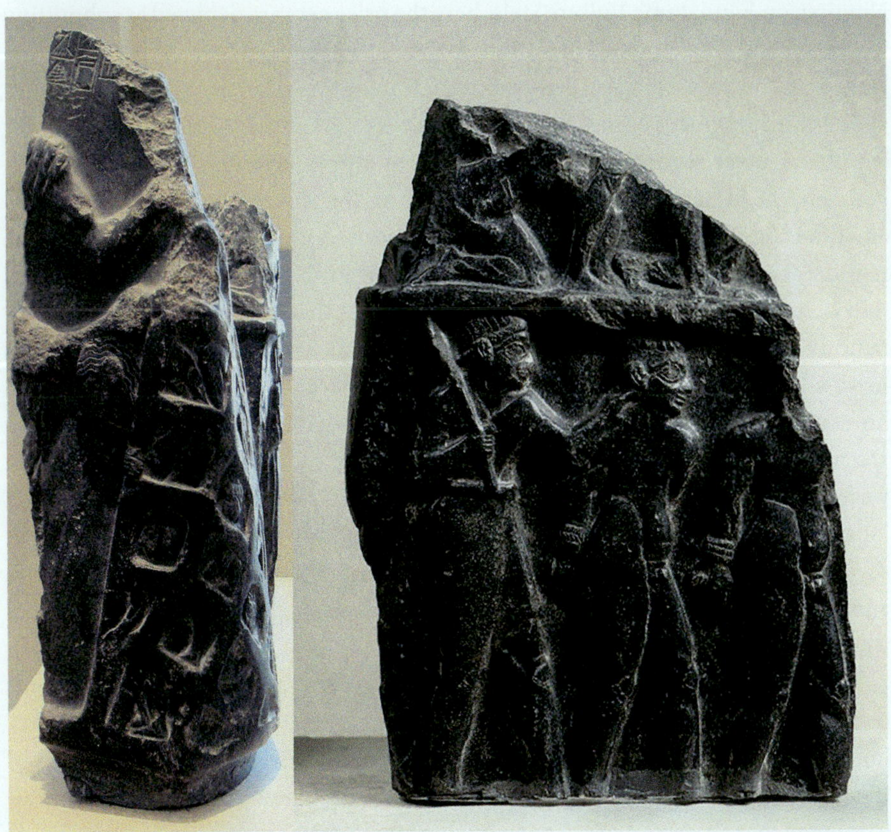

Fig. 1.5 Two fragments from Sargon's stele to Ishtar: prisoners in Sargon's war net (left) and Akkadian soldier with bound prisoners (right) (ca. 2300 BCE). Paris, Musée du Louvre Sb 2/6053 and Sb 3. Photos: Herve Lewandowski for Wikimedia Commons

and stripped of their weapons. Their hair, pulled into a knot at the top of their heads, identifies them as foreign enemies. In contrast, the Akkadian wears a knee-length loincloth, his upper body protected by a wide, thick scarf, which served as a breastplate.[22] He shoulders a curved blade fixed into a handle. The poorly preserved upper level depicted the preceding battle; one can just make out the legs of a collapsing figure struck by a spear. In the frieze above, broken in the middle, the lower part of Akkadian warriors in battle kilts push forward another row of naked captives bound at the wrist. On the opposite side of the fragment warriors beat naked prisoners who collapse. In Akkadian art nudity becomes an iconographic device to indicate the stages of defeat and death.[23] In the fragmentary lower register vultures and dogs circle the battlefield littered with dead bodies; the inscription below confirms a military victory. The second fragment shows Sargon using a mace to strike a prisoner who attempts to escape from his vast war net; attributes like the beard and long hair suggest that he is the enemy leader. Of the king, only the left arm holding the net and the right hand smiting the prisoner's protruding head survive; three undulating rays rising from his left shoulder may be an attribute of the Akkadian warrior deity Ishtar.[24] Although the net recalls the image of the war god Ningirsu on Eannatum's Vulture Stele, here the prisoners are depicted as submitting to Sargon with outstretched arms rather than as heaped-up bodies, implying that Akkadian conquest brings order over the defeated.

The third fragment comes from an obelisk-like monument (Fig. 1.6). At the far left of the lower register, Sargon (identified by the inscription "Sargon the king" beside his head) leads a procession of five figures that circles the stone. Larger than any other figure, he breaks loose from his apportioned space and pushes into the register above. He wears a tufted raiment, and his long hair is braided, drawn back into a chignon held in place by a diadem, attributes that compare with those of the famous Akkadian ruler sculpture often identified as Sargon. He holds in his right hand a battle-mace, which also serves as a kingly scepter. The first figure behind him carries a parasol to shade the king, another attribute of authority. Marching warriors follow wearing thick cloaks covering one shoulder and carrying raised weapons. Their shorter hair and lack of beards contrast with the luxuriant hair and long beard of the king, which emphasize his masculine power. In the upper register seven bound prisoners march before an Akkadian soldier; a kneeling prisoner and another marching before two additional Akkadians suggest scenes of the conflict were shown sequentially.[25]

Although the composition in superposed registers and the pictorial elements of the scenes follow the stylistic conventions of earlier Mesopotamian art, the refinement of the drawing, the forceful modeling, and the sculptural comeliness of the nude bodies on these fragmentary reliefs reveal a new concern with naturalistic detail that characterizes Akkadian sculpture. Artists working in the royal shops demonstrated their skill in carving hard stones like diorite and basalt, which are more challenging to work with than such stones as marble, and confirmed their virtuosity by incising anatomically correct details with sharp lines that emphasize

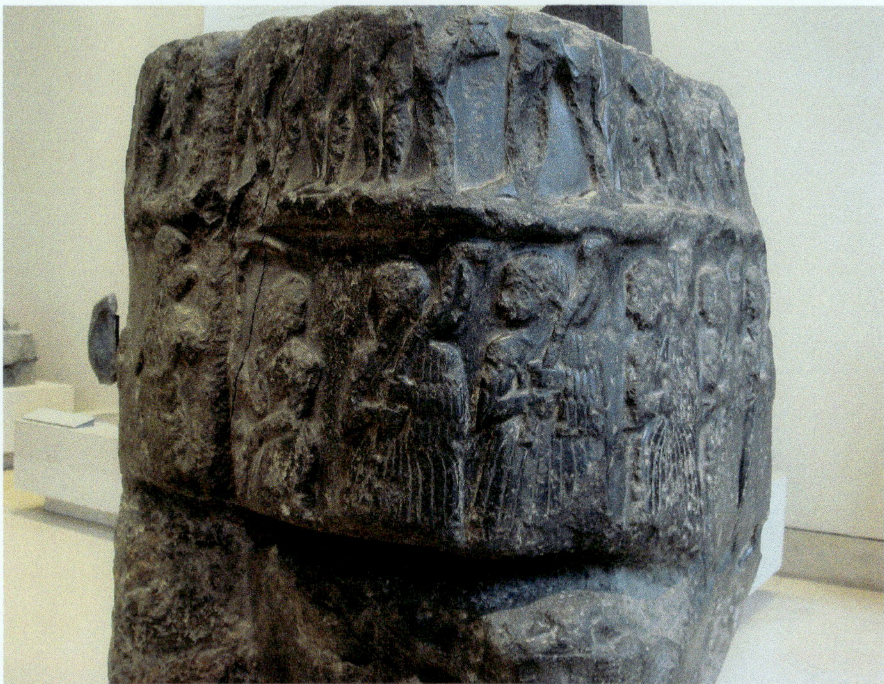

Fig. 1.6 Victory obelisk of Sargon leading a triumphal procession (ca. 2300 BCE). Paris, Musée du Louvre Sb 1. Photo: Wikimedia Commons

the body's rounded forms.[26] Such vivid displays of technical proficiency make the monuments truly remarkable, and thereby enhance their commemorative function by first enticing viewers and then leaving them more receptive to the ideological content—the Akkadian expansionist policies—they embody.[27]

The Victory Stele of Naram-Sîn

Naram-Sîn, the grandson of Sargon, used the established form of the stele to celebrate his victory over Satuni, king of the Lullubi, a neighboring tribe in the Zagros Mountains northeast of Mesopotamia in modern Kurdistan in Iraq (Fig. 1.7). He modifies the type significantly, however, to promote his radical personal agenda. The sculptor adapted traditional Mesopotamian pictorial conventions to a new compositional format and introduced novel representational attributes and stylistic nuances in fashioning his narrative. Carved of pink limestone of exceptional quality, the stele disseminates a new visual rhetoric that links commanding yet mortal kingship with the concept of the divine.

Rather than employing horizontal registers, the artist organized the narrative in a series of rising diagonals that echo the mountainous landscape setting. Figures in three tiers indicate the field of battle. Akkadian soldiers march in orderly ranks, an

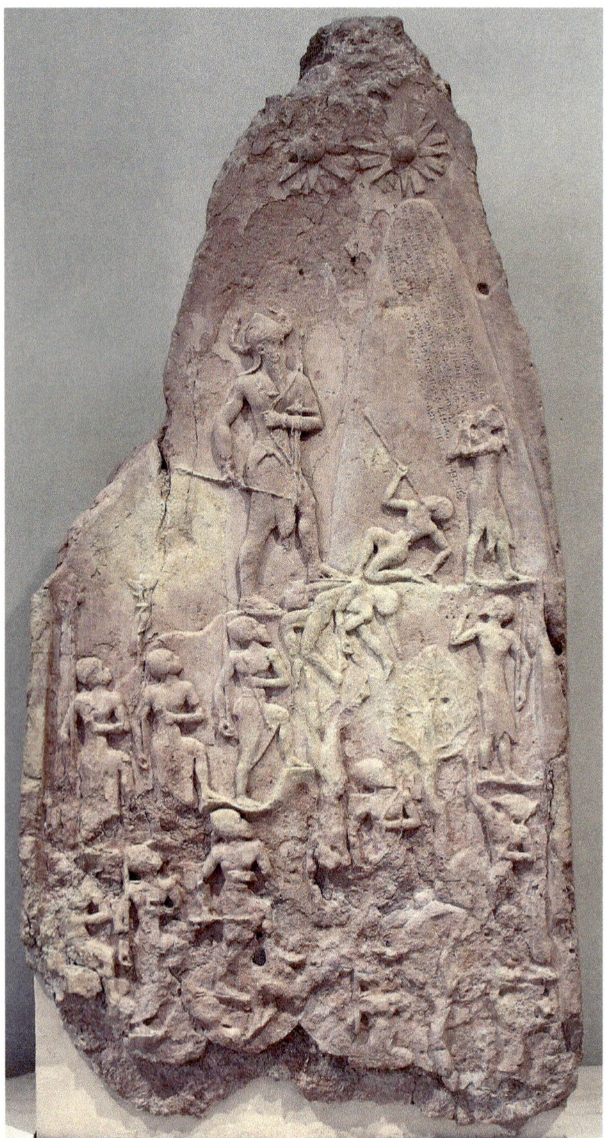

Fig. 1.7 Victory Stele of Naram-Sîn (ca. 2250 BCE). Paris, Musée du Louvre. Photo: Fred Romero for Wikimedia Commons

invincible force trampling the disordered enemy beneath their feet as they ascend the steep side of the mountain. The composition culminates in the iconic image of the king ascending the hills to enter the territory of his vanquished enemy, his towering scale proclaiming his dominant position within the state order. He stands apart from his army against the open sky where three stars appeared in the arc at the stele's top. (A third star is now missing on the damaged stele.) The novel diagonal composition compels his soldiers to look up to Naram-Sîn, while the king himself gazes toward the celestial emblems of the gods that empower him.

Animal-hide clothing and long hair worn in a single braid distinguish Lullubi soldiers from the Akkadian forces; they also expose different stages of undress, their nakedness depriving them of the power to fight and marking their imminent demise. In contrast to the disciplined Akkadians, their disorganized rout is weak and chaotic, signifying an uncivilized and barbaric people who deserve to be conquered. Naram-Sîn, armed with a battle-axe, spear, and bow and arrow, shows no pity. He steps upon the bodies of vanquished soldiers who collapse before him; he impales one soldier with a spear, kicks the body of another off the side of the mountain, and has an arrow ready to dispatch a Lullubi commander who turns to plead for mercy. The artist maintained the older convention of a composite view to depict the figures from several different viewpoints: although Naram-Sîn's legs are shown in profile, his torso turns frontally, his head again in profile crowned by his frontal two-horned helmet. This is a remarkable attribute for a mortal king.[28] Horned crowns were usually the exclusive preserve of the gods; prior to this time only deceased kings had achieved this status, so its depiction here is a sign of the king's assumption of divine power.[29] Nevertheless, he is not shown as the most powerful god. He *ascends* toward the heavens, his upward gaze conveying respect to those astral bodies above him that sanction his triumph.

The rendering of the Naram-Sîn's virile body is noteworthy. Very little distinguishes the figure of Eannatum from the phalanx he leads into battle; he is characterized by his distinctive enveloping garment and by his inscribed name. In contrast, the short kilt and diaphanous cloth draped over the left shoulder and tied in a knot at the hips reveal the broad chest and carefully articulated buttocks of Naram-Sîn's well-formed body, along with an abundant beard: all features found in earlier Mesopotamian representations of semidivine hero types on cylinder seals.[30] As with earlier Akkadian sculpture, it is carved in high relief to emphasize the body's corporeality; here, however, it not only invokes the king's physical presence, but the idealized form also draws attention to the king's physical perfection. The erotically charged image denotes the male potency and vigor that were associated with the portrayal in Mesopotamian literature of Gilgamesh, the archetypal semidivine king. Irene Winter has established that the "new" body of the king in Akkadian art coincides with the equally new elevation of kingship to divine status.[31]

Naram-Sîn's strategic claim to divinity was a decisive event in his reign; the decision to visually affirm it in the commemoration of a significant victory renders that provocative assertion more acceptable. Earlier Mesopotamian works attributed a king's military success to the actions of the gods in the divine realm, underscored by their physical presence in battle. On the Victory Stele the deities are reduced to astral symbols that merely witness the king's heroic actions, underscoring the active role of the newly deified king as both conqueror and mediator between earth and heaven: Naram-Sîn alone emerges as responsible for his victory. Rather than separating the pictorial surface into neat registers, the new arrangement reinforces hierarchical separation by elevating Naram-Sîn above other figures. He echoes both the tapered shape of the stele and the mountain depicted within it, thereby increasing his significance.[32] The mountainous terrain with coniferous trees allows the viewer to identify a specific foreign and hostile territory, which heightens the sense that this is a particular event and not a generic battle scene. This naturalism adds another layer of reality to the scene that authenticates Naram-Sîn's domination over foreign peoples and the landscape itself. Even the pink sandstone of the stele is distinctive to the region where the Lullubi lived, and its use for a monument commemorating their defeat underscores Naram-Sîn's control of the region. The king's claims of divinity further justify his ideological ambition for imperial expansion into those lands.

Naram-Sîn deployed the traditional form of the stele to commemorate his victory over a neighboring people. He used that event to tell a story that illustrates the Akkadian ideal of a unified empire under the control of a single charismatic king. Both its narrative imagery proving the seemingly invincibility of his army and its inscription commemorating this glorious triumph forewarn any insurgents who dare to oppose Akkadian rule that resistance is futile. Yet there are two different inscriptions on the stele. The first, in Akkadian at the upper left, is fragmentary, having been purposely abraded, and affirms that the stele was made to celebrate Naram-Sîn's victory over the mountain people of Lullubi.[33] The second, clearly visible on the mountaintop at the right of the stele, above the imploring Lullubi commander, was added by stone carvers in the service of the Elamite king Shutruk-Nahhunte in the twelfth century BCE.[34] It declares that Shutruk-Nahhunte seized the stele after capturing the city of Sippar and set it up in the temple of Inshushinak in his capital at Susa.[35] Circumstantial evidence (including the Elamite inscription) suggests that Naram-Sîn had originally set up the Victory Stele in the temple precinct of the sun god Shamash in his city of Sippar in southern Mesopotamia, a sacred setting that further substantiated the righteousness of Akkadian expansion. It was still visible a thousand years later when it was taken.

Reaffirmation and Survival

Naram-Sîn's storied reign was followed by that of his son, Shar-Kali-Sharri, who began his rule by putting down revolts sparked by his succession. Despite his labors and several victorious military campaigns, the state disintegrated when he was unable to maintain internal order or to stop attacks on the empire by foreign enemies. He reconstructed the Temple of Enlil at Nippur; possibly this event, combined with the invasion of the Gutians and a devastating famine, helped give rise to subsequent legends concerning the collapse of Akkad. Succeeding generations associated Naram-Sîn with *The Curse of Agade*, a later literary text in which the king is presented as a victim of his own hubris.[36] The tale recounts how an impious king committed crimes against the gods leading the deities Enlil and Ishtar to cause the destruction of Agade (Akkad) and its empire. It may also recall how Naram-Sîn's unprecedented claims to divinity exacerbated tensions between the city temples and the Akkadian centralized state. The unpopularity of Naram-Sîn's policies appear to have had more power than even his splendid commemorative monuments to affect Mesopotamians' memory of his reign.

With the downfall of the Akkadian Empire came a reaffirmation of the traditional Sumerian concept of the monarch. The practice of exaltation came to an end and historical subjects disappeared from Mesopotamian art until the end of the second millennium, when a new political ideology appeared in Assyria. Then the king was conceived primarily as a military leader, the implacable destroyer of his enemies in great conquests. This was essentially a secular conception of power, so Assyrian commemorative monuments were largely secular, but with military victory depicted as the inevitable realization of the will of the national deity. Although the king appeared with all the insignia of his rank, he was not represented as larger than other men.[37] Later still, the official relief programs of Achaemenian Persia, which include scenes of war, adapted the traditional poses and compositions of Mesopotamian commemorative art to glorify their empire and acclaim their ruler.[38] When Persian armies invaded the Assyrian empire in the seventh century BCE and destroyed the great library of King Ashurbanipal at Nineveh, Assyrian texts on clay tablets recounting tales of Naram-Sîn were preserved beneath the rubble of the burning buildings so that across the millennia, people today remember his name and deeds.[39]

2

The Temple of Ramses II at Abu Simbel

Message Control in Ancient Egypt

It can be argued that Egypt's political and art histories both begin with the Palette of Narmer, a work that exemplifies symbolic forms of representation (Fig. 2.1). Both its discovery in the temple of Horus at Hierakonpolis and its size—more than 2 feet (63.5 cm) high—indicate that the piece embodies a utilitarian object (a tablet used for grinding protective eye paint) adapted to ceremonial rather than practical use. Made of schist, it uses many of the conventions that would govern royal Egyptian art—including the new hieroglyphic writing to label figures[1]—to commemorate the Narmer's defeat of the Delta People of Lower Egypt and unifying it with Upper Egypt and the start of the country's development as a powerful nation-state.

On the front side, the king's importance is signaled by his hierarchical scale and boldly silhouetted form against a blank ground (both practices that Akkadian artists used to effect on the Victory Stele of Naram-Sîn). Narmer wears the white crown of Upper Egypt while brandishing his mace above a captive who kneels before him, an early version of the formulaic smiting scene. Above this foe at the right the god Horus, portrayed as a falcon whose human hand holds a cord tied around the head of a bearded man, forming the sign for "land," out of which sprouts stylized papyrus signifying Lower Egypt. These are pictures that speak. The symbols combine to spell out the main celebratory message: Narmer, ruler of Upper Egypt, now also controls Lower Egypt. In this way an early form of writing clarifies the image for the viewer. To the king's left an official, shown in smaller scale and on his own groundline, holds Narmer's sandals and a pail with sacred oil for purification. Narmer is barefoot because he stands on sacred ground (beneath which lie two enemy dead) performing the ritual execution of the defeated leader to conclude the war.

On the reverse side Narmer, again shown larger than the other figures and now bearing the red crown of Lower Egypt, joins in a procession of officials and standard bearers to inspect the enemy dead. At the bottom a bull symbolizing the power of the king tramples another enemy before a fortified city. In the center the elongated necks of two leonine dragons create the saucer for mixing mascara. In addition to Horus, Narmer identifies himself with the goddess Hathor, represented by the cows at the top corners on both sides. Between the cows are enframed images of a catfish and a chisel, a *nar* and a *mer* in ancient Egyptian, a rebus forming the king's name when sounded out. As in early Mesopotamia, Egyptian historical subjects are, from

Power, Image, and Memory. Peter J. Holliday, Oxford University Press. © Oxford University Press 2024.
DOI: 10.1093/oso/9780190901080.003.0003

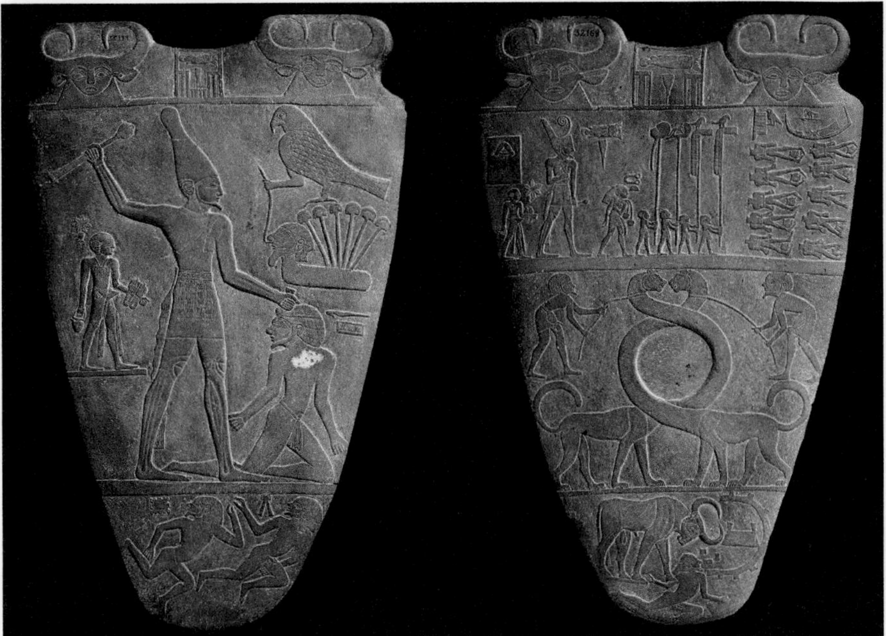

Fig. 2.1 Palette of Narmer, recto (left) and verso (right) (ca. 2950 BCE). Cairo, Egyptian Museum. Photo: Wikimedia Commons

the thematic point of view, dominated by the theme of battle victoriously waged by the king, whether the scene is reduced to a symbolic, almost emblematic, presentation as here or extended to a series of narrative episodes. By offering an image of kingship in words and pictures that transcends earthly power, the palette not only established a model for the kings of the Old Kingdom (Dynasty III to Dynasty VI, ca. 2649–2150 BCE), but also for rulers of later dynasties.[2]

The divinity of the Egyptian king was never in doubt. Already by the Early Dynastic Period (2950–1575 BCE), he was revered as a god in human form and served as mediator between the divine and human worlds. He preserved the union of Upper and Lower Egypt, which was secured in his name, by crushing Egypt's enemies, defined as the forces of chaos, and by lavishing care and attention on the myriad gods who oversaw Egypt's proper functioning. Doing so preserved the proper order of the world (*Ma'at*).[3]

Egypt's political and religious systems were remarkably conservative, and because art was believed to play a crucial role in maintaining *Ma'at*, it was conservative as well. Art functioned to transmit essential information about a subject, and Egyptian artists developed its underlying conventions early and followed them with subtle but significant variations for almost three thousand years. They tended to rely on conceptual principles rather than on the observation of the natural world; rigidly formal and stylistic practices, such as composite views of the figure, predominated over those rendering subjects naturalistically.[4] A system of mathematical formulas determined proportions. Rules of decorum circumscribed a work's content and iconography and dictated what forms could be shown in what context. Thus, profane subjects were generally relegated to the exterior walls of temples and sacred subjects to its interior. Rather than movement, artists tried to express timelessness and immortality. They tended toward diagrammatic linear compositions, often organized through the use of registers, which also helped fix subjects in a hierarchical manner.

Convention and Innovation in the New Kingdom

The New Kingdom (Dynasties XVIII, XIX, and XX, ca. 1550–1070 BCE) constituted a period of territorial expansion and tremendous prosperity for Egypt. Magnificent architectural projects arose along the full length of the Nile. At Karnak and nearby Luxor, successive kings assembled two immense temple complexes that retain much of their glory today. Called "pylon temples" after their massive stone gateways,[5] ceremonial processions passed pillars built as monuments to individual pharaohs to move deeper through sundrenched courts and shadowed halls until reaching the vast hypostyle hall (many-pillared hall), which was the furthermost point of admittance for all but priests and royalty; away from the public eye in the further sanctuaries they conducted sacred rituals before images of the gods. Artists employed a distinctively Egyptian form of decoration throughout the complex: sunken relief. In this technique, sculptors used chisels to delineated sharp outlines into the stone's surface and modeled figures within their contours, below the level of the background, rather than chiseling away the stone around the figures and thus allowing them to rise from the stone (as in the more common raised or bas-relief). Light raking across the relief's surface casts shadows into the outlines, bringing out the figures without compromising the visual integrity of the wall; Egyptian artists also painted reliefs to enhance their visibility. This type of relief required less carving in the hard Egyptian stone to adorn large surfaces.[6]

Such economy was especially advantageous, not least because the process of making a wall relief entailed a complicated sequence of negotiations. The pharaoh first stated his wishes by decree. A suitable space—the blank wall—was then appropriated or constructed. The chief draftsmen developed a design, and if there was an inscription, scribes had to compose the text. These had to receive both royal and priestly approval. The inscription or image (or combination of both) was laid out and executed by carvers. Painters finished the work.[7] The complexity of the final monument depended on the availability of time, finances, talented and skilled workers, and other variables.

The subject of the relief programs at Karnak emphasized the king's relationship with the gods.[8] The Egyptian idea of a divine king favored the repetition of unvaried iconographic formulas removed from the world of time and thus from the specific historical event. Therefore, the symbolic character of the image—especially in monumental sculpture—tends to prevail over narrative. Egyptian conventions dictated that the god-king be represented in a series of preset iconic images, portrayed in larger dimensions than other men and in rigidly fixed poses, even when the surrounding scene was enlivened by a more realistic depiction of action. The reliefs of Dynasty XIX king Seti I on the exterior walls of the hypostyle hall commemorate a succession of his military campaigns.[9] A series of established scenes surrounded by the trip out and the return trek home describe a step-by-step account featuring the central theme of the king in battle (Fig. 2.2). The king and his chariot stand against a background covered with hieroglyphic inscriptions and soldiers whose smaller scale intensifies the king's authority; sculptors cut his form more deeply than the surrounding figures to give the king a bolder outline. Hierarchical scale impairs any descriptive realism; the action emerges most strongly in those instances where difference in proportions is reduced. The figure of the pharaoh in his chariot conforms to the traditional composition, but the position of his body changes from scene to scene, adjusting to the course of the narrative. The reins are knotted around his waist in order to free his hands to draw his bow and shoot arrows into the enemy forces. In reality a charioteer would have driven the team, but to depict a second figure in the chariot would have spoiled the dramatic effect and reduced the heroic image of the king.[10] The images also reveal an unusual interest in the landscape in which the scenes take place. For the first time in the history of Egyptian art we confront a narrative that can be called complete, even if any desire for realism is tempered by conventions expressive of the symbolic and timeless invincibility of the pharaoh. The king's power and the merciless efficiency of his forces secure victory that will maintain order, *Ma'at*, over the terrestrial realm in harmony with the gods of Egypt.

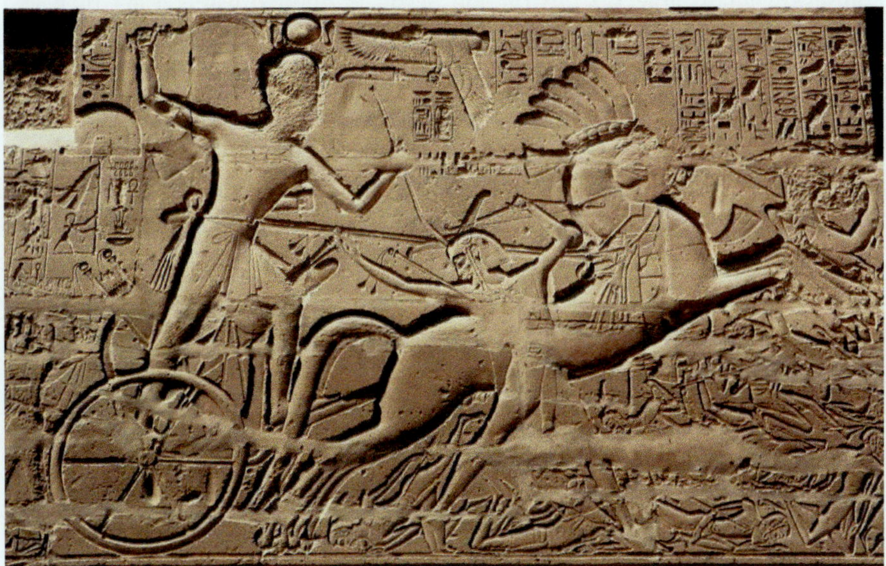

Fig. 2.2 Seti I battles the Libyans (ca. 1290–1279 BCE). Karnak, exterior wall of the hypostyle hall. Photo: author

Ramses II's Nubian Temples

During his sixty-seven-year rule, Seti's son, Ramses II, authorized more architectural projects than any other Egyptian king.[11] Like every other pharaoh, Ramses was represented as the product of the union between a heavenly father and an earthly mother. Certain statues of pharaoh represented his kingly office deified, and they, too, were regarded as divine.[12] The colossal pairs of statues of Ramses II that once stood outside temples throughout Egypt acted as intermediaries between passers-by and the great gods at home inside. Pious villagers and high officials alike might offer a petition or erect a stele to the cult of the king; in this manner Ramses II was a benefactor to all.

Within Egypt proper Ramses's programs of self-glorification were governed by tradition and restrained by the powerful temple priesthood. In far-off Nubia, however, Ramses felt no constraints and established or embellished over a dozen temples there, ultimately becoming their resident deity. The location made an eloquent statement: the temples were meant to reinforce the dominance of Egypt's state religion in the region, but also to impress Egypt's southern neighbors. Furthermore, with these temples Ramses solemnized his claim to the ancient land of Kush in Lower Nubia, which was the source of such valuable assets as gold, ivory, and animal skins. Although the Nubian temples replicated most components of temples found in Egypt proper, six original rock-cut temples incorporated the sandstone cliffs as part of their matrix and incorporated colossal royal images serving as pillars into their architecture.[13]

Two massive temples at Abu Simbel, a village on the Nile's western bank, about 142 miles (230 km) southwest of Aswan, are generally considered the grandest of Ramses's Nubian project. Construction began in approximately 1264 BCE and lasted about twenty years. Carved straight into the living rock of the site's sacred hills, the sloping façade of the Large Temple is 114 feet (35 m) wide and conceived as a pylon gateway with four colossal seated statues of the king flanking the doorway; at almost 70 feet (21 m) high, they dwarf any approaching visitor (Fig. 2.3).[14] His original purpose here was to honor Egypt's major gods and their Nubian variants; however, as the impressive images of himself were carved on the façade and pillars of the first temple and its walls were covered with a record of his military exploits, Ramses's ideas about who he was began to change.[15] Relatively small statues of family members reaching no higher than the king's knees flank the colossi of the main temple. A frieze of baboons (originally twenty-two), worshippers of the sun, crowns the façade. Above the entrance itself a bas-relief represents two images of the king worshipping the falcon-headed Ra-Horakhty standing between them in a large niche. The god holds a feather and the hieroglyph *User* in his right hand and that of *Ma'at* in his left, forming a gigantic rebus of Ramses's throne name, *User-Ma'at-Ra*.[16]

The inner configuration follows the same basic layout of most Egyptian temples. The hypostyle hall is 59 feet (18 m) long and 54 feet (16.7 m) wide and supported

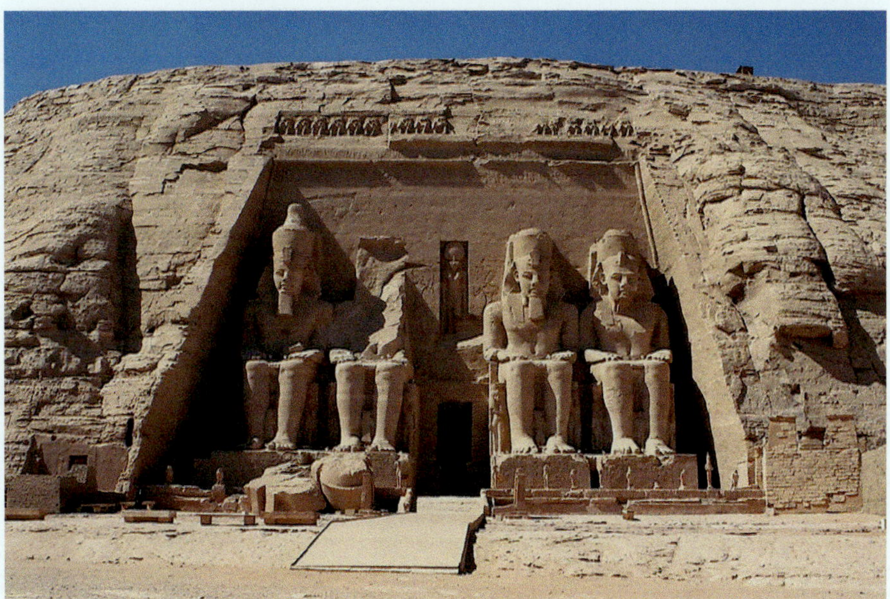

Fig. 2.3 Large temple of Ramses II (ca. 1264–1244 BCE). Abu Simbel. Photo: author

by eight 23-foot (7 m) pillars depicting the Underworld-god Osiris with the face of Ramses, signifying the eternal nature of the pharaoh (Fig. 2.4). The four colossi along the left-hand wall wear the white crown of Upper Egypt while those to the right wear the double crown of Upper and Lower Egypt, underscoring the location of Abu Simbel on Upper Egypt's borders. This space leads to a second hall, which has four pillars adorned with offerings to the gods, including representations of Ramses and Nefertari with the sacred boats of Amun and Ra-Horakhty. Ramses receives prominence equal to that of his fellow gods from this hall back through a transverse antechamber and culminating in the sanctuary itself. There against the back wall of the innermost chamber, a full 196 feet (60 m) into the heart of the mountain, he ordered his artists to carve four rock-cut sculptures—Ra-Horakhty, Ramses II, Amun Ra, and Ptah—showing the pharaoh enthroned in splendor beside his fellow gods.[17] Facing east, every morning the rising sun animates the entire façade. On the upper frieze the baboons raise their arms to greet the sun's first rays, which then slowly proceed downward to highlight the *User-Ma'at-Ra* cryptogram, and finally break into the temple itself to illuminate its interior. Twice each year the sunlight reaches the sculptures on the back wall, illuminating Ra-Horakhty and Amun Ra and energizing the image of Ramses, whereas Ptah's Underworld associations demand he remain shrouded in darkness. This creates a symbolic fusion of the solar and chthonic forces celebrated in the temple, upon completion called *Hut Ramesses Meryamun* (The House of Ramses, Beloved of Amun).[18]

The walls of the hypostyle hall are covered with sunken-relief battle scenes from Ramses's military campaigns, including those in Libya to Egypt's west, Nubia to the south, but most importantly the Battle of Kadesh to the east. Here

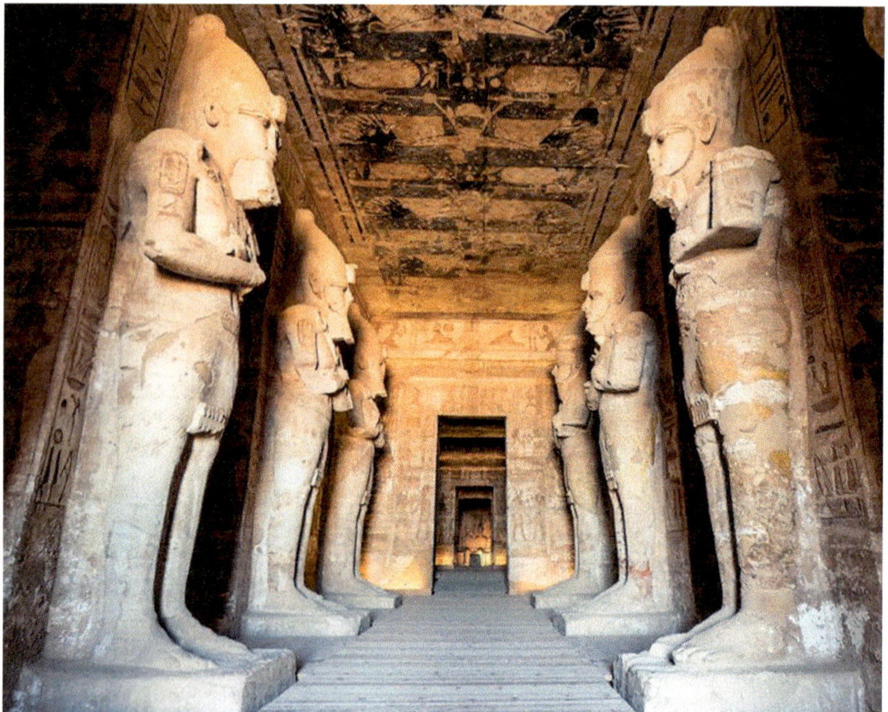

Fig. 2.4 Large Temple of Ramses II, hypostyle hall. Abu Simbel. Photo: author

the internal tensions observed in the reliefs celebrating Seti's victories disappear. The atemporal aspect of the royal victory is abandoned in favor of a pictorial epic diametrically opposed to the principles that had previously motivated the art of Egypt. The artists instead focused their attention on the historical content in a narration that is remarkably discursive. The vast representation of the battle is packed with details, which are, moreover, described at length by accompanying inscriptions.

The Battle of Kadesh

During this period the Anatolian Hittites were one of the great players of the ancient world, equal to the Egyptians and surpassing the power of the Mitannians, Assyrians, Kassites/Babylonians, and Cypriots. Under King Muwatalli II, the growing strength of their empire threatened the stability of Egypt's subject states along the eastern Mediterranean coast and control over vital Near Eastern trade. Ramses longed to restore the stature Egypt's empire had enjoyed under the Thutmosis kings almost a century before.[19] Rumors of renewed Hittite incursion forced Ramses to turn from his massive construction projects and focus on war. As Prince Regent, Ramses had accompanied his father on the Levantine campaign commemorated at Karnak to reclaim command of the coastal area and dominion over the fortified city of Kadesh, an important commercial center strategically located near the headwaters of the Orontes River in modern Syria. There the two great empires would again meet in an epic encounter.

The Battle of Kadesh is one of the most extensively chronicled conflicts in ancient history;[20] the reliability of that evidence, however, is uncertain and reflects the imperatives of the dominant elites who recorded it. Ramses gives his version of the battle in two distinct though overlapping textual accounts: the lengthy *Poem of Pentaur* and the shorter *Bulletin*, which survive on temple walls at Abydos, Luxor, Karnak, the Ramesseum (Ramses's temple near the Valley of the Kings), and Abu Simbel.[21] The battle is also depicted in relief programs at Abydos, Karnak, twice at the Ramesseum, three times at Luxor, and at Abu Simbel.[22] This Egyptian version had long dominated histories of ancient Egypt, but excavations at the Hittite capital of Hattusa (modern Bogazköy) begun by German archaeologists in 1906 have yielded thousands of clay tablets comprised of what must have been the official state archives, as well as letters, inventories and administrative texts, poems, mythological texts, histories, and religious rituals. Included among these tablets—which are still being pieced together and translated—are accounts countering the Egyptian story.[23]

Both the *Poem* and *Bulletin* describe Ramses's victory against "overwhelming odds." At the same time they reproach the king's officers for their "failure," which is connected to one of the key scenic events present in all the pictorial representations. In the Egyptian telling, Ramses left Egypt with one of the largest armies the Near East had ever seen. Four divisions recruited from Egypt's major cities traveled under the protection of one of Egypt's main gods and under the command of Ramses or one of his sons: the division of Amun from Thebes, followed by the divisions of Ra from Heliopolis, Ptah from Memphis, and Seth (or Sutekh), probably from Tanis in the Delta. Each division probably consisted of five thousand soldiers, including infantry and chariotry, but with herald trumpeters, supply wagons and camp followers, the long drawn-out columns stretched for miles. Yet Egyptian accounts only mention the size of the Hittite forces, which Ramses estimated at 47,500, including some 37,000 infantry and 3,500 chariotry.[24] It was a standard practice to exaggerate the number of foes faced on the battlefield in order to heighten one's own achievements, but even if Ramses inflated the figures, it is conceivable that King Muwatalli did in fact amass a great army by hiring mercenaries from his vast empire.

Within a month Ramses reached Shabtuna on the Orontes River, some four hundred miles from the Egyptian frontier and less than ten miles from Kadesh.[25] As Ramses waited for his entire force to catch up to him, he interrogated two captured Shosu (Semitic nomads), who asserted that King Muwatalli had retreated to Aleppo, about 120 miles (200 km) to the north: " 'Where are they, your brothers who sent you to report this to His Majesty?' And they said to His Majesty: 'They are where the wretched Ruler of Hatti is, for the Fallen One of Hatti is in the Land of Aleppo to the north of Tunip, and he feared Pharaoh [too much] to come southward when he heard that Pharaoh had come northward.' "[26]

Emboldened by this intelligence, Ramses divided his forces to cover more ground, ordering the division of Amun, closely followed by that of Ra, to cross the Orontes and establish camp just west of the walls of Kadesh without waiting for the rest of his army. The Amun division was to cut off any retreat to the northwest and to prevent any assistance coming from that direction. While enjoying a feast in anticipation of a triumphal entry into Kadesh, Egyptian scouts captured two Hittite spies who, after a severe beating (portrayed on the reliefs) confessed that the Hittite army was in fact only moments away on the other side of Kadesh. "See, the wretched Chief of Khatti is come together with the many foreign countries who are with him . . . and they are more numerous than the sands of the riverbanks. See, they stand equipped and ready to fight behind Kadesh the old."[27] Ramses found himself with only one division to face Muwatalli and the entire Hittite army. He immediately sent mounted messengers to gather his troops, half of whom had not yet crossed the river. Minutes later, the Hittites attacked.

The Hittite chariotry crashed into the unprepared division of Ra, which in panic stampeded into the Amun camp, hindering their movement. Ramses was caught completely by surprise, abandoned by all but his personal guard and shield-bearer Menna. He prayed: "I call upon thee, my father Amun, for I am in the midst of a multitude of foes."[28] The advancing Hittite chariots had pursued the divisions of Ra and Amun to exhaustion and, according to Ramses, were unprepared for any resistance when in his chariot he made a series of headlong attacks and drove the them back to the riverbank; Muwatalli, watching the battle from the eastern bank of the Orontes, failed to deploy eight thousand spearmen that he had kept in reserve. Ramses held the Hittites until the Egyptian divisions of Ptah and Seth arrived and joined the melee. Now attacked from two sides, the Hittites hastily retreated from the field and sought refuge in Kadesh. Muwatalli finally sent auxiliaries, but to no avail.

What we can establish with certainty is that there was no clear winner, as each army was able to withstand the other's tactics, and neither could surpass the other.[29] At a certain point both sides accepted that the battle would be a stalemate and a truce was devised. Ramses did not remain to take Kadesh for these negotiations but headed back south to Egypt as rapidly as possible to relate the story of his great victory, which, in fact, was nothing more than the story of his personal valor in the face of adversity overcoming his bad generalship. Nevertheless, he would tell it first.[30]

"Here I Stand, All Alone"

In Egypt, as later in Assyria, visual and textual narratives move in strict parallelism, the two languages of the figural and the verbal at times in significant intermixture. Rather than following conventional scenes like those deployed by his father,

Ramses's pictorial account of the Kadesh campaign at Abu Simbel instead parallels the dramatic narratives of the *Poem* and the *Bulletin*. The *Poem* is remarkable among Egyptian commemorative texts in providing an unusually comprehensive account that manages to follow a swift trajectory; the pictorial rendition deploys the same tactic.

Immediately to the right of the entrance of the hypostyle hall is a conventional smiting scene: Ramses's mace strikes the heads of a composite group of diminutive kneeling Asiatic prisoners (Fig. 2.5). Above Ramses flies the vulture Nekhbet. Below the ground level on which he stands a row of his numerous daughters plays the sistrum and sings songs praising the accomplishments of their father. Continuing to the right is the march of the Egyptian army under Ramses to Kadesh. The scenes of

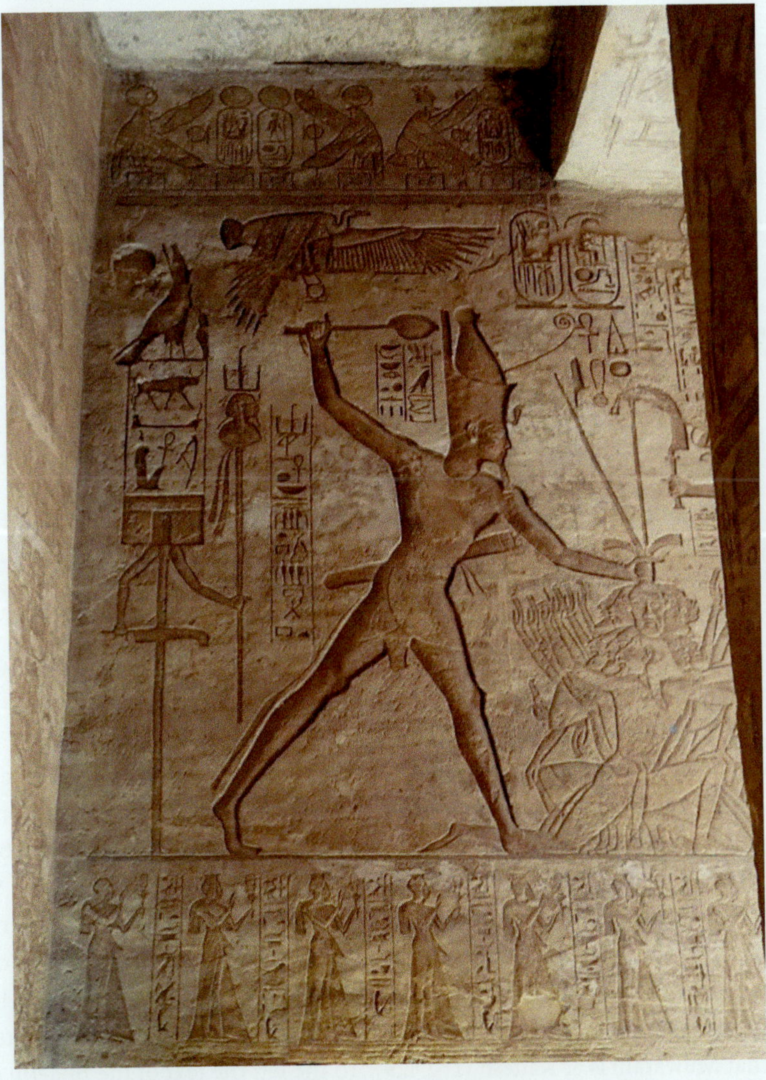

Fig. 2.5 Ramses smiting Asiatic prisoners. Abu Simbel. Photo: author

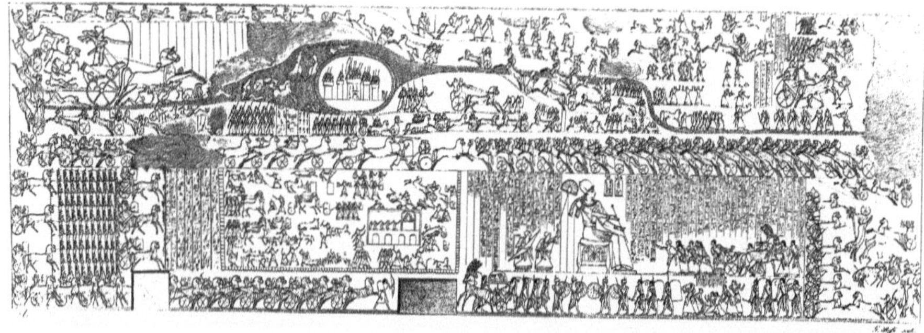

Fig. 2.6 Drawing of the north wall of the hypostyle hall at Abu Simbel by Giuseppe Angelelli. From Ippolito Rosellini, *I monumenti dell'Egitto e della Nubia* (1832–1844), Plate LXXXVII.

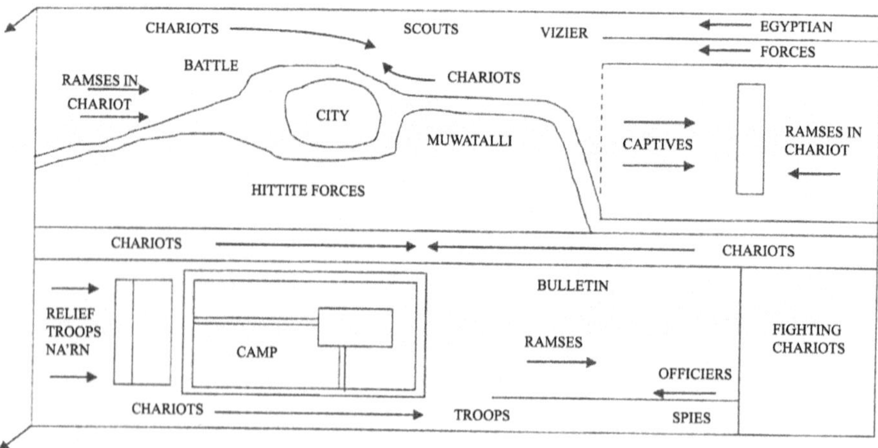

Fig. 2.7 Diagram of major events represented on the north wall of the hypostyle hall at Abu Simbel. Drawing: Jeffrey Ryan

the actual battle cover the hall's north wall and stand out from the stylized and repetitious imagery of most ancient Egyptian art (Figs. 2.5 and 2.6; Fig. 2.7 is a diagram of the major events).[31]

By dividing the long north wall into two long horizontal registers (that are then subdivided to contain discrete scenes) the designer invents an unusual panoramic design: the viewer's attention is drawn to the key dramatic elements of the battle, all of which are shown in the environs of the moated enemy city (Fig. 2.8).[32] Since this single "frame" contains multiple scenes, many featuring Ramses, the innovative narrative type is probably best characterized as continuous. At the right of the bottom register the Egyptian war chariots are aligned as for battle. To the left is the surprise revelation of affairs: after beating the spies Ramses and his officers discover that Muwatalli is at Kadesh (Fig. 2.9). To the left the text of the *Bulletin* gives its account of the accompanying scene. The Egyptian camp is just left of center in

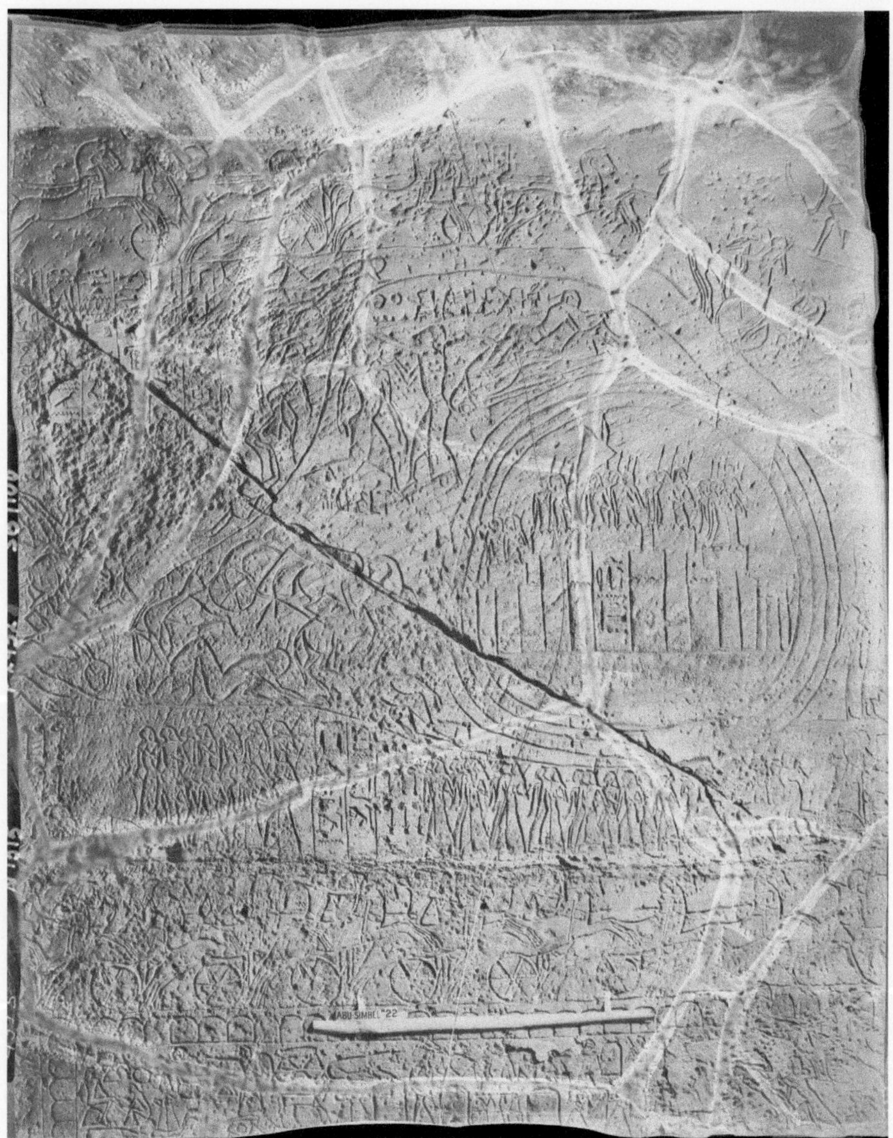

Fig. 2.8 Fighting surrounds the walled city of Kadesh. Photo: Courtesy of the Oriental Institute of the University of Chicago

the register, encircled by charging Hittite chariots. The relief troops arrive at the extreme left, thereby allowing one to read the major events surrounding the Egyptian camp and visually connect them with the account of the *Bulletin*.

At the upper right of the top register the Egyptian army under Ramses marches to Kadesh. Then to the far left (or west, from where the Egyptians came), the surprised Ramses counterattacks (Fig. 2.10). This motif, with the hierarchically larger king charging forth in his chariot, derives from a standard icon of power in Egyptian art; here, however, it takes a rather subordinate role in the overall composition. Small

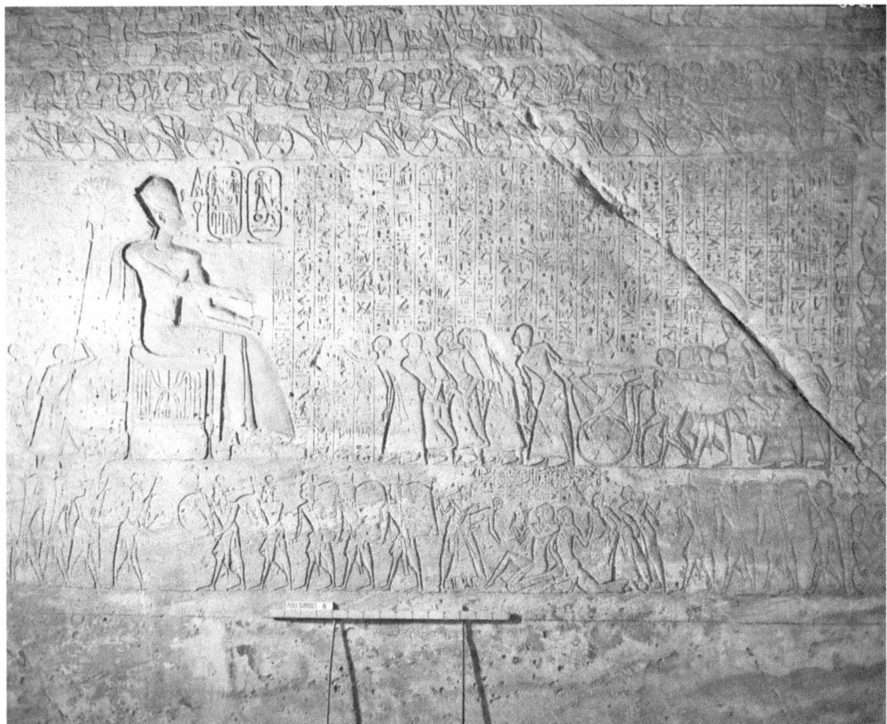

Fig. 2.9 Enthroned Ramses confers with his officers; beating of spies (lower register to right). Abu Simbel. Photo: Courtesy of the Oriental Institute of the University of Chicago

figures of Hittite soldiers fall flat before and behind Ramses's chariot, suggesting the momentum of his route to the city over their trampled bodies, a route that also connects with a border of repeated Hittite soldiers enframing this section. The artists invent an expression of movement that breaks with traditional Egyptian practice. The imagery provides a visual reference to the moment in battle when, according to Ramses, the king, isolated through trickery, was able to overcome the surrounding enemy single-handedly:

> Not one of my princes, of my chief men and my great,
> Was with me, not a captain, not a knight;
> For my warriors and chariots had left me to my fate,
> Not one was there to take his part in fight.
> . . .
> Here I stand,
> All alone;
> There is no one at my side,
> My warriors and chariots afeared,
> Have deserted me, none heard
> My voice, when to the cravens I, their king, for succor, cried.

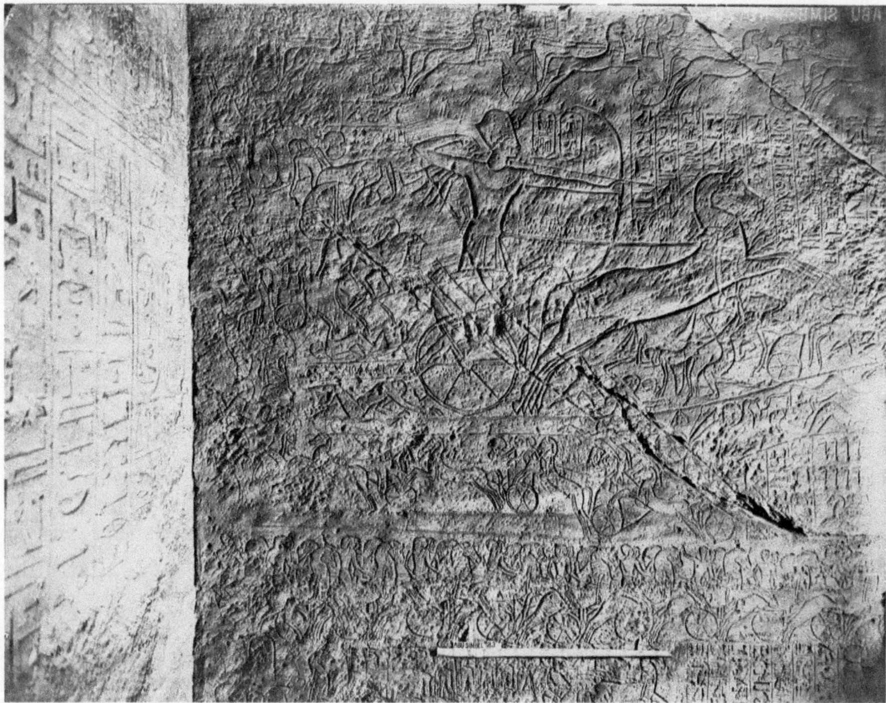

Fig. 2.10 Ramses counterattacks. Abu Simbel. Photo: Courtesy of the Oriental Institute of the University of Chicago

But I find that Ammon's grace
Is better far to me
Than a million fighting men and ten thousand chariots be.[33]

Topographic details identify specific incidents during the battle: to the right of the charging king is the Orontes River where the enemy plunge and the walled city of Kadesh where they seek refuge.[34] These landscape features also separate the valiantly fighting Ramses from Muwatalli, who passively observes from his chariot on the right (or eastern) side of the river. At the right end of the upper register a victorious Ramses dismounts to survey Hittite captives. Although the Kadesh reliefs follow the Egyptian tradition of depicting the king in each major scene—camp, battle, and postbattle presentation—the dramatic rendering of the chariot mêlée underscores Ramses's personal success through the wild flight of the Hittites into the river and their failure to withstand the young king's merciless assault. The inspired execution of an energetic and vivid pictorial narrative stands out from the stylization and repetition of typical Egyptian relief programs.

The tension between convention and desire for specificity here is also exceptional. The lack of structural harmony—the overloaded subject matter and varying orientation of figures leading to a sense of chaos with little empty space—contrasts with the typical orderly decorum of Egyptian compositions. Yet despite the design's thematic approach and the innovative addition of specific details, Ramses's martial triumph remains the dramatic center of action. The "eternal" presentation of the victorious pharaoh retains its visual rhetorical purpose (and ideological aim), namely, to reveal Ramses as the one and only heroic protagonist operating as Amun's son. The unusual placement of such battle scenes inside the temple—here beyond the power centers of objecting priesthoods—enlarges the significance of this victory. These breaks with Egyptian artistic tradition and religious practice reveal the king's power to command them.

Disputed Accounts

Many aspects of Ramses's account are now disputed, including the date of the battle and the size of the armies. Ramses undoubtedly enjoyed substantially more military support than he claimed to have lived to tell the tale. Some question the credibility of the two nomads who tricked Ramses, a trope in Bronze Age epic (such as the Greek soldier Sinon, who was "abandoned" at Troy to explain the wooden horse). It was extremely foolish for the king to divide his army at Kadesh based on information from two strangers, and yet the story comes from Ramses himself. Although we cannot diminish his personal leadership in a moment of crisis, the Egyptian forces might well have been routed but for the timely arrival of reinforcements. For his own purposes, however, Ramses downplayed their role; they are not mentioned in the literary record, and the reliefs illustrate nothing more than a large orderly array of troops approaching the Egyptian camp.[35]

The departure of Egypt's massed armies would have been spectacular, and the nation anxiously awaited news of the expedition. Although the Egyptians were able to survive a terrible predicament at Kadesh, we now know that it was not the splendid victory Ramses claimed. Nevertheless, his decision to represent his version of events in words and images at multiple locations throughout Egypt was a propaganda tour de force. (Although Ramses's position would seem secure, the instability of the previous century's ruinous Amarna Period cast a long shadow.)[36] Repetition, amplified by scale and placement in a sacred context, make Ramses's account true. That it had been accepted across the millennia is perhaps his true victory. Had the Hittite version of the battle been rendered on something more conspicuous, more memorable than clay tablets, the standard narrative of the battle might be quite different. Although Egyptian accounts describe the battle as a near disaster for the Hittites and portray Muwatalli begging for peace, in the longer term he may have been the ultimate victor.[37] Muwatalli retained control of Kadesh and gained additional territory in the kingdom of Amurru, extending the buffer zone with Egypt farther south and thereby safeguarding his empire.[38]

Skirmishes and shifting alliances menaced Egypt's borders for fifteen years following the battle. Although Ramses eventually took back Canaan, Lebanon, and Syria, minor kingdoms resisted Egyptian authority and refused to send tribute.

Following Muwatalli's death his brother assumed power as King Hattusilis III. In order to secure his precarious position internally and to counter Assyria's growing strength to his east, Hattusilis, according to Ramses, sent an embassy to Egypt to propose a formal peace treaty.[39] In 1259 BCE, three envoys arrived in Pi-Ramesses (his capital in the Delta) bearing two silver tablets inscribed in Akkadian cuneiform (the lingua franca of the day) from the Hittite court with the final terms of a treaty between the two monarchs. At about the same time, three Egyptian officials arrived in Hattusas, the Hittite capital, with two similar tablets. Although it is not the earliest ancient treaty, nor wholly original in content, it is the sole ancient treaty for which versions from both sides survive.[40] It demonstrates that regardless of his failings as a general in war, Ramses was definitely an effective statesman.[41] Both sides respected the treaty, allowing Ramses to return to his building projects. When the Hittites suffered famine fifty years later, Ramses's son and successor, Merneptah, recorded on the walls of Karnak his aid to his brothers, the Hittites.

3

The Alexander Mosaic

Commemorative Practice in Greek Polis and Macedonian Empire

The monumental art of the ancient Greeks tended to be primarily religious or funerary. In archaic Greece, votive monuments and sculptural ornamentation on temples generally perpetuated the memory of important events in an allusive manner through the great epic cycles or local myths, giving them a suggestive religious association. To represent historical events realistically would court hubris—reckless or prideful behavior—a transgression met by punishing nemesis.[1] Yet at the same time the writing of history—the process of critically examining sources for authenticity, selecting details considered reliable, and synthesizing those materials into an accurate narrative—joined rational philosophy and science as the major intellectual achievements of the classical Greeks; in fact, the Latin *historia* derives from the Greek *istoria*.

History aspired to make sense of the present, not just venerate the past, so it was essential that fact be distinguished from fiction, the real from myth and legend. Hecataeus of Miletos traced the ancestry of then-prominent families in his *Genealogies* and cast a skeptical eye at the traditions of families who claimed to be descended from gods. "I write what seems to me to be true; for the Greeks have many stories that, in my view, are absurd" (*Fragmente der griechischen Historiker* 1, frag. 1). Using the past to offer advice about the present, he was unsuccessful in dissuading the Ionians from revolting against Persia in 499 BCE. Although Herodotus related many dubious legends in his *Histories*, he also examined his materials critically to explain the origins of the Persian Wars,[2] the second and greatest of which he witnessed; later Thucydides reflected on the Peloponnesian War, in which he had fought. Representations of historical subjects, however, remained exceptional in Greek art.

Early Historical Subjects in Greek Art

A bronze sculptural group known as the *Tyrannicides* (Tyrant-Slayers) may represent Greece's first purely civic and secular representation (Fig. 3.1). In archaic times, "tyrant" described a leader who had seized power outside normal legal means, but it did not necessarily imply malevolence. Hippias, assisted by his brother,

Power, Image, and Memory. Peter J. Holliday, Oxford University Press. © Oxford University Press 2024.
DOI: 10.1093/oso/9780190901080.003.0004

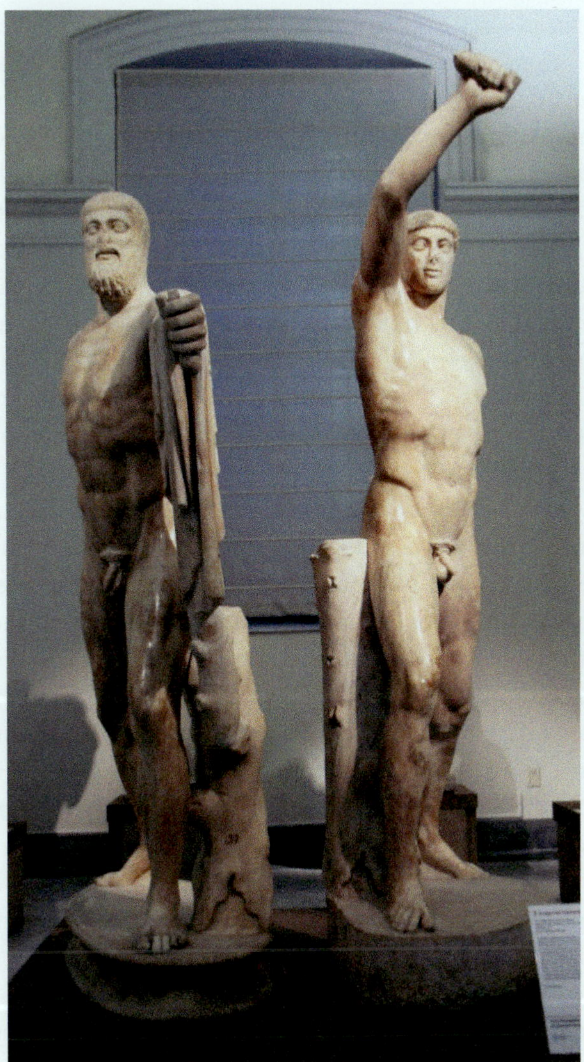

Fig. 3.1 Kritios and Nesiotes, Harmodios and Aristogeiton, the *Tyrannicides* (second-century AD Roman marble copies after Greek bronze originals of 477/76 BCE). Naples, Museo archeologico nazionale. Photo: author

Hipparchus, succeeded his father Peisistratus as tyrant of Athens; their popularity declined as they abused their power. It was the practice of Athenian elites to strengthen their patriarchal domination over archaic society through the establishment of private homoerotic bonds. According to Thucydides, Hipparchus publicly shamed the family of the young aristocrat Harmodius and also made unwanted advances on him. With his older lover Aristogeiton, Harmodius plotted to assassinate both Hippias and Hipparchus and overthrow their rule. They succeeded in killing Hipparchus during the Panathenaea religious festival of 514 BCE, but were struck down by bodyguards. Hippias escaped, remaining in power another four years until deposed after exhibiting even harsher authoritarianism, leaving tyranny with its malign connotations. Although Harmodius and Aristogeiton were unsuccessful and operated with conflicted motives as personal as they were political, the Athenians transformed them into populists who overthrew the tyranny.[3] Herodotus and Thucydides attempted to correct the record but failed.[4]

In 508/7 BCE, the magistrate Cleisthenes instituted the constitutional reforms credited with establishing Athenian democracy.[5] He commissioned Antenor to produce a bronze sculpture group honoring Harmodius and Aristogeiton to celebrate the new polity. Its significant placement in the Agora, Athens' central public space and the site of the assassination, cemented the association of the event and its protagonists with democracy in the Athenian consciousness.[6] At that time the figures would not have been portraits in our modern sense of life-like representations; rather, the dedication probably took the form of a pair of *kouroi* (cf. Fig. 3.2). Archaic elites set up these freestanding statues of male youths for votive and funerary display to bolster their claim to power as heirs of a Homeric ideal, implementing a heroic and poetic past—the *arkhaîa*—that was part of Greek cultural memory.[7] Conventional figures, kouroi literally embody the epitome of a youthful athletic warriors rendered heroic through their over life-size proportions, striding stance, and nudity.[8] The *Tyrannicides* appropriated a pre-existing aristocratic image and refashioned it to signify democratic rule by commemorating its (near-legendary) foundation, and thereby became a central source of Athenian identity. An epigram by the poet Simonides inscribed on the base of the Antenor group partially survives:

> A marvelous great light shone for the Athenians when Aristogeiton and Harmodius slew Hipparchus . . . and established the fatherland.[9]

The sculptures were seized as war booty in 480 BC by Xerxes I during the second invasion of Greece and installed at the Persian capital at Susa.

After decisively defeating the threat of Persian enslavement at the Battle of Salamis in 480 BCE, the victorious Athenians hailed Harmodius and Aristogeiton as Liberators (*eleutherioi*), casting their local heroes as the epitome of Athenian freedom as well as equality.[10] The city commissioned Kritios and Nesiotes to sculpt a replacement group to preside over the restoration of the city's ruined temples (Fig. 3.1).[11] Neither Antenor's original nor the second group survives, but the latter was copied in Hellenistic and Roman times. Their heavy chins and overemphatic musculature in the abdomen place them stylistically in the transitional period between archaic and classical art. In contrast to the frozen stride of archaic kouroi, the later figures lunge forward dramatically to attack. They also are not true portraits, but use the stylistic innovations of early classical art to characterize the two men: a mature and bearded Aristogeiton, the *erastes* or lover, brandishes a sword, with a cloak (*chlamys*) draped over his left shoulder, perhaps for defensive use as a kind of shield or as a reference to the concealment of his weapon; and a youthfully lean and

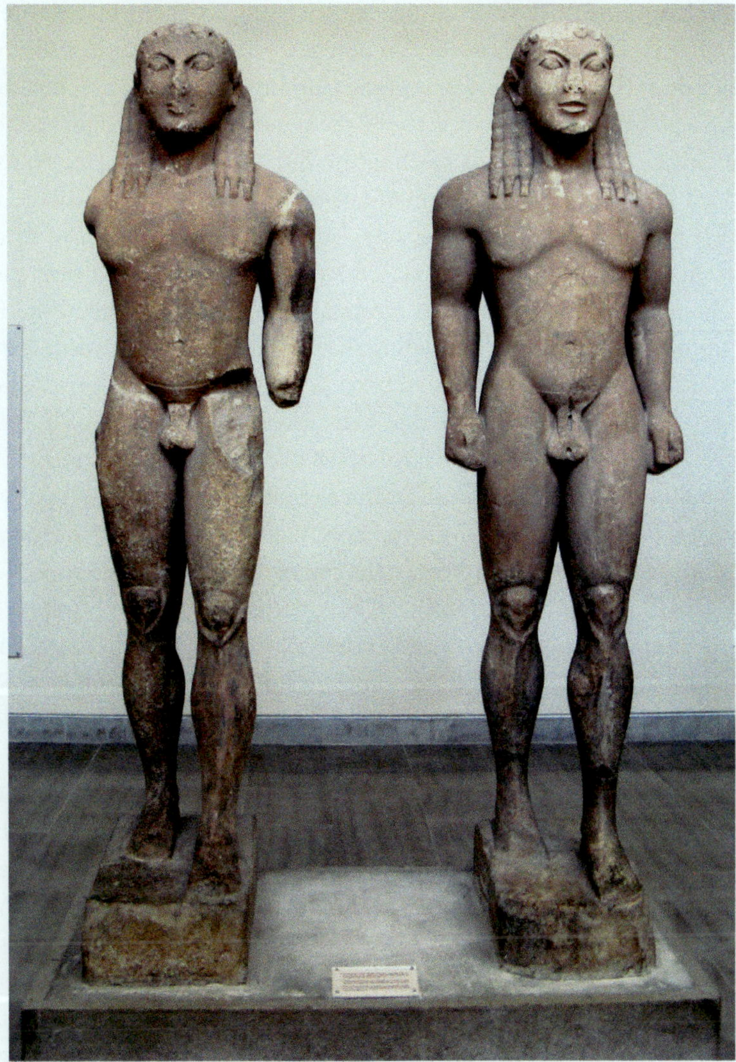

Fig. 3.2 Kleobis and Biton (ca. 580 BCE). Delphi, Archaeological Museum. Photo: author.

clean-shaven Harmodius, the *eromenos* or beloved, thrusting a sword forward in his upraised right hand, another sword in his left.[12]

Their pose, gestures, and attributes allude explicitly to their deed. Depending on the positioning of the two figures, one of two moments from the attack is possible. If placed facing one another they suggest the act of assassinating Hipparchus; back-to-back they appear to protect themselves against the bodyguards who struck them down. This desire for clarity and specificity in representing an actual event is significant; the group's innovative narrative qualities at the hallowed site revivified the event for viewers. Naram-Sîn personified the eroticized body of Mesopotamian heroes to underscore his claim to divinity; the *Tyrannicides* preserves the nudity of archaic kouroi because their courageous act propels them into the realm of heroes.[13] The *Tyrannicides* illustrates a momentary loosening of the traditional religious bonds of Greek art. Neither a grave monument nor votive in function, the group was a political dedication erected by the state to shape Athenian memories.

All of Greece suffered for not heeding the counsel offered by Hecataeus when Darius I led the first Persian invasion of Greece in response to Athenian interference in the Ionian Revolt. The Athenians, led by Miltiades and joined by a small cohort from Plataea, routed the Persian forces where they landed near the town of Marathon. The site's marshes and mountainous terrain prevented the Persian cavalry from joining the infantry, leading the Persians to flee in panic toward their ships, where a large number was slaughtered. Won in the face of overwhelming odds, the battle quickly attained mythic status, convincing the victors of the virtuousness of their democracy and the favor of the gods. The Athenians erected a great tumulus at Marathon as both a tomb and a celebratory monument of their victory; it remains a striking element in the landscape, intended to preserve the memory of an extraordinary event.[14] When Xerxes, the son of Darius, mounted a second invasion in 480 BCE, Athens fell. According to Herodotus (8.53): "Finally some Persians climbed the Acropolis and let the rest in. They massacred the Athenians, and then plundered the temple and set the Acropolis on fire." The naval victory at Salamis later that year thwarted the second invasion, which was finally halted the following year with a Greek victory at Plataea.

Around 460 BCE, Kimon, the son of Miltiades and a fervid advocate for the continuation of the Persian Wars, erected on the north side of the Agora the Stoa Poikile (Painted Colonnade), famous for its display of war booty and the celebrated paintings that gave it its name.[15] These included an *Amazonomachy* (by Mikon) and *Sack of Troy* (by Polygnotos), two traditional themes bracketed by two historical subjects: the *Battle at Oinoe* (artist unknown, and a subject of uncertain interpretation, although perhaps between Athenians and Spartans) and the *Battle of Marathon* (by Panainos, the brother of Pheidias, but also ascribed to Mikon and Polygnotos, who may have assisted). In his description of the Stoa Poikile, Pausanias (1.15.3) suggests the Marathon painting portrayed the battle in three phases. He describes a sequence opening with the Greeks joining battle from the left chasing the Persians to their ships at the right:

> Completing the painted program are those who fought at Marathon; the Boeotians who inhabit Plataea and the Attic force battle the foreigners. In this section neither side surpasses the other, but the center of the battle shows the foreigners fleeing and pushing one another into the marsh, while at the end of the painting are the Phoenician ships, and the Greeks slaying the foreigners who clamber into them. Here too is a portrait of the hero Marathon, after whom the plain is named; Theseus is shown rising from the underworld, and Athena and Heracles are also here. The Marathonians, according to their own account, were the first to regard Heracles as a god. The most prominent combatants in the painting are Callimachus, who was

chosen commander-in-chief by the Athenians, the general Miltiades, and a hero called Echettus.

Although now lost, art historians discern what may be echoes of the famous mural in other artworks. Elements shown on a nearly contemporary Greek vase, the so-called Niobid Vase, correspond so closely to Pausanias's description that many believe the vase painter borrowed from the muralist (Fig. 3.3).[16] Attributes identify the figures of Herakles and Athena among Athenian soldiers (one of which may represent Theseus).[17] The vase painter's attempt to locate the scene in a three-dimensional space defined by multiple levels of landscape was probably also inspired by innovations ascribed to contemporary wall and panel painters.

According to Pliny (*Naturalis historia* 35.57), other historical figures were portrayed, including the Persians Datis and Artaphernes.[18] The inclusion of the

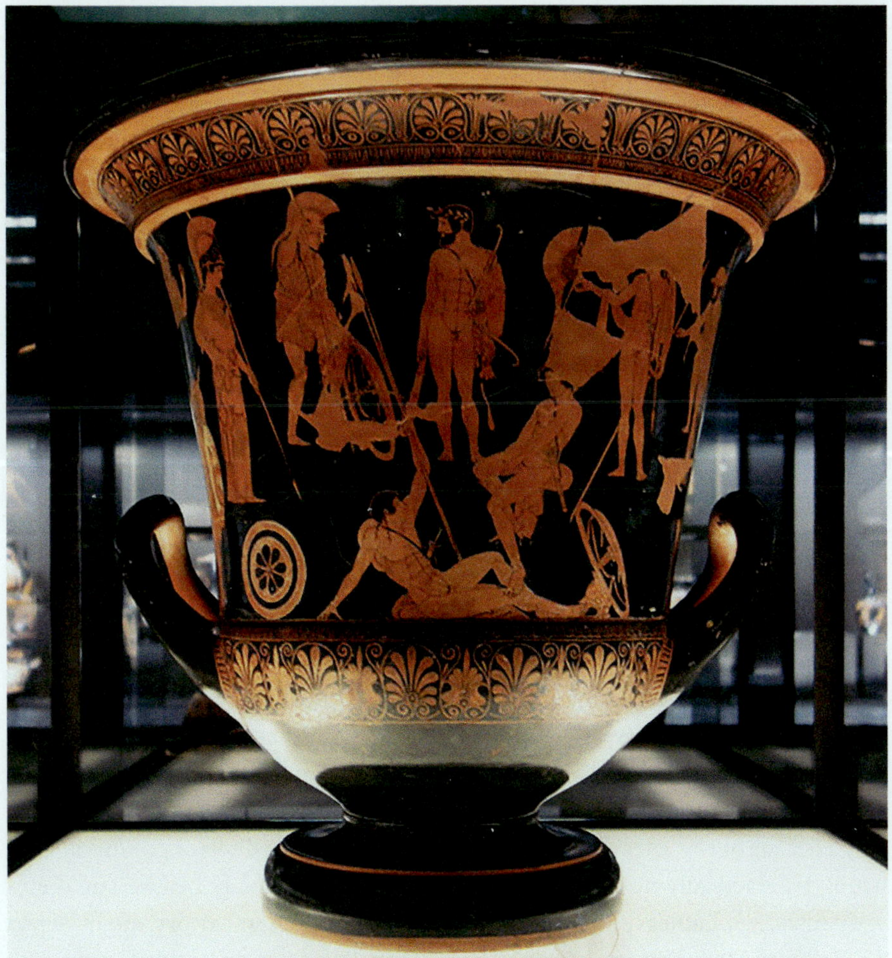

Fig. 3.3 Niobid Vase, figures perhaps based on the Marathon Painting (ca. 460–450 BCE). Paris, Musée du Louvre. Photo: author

portraits of important leaders stemmed from the same early classical experimentation that had produced the figures of Harmodios and Aristogeiton, and these figures may also have been characterizations identified by inscriptions (as used on vase paintings).[19] Iconographic details (such as distinctive helmets identifying the Boeotians) and topographical features (the marshy shore at the Phoenician ships) lent further specificity to the scenes depicted. The intermingling of mortals and immortals who observe or fight alongside them cast history as heroic epic and helped overcome the apprehension of showing hubris by representing actual events. It further suggests the gods sanctioned the Greek cause, and that victory came through their intervention, a rhetorical mode echoing Near Eastern and Egyptian monuments that depict the direct agency of the gods in ensuring victory, and also presaging the development of sophisticated allegorical representations in later Hellenistic and Roman art.[20] Vase painters had depicted Greeks fighting Persians for a generation, but a public monument displaying the pictorial commemoration of historical events was unprecedented. Kimon's stoa and its decoration amplified public oratory to mold individual and collective memories of recent threats in order to persuade public opinion to pursue a course of action in the present.

Most of the surviving structures on the Athenian Acropolis date to the ambitious rebuilding program directed by the statesman Pericles, from roughly 448 to 406 BCE. This project beautified and protected the city, exhibited its glory, and provided jobs. The new temples, most notably the Parthenon, served as a thanks offering to Athena and commemorated the Greek victory over the Persians. The sculptor Pheidias oversaw the sculptural program of the Parthenon, which depicted the sack of Troy, Greeks battling Amazons, Lapiths fighting Centaurs, and Olympian deities vanquishing rebellious Giants. These are all conflicts in which civilized order overcomes the chaos of barbarian foes, whose hubris is rightly punished. Both the Trojans and Amazons, purportedly emanating from the East, played on anti-Asian sentiments and were easily understood as metonyms for the recently defeated Persians; the Amazons also played to Athenian anxieties about women and social control. Centaurs, hybrid human-animals, and giants are lower forms of life that threaten order. Sculptors repeated conventional mythological narratives over and over on temples commemorating different incidents; the strategy allowed Greeks to allude to actual events without risking hubris themselves.[21] The association between contemporary Athens and these ancient stories—a blurring of the boundaries between actual fact and legend—was already well-established in Athenian art, and it would have been natural for Pheidias to develop the connection further.[22]

Finally, the frieze of the small Ionic temple dedicated to Athena Nike, completed only a decade or two after the Parthenon, features a series of duels or group combats, strung paratactically next to each other, which some scholars believe could embody historical battles: an encounter with Greeks entailing cavalry might depict the Battle of Marathon, and on the south side reliefs featuring nude Greeks with flying cloaks fighting an enemy whose sleeved tunics, trousers, and crescent-shaped shields are usually identified as Persian could depict the decisive Greek land victory

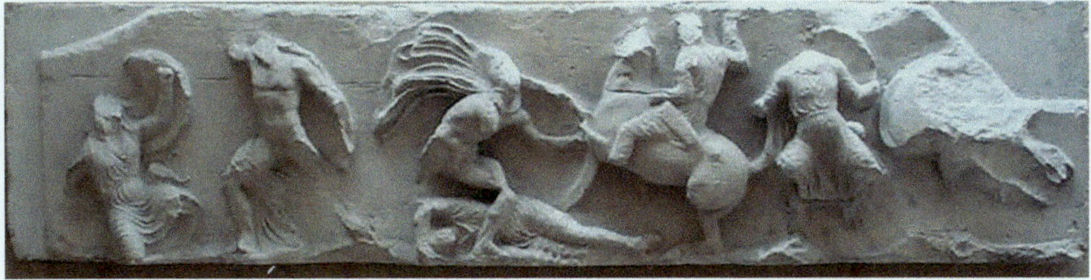

Fig. 3.4 Frieze section from the Temple of Athena Nike in Athens (ca. 426–421 BCE). London, British Museum 424. Photo: author

at Plataea (Fig. 3.4). The historicity of these scenes remains controversial, however, and most scholars interpret them as representing the Trojan War and other traditional mythological subjects. Greek battle imagery traditionally depicted duels that recall the agonal warfare of the hoplite phalanx but also evoke "memories" of Homeric combat, the Greek combatant's physical prowess expressed in his nude body leading to ambiguity. If these works are historical, then, as with the earlier *Tyrannicides* and *Battle of Marathon*, they celebrated the achievements of an earlier generation that had begun to acquire the aura of legend (helping explain the unrealistic nudity of the Greek soldiers). By the time the friezes were carved, Athens was waging the Peloponnesian War against Sparta, a disastrous conflict that would leave Athens reduced to a state of near-complete subjection. The celebration of those long-ago victories over the Persians in the face of current reality would have been as elegiac as they were stirring.

Tentative experiments in historical commemoration in the classical period were sporadic. There was resistance in democratic Athens to the kind of individuality necessary for true historical subjects. Since the days of the Peisistratid tyranny, the Athenians had been mistrustful of the concentration of power in any individual or family. Aeschines (*In Ctesiphon* 186) used the representation of Miltiades in the *Battle of Marathon* in his exploration of how an interest in the individual develops during times of crisis when a single man will stand out in contrast to the community. When a high proportion of personal pride became apparent, Greeks grew apprehensive over the emergence of hubris. Therefore, Greek custom promoted the representation of archetypal battles on temples to commemorate historical events, casting them within an epic struggle for civilization.

Alexander the Great and a New Spirit

A truly historical and commemorative iconography in Greek art appeared with the establishment of the dynastic spirit in the Hellenistic period: the age of Alexander the Great—heir to a Macedonian kingdom rather than a democratic leader—and his successors. After defeating the Greek city-states at Chaeronea (338 BCE), Philip II attempted to supplant the dominance of the *polis* with a shared identity by evoking the memory of the Greek alliance against Xerxes's invasion (necessarily avoiding Macedonia's problematic fifth-century role) with only limited success, as did his son Alexander with a similar program to rally the Greeks to his vision of imperial conquest.[23] The Greeks eventually embraced historical subjects in the wake of Alexander's victory over the Persian Empire (which then included Egypt), along with many Near Eastern artistic traditions they expressed in a Hellenized form.

Alexander deployed commemorative monuments to forward his personal agenda early in his career. In 334 BCE, at the age of twenty-two, he scored his first decisive victory in Asia at the River Granikos. To celebrate he commissioned a bronze statuary group from the sculptor Lysippos. Ancient sources tell us that rather than employing a traditional mythological theme, Lysippos appropriated the image of the single rider traditionally represented on tomb monuments in northern Greece to portray Alexander and twenty-five mounted *hetairoi* (Companions) who fell in the battle.[24] Its historicity, heightened by the inclusion of credible portraiture (an innovation of the later classical period) and purported battlefield realism, appealed to the era's new propensity for individualism and preference for drama over restraint (Fig. 3.5).[25] The scale of the monument and amount of bronze it demanded were unprecedented, as was its lavish expense.[26] The Granikos Monument epitomized Alexander's care for his men by celebrating the glory and honor they had won alongside their commander while also acknowledging the grief of their families, which may reflect a lingering influence of Greece's democratic experiment. Strategically displayed at the Macedonian national sanctuary at Dion, these entwined messages cast Alexander's personal ambition as national imperative and anticipated any possible criticism of his relentless campaigns and their mounting casualties.[27] The memorial proved extremely influential for succeeding Hellenistic and Roman rulers. In 146 BCE, the Roman general Metellus Macedonicus removed it to Rome; no trace of it remains today.[28]

Perhaps the finest representation of battle to survive from antiquity, the Alexander Mosaic conveys all the confusion and violence of ancient warfare (Fig. 3.6). It was discovered in the House of the Faun in Pompeii in 1831. Properly speaking its manufacture comprises Roman work, but it has long been recognized as a copy of a Greek painting of the early Hellenistic period. Monumental in scale—measuring just over 19 × 10 ft. (5.8 × 3.1 m)—its larger than life-size figures are made from about one and a half million tiny *tesserae* (colored tiles). The mosaic did not quite fit its allotted space in the house, so decorative borders were added to help reconcile the composition to its location. Large sections of the mosaic were lost to the very volcanic debris that also preserved it, but the bulk of the composition, including portraits of the two main protagonists, survives.[29]

A youthful and bareheaded Alexander leads his cavalry into the fray from the left, riding his celebrated horse Bucephalus (Fig. 3.7). He is clearly distinguished by his dramatically leonine hair marked at the midpoint by his trademark *anastole* (cowlick). His furrowed brow frames wide bulbous eyes. Alexander charges forward, forcing all in his path to fall or flee. With his 18-foot Macedonian *sarissa* (lance) he

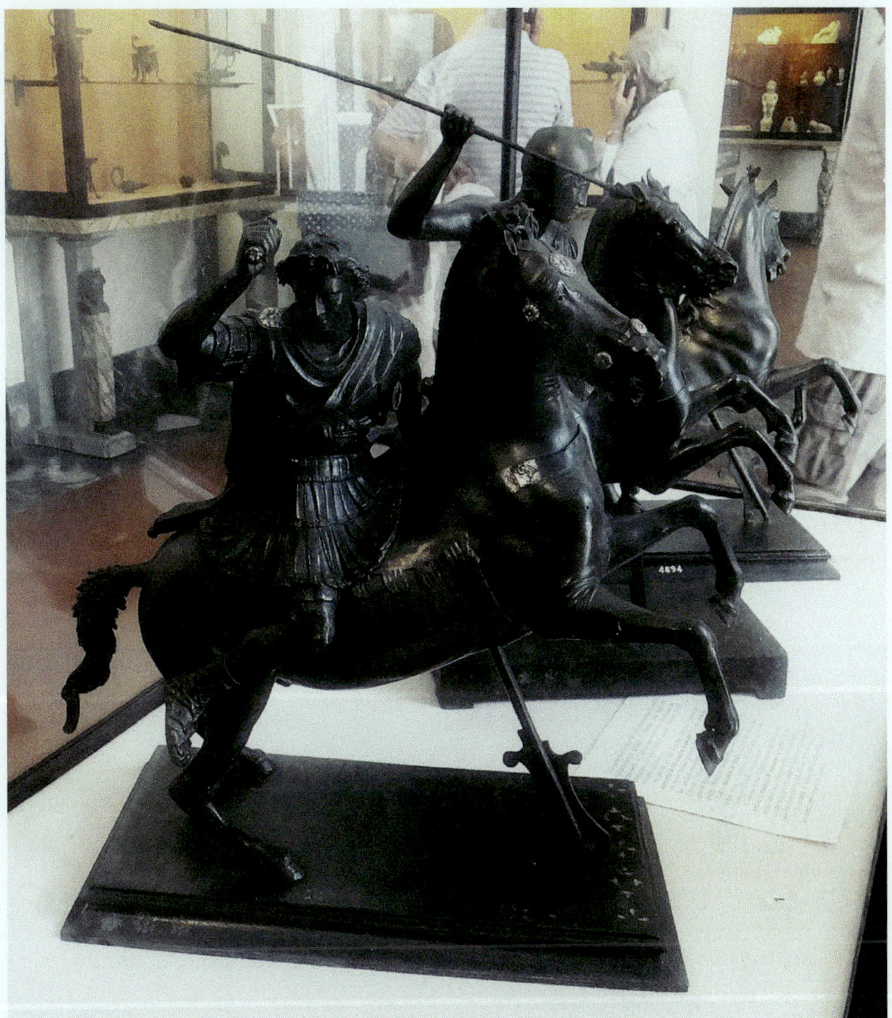

Fig. 3.5 Bronze statuette from Herculaneum of Alexander the Great (ca. first century BCE). Naples, Museo archeologico nazionale 4996. Photo: Wikimedia Commons

dispatches a Persian nobleman who slips from his wounded horse and falls to its knees, clutching at the lance with his right hand while bending his left arm up over his head in a formulaic gesture of immanent death. Alexander no longer notices him: with a dramatic turn of his head, he fixes his gaze—filled with pathos—toward his opponent, Darius III, whose worried eyes meet those of Alexander. Their gazes pull them across the field of battle to unify the composition's disparate elements. The king rides high in his chariot, standing out in a yellow Persian tiara, surrounded by his royal guard. His quiver empty of arrows, Darius can only stretch out his hand in mute gesture to yield the field to Alexander. The diagonal lines of the spears shown against the blank sky belong to Macedonian soldiers, their plumed helmets seen beneath Darius's outstretched arm. The red cloth attached to one spear signals the

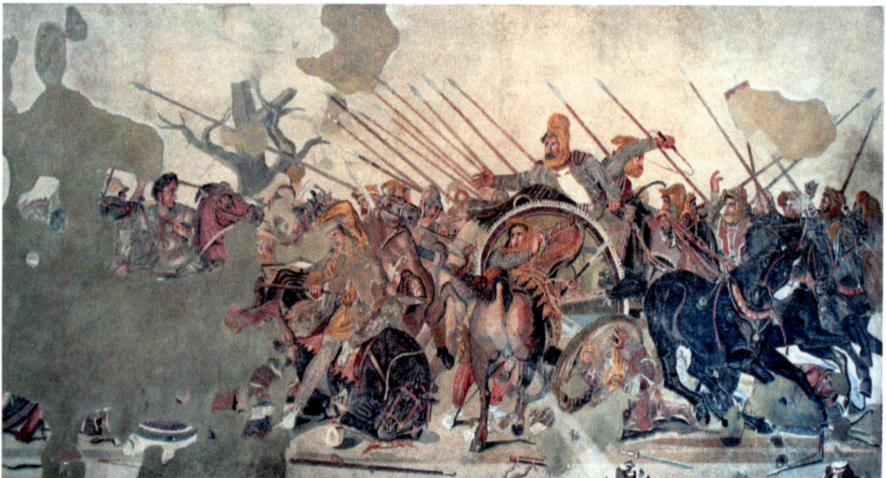

Fig. 3.6 *The Alexander Mosaic* (ca. 100 BCE). Naples, Museo archeologico nazionale. Photo: Amphipolis on Wikimedia Commons

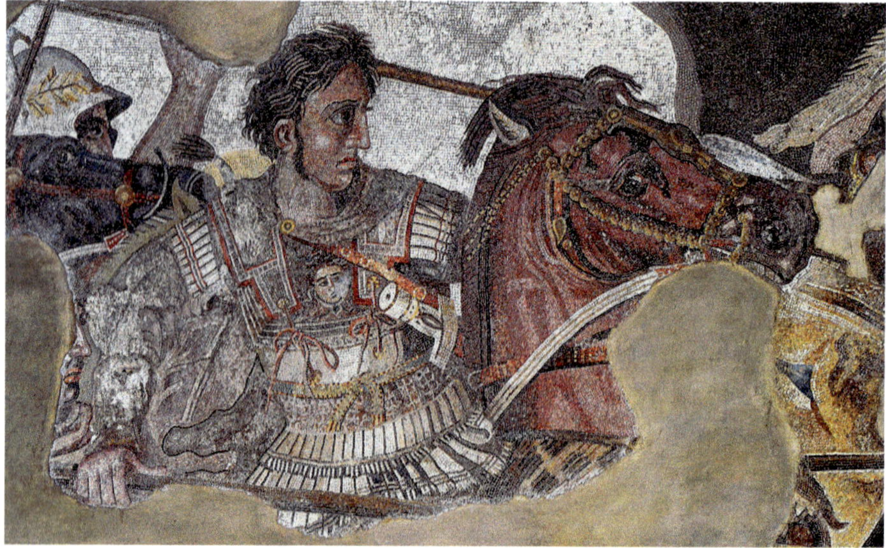

Fig. 3.7 *The Alexander Mosaic*, detail of Alexander. Naples, Museo archeologico nazionale. Photo: Wikimedia Commons

Macedonian squadron to circle around to cut off a Persian retreat (largely obscured by a damaged section of missing tile).[30] To the right under the charioteer's hand Persian soldiers stare in the direction of those helmets with expressions ranging from determination to consternation; one Persian soldier clenches his right hand to his brow in a conventional gesture denoting despair. The charioteer furiously whips the terrified horses about to secure Darius's escape from the lower right corner, directly into our space. The mosaic does not indicate that Darius ordered the retreat; rather, it implies his charioteer pulls the king from the battlefield: Darius is represented as a mere victim of his position.[31]

Pausanias described the *Battle of Marathon* as a clash between East and West, unfolding successively as the Greeks join the battle from the left to chase the Persians to their ships at the right. Similarly, the Alexander Mosaic appears to follow a left-to-right course, but featuring an even more complex compositional structure that can be read as both an unfolding frieze and as a monoscenic composition. As a frieze it cannot be grasped in a single moment but must be viewed as a narrative of successive scenes, from Alexander's charge to the death of the Persian he impales to Darius's recognition of his immanent defeat; monoscenically, the viewer grasps it all at once as a concentrated and autonomous image. The great wheel of the turning chariot signals that the battle is at the turning point, and by extension the decisive moment in the entire Persian campaign. It conjures the wheel spun by *Tyche* (Fortune) and the impermanence of all human endeavor.[32]

This battle is between professional armies belonging to vast empires, not the archaic Greek contest fought among the citizens of city-states. Fighting and dying soldiers fill the composition. Discarded weapons, the future spoils of the victors, litter the foreground. The mosaic emphasizes gritty, hard-hitting realism to highlight the triumphs and tragedies of its two royal protagonists as they struggle for world domination in far-off Syria, rivals characterized by dress, gesture, movement, and position. Their confrontation dominates the composition, which concurs with written histories of Alexander's campaigns, like that of Diodorus Siculus, who narrated the war as a series of *agones* between Alexander and Darius.[33]

Although its popular title gives prominence to Alexander, Darius is truly the emotional center of the image (Fig. 3.8). Some writers construe him as reaching out toward the slain Persian directly in front of him, a figure who could represent his brother Oxyathres. According to the Roman historian Quintius Curtius Rufus (3.11.8), at the Battle of Issus: "His brother, Oxyathres, saw Alexander bearing down on Darius and moved the cavalry under his command right in front of the king's chariot. Oxyathres far surpassed his comrades in the splendor of his arms and in physical strength, and very few could match his courage and devotion to Darius. In that engagement especially, he won distinction by cutting down some Macedonians who were recklessly thrusting ahead and putting others to flight." To his right another Persian struggles to control his panicked horse, which is shown from the rear and masterfully foreshortened to establish the density of the combat. Still another Persian has fallen beneath the crushing wheel of the turning chariot; in a tour de force passage we see him observe his own death throes reflected in his polished shield.

The mosaic portrays the Persians as utterly human. Some are unwavering, others fearful; one sacrifices himself for his king before Alexander. They are nothing like the Akkadian depiction of uncivilized Lullubi or the Egyptian representation of feckless Hittites. By dignifying them as an enemy worthy of respect, the artist increased the significance of Alexander's triumph.[34] The Greeks perceived the Persians as victims

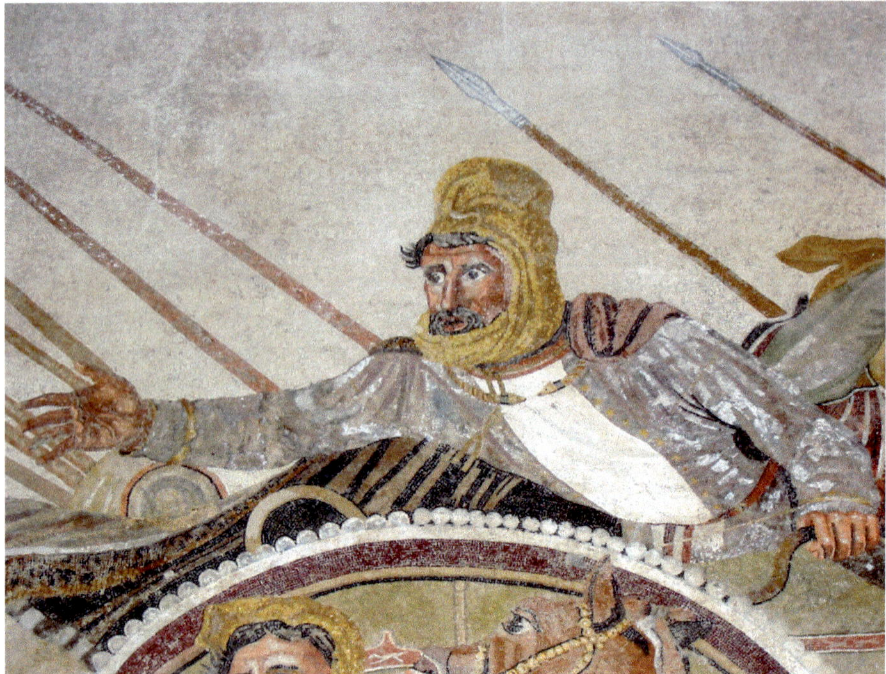

Fig. 3.8 *The Alexander Mosaic*, detail of Darius. Naples, Museo archeologico nazionale. Photo: Hibernian on Wikimedia Commons

of their own customs, of a flawed system of governance and social organization that afforded the Great King godlike reverence. Even the loftiest of Persian nobles had to accede to *proskynesis* (prostration) before the king. In contrast, the Macedonians perceived themselves as fiercely equal, at least among the elite. Andrew Stewart describes how this is displayed on the battlefield where Alexander rides *with* his Companions, whereas Darius stands *above* his troops.[35] Nevertheless, by showing the king not thinking of himself but turning back toward the dying men who enable his escape, the mosaic treats Darius with the same humanity as Alexander, which corresponds with Alexander's later politics of integration following conquest.

The surviving accounts used to reconstruct Alexander's campaigns were written hundreds of years later and are therefore of uncertain reliability. Arrian's *The Campaigns of Alexander* (*Anabasis*), written around 140 by a Roman senator and historian, are considered the best evidence; Plutarch's *Life of Alexander* and Diodorus Siculus's *Library of History* also provide abundant material.[36] Three major encounters between Alexander and Darius are recorded: the battles at the River Granikos (334 BCE, the battle commemorated in the bronze sculpture group by Lysippos), at the town of Issus in southern Anatolia (333 BCE), and at Gaugamela in Iraqi Kurdistan (331 BCE). We are told that it was at the Granikos that Alexander plunged into the midst of the fray, bareheaded so that his men could see him and follow. The dramatic retreat of Darius in his chariot following the death of his brother took place at Issus, a victory that gave Alexander control of southern Asia

Minor. Two years later Darius mustered his vast forces for one final, decisive battle at Gaugamela (also called the Battle of Arbella). There, Alexander charged through a gap in the Persian lines toward Darius after deploying his light infantry to cut off a retreat. As at Issus, the Great King fled the battlefield. With this admittedly sparse ancient evidence to go on, modern scholarship tends to favor Issus over Granikos and Gaugamela as the subject of the mosaic.[37]

We are told that Darius cleared the plain at Gaugamela of all trees and other obstructions and leveled so that his scythed chariots could move freely.[38] Left of center in the mosaic stands a dead, bare-limbed tree. This could be a topographic detail meant to identify that battle, or an artistic flourish, a motif rising above the action to offer a visual counterpoint to Darius. After Gaugamela, Darius—descended from Cyrus the Great, who had conquered Mesopotamia and claimed royal titles such as king of Sumer and Akkad, and king of Babylon—sought to muster another force, but his losses to Alexander had crushed his personal authority and he was assassinated by a faction of his own officers, ending the Achaemenid Dynasty. The tree could therefore symbolize the waning and imminent death of the Persian king and his empire, a meaning that is underscored by the fact that the tree is not merely dead but has lost its crown, as Darius will lose his. Elements from literary descriptions of each of these battles are found in the mosaic, making it almost impossible to determine which—if any—specific battle was represented.[39] It may be that the original painting contained more distinguishable details that identified the specific battle, and that these were somehow lost during the process of transposing from original to copy.[40] Alternatively, the mosaic may adhere to the older Greek practice of subordinating specific episodes to a more general type and thus represent an amalgamation of several battles.

The richness of various discursive passages forces us to consider again the discrepancies between historical narrative and artistic tradition. Specific details such as the elaborate corset, weapons, and harness of Bucephalus are realistically depicted; they are probably based on originals that could have been studied in Athens or Macedonia. Incidents such as Alexander's killing a Persian in attempting to reach Darius were recorded. But the need to illustrate an intelligible narrative within a complex composition demanded the use of conventional motifs and adaptation of recognizable schemata or stock formulae (such as the gesture of the dying Persian). The skillful handling of recent innovations—radical foreshortening, as in the panicked horse shown from behind, and the use of shading to convey a sense of convincing mass and volume—heighten the naturalistic effect of the representation to assure the viewer of its authenticity. The other horses stare directly at us, turning us into eyewitnesses of the struggle and compelling us to believe the significance of the scene before us.[41]

Questions about the original pictorial source are unresolved. If the Alexander Mosaic does record a single battle, the original painting was probably commissioned by Alexander or one of his generals to commemorate that event. That painting would date to ca. 330–310, when memories of the battle were still fresh, and its propaganda value would be most effective. Pliny (*Naturalis historia* 35.110) states that "Philoxenos of Eretria painted a picture for King Cassander which must be considered second to none, which represented the battle of Alexander against Darius." This would have been Kassandros son of Antipatros, the regent Alexander left behind in Macedonia, though Cassander took the royal title only in 303. Most scholars believe the mosaic reflects this lost painting acclaimed by Pliny, but arguments have been made for attributions to works by Aristides of Thebes and Helen of Alexandria (one of antiquity's few attested women artists), who painted a *Battle of Issus*.[42] Whatever the ancient painted source, it may have been brought to Italy as plunder after 146 BCE, when the Romans conquered Macedonia.

Rome's Alexander

Both the themes so brilliantly explored in the Alexander Mosaic and the artistic conventions used to represent them exemplify a disruption of previous Greek practice. Greek makers no longer produced art for the small, tightly knit *polis* with its cohesive citizenry; it now flourished in large urban centers with mixed populations that were spread over broader geographical expanses. Hellenistic kingship replaced experiments with democratic rule. In the Hellenistic period a ruler's legitimacy was tied to his person and established through military victories ("spear-won land"). Alexander initiated a *Kulturpolitik* that utilized coinage, building projects, and artistic commissions to promote a ruler's reputation as a dynamic commander and underscore his claim to legitimacy. There was a new interest in individual character and personality as opposed to the more generalized classical types. Portraiture began to flourish as a separate branch of art at this period—not only in Greece, but also to the west in Italy. The mosaic's—or perhaps more accurately, the painted prototype's—combination of specific, almost anecdotal details with stock types to commemorate a historical event that at the same time creates a politically potent character portrait of a leader would become the dominant theme of Roman Imperial state reliefs.

All of the surviving accounts of Alexander's conquests were written against the background of Roman imperialism, and ancient readers necessarily adjusted and interpreted what they read in the light of the social and political structures that characterized the imperial expansion of their age. Alexander "the Great" was a Roman creation: the title first appears in a Roman comedy by Plautus in the early second century BCE.[43] For a Roman audience commemorative specificity of the battle scene was probably less important than celebrating the qualities of Alexander's personality that spoke to them: his ferocity in battle, his charisma (from the Greek for "bestowed with grace," as close a claim to divinity as a Greek leader might make), and his military genius.[44] Alexander was as much a part of the cultural memory of Rome as Homeric epic was for Greece, providing a paradigm for their own military triumphs.[45] To display a mosaic of this scale, quality, and subject matter in a private house brought immense cultural capital to its Roman owners.

4

The Column of Trajan

Images of Power at Rome's Center and Periphery

With the death of Cleopatra in 30 BCE, the last kingdom ruled by Alexander's successors fell to Rome's expanding empire. Even before then Rome participated fully in the international cultural politics of the Hellenistic age. In addition to the kind of evidence suggested by the discovery of the Alexander Mosaic in a private residence, Roman political leaders commissioned public monuments to commemorate their achievements for both self-promotion and to persuade other Romans to embrace their policies.[1] In order to reach diverse urban and provincial audiences Roman makers drew upon different artistic traditions to fashion their works, including temporal and regional styles and such distinct modes of representation as sophisticated allegories and seemingly documentary depictions of events—sometimes simultaneously in the same monument.[2]

Roman Allegory: The *Cancelleria Reliefs*

Allegory is a mode of communication that combines symbolic figures with actual persons to convey complex moral, political, or religious messages. In 1938, two marble reliefs that epitomize Roman commemorative allegory were found under the Palazzo della Cancelleria in Rome, giving them their modern name (Fig. 4.1 and Fig. 4.2).[3] Frieze A (as it generally known) depicts Domitian's ceremonial departure (*profectio*) for his Sarmatian Campaign in 92–93. The emperor is led by a personification of Victory, of which only her left wing survives, a ceremonial bodyguard (*lictor*) identified by his bound fasces and axe,[4] the armed god of war Mars, and Minerva, also armed in her guise as a warrior goddess. Domitian, dressed in his traveling costume of short tunic covered by a military cloak (*paludamentum*), is propelled forward by the Amazonian personification of Virtus (military prowess). Two other personifications, the bearded Genius of the Roman Senate and the youthful Genius of the Roman People (identified by his attribute, a cornucopia), bid the emperor farewell. The figures are classicizing in style, carefully modeled and idealized, and with those in the foreground carved in high relief and those appearing behind them in low relief. The body language suggests that Domitian, peace-loving yet ready for warfare, is reluctant to set out for the frontline.

Power, Image, and Memory. Peter J. Holliday, Oxford University Press. © Oxford University Press 2024.
DOI: 10.1093/oso/9780190901080.003.0005

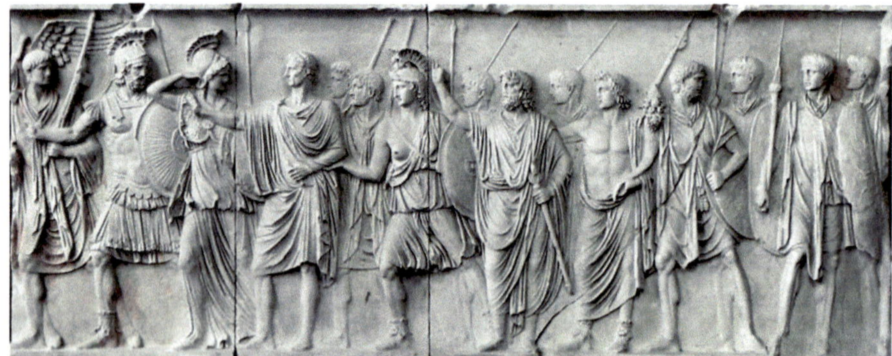

Fig. 4.1 *Cancelleria Relief*, Frieze A: *profectio* of Domitian (ca. 93–95). Vatican, Museo Gregoriano Profano. Photo: author

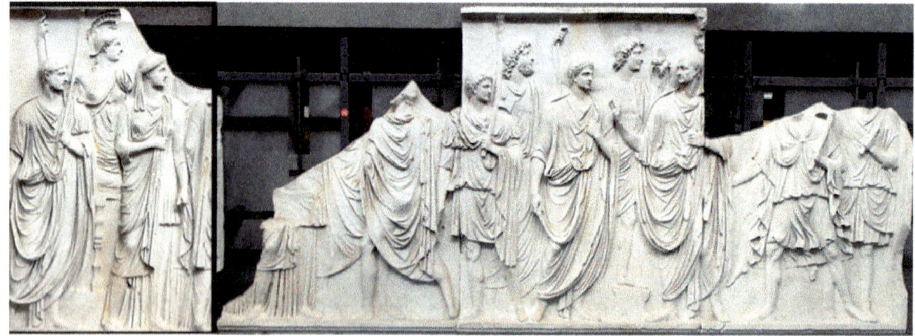

Fig. 4.2 *Cancelleria Relief*, Frieze B: *adventus* of Vespasian (ca. 93–95). Vatican, Museo Gregoriano Profano. Photo: author

Frieze B is usually interpreted as representing Emperor Vespasian's return to Rome (*adventus*) after his victory in the civil wars of 68–69. (A flying Victory held a laurel wreath above his head.) Seated on a raised throne, the goddess Roma greets him at the far left of the panel; before her are figures of Vestal Virgins escorted by lictors. Just right of center are the Genius of the Senate and of the Roman People; some scholars identify the young man before them as Vespasian's son, Domitian. Like Frieze A, the background is completely neutral, the absence of distinguishing landscape or architectural elements confounding a definite identification. Together the panels extoll the imperial virtues of the ruling family: *virtus* in war and filial *pietas* (devotion). The combined representation of members of the imperial family, gods, personifications, and various symbolic figures, attributes, and adjuncts forms a highly complicated allegorical message, perhaps a program to convince a war-weary populace of the necessity of taking action on the frontier.[5] The underlying conception is subtle and half-spoken and perhaps not even entirely clear. The delicate technique and luxurious character indicate a continuation of Hellenistic court practices assimilated to Roman needs.

Careful examination reveals that the reliefs were recut to celebrate another regime after the assassination and *damnatio memoriae* of Domitian. The head of Domitian on Frieze A is too small for the body, implausible for a work of such high artistic quality. In fact, the facial features conform more closely to those of Nerva, Domitian's successor. Recent analysis suggests that the head on Frieze B was also recarved and the figure greeting him may simply be a young priest. Only the heads were recarved on the reliefs, indicating that Roman historical reliefs were governed by an interchangeable visual language: the surrounding gods, attributes, associations, and types of events stay the same; only the identities of the protagonists need be altered. That Nerva is shown taking part in a *profectio* even though there is no record of his departure for a campaign suggests that precise historical reference was secondary to the symbolic potential of imperial allegories.[6] The decision to recast these reliefs not only speaks to how contemporary viewers appreciated their exceptional quality, but also indicates that those with the power to commission such artworks also recognized their program as being highly effective. Nerva, however, died sixteen months after assuming office. Since the heads would be too small to recarve yet again with another figure's features, it was probably decided to discard the panels.

The interaction of divinities and personifications with historical persons on these reliefs allows the artists to glorify imperial virtues in relation to real-world events that far surpasses the capacity of purely documentary description, subject to the viewer's ability to construe their metaphors. Whereas the obscure complexity of the allegorical mode may have hindered the propagandistic power of the reliefs for some audiences, the realistic imagery employed on the Column of Trajan is easily understood.

Trajan's Dacian Wars

Trajan came to power in a challenging time. The Roman state carried out building programs of unprecedented scale and complexity. Since the reign of Nero emperors had removed gold from Roman coinage to help finance such projects, a practice that destabilized the economy. The treasury was further encumbered by military campaigns throughout Europe, forcing Nerva, Trajan's predecessor, to accelerate the devaluation of the currency. Conquering Dacia (located in modern-day Romania), celebrated for its productive gold mines, presented Trajan with the prospect of restoring the Roman economy and proving his military prowess. Under pretext of protecting the Danubian province of Moesia (in modern-day Serbia and Kosovo, and the northern part of the Republic of Macedonia and Bulgaria) from persistent Dacian incursions, in 101 the Senate sanctioned Dacia's invasion.[7] As Roman soldiers pressed toward the capital of Sarmizegethusa, they erected strategic forts and bridges while incinerating Dacian villages. The Dacians were forced to surrender following the Battle of Tapea in 102, but their king, Decebalus, was permitted to retain his title to ensure the supply of gold.

By 105 Decebalus had reestablished his power, reorganized his people, and launched attacks on Roman garrisons. In response Trajan mounted a new campaign. This second Dacian War lasted longer than the first and brought Rome higher casualties. During the decisive assault the Romans burned Sarmizegethusa to the ground. Decebalus committed suicide to avoid capture, but his treasure was found in the River Sargesia (Sargetia). Rome incorporated Dacia into the empire. Her rich mines added 700 million denarii a year to the Roman treasury,[8] financing both Trajan's later campaigns to expand the empire to its greatest extent (Armenia in 114 and Parthia in 115) and his incomparable urban program.

The Forum of Trajan

By the late Republic, the venerable Roman Forum was no longer capable of encompassing all its traditional activities. Julius Caesar, Augustus, and Nerva each built supplementary venues for judicial proceedings, business affairs, and public assembly to the northeast of the old Forum, self-contained but still connected to it and each other; Trajan used the vast Dacian spoils for the construction of a massive building project that dwarfed all earlier imperial endeavors: it included an immense plaza, a basilica, libraries, a multi-level market in which spices and other luxuries were sold, and a monumental column with sculpted reliefs commemorating the Dacian Wars (Fig. 4.3). It not only provided additional space to conduct Rome's public business, but it also served as a monument to Trajan and to the glory of the empire. For Roman viewers, the fruits of Roman imperialism surrounded them in the new complex. So esteemed were his victories and civic munificence that he was acclaimed *optimus princeps*: the best emperor.[9]

Trajan began his forum in 107, the same year he celebrated his victory over Dacia; most of the work was completed by 112. Designed by Apollodorus of Damascus, the complex is modeled on the earlier and smaller Forum of Augustus. The main gate to the forum is similar in form and sculptural program to a Roman triumphal arch, underscoring Apollodorus's attempt to cast the complex as a victory monument. This entrance led into a great open rectangular plaza with an equestrian statue of Trajan as its centerpiece. On the upper stories of the flanking colonnades captive Dacian prisoners alternated with portrait shields (*imagines clipeatae*). The basilica or law court dominated the north end of the forum rather than a traditional temple; it was named for Trajan's family name, *Ulpias*. Like the forum, the Basilica Ulpia was fronted with a monumental doorway in the form of a commemorative arch with three entrances. The basilica led to a small colonnaded rectangular court flanked by Greek and Latin libraries and on the fourth side a monumental gateway that opened to the northwest side of the forum complex (not the temple as often shown in reconstructions) with the column as its centerpiece. Beyond the eastern end of the plaza Trajan's market nestles against the flank of the Quirinal Hill; the

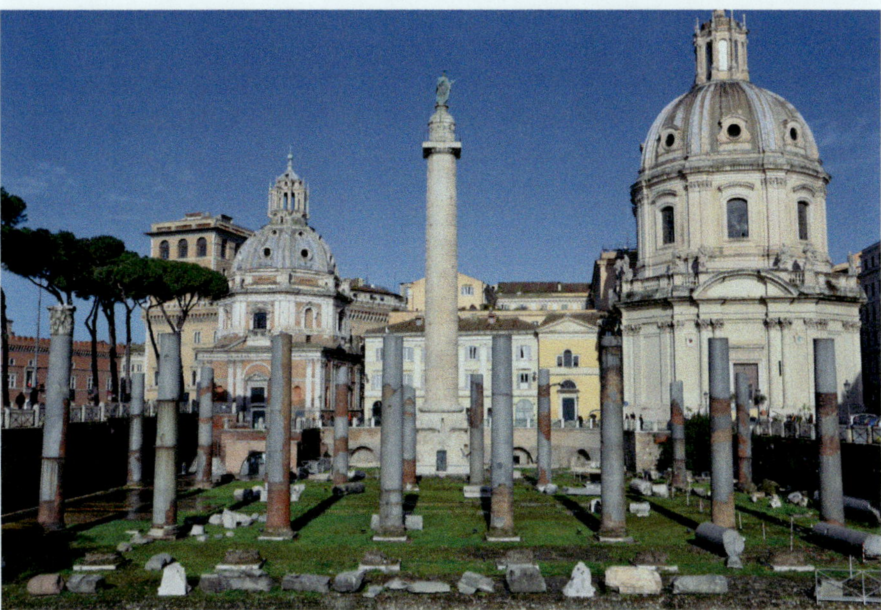

Fig. 4.3 Ruins of the Basilica Ulpia and the Column of Trajan. Rome. Photo: author

solid brickwork of this structure is so enduring that except for the column, today it is the best-preserved element of Trajan's complex.

The Column and Frieze

The column was dedicated in May 113, more than sixteen months after the forum. The first thing a visitor saw entering the small court was the column's large base made of eight marble blocks topped by a two-block pedestal (Fig. 4.4). The pedestal frieze depicts the spoils of captured Dacian weapons and armor in wonderfully detailed low relief; on the cornice four eagles (two of which survive) carried victory garlands of oak leaves. An inscription on the southeast side of the base indicates that the Senate and People of Rome dedicated the monument in honor of Trajan. A door at one side of the base opens to a chamber that on the right side leads to stairs and on the other side, behind another set of doors, to the sepulcher. The 185 spiral steps within the hollow column, illuminated by forty-three small windows set at regular quarter turns, climb to a viewing platform at the top.[10] This originally had a metal rail and could accommodate up to fifteen people who would have admired breathtaking views in all directions. A 16-foot (4.8 m) bronze statue of Trajan crowned the top pedestal.[11]

The monument stands 126 feet (38.4 m) high from ground level to the top of the statue base.[12] The column shaft consists of 29 stacked drums of Luna (Carrara) marble, weighing more than 1,100 tons that rise 100 Roman feet (97.64 British feet

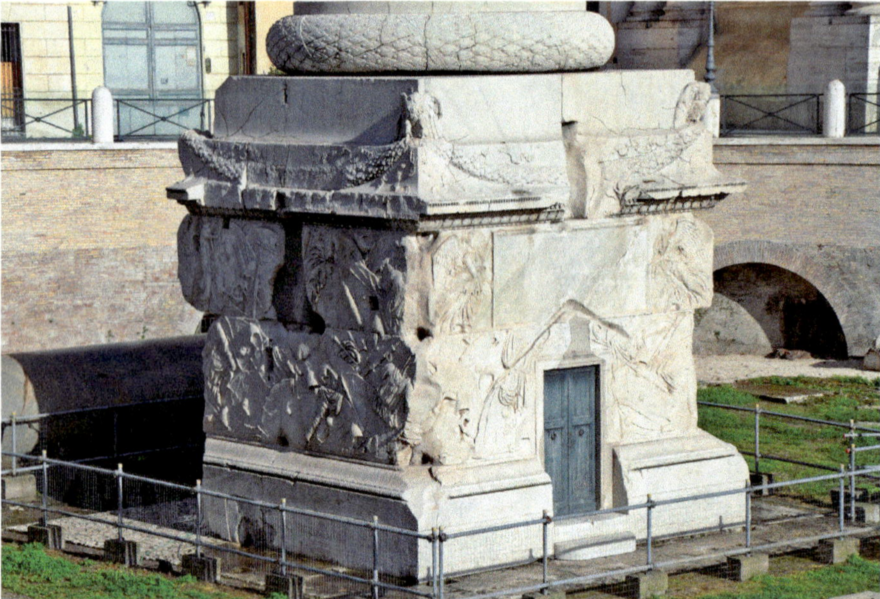

Fig. 4.4 Base of the Column of Trajan (dedicated 113). Rome. Photo: author

or 29.76 m). Its execution represents an immense engineering challenge that required careful planning. Materials had to be obtained and transported to Rome, some across vast distances. Ancient sources indicate that Roman engineers designed complex devices that were capable of raising large weights for architectural projects, and it is likely that cranes lifted the column drums into place.[13] Its successful completion stands as a monument to the complex tasks Roman architects could successfully complete.

During the Republic, Romans initiated a rich tradition of celebratory monuments, which they continued into the imperial period. Here the designer drew on a longstanding practice of honorific columns surmounted with statues of famous men or divinities that adorned the fora of Rome and provincial cities.[14] Truly innovative, however, is the helical frieze narrating Trajan's campaigns, which winds around the column twenty-three times from its base to the capital.[15] Giovanni Becatti called the *colonna coclide istoriata* "the most original monument of Roman art."[16] Today we are uncertain who was responsible for designing and overseeing the carving of the column and its remarkable reliefs. In modern scholarship he is called the "Maestro" or "Master of Trajan." The forum's designer Apollodorus has been suggested, for it is generally agreed that the column was a part of his original program.[17]

The reliefs portray some 155 scenes that by and large appear to follow one another in true temporal and spatial sequence to present a chronicle of the major events of Trajan's Dacian campaigns; the lower half illustrates the first war (101–102), and the top half illustrates the second (105–106), separated by a scene with the personified Victoria writing on a shield flanked by trophies. The narrative technique involves

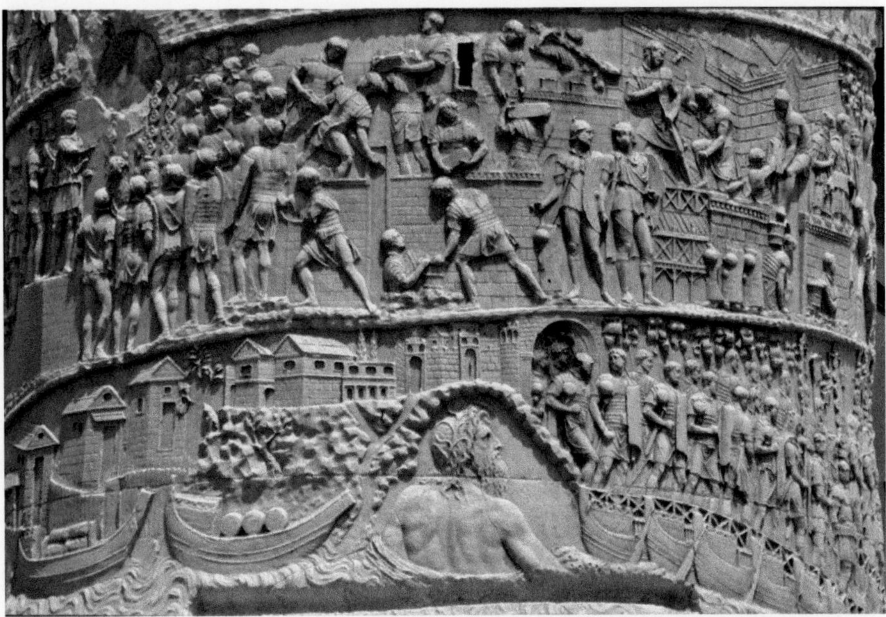

Fig. 4.5 Column of Trajan, Romans cross the Danube; (lower register) Trajan addresses his troops (*adlocutio*) and Roman soldiers engaged in construction (upper register). Rome. Photo: author

a skillfully arranged alternation of a few recurrent motifs, the story told in an epitomized matter-of-fact manner. Significant historical and topographical points are organized on vertical axes to enhance viewer comprehension and to emphasize principal achievements, such as building the Danube bridge (Fig. 4.5), the capture of the Dacian treasure, the death of Decebalus, and the presentation of his severed head to the emperor. The innumerable details of the narrative are stamped with the authenticity of realistic observation; divine figures are used sparingly, and then only to describe natural phenomena such as thunder, night, and water (a personification of the Danube watches Roman soldiers cross their bridge). Although some scenes sometimes unfold continuously, even running into each other, in most instances landscape features such as rocks, trees, or buildings separate individual scenes to indicate narrative changes, making this predominantly an example of sequential narrative (Fig. 4.6). The upward flow of the story lends a sense of historical inevitability to both Trajan's achievement and Rome's dominance, a rhetorical strategy echoing some Mesopotamian and Egyptian monuments.

Ethnic typing distinguishes Dacians from Romans in battles and other thematic episodes, and distinctive headgear and dress (such as leggings) further differentiate figures in terms of rank and class (Fig. 4.6). In a scheme that recalls the Victory Stele of Naram-Sîn, the Romans are shown as clean-shaven and orderly and uniform, whereas the Dacians appear disorganized and unkempt. Regular Roman legionaries consistently wear their distinguishing body armor (*lorica segmentata*)

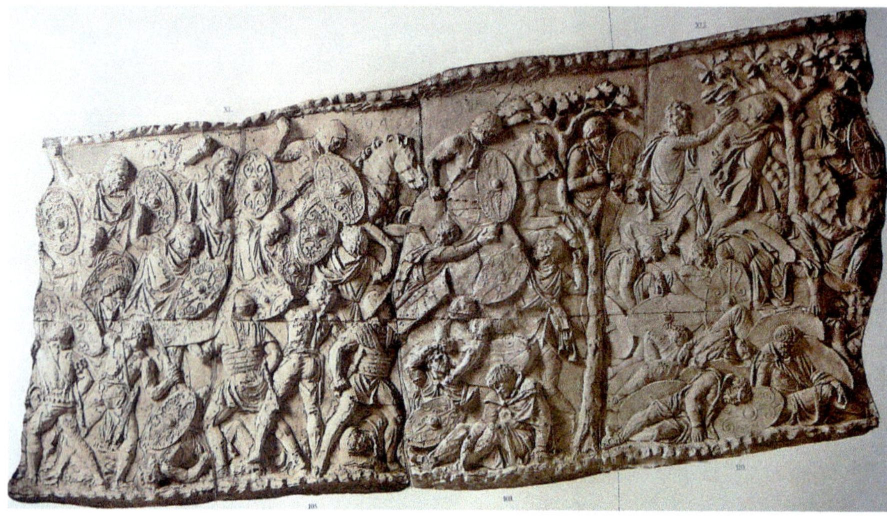

Fig. 4.6 Column of Trajan (cast), battle scene between Roman and Dacian armies; retreat of defeated Dacians. From Conrad Cichorius (1896), scenes 40 and 41.

and carry rectangular shields, while auxiliaries wear leather or chain mail tunics and carry oval shields. Sculptors adhere to this convention even when soldiers appear engaged in pursuits that would not require the wearing of armor, such as cutting down trees, setting up a camp, or being employed in construction. The detailed depiction of siege engine like the ballista and catapult provides an extraordinary visual resource for studying the iconography of both the Roman and barbarian armies and contributes valuable information about their equipment and tactics of warfare; overall, however, representations of battle are downplayed in favor of scenes of disciplined soldiers executing ceremony and construction.[18] There are also near genre-like scenes such as the army on the march or grazing animals.[19] Within the numerous scenes of Roman soldiers building or fortifying camps, their buildings are shown as solid, regular, and well-designed, contrasting sharply with the humble structures of the Dacians. Very likely the emphasis on representations of building instead of battle scenes and the restrained portrayals of the collateral damage of war—depictions of violent actions against the civilian population, especially women and children, are not shown—is a thematic choice aimed specifically at the urban population of Rome tired of generations of expensive conflict.[20] The Dacian Wars are portrayed as campaigns of conquest and expansion of civilization into *barbaricum* to incorporate the new province into the Roman Empire.[21]

Over a century ago, Franz Wickhoff noted that "whatever war is going on we want to know what [Trajan] is doing, and in every fresh event we are dissatisfied until we have found out his striking person."[22] Trajan is generally portrayed as clean-shaven with medium-length hair reminiscent of representations of Rome's first emperor, Augustus.[23] He is shown on the column nearly sixty times in such diverse yet consistent roles as leading the army as it sets out on a campaign (*profectio*), addressing

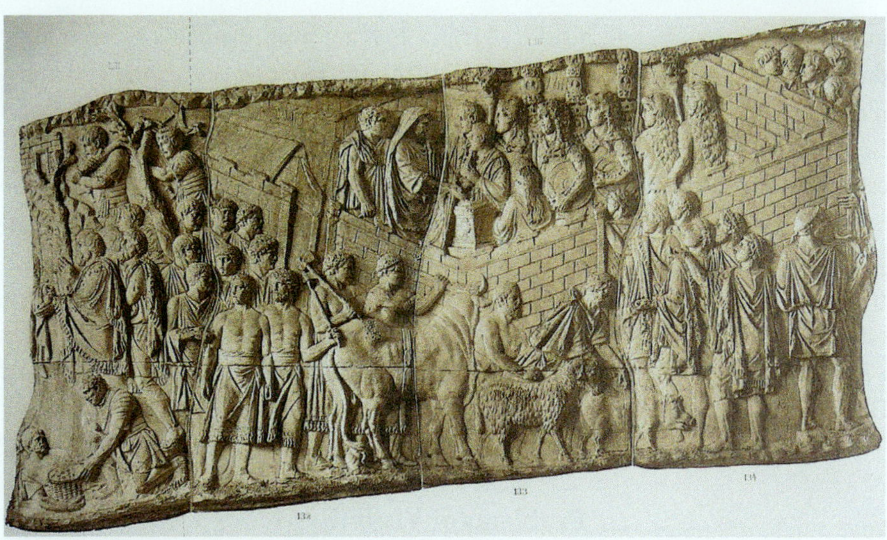

Fig. 4.7 Column of Trajan (cast), procession and sacrifice of a pig, sheep, and bull (*suovetaurilia*). From Conrad Cichorius (1896), scenes 52 and 53.

the troops (*adlocutio*, Fig. 4.5), conducting sacrifices (*lustratio* demonstrating his *pietas*, Fig. 4.7), overseeing building operations, and receiving embassies or captives, always commanding and the iconographic focus of attention. He is routinely shown in profile or three-quarter view; when flanked by his lieutenants, he is generally placed in the middle of the group or shown just slightly taller (in contrast to the unnaturalistic hierarchical scales deployed by Mesopotamian and Egyptian artists). Figures in the scenes turn toward Trajan, further drawing the viewer's attention to him. He is portrayed armed for battle in about half the representations, and like Alexander's image, his head is usually bare, making him easier to identify.[24] He is portrayed nineteen times on the principal (southeast) face of the column, which faced the Basilica Ulpia; although the basilica would have blocked this side of the column from those standing in the forum square, its scenes would have been visible from viewing platforms on the basilica. The emphasis on Trajan as the heroic protagonist is fundamental to the monument's commemorative function.

While some scenes may be inventions, others are corroborated by literary sources, and most surely conformed to the ancient viewer's knowledge and expectations of the Roman army. Since the Dacian Wars had occurred only a few years earlier, many of those who had fought in the campaigns would have been able to see the completed monument. Sculptors carefully rendered details to identify particular combatants, and settings for scenes—including natural backgrounds—denote precise locales; such specificity suggests that the designer worked from eyewitness accounts and maybe even drawings made in the field during the campaigns. Sculptors made provisions in many places for adding metal attachments, mainly tools and weapons held by soldiers.[25] The precision with which the details are rendered creates the strong effect of authenticity, reinforcing the idea that the images describe objective historical truth, making even elements of seemingly doubtful accuracy appear convincing. Trajan's triumphal celebrations and commemorative coin issues had already educated Romans about conflict incidents and Dacian culture. Representing the ethnically specific barbarian *spolia* on the pedestal reliefs with veristic detail gives them particular immediacy; sculpted reliefs on the Basilica Ulpia façade and the statues of bound captives around the forum plaza further advance the message. Nevertheless, it was not an unimaginative retelling of historical events, but a monument carefully calculated to combine narration with imperial symbolism. Documentary accuracy was deployed to convince a Roman audience that had grown cynical with the fabrication and exaggeration of Domitianic allegories.

Problems of Visibility

The column's great height and the acute angle of view thwart any attempt to follow the scenes without interruption: a viewer has to walk around the column twenty-three times looking upward to follow the narrative from bottom to top. The designer may have taken these problems into account, for the band's dimensions change slightly as it reaches the top: the frieze expands from about 3.3 feet (0.8 m) at the base to slightly over 3.9 feet (1.5 m) in height, as do the heights of the individual figures, from 0.60 m to 0.80 m., perhaps with an aim of making the higher scenes more visible from below.[26] Some scholars argue increased visibility was not the reason for these changes. Instead, they note that the spiral keeps roughly the same width (1.1 to 1.2 m) between the first and thirteenth turn, then narrows as it continues up the column, contracting to its narrowest at the nineteenth spiral and then attains its greatest width on the last two drums. They therefore posit that the sculptors were not sure just how much space they were going to have to fit in all their scenes, and only once the final drums were placed on top of the column were they sure of how much space they had, increasing the height of the last spirals to take up space they did not know they would have.[27] If this were indeed the case, it raises questions about how closely Apollodorus, the draftsmen he directed, and the sculptors collaborated.

All the same, the higher scenes remain barely legible from the ground. Ancient viewers could probably observe the sculpted reliefs from multiple vantage points from the top floors of the two libraries flanking the column, which may have provided viewing platforms in addition to those on the nearby basilica, making some of the higher scenes somewhat more discernable.[28] Nevertheless, viewers could only observe one side at any time, and recent reconstructions of the forum have determined that the two libraries would have further obstructed the viewer's ability to follow the reliefs by circling the column. Even if it was impossible to follow the narrative from beginning to end, the viewer can form associations among the different scenes and recognize the figure of Trajan stacked vertically from band to band.

The design gives prominence to the column's narrative function. The dominant perspectival convention represents scenes as though they have been tilted toward the viewer so that figures in the background appear above those in the foreground, but other perspectival views are also deployed to present the maximum level of detail. Sometimes multiple perspectives are used in a single scene so that more can be shown, such as mixing different angles to reveal two men working behind a wall. In addition, the reliefs were initially painted in bright colors, making the column all the more impressive while also making details (including the image of Trajan) on—at least the lower, if not higher—spirals easier to discern. Both the use of different perspectival schemes and color call attention to the use of painted pictorial sources.[29]

The column's location between two libraries and the appearance of the spiral frieze winding around it have led some authorities to believe that the reliefs were meant to evoke the impression of a book or unrolled scroll in the mind of the ancient viewer.[30] A rolled scroll (a *volumen* or *rotulus*) was the standard format for literary works in the second century. Following the model of predecessors like Julius Caesar, Trajan himself wrote an account of his military exploits, the *Commentarii*, to influence how they would be remembered;[31] although readership would be limited to literate elites, many more could hear it read at private or public recitations throughout the Empire. Some Greek and Latin scrolls were richly illustrated, with integrated text and images, leading some scholars to believe that the reliefs—especially in light of the apparent accuracy of their detail—provide a precise visual illustration of Trajan's text.[32] Text in the form of explanatory inscriptions for the reliefs, like those on the Kadesh reliefs, was unnecessary because it was available right next door at the library. Although problems of visibility may limit the column's narrative power for modern viewers, ancient Roman observers were already familiar with the story and would not have needed to see all the scenes to comprehend the monument.

Commemorative Significance

The column's ultimate significance did not lie in its recording of individual scenes; ancient sources do not even mention its helical frieze. Unlike Ramses's Kadesh reliefs, the column did not need to convince viewers of a victorious outcome, because the fruits of victory were all around them; rather, through multiple layers of honorific allusions it affected how Romans remembered the war and thereby increased their esteem for the *optimus princeps*.[33]

First, the column served as an engineering marvel that marked where the Quirinal hill had been cut back one-hundred Roman feet to afford level ground for Trajan's market, a statistic commemorated by its height (*columna centenaria*).[34] According to Cassius Dio (68.16.3): "And he set up in the forum an enormous column to serve at once as a monument to himself and as a memorial to the work in the forum. For that entire section had been hilly and he had to cut it down for a distance equal to the height of the column, thus making the forum level."[35]

Second, the column honored Trajan's virtues and accomplishments in a monumental and figural eulogy. The helical frieze and crowning statue both promote the emperor and advertise his victory in the wars that financed the forum. He is represented as exhibiting formulaic Roman leadership qualities of *pietas*, *liberalitas*, and *clementia*. He maintains control over a disciplined, multicultural army, and—echoing Alexander's self-representation—demonstrates concern for his soldiers through campsite scenes, *adlocutiones*, and commanding victories with no apparent the loss of Roman life.

Third, the scenes honored the achievements of the Roman army. Soldiers are paramount. Represented as disciplined and skillful in technologically challenging sieges, they disseminate Mediterranean urban civilization through their clearance of forests, construction of military installations, and building of roads and bridges. They are attentive to both the gods and the emperor, while the diversity of troop types reinforced the eulogy of Trajan's leadership virtues. Contemporary and later Roman viewers shared in a sense of collective purpose—this was their victorious army, their empire—and were undoubtedly relieved by the minimal depiction of violence in achieving their goals.

Fourth, the column functioned as a funerary memorial. After his death in 117, the Senate had the emperor's ashes placed in a chamber at the column's base.[36] Trajan's earthly remains stay on below with his subjects, while through his triumphant Dacian campaigns he ascends heavenward to the crowning statue, his soul transported by eagles, the vehicles of apotheosis, which alight on the base. (One recalls the way Naram-Sîn was portrayed close to the heavenly realm of the gods.) Any attempt to read the narrative of Trajan's achievements demands the viewer circle around the column, which forces the viewer to re-enact the circumambulation of ancient burial processions while viewing the reliefs at the center. As Penelope Davies observes, a tomb "may be monumental and unusual . . . but it is always dependent on the passerby to read it aloud, and in the glance or the voice of the living lies perpetuation through memory."[37] The column thereby becomes memorable to each of its actively engaged viewers.

Finally, the platform at the top of the column provided optimal viewing of the Trajanic metropolis. The feat of removing the *mons* could be grasped from this height, as well as Trajan's magnificent forum complex below and the imperial city extending in all directions. The belvedere ensured the column's preservation while the rest of the buildings were stripped away over time. In the fourth century, its sculpture was despoiled for the construction of the Arch of Constantine. Earthquakes caused further damage and in the Middle Ages much of the marble of the basilica and forum was removed. The column, however, was preserved by order of a decree in 1162 under penalty of death, ensuring that its form and imagery would provide a model for commemorative monuments from the Middle Ages into the modern era. Major excavations were ordered by Napoleon from 1811 to 1814, and again in 1932 by Mussolini, who ended up covering much of the forum with the Via dell Impero, an attempt to recast the monuments of antiquity as precedents for modern empire.

Commemorating the War in Dacia

In 109, Trajan dedicated the monumental *Tropaeum Traiani* (Trophy of Trajan) at Adamclisi in modern Romania to mark a decisive if costly Roman victory there in the winter of 101/102 (Fig. 4.8). Replacing an earlier altar whose walls were inscribed with the names of three thousand legionaries and auxiliaries who had died in the battle, its visual language addresses both conqueror and conquered. The base, a large concrete drum 124.5 feet (38 m) in diameter, copies elements of the Mausoleum of Augustus in Rome and supports a conical roof with a large trophy of Dacian arms rising from the center that recall the arms carved on the base of the column, endowing this monument in newly conquered territory with unmistakable references to memorial traditions in the homeland.[38] A poorly preserved inscription in Latin appears twice that dedicates the monument to Mars Ultor (Mars the Avenger), the same god honored in the Forum of Augustus, underscoring that the tropaeum represents revenge.[39] These allusions to the first emperor, easily grasped by viewers from the capital, demonstrate the enduring practice of Roman leaders to channel layered memories of the past to inspire the present.

The sculptural decoration around the drum, however, was more likely designed to convey its messages to a local audience. A frieze comprised of fifty-four carved relief panels of local limestone, often called metopes, depict events from the war and its aftermath.[40] Generally, each consists of three or four figures to convey the message, many of which repeat scenes similar to those depicted on the column and reliefs decorating Trajan's forum. Romans and Dacians are again distinguished by details of dress and weapons: Romans appear in legionary armor while Dacians are nude or wear trousers with bare torsos. Several panels depict a mounted Roman soldier riding down a fallen Dacian, an image with vast diffusion but resonant to Romans of sculpted representations of Trajan in the frieze decorating his forum, which also evoked Alexander (Fig. 4.9). The figures are nonclassicizing in form with irregular proportions; simple lines convey interior detail rather than fully modeled musculature; poses also defy classical conventions of balance and body movement. Art historians once considered these panels crude, the "low" work of ungifted artists. Now, however, the figures are understood to be the work of sculptors trained in a local idiom that reflects regional visual expectations. The abstracted forms are bold, clear in both the individual scenes and the overall narrative. In contrast, the decorative borders that frame each figural panel are very classicizing, demonstrating the capacity of the sculptors to carve in the style current in Rome and underscoring the purposeful representational choices.[41]

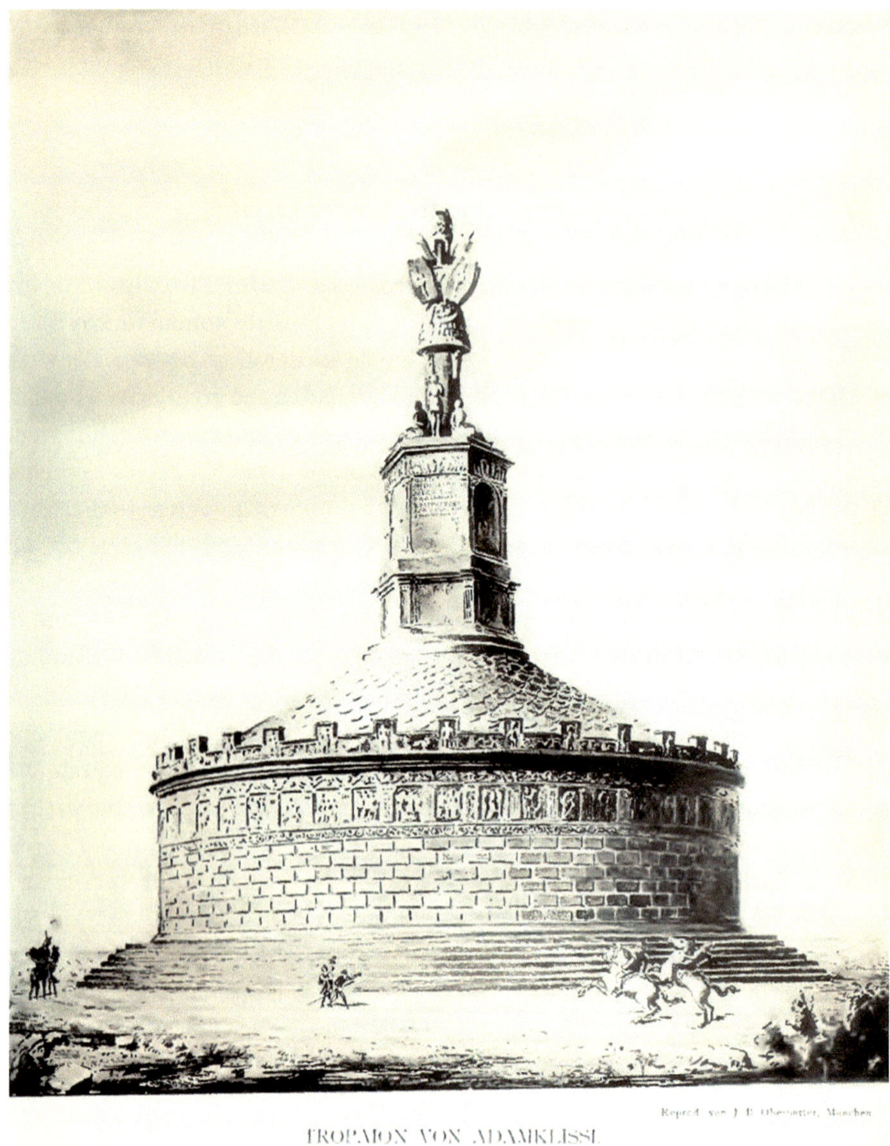

Fig. 4.8 Reconstruction drawing of the *Tropaeum Traiani* (109). Drawing from Adolf Furtwängler (1903)

In describing the tight relationship between Roman art and imperial policy, Richard Brilliant noted that "propaganda is not used, merely, to create a favorable climate of belief or opinion; it is used to channel the energies of the public exposed to it and repeatedly—a public whose beliefs are conditioned by propaganda so that they will act in concert in some desired manner, that is a manner or direction useful to the creators and disseminators of that propaganda."[42] Strategically placed along a major route at a remote edge of the empire (as were Ramses's Nubian temples),

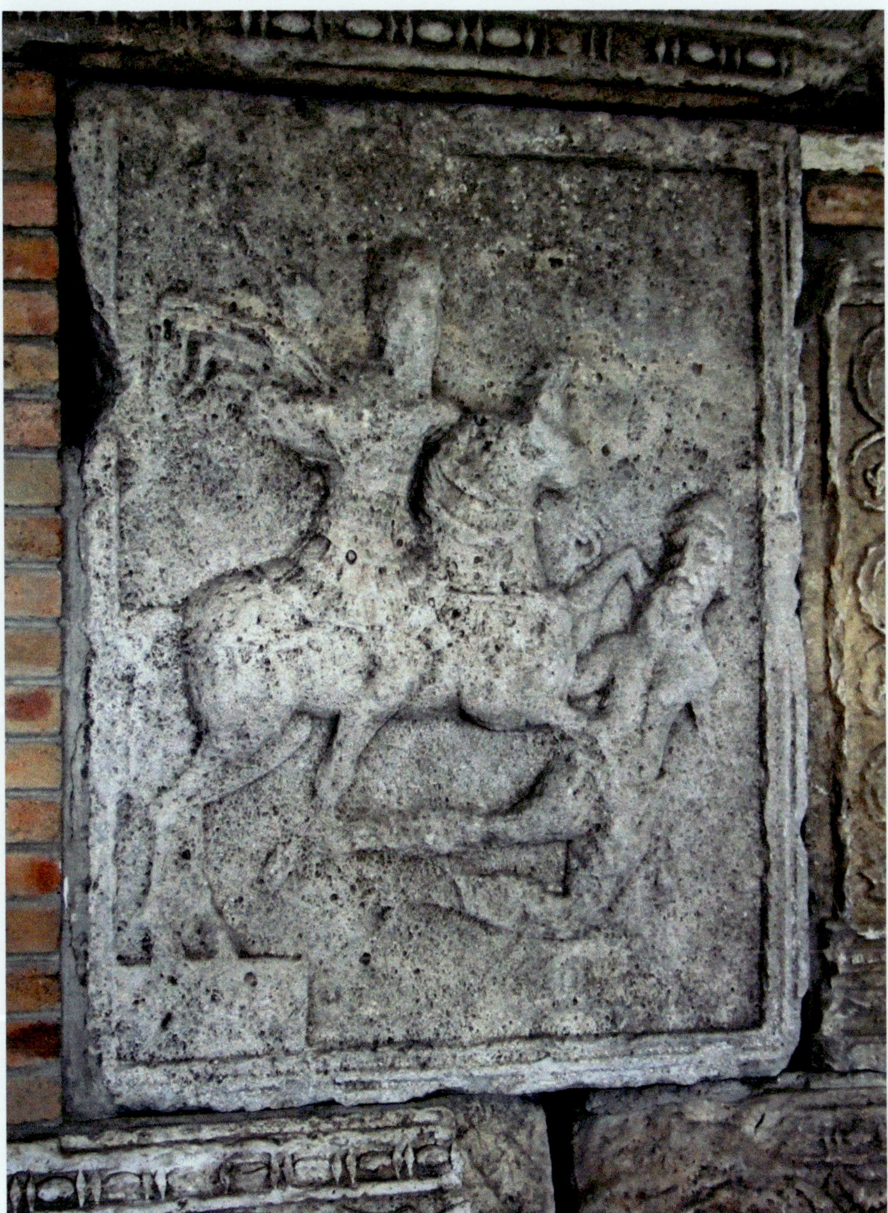

Fig. 4.9 *Tropaeum Traiani*, metope VI: mounted Roman soldier trampling enemy soldier. Adamclisi, Archaeological Museum. Photo: Christian Chirita on Wikimedia Commons

the tropaeum's form and monumentality announced that this land now belongs to Rome.[43] The commemoration not only warned tribes outside the new province about Roman dominance, it also informed Dacian viewers about their new identity as part of the empire, although it is impossible to know how willingly that identity was accepted.

5

The Bayeux Embroidery

Stitching New Identities in Medieval England

Few artworks featuring historical subjects survive from Europe's early medieval period.[1] By the middle of the eleventh century on, however, several factors contributed to a rapid increase in the production of historical representations, both as single subjects and in series. These included an increasing departure from Augustinian theology's emphasis on the role of history as part of the divine plan for salvation, but more crucially the expanding wealth, power, and self-esteem of religious and secular rulers alike who became patrons of the arts. At that time tapestries and embroideries, more highly valued than paintings and sculptures, were favored to adorn churches and the houses of ruling elites.[2] Sumptuary laws restricted the display of luxurious textiles to the nobility, signaling the owner's high ranking in medieval society.

Only a small percentage of the once large number medieval luxury objects survive, and the Bayeux Embroidery is one of the finest (Fig. 5.1). Its seventy scenes depict events related to the Norman Conquest in 1066. Like other medieval hangings, it was traditionally called a tapestry, even though it is not technically a tapestry in which the design is woven into the material; rather, the figures and decorations are embroidered with colored woolen yarns, a technique that makes the subjects stand out against the plain linen background. Consequently, in recent years the more correct name Bayeux Embroidery has come to be preferred among art historians. Controversies surrounding the distinct social groups that negotiated the embroidery's creation—who commissioned it, who made it, and who its original audience was—are all woven into how its imagery is interpreted.

The Contested Crown

King Edward of England, later hailed as "the Confessor," had no children or any apparent successor; he was about sixty at the time the embroidery begins its narration. In that period the English succession was not by primogeniture (the feudal rule by which an estate passed to the eldest son) but was selected cooperatively by the king and an assembly of nobles, the Witenagemot. Literary sources for the period are highly subjective and take either a decidedly pro-English or pro-Norman position; they could afford to be partisan since they were directed to a small, literate audience within a monastery or court. Perhaps the most complete—if not entirely reliable—is the account written by

Power, Image, and Memory. Peter J. Holliday, Oxford University Press. © Oxford University Press 2024.
DOI: 10.1093/oso/9780190901080.003.0006

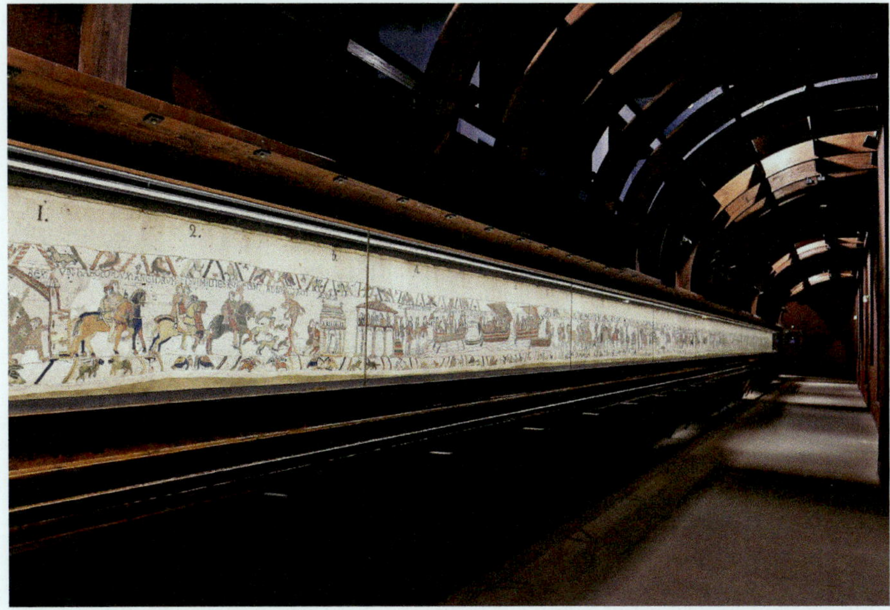

Fig. 5.1 Bayeux Embroidery, museum installation. Bayeux, Bayeux Tapestry Museum. Photo: author

William of Poitiers, which falls unequivocally into the pro-Norman group.[3] The author, who eventually took holy orders, originally trained as a knight, and that military background seems to have given him a deeper understanding of the particulars of contemporary warfare than what the typical clerical writer conveyed. His chronicle describes the contest between two claimants: Harold Godwinson, Edward's brother-in-law, Earl of Wessex, and the most powerful nobleman in England; and William, who became Duke of Normandy at the age of seven and was firmly in power by nineteen.[4]

Edward's mother, Emma of Normandy, was William's great aunt. William of Poitiers reports that Edward had earlier promised that Duke William would succeed him, a decision that Harold swore to honor, but that later Harold asserted that on his deathbed the king made him heir to the throne over William. Not surprisingly, Norman commentaries dispute the veracity of this last-minute switch.[5] William led a largely Norman force, often called the Companions of William the Conqueror, to claim his crown.[6] Given the lack of reliable literary sources, the compelling visual record of the Bayeux Embroidery has profoundly affected the traditional recounting of events—comparable to the role Ramses's Kadesh reliefs played in reconstructing Egypt's historical record.

"And the English Turned in Flight"

The embroidery is 224.3 feet (68.38 m) long and 20 inches (0.5 m) tall. It consists of nine linen panels, between approximately 9 and 45 feet in length, which were stitched together after each had been embroidered; the seams were concealed by later embroidery. The main narrative fills a broad central zone, although the action frequently spills over into the narrow decorative borders at the top and bottom, either for dramatic effect or to keep the scene from becoming too cramped. The borders included mythological creatures, animals enacting fables (e.g., the fox and the crow), and genre-like vignettes of rural and military life (a soldier and a prostitute). Latin labels or captions (*tituli*) identify people and places or briefly describe the events represented.[7] These are generally in the central expanse but sometimes appear in the top border, and their left-to-right direction helps propel the story's momentum. The scenes unroll before one's eye like the sequential narrative of the reliefs on the Column of Trajan, an echo that may be more than coincidental.

This visual chronicle opens with a scene of King Edward dispatching Harold on a mission to Normandy (Fig. 5.2). Although the embroidery does not suggest any specific reason for his mission, the Norman sources assert that it was for Harold to swear his fealty to William. By misadventure, Harold lands at the wrong place and is captured by Guy, Count of Ponthieu. Horsemen relay messages, after which William procures Harold's release, who then joins William in a struggle against Conan II, Duke of Brittany. En route, the army becomes mired in quicksand at the river Couesnon just outside the monastery of Michael's Mount (Abbey of Mont-Saint-Michel), where Harold rescues two Norman soldiers. William's forces pursue Conan from his fortified tower at Dol de Bretagne to Rennes. Conan ultimately surrenders and tenders the keys to the fortress at Dinan. William presents arms and

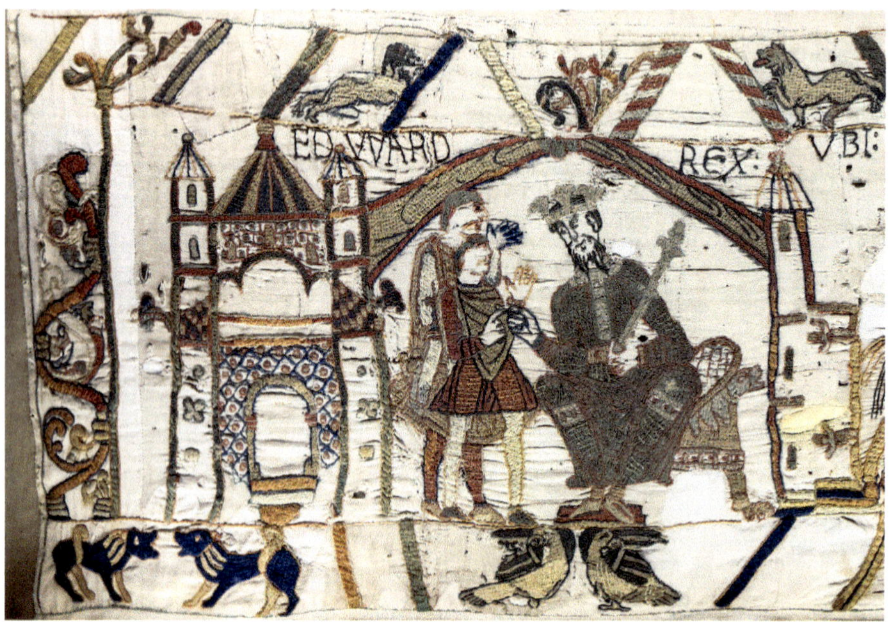

Fig. 5.2 Bayeux Embroidery, King Edward sends Harold to Normandy (scene 1). Bayeux, Bayeux Tapestry Museum. Photo: Wikimedia Commons

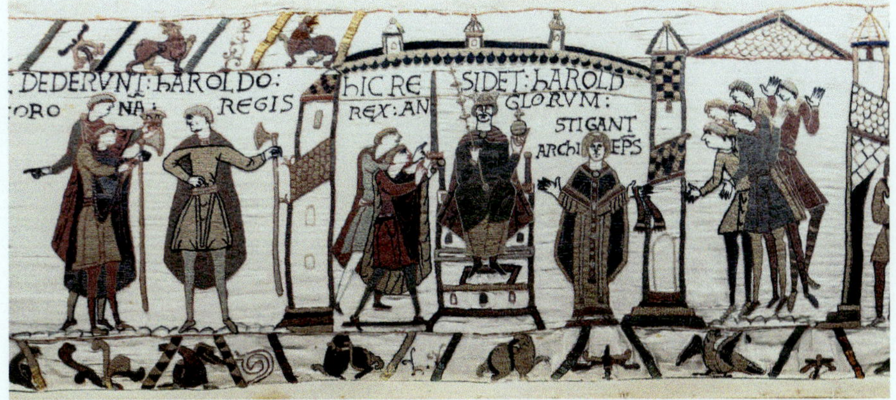

Fig. 5.3 Bayeux Embroidery, men offer Harold the crown, the coronation of Harold with Archbishop Stigand, and people acclaim King Harold (scenes 29–31). Bayeux, Bayeux Tapestry Museum. Photo: Wikimedia Commons

armor to Harold, suggesting he knighted him. They arrive at Bayeux where Harold swears an oath on saintly relics. The titulus in the embroidery clearly states Harold takes an oath, but it provides no indication as to what is being sworn.

Harold then returns to England where King Edward appears to reprimand him; Harold assumes a submissive attitude and appears to be in disgrace. And yet—possibly intentionally—the significance of these scenes is ambiguous. The narrative then moves ahead one year to when illness overcomes Edward, and his body is brought to the church of St. Peter the Apostle (Westminster Abbey). On his deathbed, Edward addresses the faithful. Two men give Harold the crown at what is possibly the coronation ceremony of January 6, 1066, celebrated by a figure identified as *Stigant Archieps* (Stigand the Archbishop, Fig. 5.3). (When serving as chaplain to King Cnut, Stigand rose in ecclesiastical rank to the bishopric of Winchester and later the archbishopric of Canterbury; by this time, however, he had been excommunicated for unlawfully holding both seats.)[8] People wonder at a star with a streaming tail: what we recognize today as the comet identified some six hundred years later by Edmond Halley (Fig. 5.4).[9] In the Middle Ages comets were considered to be omens of ill fortune. Here the lower border features five mysteriously unmanned ships that portend the coming invasion.

William of Poitiers tells us that when word of Harold's coronation reached Normandy, William ordered a fleet of ships to be assembled; the embroidery, however, shows his half-brother Odo, Bishop of Bayeux, directing workmen to chop down trees, build ships, and drag them and provisions to the sea. The Normans cross the channel, land in England unopposed, and establish a beachhead on the south coast.[10] William instructs his men to forage for food and a feast, blessed by Odo, is prepared. The Normans erect a motte-and-bailey fortification at Hastings to secure their position (Fig. 5.5). William receives news, perhaps about Harold's victory at the Battle of Stamford Bridge, although the embroidery is again ambiguous.

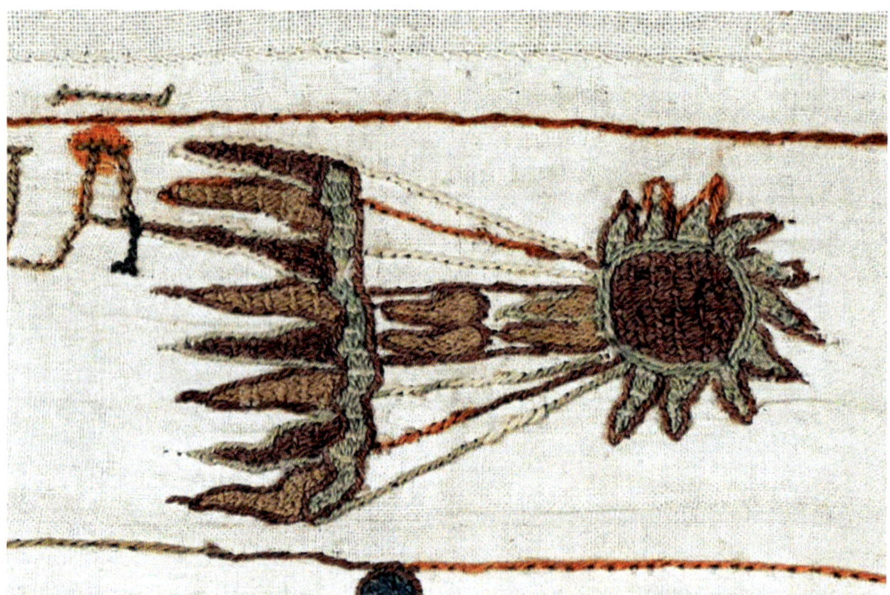

Fig. 5.4 Bayeux Embroidery, appearance of Halley's Comet (scene 32). Bayeux, Bayeux Tapestry Museum. Photo: Wikimedia Commons

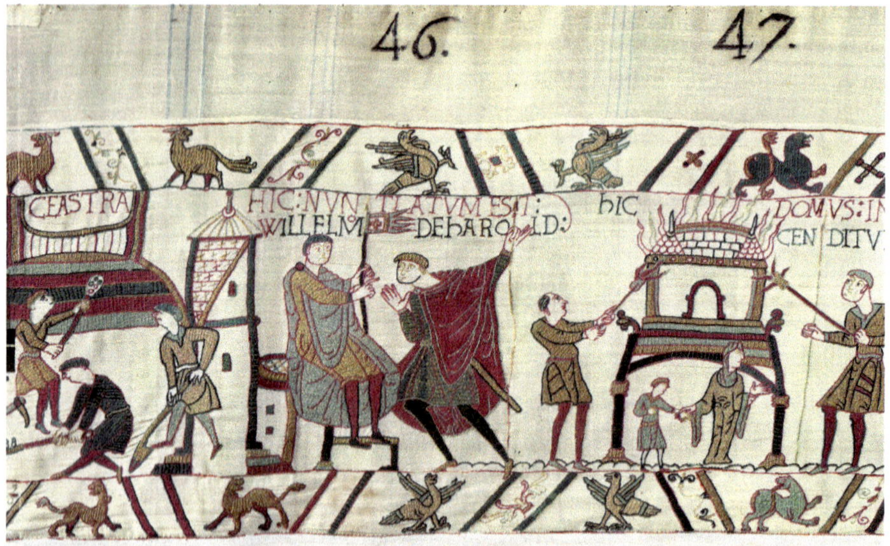

Fig. 5.5 Bayeux Embroidery, Normans build a fort at Hastings, William receives news of Harold, and Normans ravage the countryside (scenes 46–47). Bayeux, Bayeux Tapestry Museum. Photo: Wikimedia Commons

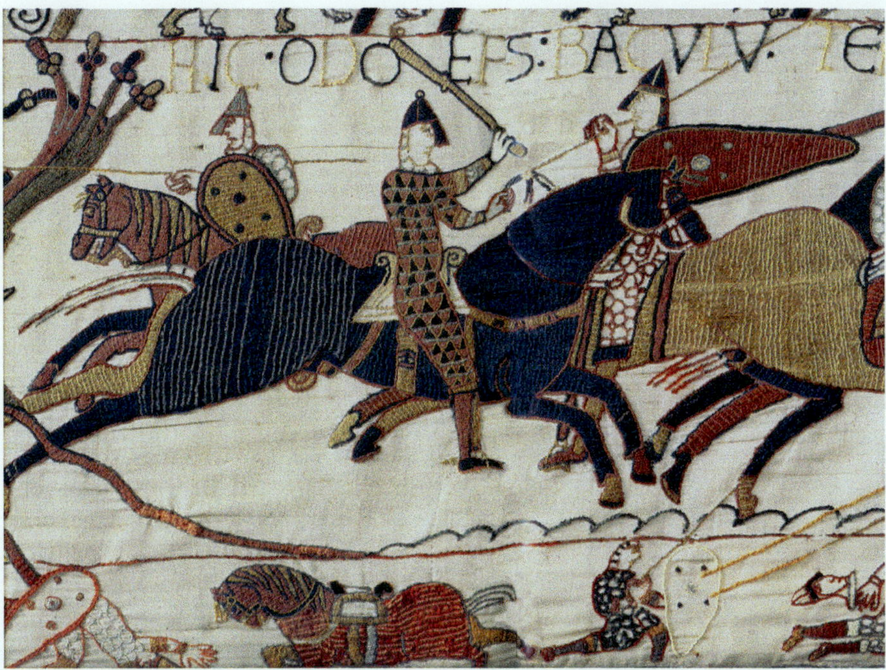

Fig. 5.6 Bayeux Embroidery, Bishop Odo at the Battle of Hastings (scene 55). Bayeux, Bayeux Tapestry Museum. Photo: Wikimedia Commons

Normans ravage the countryside. Two men set fire to a modest house, before (or within?) which a defiant woman holds a small boy's hand. The Normans then depart their fortification at Hastings for battle.

On October 24, 1066, shortly after the success at Stamford Bridge, the armies met at the Battle of Hastings.[11] Over the course of nine hours both sides fight bravely, the English on foot behind their shields and the Normans mounted on horses, a detail corresponding with reality. As a cleric, Odo's role should have been limited to praying for the Norman knights, yet he is shown riding into the heart of the fighting, brandishing a large wooden cudgel, probably a badge of office like those plied by other Normans (Fig. 5.6); taking holy orders forbade shedding blood with a sword, but not whacking opponents with an oak emblem.[12] In an echo of the heroically bareheaded Alexander and Trajan, William lifts his helmet to reveal his face and thereby reassure his troops that he is still alive and well. However, whereas the violence of combat was eschewed on the Column of Trajan, the embroidery emphasizes bloodshed with images of soldiers being slaughtered and mutilated corpses strewing the field. Two knights identified as Leofwine and Gyrth, Harold's brothers and probable successors, fall during the struggle.

A figure struck in the eye with an arrow is traditionally interpreted as showing the death of Harold, seemingly secured by the titulus *Harold Rex* (King Harold) above the figure's head (Fig. 5.7). Since medieval iconography often showed a perjurer dying by a weapon through the eye, the mortal wound shown here could

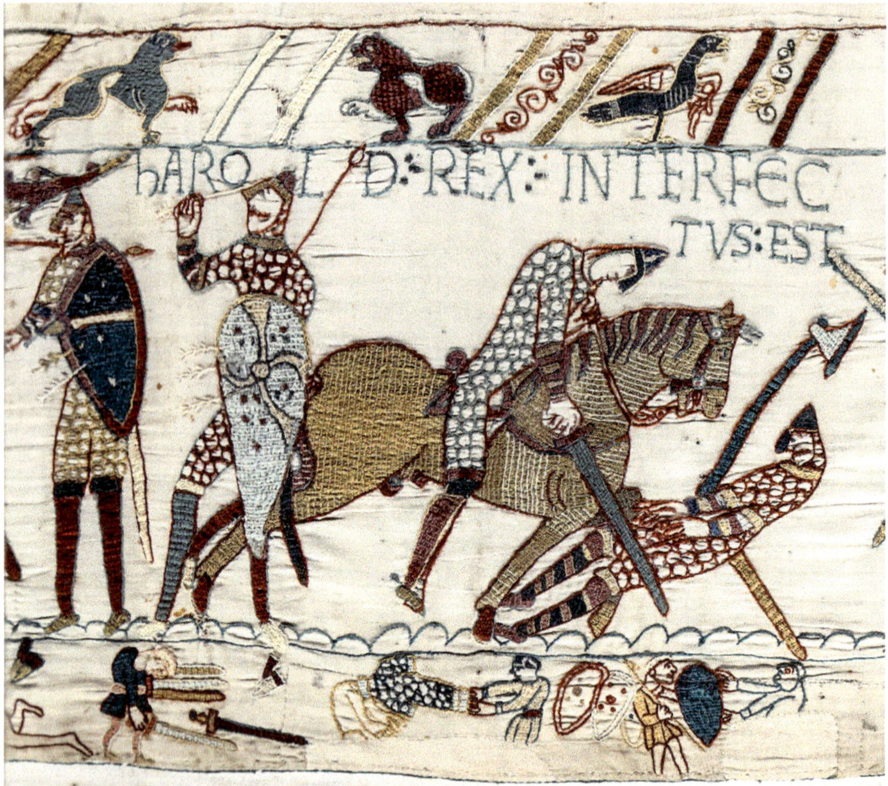

Fig. 5.7 Bayeux Embroidery, death of Harold (scene 57). Bayeux, Bayeux Tapestry Museum. Photo: Wikimedia Commons

underscore William's legitimate claim to the English throne by describing Harold as an oath-breaker. Although Harold may indeed have lost an eye in battle, it is unlikely that he actually died this way.[13] The arrow may be a later alteration following a mending to the ground, a possibility underscored by the fact that it does not appear in a suite of detailed engravings from the eighteenth century.[14] Recent conservation detected some needle holes in the linen ground suggesting something else had previously been depicted in its place, such as a lance. The entire titulus, *Harold Rex interfectus est* ("King Harold is slain") continues into the next panel, where another figure is killed with a sword. This figure may instead represent Harold's death, which would be more consistent with how tituli are used throughout in the work.

The last surviving scene shows unarmored English troops escaping from the battlefield with a titulus reading *Et fuga verterunt Angli* ("And the English turned in flight"); the caption may be a later addition since this section has been heavily restored, albeit with sensitivity to the original stitching (Fig. 5.8).[15] The last part of the embroidery—missing as long as it has been known, perhaps consisting of at least two additional panels (as much as another 7 yards or 6.4 m worth)—probably included William's coronation.[16]

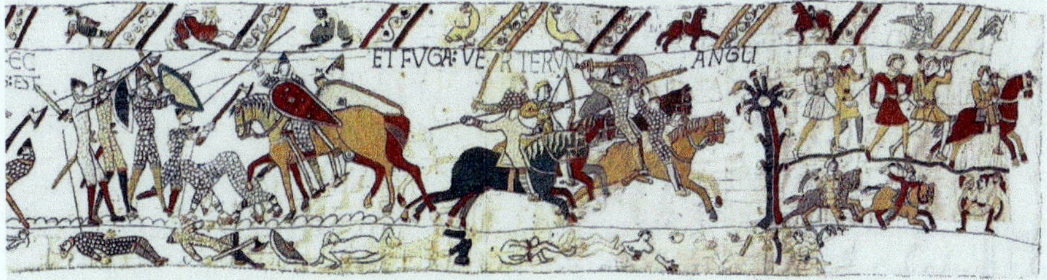

Fig. 5.8 Bayeux Embroidery, flight of the English (scene 58). Bayeux, Bayeux Tapestry Museum. Photo: Wikimedia Commons

Issues of Reliability

Like the Column of Trajan, the embroidery presents an exceptional visual document for the arms, apparel, and tactics of warfare surviving from its period. The attention to detail is such that when discrepancies with written sources are discerned, they are remarkable.[17] Although Norman written accounts are generally preferred today, the embroidery's largely Norman bias does not guarantee a wholly accurate chronicle of the events. Both English and Norman sources allege that the Harold pledged to support William's claim to the crown. The embroidery's extensive attention to Harold's activities in Normandy in 1064 argues for strong connection between that earlier mission and William's invasion two years later to depose an unworthy king. Since William needed the backing of the Church to legitimize his claim to the throne, the embroidery explicitly depicts Harold taking an oath on holy relics to defer to William, a story that seems to have originated in the court of William after Harold's coronation.[18] The embroidery also attempts to discredit Harold's kingship by identifying Stigand, the excommunicated Archbishop of Canterbury, as the ecclesiastic who officiated.[19] English sources, in contrast, confirm Harold's legitimacy by having him defer to papal authority by being crowned by Ealdred, Archbishop of York.[20] The embroidery's predominantly pro-Norman bias points to how William and his supporters would want events remembered.

And yet although the embroidery portrays William positively throughout the narrative, his adversary Harold is also represented as a decisive and capable leader; nor are his English soldiers disparaged (except for the potentially spurious final caption). In fact, some incidents clearly portray the Normans unfavorably, such as the episode showing the torching of a peasant house. The *Domesday Book* of 1086 documents the extensive damage done to the territory surrounding Hastings.[21] William's deathbed confession, as later provided by Orderic Vitalis, apologizes for actions taken in subduing and unifying England's realms: "I have persecuted the natives of England beyond all reason. Whether gentle or simple I have cruelly oppressed them; many I unjustly disinherited; innumerable multitudes perished through me by famine or the sword . . . I fell on the English of the northern shires like a ravening lion . . . Having gained the throne of that kingdom by so many crimes I dare not leave it to anyone but God."[22] Scholars dispute the authenticity of this confession; by having William express remorse, Orderic probably presents here a perspective some forty years after William's death and sixty years after the Battle of Hastings that attempts to make William, if not his deeds, more palatable to English audiences.

Although Norman audiences would regard the embroidery's narrative as largely truthful and accurate, they were undoubtedly joined by English viewers who had their own version of the conquest: one group saw their champion right a great wrong, while the other gazed upon the defeat of their unfortunate hero. Where the embroidery was displayed would generate further distinctions among viewers: men and women, nobility and commoners, laity and clergy would have each beheld the embroidery differently. One explanation for its opacities—the inclusion of what appear to be pro-English sentiments within a substantially pro-Norman narrative—is that the embroidery was knowingly designed in consideration of being seen by heterogeneous groups. Accordingly, the embroidery did not merely celebrate William's victory; rather, it might have been intended to play a role in realizing a Norman desire to fashion a unified kingdom out of its disparate populations.[23]

Possible Patrons

Whoever commissioned the embroidery had a primary role in determining what was portrayed and how. French tradition long held that Duke William's wife, Queen Matilda, worked on the embroidery with her ladies-in-waiting to honor her illustrious husband and his victory, earning it the name *La Tapisserie de la Reine Mathilde*.[24] Indeed, the role of aristocratic women in the social and cultural patterns of medieval Europe assured this explanation would endure. When the game of chess was introduced to Western Europe from the Islamic world (probably via Iberia) toward the end of the ninth century, the queen replaced the original vizier piece. She combines the power of the rook and bishop with the ability to move any number of squares along a rank, file, or diagonal, her versatility making her the most powerful piece on the board, but with the ultimate objective of defending the king.[25] Women of high rank frequently commissioned works of art, especially those that glorified their families and promoted the reputations of husbands and sons.[26] Furthermore, such women were generally carefully instructed in all aspects of sewing and textile work. Although the romanticized—and wholly incorrect—notion of aristocratic women collaborating to stitch this piece while the men ran the affairs of state can no longer be accepted, there is still validity in envisaging women as closely involved in aspects of its creation: at this time women in nunneries usually undertook large-scale sewing projects of this sort, and it was a queen's responsibility to superintend the nunneries.

Another candidate for commissioning the embroidery is Queen Edith, Edward the Confessor's wife and later widow, sister of the determined Godwinson boys (including Harold), and also the daughter of the formidable Earl Godwin who had been a kingmaker in his day. Mariah Proctor-Tiffany observes, "As they moved into widowhood, queens often found this period more treacherous than the years of their reigns. More than ever, the widow's influence and reputation were closely related to her skill in negotiating the political landscape."[27] Edith was a survivor. After the Conquest she appears to have refashioned herself as the beloved kinswoman of William. Carola Hicks argues that the fact that the embroidery's narrative presents sympathetic consideration to both the Norman and English sides suggests that Edith may have had it made to reinforce her new position in the Norman hierarchy by displaying her backing of the new king, while at the same time acknowledging her past allegiances.[28] Edith is conspicuous in the crucial scene at Edward's deathbed. She was probably also the patron of a book promoting herself and her family's achievements, the *Vita AEdwardi Regis*, and like Queen Matilda, she oversaw nunneries where such textile works were undertaken.[29] She could have commissioned the embroidery an offering to William, perhaps as a token of reconciliation following the invasion.[30]

Most scholars, however, now attribute the commission to William's half-brother, Bishop Odo of Bayeux, who was also made Earl of Kent following the Conquest. In that position he was a strategic ally of William, even acting as regent of England when William was absent in Normandy. He might have ordered the embroidery to demonstrate his support for his king, perhaps in order to curry favor and regain William's esteem after Odo had fallen from favor in 1082.[31] Details depicted within the narrative that support this contention include the central role played by Bayeux, with Harold taking his famous oath to William there (in contradiction to other contemporary accounts). Odo is shown prominently in both heroic and advisory roles, and three of the Bishop's retainers, who are also mentioned in the *Domesday Book*, appear with labels in the embroidery. Although the idea that the embroidery was commissioned for display at Bayeux Cathedral, also built by Odo in the 1070s, possibly to be finished in time for its dedication in 1077 (a ceremony attended by William, Matilda, and their sons), is no longer accepted, Odo could have commissioned it for display in his baronial hall and then bequeathed it to his ecclesiastical seat.[32] This would also be consistent with Norman programs working at integrating the English and Norman peoples.

Nevertheless, elements in the embroidery's imagery—such as hints in the narrative that could support Harold's claim to the throne—do not necessarily justify the Conquest in a way that would have satisfied Odo. Elizabeth and Stephen White suggest instead that the embroidery was made for the monks at the Benedictine St. Augustine's Abbey near Canterbury who would have appreciated "its multi-layered narrative in a variety of ways."[33] In support of this attribution they argue that many of the figures depicted in the embroidery were benefactors of the abbey, that places shown also have reference to the history of St. Augustine's, and that the structure and sequencing of the pictorial narrative follow models in book illuminations found at the abbey. There, any viewers' affiliations previously defined by virtue of kinship or language would be subordinated to their common identity as monks, "separate from and superior to the secular world."[34]

Where Was It Made?

Determining where the embroidery was made has proven as challenging as establishing its patron. Current discussion focuses on England (including Canterbury in Kent, Wilton in Wiltshire, and Winchester in Hampshire) and France (Bayeux in Normandy and Saumur in the Loire Valley). Arguments in favor of French fabrication generally start by interpreting its content to identify French patronage, and from there determining a location under that person's control. For example, George Beech makes the case that the Abbot of St. Florent at Saumur in the Loire Valley knew William before the Conquest and that the duke, being familiar with the tapestry workshop in his abbey, commissioned the abbot to create the piece.[35] Central to Beech's argument is the generous depiction of Brittany in the embroidery. The abbot came from the small town of Dol de Bretagne in northeastern Brittany, which had backed William against the Bretons in the campaign of 1064. The prominence given to the Breton campaign on the embroidery has long perplexed scholars; it does not really impact William's later conquest of England, but it does fashion a narrative championing the lords of Dol.

Such arguments, however, ignore the internal evidence of the embroidery's manufacture. Most experts today identify the work as being made by English embroiderers in England. They used two distinct methods of needlework, done in crewel (wool yarn): a stem stitch for lettering and outlining the images and couching or laid work for filling them in, a detailed type of stitching later called *Opus Anglicanum*, or English work.[36] During the Middle Ages, *Opus Anglicanum* was internationally recognized as exceptional, and it conferred prestige upon its owners. William of Poitiers stated, "everyone attests to the fact that English Women are very skilled in needlecraft and embroidery."[37] Furthermore, English needleworkers were even singled out in the *Domesday Book*. One, Leofgyd, was successful enough to hold a modest estate at Knook in Wiltshire because "she made and makes the gold fringe of the king and queen."[38]

Unfortunately, little earlier medieval textile work survives for comparison, but the tituli have long been adduced as evidence for an English origin. Although they are always in Latin, the character of the words and their spelling are how an English manor woman would have written them in the Middle Ages.[39] As noted above, the claim for English fabrication is further bolstered by the fact that its pictorial style is similar to that found eleventh-century English illuminated manuscripts. Specific motifs in the embroidery are taken from manuscripts in St. Augustine's, leading authorities to believe that the intellectual creator and designer and his assistants worked at Canterbury, or at least had access to the abbey's library, although it does not guarantee that the embroidery was actually worked there.[40] Howard B. Clarke proposed that the designer of the embroidery was Scolland, the abbot of St. Augustine's Abbey, because he had previously overseen the scriptorium at Mont-Saint-Michel, famed for its manuscript illumination; his connections to Wadard and Vital, two individuals prominently identified in the embroidery; and his travels to Rome where he would have seen the Column of Trajan, one of the most prominent marvels listed in medieval guidebooks for pilgrims and tourists (*Mirabilia Urbis Romae*).[41] The former librarian may even have seen surviving illustrated scrolls, although that must remain highly uncertain. Accordingly, even if the embroidery was commissioned by Bishop Odo or another Norman patron, it was probably designed in England and undoubtedly made there by women, perhaps in a nunnery under the direction of a queen, and only later taken to France.[42]

Richard Gameson argues that the making of the embroidery in England for a Norman patron explains its "bicultural" nature.[43] Its narrative and imagery represent the Norman Conquest figuratively, while its commissioning represents the conquest materially: both the art form and the makers were of the conquered English people, establishing a connection and continuity that help authenticate its predominantly Norman narrative.[44] Thus the descriptive detail of the Bayeux Embroidery affirms the legitimacy of William's rule in England, its display propagates that message to diverse audiences, and by employing local traditions as a means to celebrate their history and fashion their own identity, the Normans integrate themselves into the history of their new subjects.[45] R. Howard Bloch eloquently describes the embroidery as "a suture for the wound of 1066."[46]

Although the identity of its designer is unlikely to be truly settled, some critics surely go too far when speculating that its "pacifist" details must reflect the attitudes of the English female needleworkers who did the actual physical work of stitching and filled it with seditious subtexts. The depiction of so many dark turns in this story of men's pursuit of power may suggest the perspective of skeptical women embroiderers, but it could equally reflect that of monks scornful of worldly dominance. In fact, the embroidery's ambivalence increases its mystery and grandeur. Today it represents more than a narrative to legitimize a claim to the throne or even the attempt to forge a unified national identity; rather, the Bayeux Embroidery is one of the most immediate and sensitive depictions of war ever created, equaling the horror evoked by Picasso's *Guernica*. The burning house challenges myths of chivalry. At the height of the battle, what started in the lower border as a parade of fantastic beasts turns into a grisly field of the wounded and dead, with victimized horses running wild with terror and taking terrible falls. Although such scenes seem to run counter to a work meant to shape positively the collective memory of an event—passages making this a disturbingly human document that rings true to modern eyes—such assessments may itself merely betray modern sensibilities.

The Threads of Memory

Controversies about the embroidery's origins and its reception began with its modern rediscovery. In 1724, Antoine Lancelot reported information to the Académie Royale des Inscriptions et Belles-Lettres regarding a series of colored sketches depicting scenes involving William the Conqueror. He wondered whether the original source might be a tapestry or a sculpted frieze, perhaps from William's tomb, which had been in a church at Caen before its destruction in 1562, or alternatively from a set of commemorative stained-glass windows in that church. The Benedictine scholar Bernard de Montfaucon (1655–1741) copied the drawings and asked his Benedictine colleagues in Normandy to uncover the original work, which they determined to be a tapestry preserved at Bayeux Cathedral. In 1729 and 1730 he published a detailed description of it, illustrated with drawings by Antoine Benoît, one of the most skilled draftsmen of the day, in the first two volumes of his *Les Monuments de la Monarchie française*.[47]

Contemporary critics considered the artistry to be exceedingly coarse: the red and yellow multicolored horses were especially offensive to the tastes of that time. Nevertheless, Montfaucon instructed Benoît not to change the style in any way, even though it was "extremely vulgar and barbarous," because "in my opinion decadence and the revival of the arts constitute an important historical fact."[48] Montfaucon lamented how the testimony of monuments from the earlier Merovingian and Carolingian periods had not survived, for "crude as they are, they instruct us on many things that we cannot find elsewhere."[49] But tastes change. By 1829, A. L. Léchaudé d'Anisy claimed to find "a sort of purity in its primitive forms, especially considering the state of the arts in the eleventh century."[50]

The Bayeux Embroidery would certainly have impressed its contemporary viewers, commoner and noble alike, with its vivid color, scale, and costly *Opus Anglicanum* workmanship. It is doubtful that many of them would have occasion to study the piece carefully or follow its narrative from beginning to end wherever it was originally displayed, for great halls were always full of people conducting business and cathedrals with pilgrims and worshippers; whether monks enjoyed the time for the delectation of decorative wall-hangings of secular subjects is uncertain. This might be one reason scenes with subversive content, if that is what they actually are, went unnoticed, if indeed they did. During the following centuries European elites continued to prize sumptuous textiles. Hung in great houses, representations drawn from diverse traditions transmitted the cultural memory of such historical figures as Charlemagne, Godefroy de Bouillon, and Bertrand Du Guesclin alongside legendary heroes like Roland, Arthur, and Tristan, all providing *exempla* worthy of emulation.[51] History and pious legend also mingled in cycles taken from the lives of saints, as recalled in the stained-glass window at Saint-Denis and manuscript illuminations in several versions of the *Grandes Chroniques de France* that preserve the story of St. Louis. Only in the fifteenth century did paintings begin to supplant wall coverings among elite commissions.

6

Night Attack on the Sanjō Palace

Unscrolling the Warrior Ethos of Medieval Japan

Splendor and elegance distinguished the four centuries of Japan's Heian period (794–1185). The development of an efficient manner of writing the Japanese language generated the creation of Japan's famous vernacular literature chronicling the era.[1] These accounts reveal that medieval Japan, like many premodern societies, was prone to ever-changing allegiances, treachery, and divisive ruptures among ruthless elite families. Although power was technically vested in the Imperial House of Japan, the aristocratic Fujiwara clan had intermarried with the imperial family and wielded true power; the Fujiwara functioned as imperial regents and were unrivalled in suppressing and sometimes selecting a succession of emperors. Emperors, in turn, had numerous consorts, and high-born daughters were mere instruments in political marriages to placate contentious families and warrior factions.

Nobles, including current and retired emperors, increasingly depended on warrior clans led by provincial lords—samurai—to resolve bitter rivalries. Two military clans, the Minamoto (also known as the Genji) and the Taira (or Heike), were remarkably powerful and took opposing sides in factional disputes at the imperial court, hoping to influence the undermined emperor and control the government. When intense disputes arose over which son of which wife of which current or retired emperor would succeed to the throne, the Minamoto and Taira clans chose who they would support with an eye to their own ambitions as bitter competitors. Over time patriarchs of these military clans succeeded in pre-empting imperial authority and consigning the emperors to numbing ceremonial functions. In response, however, Japanese emperors found that stepping down in favor of a successor could free them from arduous ceremonies and allow the "retired" emperor to assert himself and reclaim some of his lost power. The authority of the court further declined as courtiers became absorbed in their own refinement and neglected their administrative obligations, hastening the rise of autocratic rule by a series of samurai who would lead Japan, or factionalized areas of it, for the next eight hundred years.

The Kamakura period (1185–1333) began when the leader of the Minamoto clan, Yoritomo (1147–1199), routed the Taira family and commanded the emperor to appoint him as *shogun* (general-in-chief). Yoritomo disdained what he saw as the softening influences of courtly life in Kyōto, and therefore established his military headquarters in Kamakura (on the coast to the south of modern Tōkyō), allowing the emperor to continue to reside in Kyōto. Yoritomo's newly conceived

Power, Image, and Memory. Peter J. Holliday, Oxford University Press. © Oxford University Press 2024.
DOI: 10.1093/oso/9780190901080.003.0007

designation as shogun technically acknowledged the authority of the emperor, but it actually secured Yoritomo dominant military and political power. The shogunate he initiated persisted in various forms until 1868.

Gunki Monogatari

The Japanese developed strategies to capture, preserve, and disseminate the crucial elements of their commonly accepted history: collective memories that became central to their national identity. Written sources include chronicles of sovereigns and events, biographies of prominent individuals, and the military epic or *gunki monogatari* ("war tales" or "warrior tales"). The *gunki monogatari* comprise a group of Japanese literary works written primarily during the Kamakura and later Muromachi (1336–1573) periods whose subjects focus on historical wars and conflicts, especially the civil wars that occurred during the collapse of the Heian period in the late twelfth century.[2] Although they are called *gunki* (literally, "military chronicles"), they do not document or faithfully record facts but rather provide narratives, sometimes based on oral tradition, that emphasize heroic episodes and even love stories for posterity, hence the rendition as "tales." Despite their exaggerations they are sometimes useful as reference when exploring the historical background of military events.

Gunki monogatari inspired a huge body of art, appearing in scrolls and screen paintings and on objects used by samurai. The major battles, small skirmishes, and individual struggles of the three major conflicts that precipitated the collapse of the Heian period—the Hōgen Rebellion (1156), the vicious Heiji Insurrection (1159–1160), and the Genpei War (1180–1185)—have been passed down in the narrative formats of the *Hōgen monogatari*, the *Heiji monogatari*, and the *Heike monogatari*. In each of these works the protagonists are easily recognized, the events are commonly familiar, and the dangers are as they were conventionally understood at the time. Their texts are mainly written in prose, although they sometimes incorporate poems, usually *waka*.[3] Their correctness as historical records has presented an absorbing subject for further study; whereas some accounts have withstood close examination, other reputed deeds have been shown to be erroneous.[4]

In detailing events of the Heiji Insurrection, the *Heiji monogatari* recounts how during an imperial succession dispute the samurai clan head Minamoto no Yoshitomo laid siege to Kyōto, in which he was opposed by Taira no Kiyomori, head of the Taira clan. Only three scrolls survive, together with several fragments, of the many original scrolls made in the late the thirteenth century, probably over the course of several decades. The first of these represents the siege of the Sanjō Palace, an act of violence culminating in a great fire that destroys the palace and sweeps over almost the whole height of the scroll (Fig. 6.1).[5]

The Sanjō Palace was the residence of the Retired Emperor Go-Shirakawa, recognized as the most devious and long-lived of the monarchs who had abdicated.

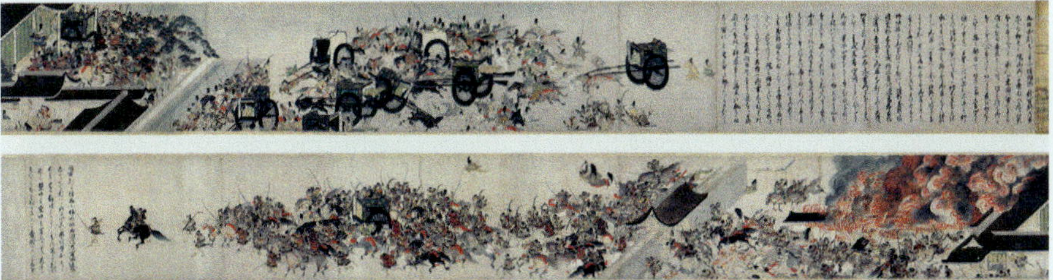

Fig. 6.1 *Night Attack on the Sanjō Palace* (thirteenth century). Boston, Museum of Fine Arts. Photo: Wikimedia Commons

His son the Emperor Nijô had just succeeded him on the throne. The two emperors supported opposing sides of the conspiratorial Fujiwara clan; one member of this family, the notorious Fujiwara no Nobuyori, schemed against everyone.[6] In 1159, Taira no Kiyomori, leader of the Taira clan and supporter Emperor Nijō, left the capital Kyōto with his family on a pilgrimage to the Kumano-jinja Shrine. Fujiwara no Nobuyori, who had been involved in the struggle to win Go-Shirakawa's favor against Fujiwara no Michinori (also known by the priestly name Shinzei), raised an army and joined forces with Minamoto no Yoshitomo, head of the Minamoto clan that felt oppressed by the Taira family, particularly with what Yoshitomo considered an inadequate reward from his service in the earlier Hōgen War. Together they raised a force of about five hundred. Fujiwara no Nobuyori attempted to take power by attacking the palace on a December night in 1160 and seizing both the current and retired emperors. They confined the retired emperor to the Daidairi (the Greater Imperial Palace), killed Shinzei, and briefly held power until Taira no Kiyomori returned from Kumano and defeated them. Nobuyori was executed and Yoshitomo was assassinated.

Night Attack on the Sanjō Palace

The scroll known as *Night Attack on the Sanjō Palace* is almost 23 feet long and 17 inches high (774.5 x 45.9 cm). It was designed to be unrolled a section at a time to facilitate viewing up close; between the written introduction and conclusion it features a bird's-eye view of the pictorial imagery, the figures and motifs depicted in vivid outline and washes of color, basic characteristics of this pictorial form. The characters appear multiple times as the story unfolds sequentially. At the scroll's far right the introductory text reads:

> At about the hour of the ox [2:00 a.m.] on the ninth day, Lord Nobuyori proceeded with several hundred mounted soldiers to the Sanjō Palace, the residence of the Retired Emperor, and said, "Since I have heard that I am to be struck down, I intend to go to the east. I have served you close at hand for years and have been

> favored more than others by your Majesty, and so it is indeed sad for me to part from my lord and abruptly leave the capital."
>
> Then the Retired Emperor said, "What sort of affair is this? Who would strike you?" But without hearing him out, soldiers hastily brought up the Imperial carriage. "You must hasten into the Imperial carriage. Now, set fire to the Palace," ordered Nobuyori, and His Majesty unwillingly got into the Imperial carriage. Jōsaimon'in had already gotten in. It was Lord Moronaka, who had brought up the Imperial carriage. Nobuyori, Yoshitomo, Shigenari, the Sado Vice-Minister of Ceremonial; Minamoto Mitsumoto, the Commissioner of the Police; Suezane, the former Commissioner of Police; and the others surrounded the Imperial carriage and took it to the Imperial Palace. They shoved him into the Palace Single-Copy Library, where Shigenari and Mitsumoto guarded him.
>
> Soldiers blockaded the Palace on all four sides and set fire to it. Those who fled out they shot or hacked to death. Many jumped into the wells, hoping that they might save themselves. The ladies-in-waiting of high and low rank and the girls of the women's quarters, running out screaming and shouting, fell and lay prostrate, stepped on by horses and trampled by the men. It was more than terrible. No one knows the number of persons who lost their lives.
>
> Some said that Yoshitomo had raised a rebellion and had broken into the Sanjō Palace in a night attack and set it on fire and that even the Retired Emperor had not escaped the flames. Some also shouted His Imperial highness had gone to the Imperial Palace. Consequently, the "Great Lord" the Lord Chancellor, and all the other nobles and courtiers came in a crowd. The noise of their horses and carriages rushing back and forth was like thunder, and greatly did it resound in heaven and on earth.[7]

The account provides both the overall context and details, such as the names of the participants, that allow the viewer to properly interpret the imagery that follows. To the left, the first scene opens with an ox cart rushing toward people hurrying farther left into a confused swarm of warriors and various nobles (Fig. 6.2). The same carts and people are shown multiple times within this mass, the confusion exemplified by an errant bystander being crushed by one ox cart. The violence heightens with shoving and colliding carts and warriors. Reaching to the left edge of the mass, attention shifts to a group of rebels gathered outside the palace grounds. Farther to the left, the rebels have now penetrated the precinct and proceed to enter the royal mansion (Fig. 6.3). Historians find the attention to detail to be so precise that its imagery provides an extremely important reference for this period. For example, the enclosed portals of the palace, its bare wooden structures connected by passageways, bark roofs, sizable shutters, and bamboo blinds that open to loggias, offer evidence for contemporary architectural forms and materials.

Fujiwara no Nobuyori directs the retired emperor into the waiting cart. Wisps of smoke rise as the palace buildings are set alight (Fig. 6.4). (The blaze echoes that in another, earlier scroll, the *Ban Dainagon ekotoba*, which is celebrated for

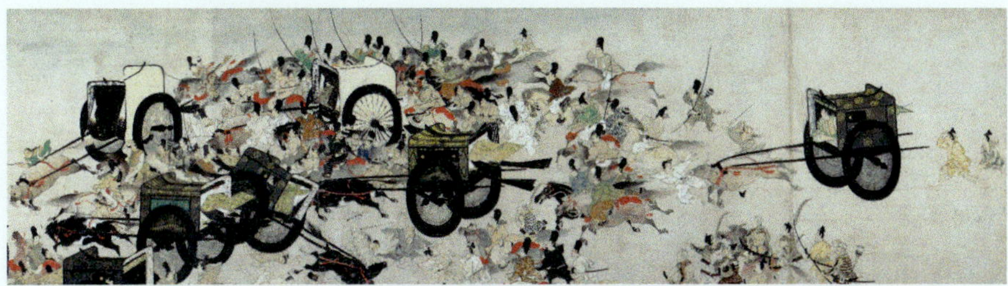

Fig. 6.2 *Night Attack on the Sanjō Palace*, ox cart amidst confused throngs of people. Boston, Museum of Fine Arts. Photo: Wikimedia Commons

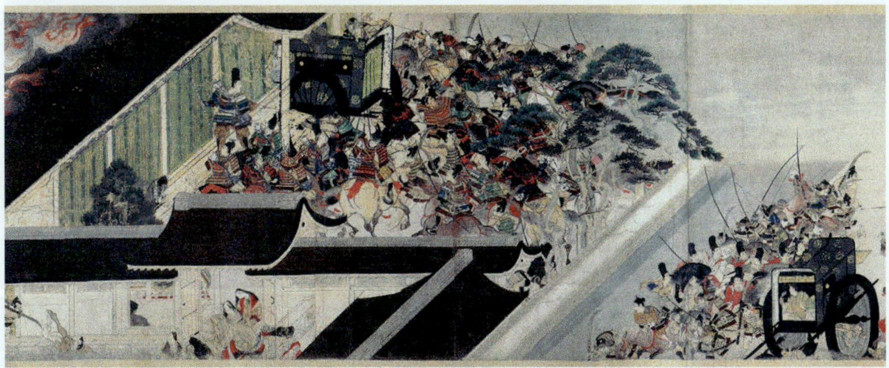

Fig. 6.3 *Night Attack on the Sanjō Palace*, rebels storming the royal mansion. Boston, Museum of Fine Arts. Photo: Wikimedia Commons

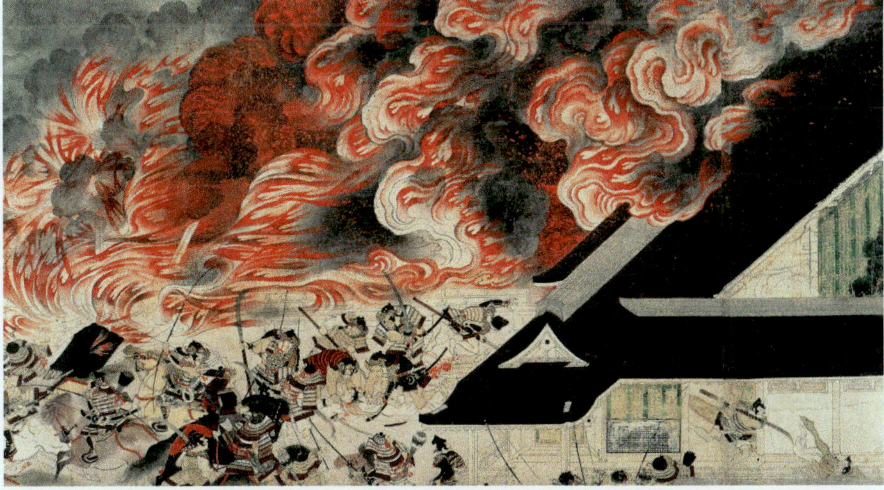

Fig. 6.4 *Night Attack on the Sanjō Palace*, fire consumes the royal mansion. Boston, Museum of Fine Arts. Photo: Wikimedia Commons

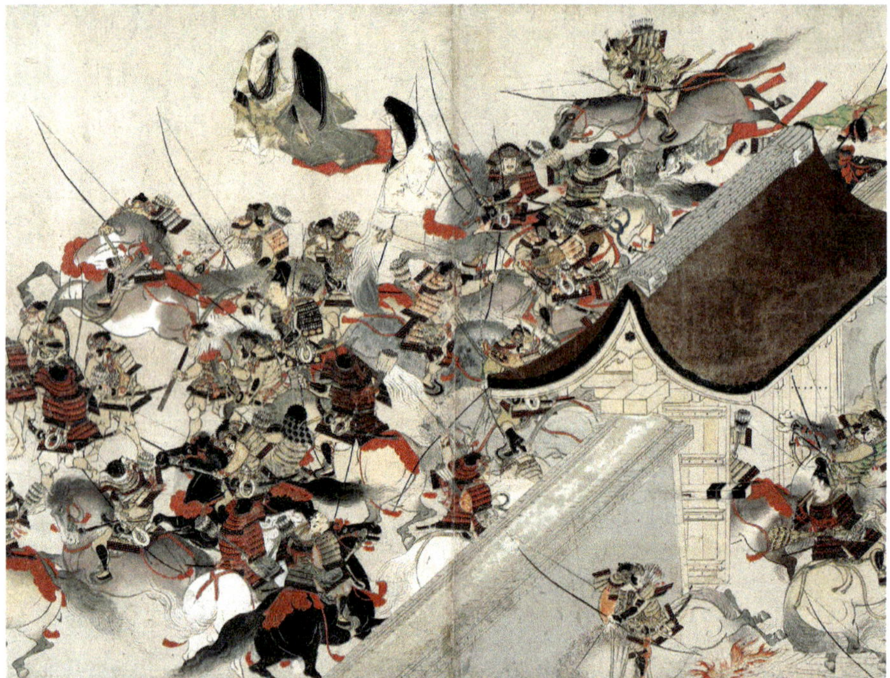

Fig. 6.5 *Night Attack on the Sanjō Palace*, massacre as people flee the royal mansion. Boston, Museum of Fine Arts. Photo: Wikimedia Commons

its combination of lively and refined scenes.)[8] Realistically represented infantry, cavalry, imperial police, courtiers, priests, and women of the palace are easily differentiated by armor, weaponry, and robes according to rank, style, and type.[9] In several cases, these carefully rendered details distinguish particular individuals, even without identifying inscriptions. For example, Suzuki Keizō determined that the particular kind of black armor worn by two warriors among the group in the garden distinguishes them as Minamoto Yoshitomo and Mitsuyasu.[10] The scores of figures are further characterized by gesture and facial expressions that range from shock to macabre humor. Amid the growing conflagration hapless supporters of the Taira clan are savagely massacred, represented by figures that are drawn from a repertoire of that reappears throughout numerous illustrated scrolls.[11] Women (distinguished by their flowing hair) attempt to flee the intense flames and billowing smoke through the palace gate with mixed success (Fig. 6.5).[12] The escalating violence includes stabbing and slashing; rebels parade the severed heads of Taira courtiers. Gradually, as the fire dies out, the rebels depart the palace ground. Meanwhile, Fujiwara Nobuyori and his coconspirator, Minamoto Yoshitomo lead a gang of warriors in taking Go-Shirakawa's carriage, which is led away in a triumphant procession (Fig. 6.6). At the vanguard is a single warrior mounted on horseback led by lone archer walking to the left where there is an additional section of text, which reads:

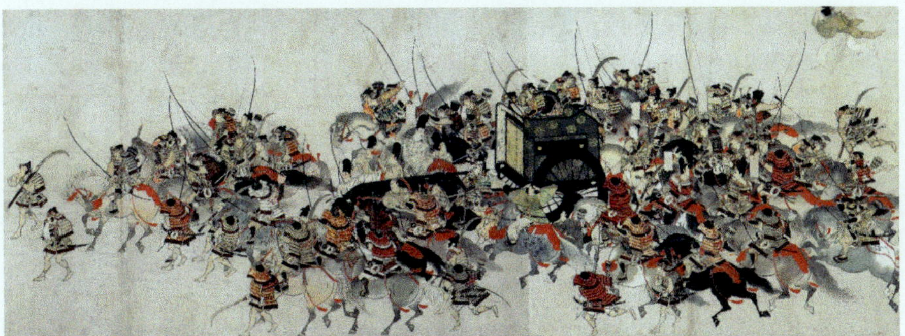

Fig. 6.6 *Night Attack on the Sanjō Palace*, Go-Shirakawa's carriage led away. Boston, Museum of Fine Arts. Photo: Wikimedia Commons

> At the hour of the tiger [4:00 a.m.] the same night, they seized the dwelling of the Shinzei at Anegakoji Nishinotoin and set fire to it. For the last three or four years arms had been banned, and the Empire had been at peace, but now suddenly this disturbance had broken out, and both the Imperial Palace and the capital were filled with soldiers. The noble and lowly lamented together, wondering what had happened.[13]

The illustration thus ends as it began with a single figure moving left, but now the excitement of impending battle shifts into a kind of weary acceptance of war's cost.

Nobuyori and Yoshitomo were victorious in the Heiji disturbance, but were later defeated and executed by their rival Taira Kiyomori. Kiyomori secured authority as a trusted counsellor to Go-Shirakawa and staged his own rebellion some twenty years later, unleashing the final phase of the civil war, known commonly as the Genpei War. One of Yoshimoto's sons, Minamoto Yoritomo, prevailed in this drive, and condemned Taira Kiyomori's family to death or exile. It was then when Yoritomo established the Kamakura *bakufu*, the Japanese feudal government headed by a shogun, which provided judicial and policing authority from 1185 to 1333.

Formal Structures and Narrative Strategies

The *Heiji monogatari* portrays the struggle between old aristocratic and new military elites. It follows the traditional tripartite structure of *gunki monogatari* with sections to describe the origins of the conflict, the actual battles, and an enumeration of the war's consequences. The texts are mostly episodic, divided into numerous small tales that concentrate on specific warriors or events. It is written in thirty-six chapters, which may reflect the text's oral transmission (as discussed below). As in other *gunki monogatari*, multilevel and interrelated rivalries are presented as the cause of war. The scroll presents the main characters according to traditional Japanese hierarchical ordering: emperors and former emperors first (cloistered Retired Emperor Go-Shirakawa and Emperor Nijô), aristocratic ministers second (Fujiwara no Michinori and Fujiwara no Nobuyori), and military clan warriors third (Taira no Kiyomori and Minamoto no Yoshitomo).[14] The *Heiji monogatari*, however, progresses beyond the comparatively simple narration pattern of the *Hōgen monogatari* toward a more complicated and nuanced account to suggest the necessity of more flexibility in desperate times.[15]

During the Heian period (literally "the period of calm and tranquility"), the Japanese had fully assimilated and transformed aspects of culture from China and Korea, and by the late Heian and subsequent Kamakura periods Japanese scrolls reveal significant variation from those continental traditions. Of all their innovations in narrative form, their chronicles of past achievements were critical to establishing the authority of elite families and defining the martial ideals they professed. *Night Attack on the Sanjō Palace* is one of the most celebrated in the *emakimono* artform due to its technical sophistication and dynamic narrative propelling the reader to the climactic blaze.

Emakimono refers to an illustrated narration system of painted horizontal handscrolls. The term *emakimono* (sometimes shortened to *emaki*) is formed from of the kanji *e* ("picture"), *maki* ("scroll" or "book"), and *mono* ("thing"). Dating back to the Nara period (eighth century), the artform initially copied venerated Chinese precedents, combining text and illustrations. The artist constructs the story using a succession of these two components—the portions of calligraphic text (*kotoba-gaki*) and the portions of paintings (*e*)—painted, drawn, or stamped on long rolls of paper measuring from one to several meters, on average 30 to 39 feet (9 to 12 m). Traditionally, one reads an *emaki* while kneeling or seated on a mat with the scroll positioned on a low table or even on the floor. The reader proceeds to unwind with the left hand while rewinding it with the right, following the right to left direction of Japanese writing. As a result only part of the story—about 24 inches (60 cm)—is revealed at a time (Fig. 6.7). Once it has been read, the *emaki* must be rewound to its original reading direction.[16]

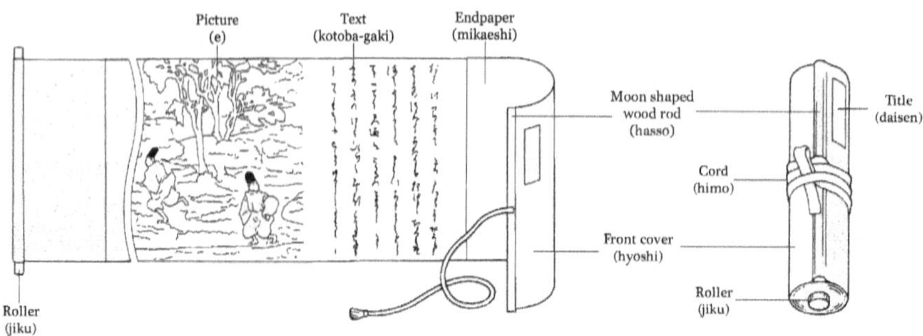

Fig. 6.7 Format of an *emakimono*. Drawing: Jeffrey Ryan, after Aoyagi (1997): 560.

Several successive scrolls can make up an *emaki* as required by the tale, although they typically number between one and three. (Their dimensions, organization, and number fluctuate, depending on the period, narrative represented, and artist.) Historically they were read by elites but could also be used to illustrate lectures by the high clergy, so-called *e-toki*. *Emakimono* paintings mostly conform to the *yamato-e* style, distinguished by its seasonal landscapes and narrative subjects drawn from Japanese literature and history, distinguished from themes imported from China, known as *kara-e* or "Tang painting."[17] From the late Heian period onward, the meaning of *yamato-e* evolved to denote not just the subject or setting of the paintings but also the formal conventions artists employed, including highly stylized figures with abbreviated facial features, an emphasis on rich colors, and a technique known as *fukinuki yatai* ("blown off roof") in which a building's roof is removed to afford a careful depiction of the interior from above. The format of long scrolls of limited height—on average 12 inches (30 cm)—requires the resolution of numerous compositional difficulties, such as making transitions between the different scenes that accompany the tale, choosing a point of view that mirrors any accompanying narrative, and creating a rhythm that best conveys the feelings and emotions of the story. When sections of text do not interrupt the paintings, various technical processes allow the artist to generate fluid transitions between the scenes; according to Melissa McCormick, such tactics allow the images and texts to function "symbiotically to shape a reader's cognitive experience of the work."[18]

Long scrolls are an impeccable medium for extensive and stunning panoramic landscapes, certainly the dominant theme developed in East Asian painting from the eleventh century. Handscrolls present a more awkward format, however, when used to depict narrative. The space in the composition of an *emakimono* constitutes an indispensable element for conveying the passage of time within the narrative. The most obvious and popular approach was to create a sequential or progressive narrative by formally structuring several scenes from a story along the length of the scroll. (Comparisons with the structure of ancient scrolls and works influenced by their form, such as the Column of Trajan and the Bayeux Embroidery, are natural and instructive, but one must remember that Japanese artists would have had no knowledge of them.) This enabled the artist to convey intricate narratives across a series of images, much as some artists in Renaissance Europe used multiple canvases (as demonstrated with Uccello's *The Battle of San Romano* in the following chapter, which again had no historical connection to Japan).

Another strategy was to use the width of the scroll itself to describe both space and time when they advance together, whereby the artist reduces the four dimensions of space and time to three dimensions, and subsequently depicts them on the two-dimensional scroll. Japanese artists developed a form of multipoint linear perspective projection to accomplish this, where individual portions of the scroll—the section of unrolled scroll visible for close viewing—share the same vanishing points, but with various groups of vanishing points plotted along the scroll's length.[19] The method for indicating temporal links was similar: what is portrayed within each section along the length of the scroll would be relatively simultaneous, and as one unrolls the scroll to reveal new sections, so too time progresses. Although compounding the progression of time and location works here, in other narratives divergences might arise that make the technique unsuitable, suggesting why there are so few specimens like this one, and instead more scrolls showing a series of temporally distinct events along its length.

According to Japanese conventions, the layout of the texts and images provides the primary narrative rhythm of the *emakimono*, constituting an indispensable marker of the story's development. *Night Attack on the Sanjō Palace* (as it survives) uses a form called intermittence, in which the texts appeared only at the beginning or at the end of the scroll, affording prominence to continuous illustrations (*rusogata-shiki* or *renzoku-shiki*).[20] Transitions in scrolls with continuous illustrations are sometimes more ambiguous, but as Elise Grilli notes, this type provides the artist with a wide-ranging "syntax of movement and time" that allows him to adapt the form to both the story and the sentiments conveyed.[21]

Since the scroll is usually read from right to left and top to bottom, artists frequently employ plummeting points of view called *chokan*, or "bird's-eye perspective." Not only does this convention correspond with the actual position of the seated reader-viewer looking down at the scroll, but it also allows the artists to make the most of the available surface, despite the low height of the scroll, even leaving part of the paper's surface visible as neutral background in the painting. At the same time, the low height of the *emakimono* encourages the painter to employ artistic conventions that include the use of extended diagonal lines or flowing curves to suggest spatial depth.[22] For indoor scenes, such diagonals are established by architectural elements (beams, partitions, doors); for outdoor settings they are organized by roads and rivers or walls and roofs arranged on several planes. The unrolling scroll evokes a parallel or oblique projection rather than the unity established by Renaissance single vanishing point perspective commonly used in European canvases.[23]

The construction of the scroll's narrative rhythm is dedicated completely to leading the reader-viewer to the dramatic climax. As the unwinding scroll reveals the main action its pace intensifies, escalating the suspense. Close-ups alternate with vast panoramas; the action of dynamic stories seems to gain momentum with the skillful use of elisions, transitions, and exaggeration. Here a dense red spreads over almost the entire height of the paper to accentuate the measured escalation of the violent battle and the pursuit of Emperor Go-Shirakawa, culminating with the palace catching fire.[24] The artist also energizes the story by representing the same characters in a sequence of changing settings (generally outdoors), a technique known as *hampuku byosha* ("repetition").[25] And the same character can also be represented multiple times in a single scene (*iji-do-zu*), a version of synoptic narrative, in order to indicate a sequence of actions with an economical saving of space.[26]

Swift, active brushstrokes enhance the dynamic composition, as do the vibrant use of outline and color. Strong diagonal lines emphasize movement; even the palace ceiling takes the shape of a lightning-bolt to divide the scene. Unfurled, *Night Attack on the Sanjō Palace* stands apart. It exploits the dramatic potential of the elongated *emaki* format with such virtuosity that the painter may have conceived occasions when it would be fully unfurled, and therefore structured what from a lesser artist might be a muddle of details into a cohesive narrative arc.

Authors, Artists, and Their Audiences

Unlike their earlier Heian counterparts, few of the warrior tales from the Kamakura period have identifiable authors; in fact, a tale is generally a collaborative work composed by several people who did not write the tales fully from start to finish but rather edited and rewrote them numerous times. It can be stated with certainty that the *Heiji monogatari* was completed at least after 1199, when Minamoto no Yoritomo passed away, because the manuscript of the first edition in the Gakushuin University Library contains an article describing the death of Yoritomo.[27] It was once believed that the author of the *Heiji monogatari* was the same as that of the closely related *Hōgen monogatari*. In recent years, however, it has generally been assumed that the two *monogatari* were the work of different authors (recognizing the difficulties implicit in that term), then rewritten and revised many times while reflecting a contemporary oral tradition as well.

Traditionally, warrior tales earned acclaim through oral performances, usually accompanied by a lute (*biwa*), resulting in the pervasive misunderstanding that the scripted texts (*yomimono*) of *gunki monogatari* were originally written exclusively for memorization and recitation; and in fact, most often the *Tale of the Heiji* would have been recited as a sequel to the *Tale of the Hōgen*. These works have characteristics of narrative recitations (*katarimono*), a practice that has a ritual component, such as the recitations by blind priests (*biwa hōshi*) that were thought to reestablish social order and placate the enraged souls of warriors killed in battle; when chanted by minstrels, however, they also functioned as popular entertainment that celebrated heroic warriors and their ethos. Such performances of the texts, however, actually transformed the material of private contemplation into the stuff of social or collective memory. Analysis of surviving original manuscripts reveal that the *Heike monogatari* was first written pseudo-historically to chronicle the later Genpei War. In devising this tale, the author drew heavily on existing oral narratives as well as from memoirs and other historical records. The account was originally written to be read privately, not recited, and therefore it had to be revised for performance; consequently, the current authoritative version of the *Heike monogatari* is a product of these intermingled practices. The *Heiji monogatari* probably results from a similar fusion.

As with the authorship of the war tales, their illustrations were also the product of collaboration, most likely by a team or workshop of artists working under the direction of a master, calligraphers, and coordinators overseeing the entire project. Although once attributed to a classical Japanese artist named Keion (perhaps a misreading for Keinin), a member of the famous Kasuga family of painters, the dearth of substantiated facts about both his work and his connection to any surviving handscrolls makes this unlikely.[28] Since reliable sources concerning the painters of the *Heiji monogatari* are so meager, specialists in Japanese art are drawn to establishing the social and artistic situation of the painters: whether they were amateurs or professionals, aristocrats or of modest birth, and whether they worked at court or in temples.[29] We can say with certainty that in contrast to the amateurs found at the imperial court during the Heian period, in the Kamakura period workshops of professional painters dominated production associated with the palace, as well as the great temples and shrines.[30]

Oral traditions and painted representations of the battle scenes present links similar to those found between oral traditions and written texts. Examination of different versions of the texts and images of the better-preserved *Heike monogatari* shows that earlier renderings, such as the *Shibu kassenjō*, contained only a general account of the actual battle, while later renderings transform the warriors from mere human combatants into idealized heroes who embody a particular martial ethos exemplified through portrayals of their individual actions. Another innovation was to have the hero introduce himself to his opponent in a speech that included his name and title, and also his lineage and achievements. (These speeches compare with those made by the Bronze Age heroes fighting before the walls of Troy, which were also formulations employed in the oral recitation of the Homeric epics.)[31] Therefore many aspects of the warrior tales are undoubtedly fictional, resulting from the propensity for oral traditions to integrate real people and events with set themes to generate successful performances, a combination of historical fact and dramatic fabrication to shape and preserve the memory of this period.

Some passages contain careful if formulaic descriptions of a warrior's apparel and armor; careful depictions of these same details in representations of battles are pictorial conventions that parallel textual practices, in both cases to identify a warrior clearly and to characterize his personality. Since most surviving picture scrolls representing warriors date from the fourteenth century, *Night Attack on the Sanjō Palace* offers an indispensable representation of Japanese armor borne during the Kamakura era. When severely damaged in the eighteenth century, a handscroll illustrating the *Tale of the Heiji* dating to the first quarter of the fourteenth century was cut into fourteen sections which were then remounted. One surviving fragment from that *emaki* now in the Metropolitan Museum represents a scene from the Battle at Rokuhara, which occurred when Yoshitomo joined forces with his son Akugenda Yoshihira to cross the Kamo River and attack the Rokuhara Mansion, Kiyomori's Taira stronghold (Fig. 6.8).[32] The scene shown here represents the life-or-death struggle. Beneath their billowing red banners two charging Taira warriors close in on a Minamoto soldier. As the latter draws his sword, one of the Taira warriors grabs for his horse's reins while the other seizes his helmet and raises his sword to behead him. The armor they wear is of the later fourteenth century, in

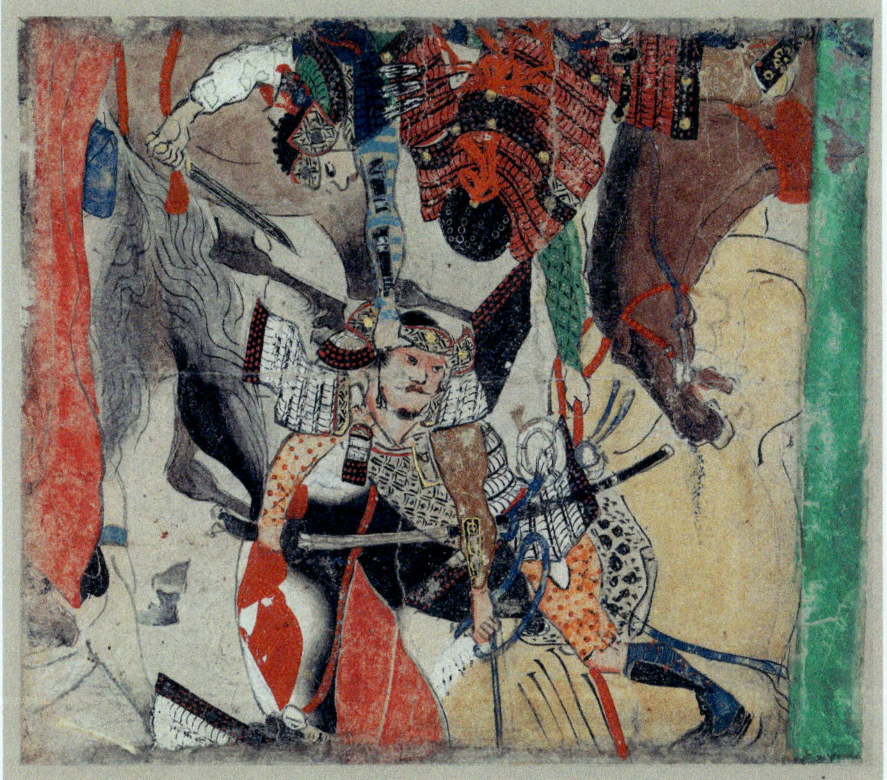

Fig. 6.8 *Tale of the Heiji*, Battle at Rokuhara (first quarter of the fourteenth century). New York, Metropolitan Museum of Art. Photo: Metropolitan Museum of Art on Wikimedia Commons

contrast to the remarkable thirteenth-century panoply depicted in *Night Attack on the Sanjō Palace*.

The production of *gunki monogatari* flourished with the backing of the newly empowered warrior elite (and also the influence of new Buddhist sects),[33] and with time their themes and techniques became more diverse.[34] The prevailing style of Kamakura period *gunki emaki* is characterized by the synthesis of older genres of the *yamato-e* style and a new emphasis placed on realism, seen in such passages as the detailed rendering of armor and weapons described above.[35] In fact, pictorial realism in representing battle imagery may well betray the tastes of the warrior patrons then in power. As McCormick observes, the text and images "contain a wealth of information about the values, interests, and aspirations of those who commissioned the work and assisted in its creation."[36]

Gunki monogatari help constitute *bushido* ("the way of the warrior"), a philosophy and code of conduct that guided the ruling military class in medieval Japan.[37] Its values and ideals demand, above all else, loyalty to one's lord and fearlessness in the face of certain death. This allegiance is firmly tied to the concept of personal honor; warriors would rather die and receive posthumous praise than survive with a tainted reputation. *Bushido* prescribes a determined course of action that warriors should follow notwithstanding their personal feelings or preferences. Accordingly, the code disallows compassion when it conflicts with duty.[38] Nevertheless, deviations between the actions of the same individuals in different versions of the narratives reveal divergences in the way diverse authors and editors understood model behavior, and therefore impede our ability to draw definite conclusions about any fixed nature of the warrior ethos.

The *gunki monogatari* are distinguished from other works in this study by the distance in time separating their manufacture from the events they commemorate. Because their historical subjects represent earlier wars and are not truly contemporary, they do not truly advance the ideological agendas of the figures portrayed in them. Rather, illustrated historical chronicles like this one preserve the memory of the heroic roles played by significant ancestors of the newly ascendant warriors in battles that precipitated the establishment of their caste. Workshops associated with the court satisfied orders for these *gunki monogatari emaki*, produced primarily for members of the Minamoto clan, the eventual winners of the final Genpei War; not surprisingly, they are characterized by a sympathetic tone toward that clan. The scrolls therefore relate the historical events chosen from these battles as stories to celebrate the values of a contemporary, that is later, audience. Although modern viewers may be inclined to interpret representations of pitiless violence in the Bayeux Embroidery as critiques of the excesses of war, in *gunki monogatari* violent acts are instead exemplary and represent the performance of the warrior ethic embraced by the protagonists and venerated by readers.

Oral performance of the texts of the warrior tales for entertainment and ritual functions ensured that their narratives were widely known and remembered; audiences were engaged by vivid yet didactic narratives drawn from their national history. Scrolls like *Night Attack on the Sanjō Palace*, however, were not made as public commemorations; rather they were intended to be collected and read privately.[39] They are known to have been prized pieces in the fifteenth century, when aristocrats refer to viewing them. *Gunki monogatari emaki* belong to a class known as *otoko-e* ("man's painting"). They exalt the martial endeavors of famous samurai who embodied *bushido* values. Illustrations of the violent actions of "those who serve," which was the original meaning of *samurai*, invite close inspection, contemplation, even revery. Crucially, the scrolls were understood as recounting family as well as national history. In many cases readers identified the protagonists as their own admirable ancestors, and consequently sought to model their personal conduct and public lives after them.[40] In this way the scrolls came to serve as manuals for personal conduct in the present with exemplars drawn from the past. By detailing heroic tales about the foundation of the system which they inherited and now managed, *gunki monogatari* justified and the sustained the power of their individual owners.

With the collapse of the shogunate in 1868 and decline of traditional feudal power alongside Japan's modernization during the tumultuous Meiji Period

(1868–1912), many privately owned scrolls became fragmented and dispersed.[41] *Night Attack on the Sanjō Palace* had been a prized possession of the Honda family before 1878, when it was acquired in Japan by Ernest Francisco Fenollosa, an enthusiastic Orientalist. In 1886 he sold it to Charles Goddard Weld, who bequeathed it in 1911 to the Boston Museum of Fine Arts, a course of transferal that brings new layers of history for interpretation.[42]

7

The Battle of San Romano

Painting and the Perpetuation of Memory in Renaissance Florence

Renaissance Italy functioned much as it had during the Middle Ages: as a group of competing city-states with their own governments driven by rival families. Each regime hired mercenaries to fight in its conflicts and *condottieri*—soldiers-for-hire who were holdovers of the medieval knights—to command. In *The Prince*, Machiavelli described condottieri as untrustworthy leaders with little loyalty to the short-lived governments that hired them:

> The fact is they have no other attraction or reason for keeping the field than a trifle of stipend, which is not sufficient to make them willing to die for you. They are ready enough to be your soldiers whilst you do not make war, but if war comes they take themselves off or run from the foe . . . The mercenary captains are either capable men or they are not; if they are, you cannot trust them, because they always aspire to their own greatness, either by oppressing you, who are their master, or others contrary to your intentions; but if the captain is not skillful, you are ruined in the usual way.[1]

Nevertheless, city-states competed fiercely for their services. Paolo Uccello's *Equestrian Monument to Sir John Hawkwood* (1436) portrays a famous English soldier-of-fortune as a Florentine hero (Fig. 7.1).[2] Larger than life-size, the fresco's prominence in the city's cathedral and allusions to public equestrian monuments conjure the rewards civic governments promised to bestow.[3] Such artistic commemorations also enhanced the grandeur of the city by decorating its public places and evoking proud events in its history. When Alberti described how paintings of deceased individuals ensured that "even after many centuries they are recognized with great pleasure," he drew attention to their power as carriers of memory.[4]

The Battle of San Romano

In the late 1420s, the republics of Florence and Lucca disputed access to the port of Pisa for trade. This quarrel escalated into a war between Florence and Lucca and its allies (Genoa, Milan, and Siena) that persisted from 1429 to 1433. Sienese

Power, Image, and Memory. Peter J. Holliday, Oxford University Press. © Oxford University Press 2024.
DOI: 10.1093/oso/9780190901080.003.0008

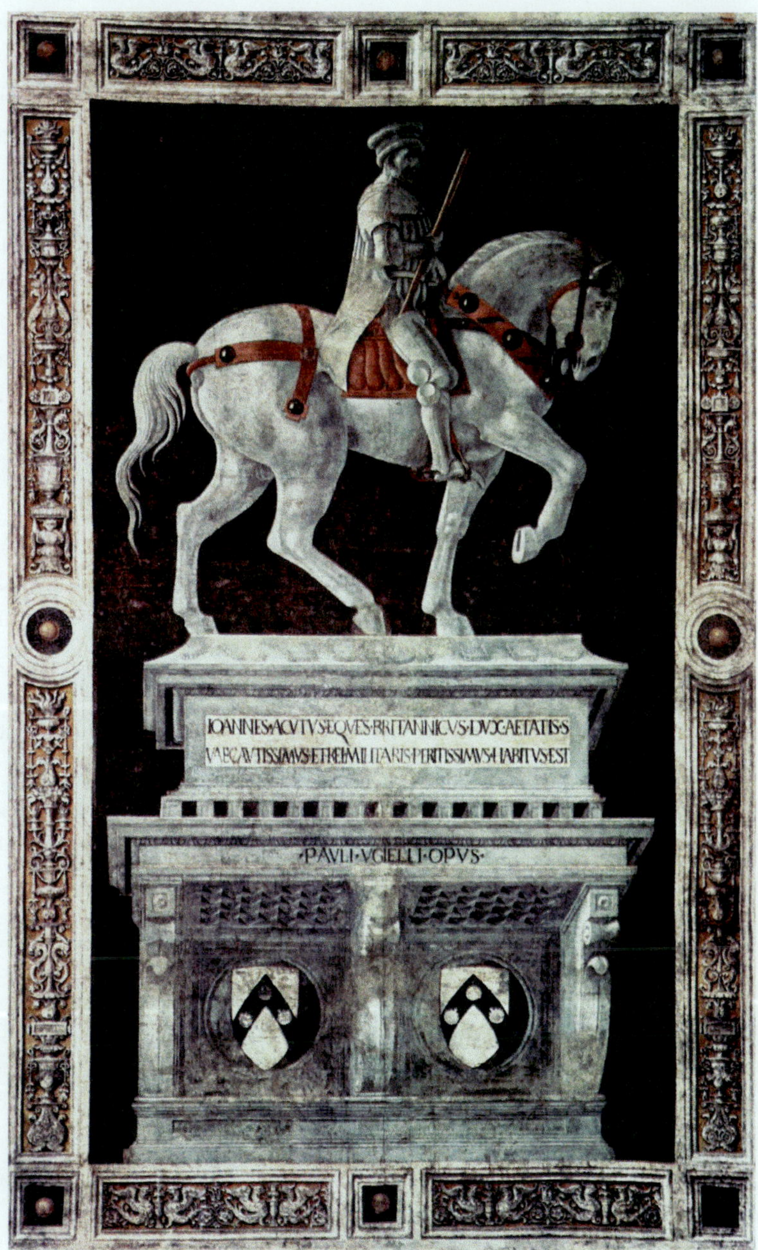

Fig. 7.1 Paolo Uccello, *Equestrian Monument to Sir John Hawkwood* (1436). Florence, Santa Maria del Fiore. Photo: Wikimedia Commons

forces led by the condottiere Bernardino Ubaldini della Carda, then in alliance with the Duke of Milan, ravaged Florentine territory. Following a series of reverses the Signoria decided that Niccolò Maurucci da Tolentino, a notorious condottiere of the day, should take command of the Florentine troops, with Micheletto Attendolo da Cotignola leading a subsidiary force.[5] The new appointment soon justified itself.

On June 1, 1432, a scorching summer day, the Florentine and Sienese armies met midway between Florence and Pisa, some thirty miles outside Florence in the valley of the Arno River, near the tower of San Romano and the town of Monopoli. The clash lasted for some seven or eight hours over the course of the day, consisting primarily of a series of cavalry skirmishes.

Tolentino, perhaps impulsively, had separated from his main force with some twenty cavalry to explore the area. The Sienese forces under Carda, seeing an advantage, attacked. Instead of capitulating, as contemporary military standards would have allowed, Tolentino and his small cohort resisted. Niccolò sent for help from Michelotto Attendolo, who led another contingent of Florentine troops some distance away. Michelotto crossed the Arno in the afternoon and set upon the Sienese rear guard.[6] When the Sienese commander eventually withdrew he abandoned numerous soldiers to be taken prisoner. (Whereas Florence had only 400 cavalry taken prisoner, Siena had 600 cavalry and an unknown number of infantry taken prisoner.) Matteo Palmieri, a Florentine historian and supporter of the powerful Medici family, went to the site of San Romano to write his account, the *Annals*. Palmieri determined that Niccolò was a strategic leader, who intentionally isolated himself to set a trap:

> Tolentino . . . sent three companies leftward through the vineyards and brambles toward Monopoli, under orders to wait until after the battle had begun and the others had all descended into the plain, and then to launch their own attack. He kept three companies in reserve on the hill. He himself advanced with two companies, and he dispatched a messenger to Michelotto to inform him that the operation had begun and that victory was assured if he would attack the enemy unexpectedly from the rear.[7]

It was one of those combats that Machiavelli dismissed as petty and trifling, fought by proxy with mercenary captains at the head of hired forces, rather than between citizen armies. Modern historians agree that it was a minor battle and offered little other than brief satisfaction, but thanks to Medici partisans, Florence celebrated the battle as Tolentino's victory and a turning point in the war; not surprisingly, Sienese accounts award victory to Carda.

The Three Panels

Three paintings, since the fifteenth century commonly referred to as *The Battle of San Romano*, depict similar subjects and are recorded in common ownership from 1480 to 1487 (Fig. 7.2, Fig. 7.3, and Fig. 7.4). Skilled workers prepared three wooden panels, each measuring approximately 6 x 10.5 feet (182 x 320 cm), for the paintings Paolo Uccello executed in egg tempera with walnut and linseed oil.[8] They are traditionally understood as a triptych—and will be discussed as such here—designed

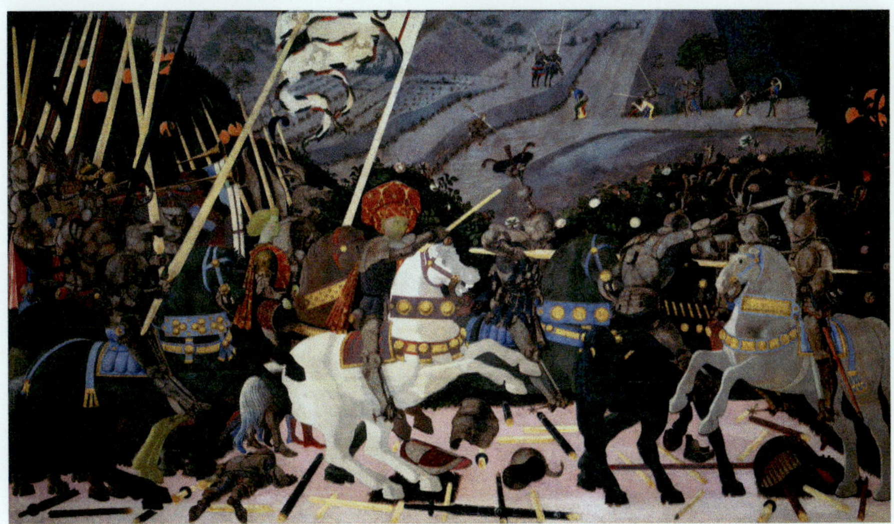

Fig. 7.2 *Niccolò Mauruzi da Tolentino at the Battle of San Romano* (ca. 1438–1440). London, National Gallery. Photo: Wikimedia Commons

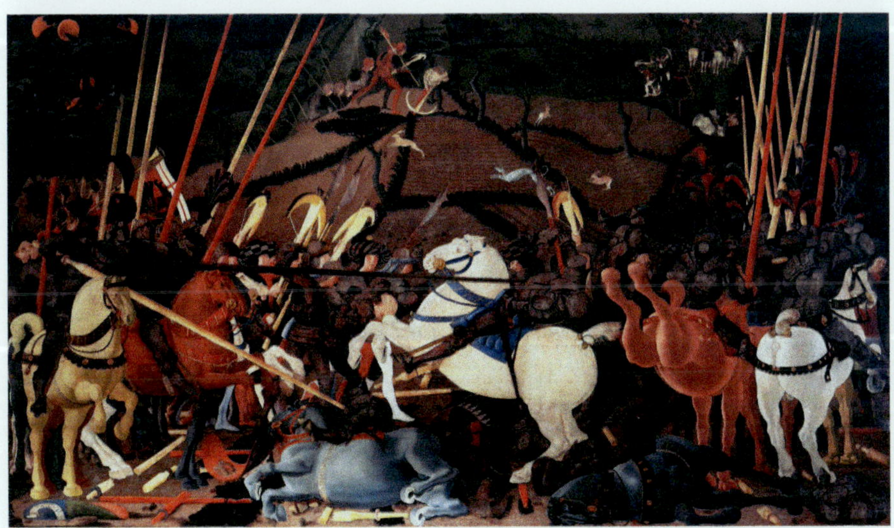

Fig. 7.3 *Niccolò Mauruzi da Tolentino Unseats Bernardino della Carda at the Battle of San Romano* (ca. 1438–1455). Florence, Galleria degli Uffizi. Photo: Wikimedia Commons

to be hung together high on three adjoining walls of a chamber and to take that height (approximately seven feet above one's head) into account, which explains several inconsistencies in the perspective when viewed in photos or at standard gallery height. They have been interpreted as each showing a specific moment from the battle. The first would be displayed at the left: *Niccolò Mauruzi da Tolentino at the Battle of San Romano* (National Gallery, London); in the center: *Niccolò da*

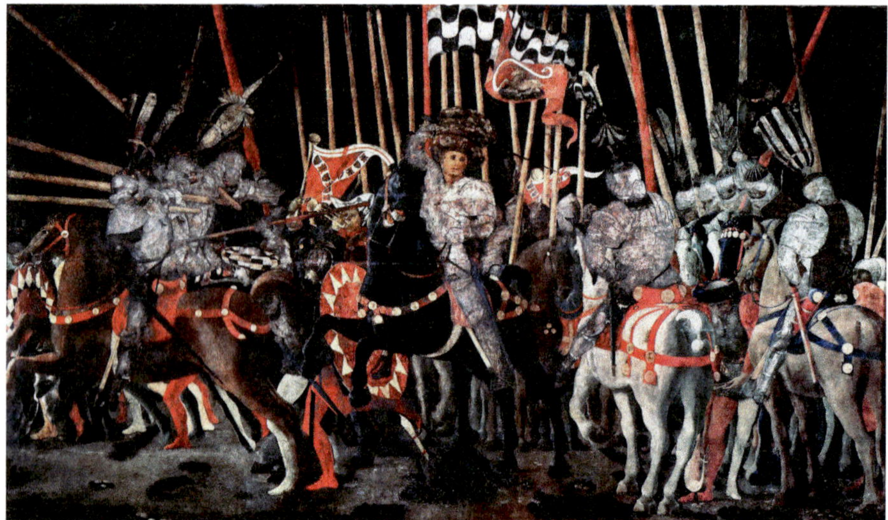

Fig. 7.4 *The Counterattack of Michelotto Attendolo da Cotignola at the Battle of San Romano* (ca. 1455). Paris, Musée du Louvre. Photo: Wikimedia Commons

Tolentino Unseats Bernardino della Carda (Uffizi, Florence); and at the right: *The Counterattack of Michelotto Attendolo da Cotignola at the Battle of San Romano* (Louvre, Paris). Most art historians agree on this sequence, although others have been proposed. The distinctly different appearance of the panels may represent different times during the day-long battle: dawn (London), mid-day (Florence), and dusk (Paris). Recent research, however, has called this traditional interpretation into question. Their dating remains uncertain, ranging from 1435 to 1455. What is not doubted is that as a private secular commission the panels are innovative for that time, and one that also demonstrates the value of historical representations to commemorate an event and shape how viewers remember it.

The Florentine commander Niccolò da Tolentino on his rearing white mount stands out at the heart of the London painting. Rather than the expected battle armor he wears elaborate ceremonial clothing, including a damask cloak and an extraordinary gold and red patterned turban; the short baton in his right hand signifies his command. Behind him to the left a blond youth holds Niccolò's banner, which is emblazoned with the Knot of Solomon.[9] Niccolò leads his men over broken lances and enemy dead toward the opposing force at the right. A barrier of rose bushes and orange and pomegranate trees enclose the battlefield action in the limited space of the foreground, completely separating it from the background where several soldiers are scattered across the rolling Tuscan hills; two, shown at the center top across the road, are probably the mounted messengers Niccolò sent to Michelotto Attendolo, connecting the left and right panels narratively and temporally. Others are dressed in colorful pants and seem to perform various training tasks, including three archers, one who uses his feet to load a crossbow, a physically demanding task.

The captain in the center (Florence) panel is usually identified as Bernardino della Carda, the commander of the Sienese mercenaries, knocked from his white horse by a lance. Written sources do not recount this incident, but instead relate that he bolted from the battle. The arms of one of the Sienese soldiers are similar in form if not in color to those of the Petrucci family, leading some scholars to suggest the unhorsed figure may represent Antonio Petrucci, who fought at San Romano.[10] The forward direction of the Florentine lances and crossbows contrasts to those of their adversaries, which are slightly drawn back and foreshadow the outcome. The crowded composition and the complex representation of space lend the atmosphere an unreal quality. Uccello placed the principal action in the foreground, consistent with the London panel's composition, but here he used a screen of greenery only on the side to direct the viewer's eye into the composition and allow the landscape to extend into the background gradually. The interweaving of narrative and landscape, with the detailed representation of subdivided fields and foot soldiers emerging on the hill in the middle distance, establish a visually teeming locale for the combat in the foreground. The scenery is also more abundant here, with a dog chasing rabbits and at the upper left a small group of winemakers who cluster around a half-barrel while holding their jugs. The dark needles and bent boughs of the pine tree evoke a pastoral beauty unmarked by the action in the foreground. Hugh Hudson submits that the maturing sophistication of the rendering of the landscape between the London and Florence works indicates that the panels were envisioned all together as an ensemble, but that they were painted in succession, with the London panel probably painted first and the Florence panel slightly later.[11]

The central figure of the third (Paris) panel is the Florentine general Michelotto Attendolo on a black horse, his large headpiece accentuating his importance.[12] Additional figures and horses in the foreground animate the painting. Michelotto raises a sword in his right hand to order the Florentine soldiers at the right to enter the fray, while behind him on the left two men trumpet his command above the din of battle. Soldiers at the left lower their lances to attack. The welter of soldiers, horse's legs, and weapons suggest the massing of forces. Uccello's virtuosity with perspective is found in the construction of the foreshortened bodies that function best when viewed from below, acknowledging the original disposition of the panels. The Paris panel was probably painted third.

The three paintings cohere as a triptych through their balance and counterbalance of form and color. Their internally episodic nature is complemented by an overall thematic and compositional unity that results from the placement of the captains close to the center of each panel.[13] The Florentines Niccolò and Michelotto face from the left and right, their mounts both rearing on their hind legs in foreshortened three-quarter view toward the center painting, thereby establishing the importance—literally and compositionally—of that panel and its representation of the unseating of the Sienese leader. In stark contrast to Niccolò's white steed, Michelotto's is black, and stands out among that panel's lighter colored horses. Like Niccolò, Michelotto also wears elaborate garments and fanciful headgear, and rides beneath a banner, his emblazoned with a unicorn. The central (Florence) panel, on the other hand, is built around a pyramid formed by the white mount of Bernardino and two flanking horses fallen to the ground.[14] Uccello carefully composed the pictorial space of each panel and teases its boundaries, yet also disposes key elements across the picture surface, demanding a mobile gaze to follow the unfolding story. Each panel features a monoscenic composition, and the viewer would follow the action painting to painting, wall to wall, much like unfolding action in expensive tapestries. As separate panels that operate together sequentially; they also recall earlier practices like those found on the predella panels of Duccio's trecento *Maestà* (cf. Fig. I.4). Nevertheless, there are differences of scale among the panels, with the figures and horses in the London and Florence panels somewhat smaller than those in the Paris painting. In addition, the viewing position of the London and Florence panels is higher, while the Paris panel also presents dissimilarities in armor and horses' equipage. Finally, the London and Florence panels feature visible landscapes, whereas a dark screen of trees forms the background for the Paris panel.[15]

Putting History into Perspective

For all their carefully rendered detail, the paintings do not establish a literal depiction of actual events. The landscapes contain no recognizable topographical references, such as the town of Montopoli or the eponymous tower of San Romano. Although the natural world dominates Uccello's landscape settings, much of the vegetation is rendered flat, and the attention given to minutiae and patterns seem to diverge from his otherwise realistic impulses. The principal figures are dressed in fantastically lavish costumes, not the armor demanded in battle. Some authorities have suggested that Niccolò's wearing of fanciful headgear rather than a helmet is meant to convey his recklessness, but that seems unlikely since Michelotto is similarly garbed, and it is doubtful that the patron would have wished to see the portrayal of any character flaws in the condottieri commemorated for Florence's victory. Uccello did not evoke the blood and chaos of the actual event; rather, he told a story that portrays the battle as a theatrical performance. Very likely the original domestic setting for these panels (see below) figured into eschewing the gruesome violence of war. The debris of conflict receding on the ground instead suggests a tournament whose pomp and pageantry are those of a glorious, chivalrous game—an ingenious transformation of war into splendid but appropriate palace decoration. To this extent Uccello follows the conventions he inherited for the visualization of battle, but he would soon begin to transform them.[16]

All three paintings have suffered from time and early restorations. Some sections show losses in modeling, contributing to a general stiffness and a lack of movement in the soldiers and horses. Details picked out with gold and silver leaf clearly recall the gold and silver threads woven into imported tapestries; Uccello's cunning visual allusions to the older art form underscore the way these paintings start to assume the value in addition to the function of textile hangings. The gold leaf—seen on the decorations of the bridles and weapons, Niccolò's clothing (London), as well as in miscellaneous and sporadic places in the foreground and background—has remained bright, whereas the silver leaf used for the soldiers' armor has oxidized to dull grey or black (especially apparent in the Paris panel). The original appearance of the burnished silver would have been stunning. Similarly, the color of the fruit, flowers, and multicolored figures decorating the Tuscan countryside are brilliant and joyful. There is a miniaturist's love of detail seen in the scrupulous description of the armor and such elements as the hunting and fighting motifs in the background. The viewer picks out decorative flourishes with pleasure and wonder; by arresting the viewer's eye they also capture mind and thereby direct attention to the artistic skill involved, all in the service of focusing attention on the image and its meaning.[17]

The Battle of San Romano paintings initially appear reminiscent of Lippo Vanni's *Battle of Sinalunga* (1373–1374), commissioned to commemorate the Sienese victory over English mercenaries in the Val di Chiana in 1363 (Fig. 7.5).[18] Both artists carefully controlled any sense of chaos caused by overlapping soldiers and horses in crowded battle scenes; both also depicted background landscapes that include elements of flat imagery and stiffness. Vanni's fresco, however, is monochromatic, and depicts the progress of the battle and disposition of the armies episodically across the wall more akin to the way the Bayeux Embroidery unfolds to provide a graphic chronicle of events rather than a naturalistic representation. In contrast, elements in Uccello's panels show a higher degree of naturalism, such as the three knights in combat on the right of the London panel. Although highly formalized, the horses (of which some two dozen are distributed over the three panels) are wonderfully sculptural.[19] Uccello rendered the lances as long, slender cones. The individualism of the figures, such as the way the seemingly jumbled soldiers can nevertheless be separated, also indicate evolving Renaissance practice.

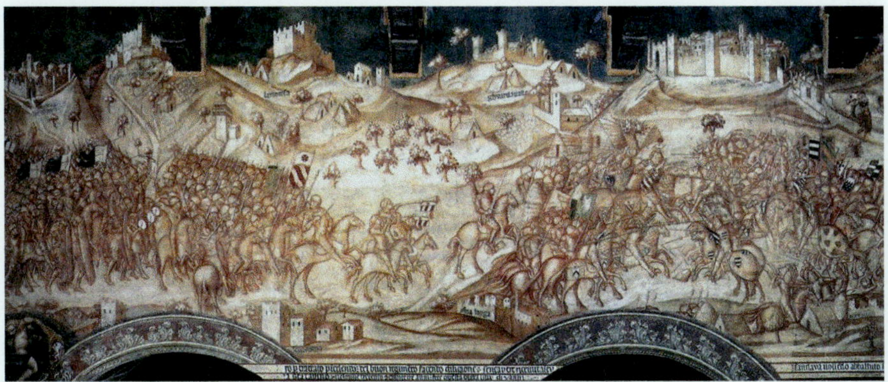

Fig. 7.5 Lippo Vanni, *The Battle of Sinalunga* (1363). Siena, Palazzo Pubblico. Photo: Wikimedia Commons

Alberti asserts that in order to substantiate the events—the *istoria*—it represents successfully, a painting needs to establish a connection and hold the eye of the both the learned and unlearned viewer. Renaissance artists seized linear perspective as an effective method to accomplish this. They were thrilled by the possibility of a geometrical precision that created the illusion of depth that could make their representations more believable by inviting viewers to feel they have entered the space of the picture where they experience the unfolding action, recounting the story to themselves as they look at the picture. The young Uccello had been apprenticed to Ghiberti, himself a formidable master of perspective and one with a serious interest in optical theory as proven by his *Commentarii*.[20] Later, under the influence of contemporaries such as Donatello, Brunelleschi, and Masaccio, he became fascinated with incorporating new discoveries in linear perspective in his own paintings. Vasari described Uccello as a man so preoccupied with studying perspective that he eventually ignored his painting, his family, and even his beloved birds, becoming "solitary, eccentric, melancholy, and impoverished." His wife "used to declare that Paolo stayed at his desk all night, searching for the vanishing points of perspective, and when she called him to bed, he dawdled, saying: 'Oh, what a sweet thing this perspective is!' "[21]

Individually, the detailed rendering of the debris scattered beneath the horses fascinates the viewer; at the same time those splintered lances and even the bodies of fallen soldiers are carefully aligned into orthogonals and transversals, establishing the receding grid of linear perspective.[22] As Patricia Lee Rubin explains, "the geometrical regularity of [Renaissance] composition—its order—acts as a visual metaphor for social order. Through this spatial organization the ideals of a given moment are fixed for all future viewers in a way that makes the very observation of that moment an acceptance of its terms and truths."[23] Here the foreground leads the eye to a tapestry-like backdrop of landscape and vegetation that rises up parallel to the picture plane rather than receding deeply into space. In each panel Uccello confined the illusion of space to a relatively narrow stage where the main action takes place. Moreover, he draws our attention to the discrepancy between the real space of the stage and its action and the false space represented on the backdrop curtain, the allusions to the stage underscoring each scene's theatricality.

Uccello breaks up and recomposes the horses, suits of armor, and standards into volumetric solids extrapolated in space not for "cubist" reasons, but as a way of inviting the viewer to reflect on the stability of appearances. Although Alberti opens his treatise with the observation that mathematical perspective is derived from the "first principles in nature," nature is not the same as unplanned and deficient reality.[24] Uccello deployed the science of perspective to bring order to what was actually chaotic and at the same time make the viewer aware of his artifice in depicting an illusion of the natural world. This convincing illusion emphasizes the reality of the events represented for both contemporary and future viewers. According to Rubin, "The use of paintings to create an immediate memory is done not by the object itself but through the interaction between the painting and the viewer in which the symbols convey a meaning particular to the content. The 'outward symbols' of memory are able to influence and create immediate memory through this dialogue."[25] In other words, drawing attention to the artist's skill persuades the viewer to pay attention to the image and make it memorable, thereby underscoring and enhancing the artwork's commemorative purpose.

The Commission and Its Fortune

Fifteenth-century Florence saw the emergence of a new ruling class, which began to take shape following the turbulence the city experienced during the mid- and later fourteenth century.[26] Amid the tensions generated as this new elite vied for power with rival social groups and political factions, Florentine humanists argued leaders should emulate the "magnificence" of ancient Romans through the lavish display of art and architecture, which could both increase personal prestige and enhance the city.[27] Competitive elites acquired splendid tapestries to adorn palazzo *salóne*, but since Italy did not have established manufactories for them, wall hangings were imported from Flanders in large quantities;[28] paintings, however, could be fashioned locally. Artworks embellishing domestic interiors were more than merely decorative; rather, they played a key role in securing the position of a powerful family by expressing its supreme prowess and that of their city-state. These panels commemorated Niccolò da Tolentino's victory for Florence, but by implication also the men of affairs whose policies secured his service. Tolentino may have been a mercenary, but he was paid by and fought for Florentines, and he fought against the enemies of their city: his victory was a civic accomplishment with which Florentines could effortlessly identify. Tradition long held that Cosimo de' Medici commissioned the paintings for display in the Palazzo Medici. Recently this belief has been doubted, raising questions over who is represented, what battle is depicted (or even if it is more than one), and when and why the paintings were altered. There has never been any question, however, regarding the authorship of *The Battle of San Romano*: the Florence panel is signed PAVLI UGIELI OPUS in the bottom left.

Archival and scientific testimony point to the panels being painted for the Bartolini Salimbeni family.[29] The patriarch, Lionardo, was a leading figure in early fifteenth-century Florentine political life. A wealthy banker himself, he was a member of the inner circle of the Medici faction and was elected to the Signoria and to the Dieci di Balìa where he was a major proponent of the war with Lucca.[30] Francesco Caglioti proposes that Lionardo commissioned the paintings in 1438, shortly after the battle. They first appear in a 1480 account describing Lionardo's bedchamber, the Camera Grande of his Florentine palazzo, at which time they were described as the *Rout of Niccolò Piccinino*.[31] (In early modern Europe the boundaries between the realms of public/business and family/private spaces in elite houses were highly porous, and bedrooms would not have been sequestered; therefore the panels could be seen by the numerous citizens swarming about the palazzo on business or for pleasure.) The panels originally had curved tops to accommodate that room's corbelled arches. Their high placement echoes the traditional preference for tapestry in elite domestic settings and helps explain the visual references to textile hangings in their backgrounds. Uccello further exploited his "sweet perspective" to establish the continuity of space between viewers and the placement of the panels above their heads, creating a system of calculated relationships to assert the endurance of the images beyond their own time and space to that of any present or future beholder.[32] The condottieri Niccolò Tolentino and Michelotto Attendolo and their soldiers had cost the Dieci vast amounts, and Lionardo may well have wanted to demonstrate that the expense was worth it.[33] Rivalries among the city's factions complicated public commemorations. It was undoubtedly easier for Lionardo to honor Niccolò in a private commission many years before he was publicly honored with a painting in the Duomo, despite any lingering resentment toward the Medici.[34] More than the memory of a single battle, however, the paintings recall a series of alliances that safeguarded the continuity of the family and its position in the city. They are significant reminders of recent events, which like memoranda of family record books, were intended to create a corporate memory for the lineage, binding future generations to the present.[35]

Uccello was a natural choice to undertake the battle scenes, for Lionardo's colleague on the Dieci and fellow Medici backer, Neri di Gino Capponi, had helped direct the commission for his *Equestrian Monument to Sir John Hawkwood*, in which Uccello had shown the skill to portray a condottiere with obligatory decorum. Many Bartolini participated in the battle, and the yellow diamond shapes on a red ground on the shield borne by an infantryman on the far left of the Paris panel may be a reference to that family's arms, which display three yellow diamonds on a red field in two of its quarters.[36] While the paintings were not a Medici commission, they do communicate a pro-Medici viewpoint that champions their role in the war. Michelotto's headdress in the Paris panel is embellished at the front by seven circles that are highly suggestive of the Medici *palle* (the balls of the Medici coat of arms), while the oranges, roses, and tripartite feather headdress in the London panel have been interpreted as allusions to Medici *imprese*.[37]

Lionardo's two sons, Damiano and Andrea, inherited the paintings jointly. Lorenzo de' Medici, obsessed with rare and beautiful things, had agents primed to find and purchase antiquities, tapestries, manuscripts, and other beautifully crafted works, especially those with historical associations.[38] Lorenzo is said to have particularly coveted these paintings, and after having purchased the first panel around 1484 he evidently appropriated the other two. Following the expulsion of Lorenzo's sons in 1495, Damiano reported to the commission hearing claims to Medici property that Lorenzo virtually stole the panels from Damiano's house, having sent a group of laborers headed by the carpenter Francione ("Big Frank") to seize them.[39] Lorenzo probably directed Big Frank to adjust their shape when he had them installed in his palace and had other painters in his employ integrate in their corners the depiction of orange leaves: the *mala medica* or sour orange, the emblem of the Medici family.[40]

Rubin observes: "Italian Renaissance art has been studied from the perspective of its use as propaganda specifically in the political realm as a way for leading families to gain political prestige, secure a position of power, and to promote a family's memory throughout time."[41] With numerous changes in ownership and relocation, it is not surprising that there was confusion about the subject matter. In 1492 the paintings were referred to as *The Rout of San Romano*, and in 1495 the older association with Piccinino returned. Although Piccinino is not mentioned in the accounts of the Battle of San Romano, he was overpowered at the Battle of Anghiari on June 29, 1440. The prominence in the Paris panel of Michelotto, who was hardly distinguished at San Romano, led Julia Lessanutti to propose that it actually depicts the Battle of Anghiari, at which Michelotto led the Florentines in defeating Piccinino. Caglioti argues that the earliest account of the subject is perhaps erroneous or that the three paintings may come from two different commissions, and only later came to be associated with each other.[42] The three panels may have come to be identified as *The Rout of Niccolò Piccinino* simply because that success was more important than the Battle of San Romano owing to the territory won for Florence and to the ultimate downfall of the Albizzi faction, Florentine rivals of the Medici.[43] As a result, identification fluctuated with the changing fortunes of Florentine families and the diverging memories they endorsed.

Legacy

By the sixteenth century in Italy, historical scenes largely belonged to predominantly celebratory cycles painted in large official spaces. They adorn reception rooms in Venice in the Palazzo Ducale; in Siena in the Palazzo Pubblico; in Genoa in the Palazzo Doria-Pamphili; in Rome on the Campidoglio, the Cancelleria, and in the papal palaces of the Vatican. In 1504 Leonardo da Vinci was commissioned to decorate the Hall of Five Hundred in Florence's Palazzo Vecchio with a representation of the *Battle of Anghiari*.[44] The central section of Leonardo's lost painting is now known through a drawing after it by Peter Paul Rubens (Fig. 7.6).[45] Rubens was a student of both Alberti's writings and Leonardo's art.[46] In what becomes a central teaching of art theory for later generations, Alberti argues that the artist must portray events in such a way that viewers will perceive how they should feel or react. He draws an analogy from classical rhetoric to claim that a painting should arouse a viewer like a good speech does; for this reason, the artist must elevate the figures above the everyday and represent their interactions persuasively to illustrate the significance of the narrative. Renaissance artists had fully assimilated the demand to portray states of mind by representing figures empathetically (*il concetto dell'anima*).[47] In contrast to Uccello's chivalric image of Niccolò Tolentino, Leonardo's head of Niccolò Piccinino, commander of the Milanese forces, portrays a desperate figure, his face contorted in a mask of fury at once terrifying and exhausted. Rubens captured Leonardo's representation of intense emotions and vivid rendering of naturalistic detail, transforming them into high Baroque complexity.

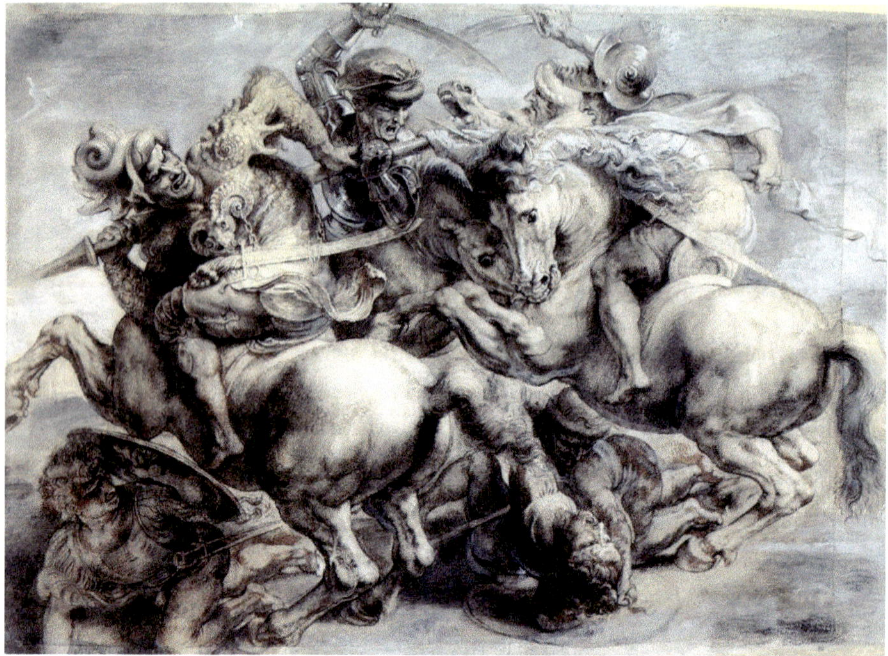

Fig. 7.6 Peter Paul Rubens, *Battle of Anghiari* (1603), after the lost Leonardo fresco (1504–1505). Paris, Musée du Louvre. Photo: Wikimedia Commons

When understood as a triptych, the three distinct moments Uccello represented in each panel create a unified narrative that elevates an otherwise inconsequential encounter to a day-long epic worthy of commemoration. They celebrate the audacity shown by Niccolò Tolentino in his stand against the Sienese army until relieved by the arrival of Michelotto's Florentine reinforcements, an account that echoes the bravery of Ramses at Kadesh.[48] Yet Machiavelli described both Niccolò and Michelotto as idiots, and their style of combat: "An art by which they contrived generally to have both sides lose, and which they had finally reduced to a level so base that any mediocre captain, with even a shadow of reborn ancient virtue, could have put to shame these men upon whom Italy was then heaping honors so imprudently."[49] Still, Medici partisans needed a victory to persuade their fellow citizens to support their expensive policies. The pomp and pageantry Uccello depicted suggest the anxiety of Florence's leaders to be perceived by their contemporaries and remembered by posterity as glorious and triumphant. Linear perspective convinces the viewer of the reality of his representation which, in the end, proves more effective than all Machiavelli's censuring judgments; today the battles of San Romano and Anghiari are remembered through vivid visual representations rather than contemptuous written accounts. The variable relations between the Medici and people of Florence, however, indicates the limitations of this or any artistic program in ensuring genuine political stability.

8

The Benin Plaques

Displaced Memories of an African Empire

Early European visitors to the Royal Palace of Benin (in present-day Nigeria) reported a dazzling assemblage there of artforms incorporating terracotta and brass royal ancestor heads, carved ivory tusks, and cast brass plaques.[1] These works, produced by the Edo people from the thirteenth century onward, recalled and refreshed events of a nonliterate society through images and storytelling, casting sacred prophecy and collective memory in material form.[2] This vital chronicle was destroyed when more than a thousand metal sculptures, including 850 relief plaques popularly known in the West as the Benin Bronzes, were looted in 1897 during events described by the British as the Benin Punitive Expedition but known in Nigeria as the Benin Massacre.[3] Shortly after seeing them in 1898, Ormonde Maddock Dalton of the British Museum explained the plaques as "a valuable manuscript"—"a new 'Codex Africanus' not written on fragile papyrus but in ivory and imperishable brass."[4] Like the capital city and palace they adorned, these objects were understood to embody, not merely mirror, the political organization of the kingdom, and consequently they cannot be understood without knowing the events that comprise Benin's distinctive history.

The Edo Royal House

The people of Benin call themselves, their language, kingdom, and capital city *Edo*. Their history is recounted in diverse oral traditions held within a small elite consisting of the king (Oba), the Ihogbe priests (genealogists of the royal ancestors), various title-holders, ritual specialists, and craftspeople centered in the royal court, and thus describe a predominantly imperial view of the past.[5] According to these sources, after the failure of Benin's earliest kings, known as the Ogiso or "Rulers of the Sky," a faction of chiefs demanded that the Oni or sovereign of Ife (the ancient center of the Yoruba people) send them a new king. He sent his son Oranmiyan to Benin, who fathered a son by the daughter of an Edo chief. That boy grew to become Eweka I, founder of the dynasty that still rules Benin today. Both this oral tradition and limited archaeological investigations point to a flourishing state by the late thirteenth or early fourteenth century.

Power, Image, and Memory. Peter J. Holliday, Oxford University Press. © Oxford University Press 2024.
DOI: 10.1093/oso/9780190901080.003.0009

During the fifteenth and sixteenth centuries, a succession of warrior kings oversaw period of consolidation and development.[6] The first of these, Oba Ewuare, transformed Benin on every level, from its physical appearance to its religious and political organization, introducing comprehensive changes to the governance of the kingdom and creating the war machine that became integral to the state's imperial expansion. He emphasized the roles of art and ritual by establishing an annual cycle of sacred ceremonies and festivals to protect and purify the nation.[7] The most important of these were Ugie Erha Oba, in which the royal ancestors were honored, and Igue, which strengthened the spiritual powers of the king.[8] The elaborate costumes worn by the king and chiefs also began in his reign.

The reign of his grandson, Oba Esigie, is remembered as one of territorial enlargement and accomplishment, but oral traditions reveal that its early years were marked by violent struggle. He fought his brother for the succession, his own nobles initially contested his authority, and Benin's subject states asserted their independence. In 1515–1516, the Atah of Idah, the ruler of the neighboring Igala (Igbon) people, attacked. It was the first time Benin City had been challenged by foreign enemies, but Esigie was ultimately victorious, driving the Igala forces across the Niger River and rendering their king a vassal of Benin. Following the precedent of Oba Ewuare, Esigie established new religious and commemorative festivals to reframe the wars at the beginning of his reign as heroic successes, rather than the near-fatal threats to Benin power they actually were.

The Royal Palace and Its Plaques

According to one oral tradition, ornamental plaques were first created during the reign of Oba Esigie, although this dating is unresolved. In a tradition recorded by Lieutenant E. P. S. Rouppell, one of the British colonial officers who occupied Benin after the Punitive Expedition, "In the time that Esigie was king, a man named Ahammangiwa . . . made a brasswork and plaques for the king. He stayed a very long time . . . [and] the king gave him plenty of boys to teach." When Esigie's son Orhogbua waged war against the Igbon and returned with his captured enemies, "Osogbua [*sic*] called Ahammangiwa and his boys, and asked them if they could put them in brass; they said 'We can try,' so they did and those are they—then the king nailed them to the wall of his house."[9] Although this ambiguous account could refer to either the origin of the plaques or their mode of manufacture, it definitely underscores their commemorative significance.[10] They recast Esigie's military near failures into legendary successes and confirmed the magnificence of his kingdom.

A plaque in Leipzig is one of only six surviving that show Benin warriors in action (Fig. 8.1).[11] According to one oral tradition, the master Ahammangiwa or his workshop crafted this plaque on the orders of Oba Orhogbua (although the scene might just as easily refer to later wars).[12] The scale and degree of three-dimensionality (relief height) of the figures indicate their relative importance. The largest represents

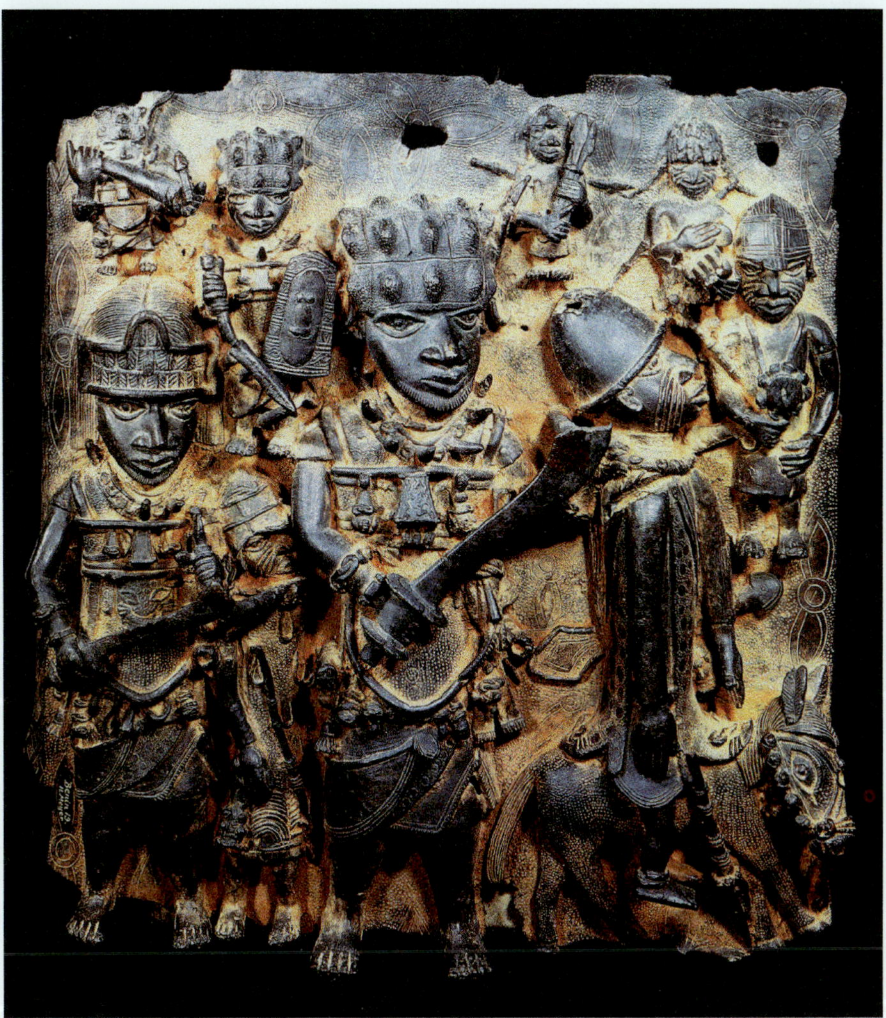

Fig. 8.1 Plaque representing a battle scene. Leipzig, Museum für Völkerkunde zu Leipzig, Staatliche Ethnographische Sammlungen Sachsen, MAf. 34549. Photo: Karin Wieckhorst

the war chief who stands at the center and prepares to behead a mounted prisoner, also of high status, with a short sword with a slightly curved blade (*umozo*). Three additional enemy soldiers, all portrayed much smaller, surround him: one in front has a drum and two above are equipped with a bow, lute, and bundle of spears. A Benin warrior at the far left holds a smaller wounded prisoner by the arm; the leopard motif on the warrior's costume reveals his importance. Above them are two smaller figures, to the left a Benin soldier with an ivory trumpet and to the right another with spear and shield. The Benin soldiers wear helmets of crocodile hide or of horsehair, necklaces of coral beads and leopard teeth, and a quadrangular bell on their chests; their enemies exhibit different facial scarifications, literally marking their "otherness." The background features the incised river-leaf (*ebe-ame*) pattern alluding to Olokun, the god of wealth whose palace is under the waters.[13]

A plaque in the Metropolitan Museum may depict the Oba returning to Benin City from war (perhaps Esigie from the Idah war) or one of the royal processions initiated by Oba Esigie (Fig. 8.2). The hieratic composition ignores the real size of figures and objects and flouts spatial relationships to emphasize the relative importance of one figure to another within court hierarchy. The central figure of the Oba rides sidesaddle on a horse whose diminutive scale allows the king to rise above the attending warriors without disrupting his connection with the

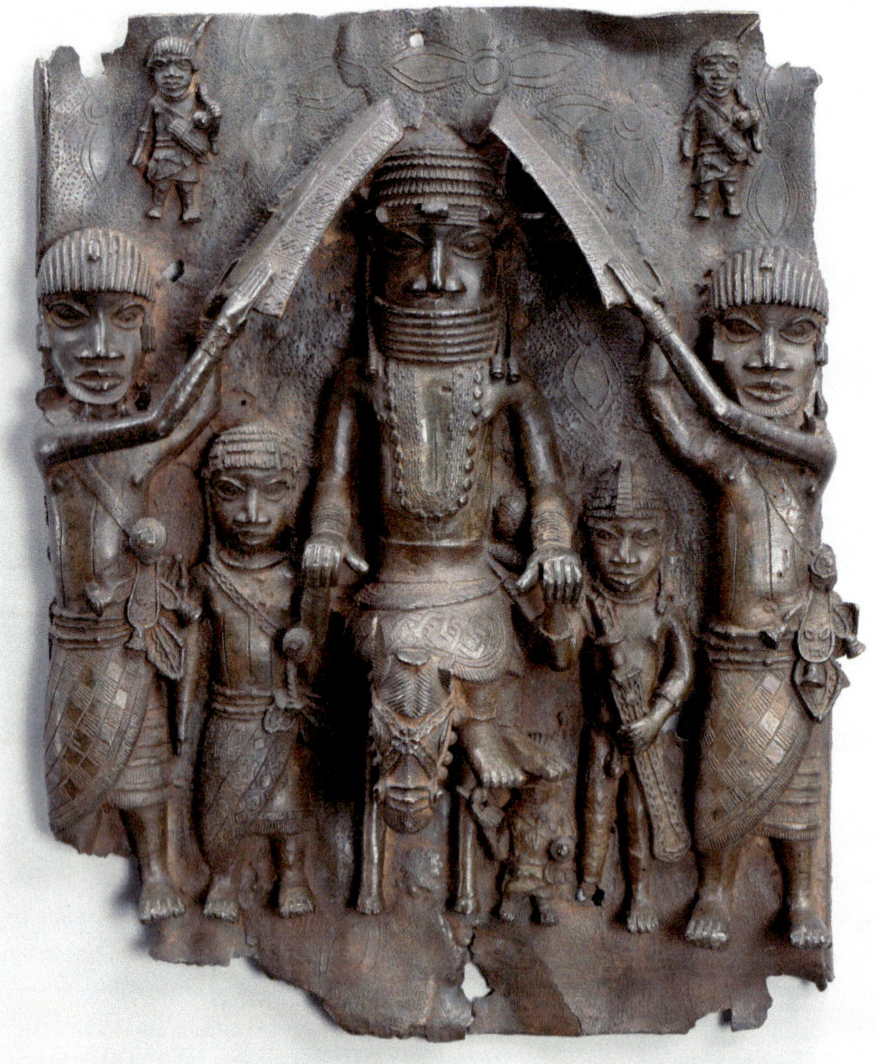

Fig. 8.2 Plaque representing Oba and attendants in procession. New York, Metropolitan Museum of Art 1978.412.309. Photo: Metropolitan Museum of Art

flanking pages who support him.[14] Detailed costumes, ornaments, hairstyles, weapons, and musical instruments make clear each figure's role and status.[15] Coral beaded regalia—the crown and high collar called *odigba*—distinguish the Oba.[16] In processions attendants wear simplified versions of the Oba's costume; those wearing sashes across their chests (and sometimes bands around their wrists and ankles) were shown special favor. Their gestures announce that they are faithful and dutiful subjects. In a tour de force of casting the thin blades held by the warriors to shield the king rise completely free of the plaque surface, a daring compositional feat that required expert control of the hot brass to fill the form. The background pattern of coral and the river-leaf designs again refer to the water deity Olokun. Even against this patterned ground, with no horizon or spatial features, the firm stance of the pages creates a sense of weight and gravity, while his horse effectively anchors the Oba.

During Esigie's reign new connections with Europeans led to increased trade and an influx of wealth, eventually securing the Oba's position. Portugal supplied Benin with valuable luxury goods: coral beads and cloth for ceremonial attire and huge quantities of manillas (torque-shaped rings of copper or brass used as a form of currency for trade in West Africa from the late fifteenth to the mid-twentieth century).[17] In return for these items, Benin delivered pepper, cloth, ivory, and slaves. According to the *Esmeraldo de Situ Orbis*, an account written in the 1490s by the Portuguese explorer Duarte Pacheco Pereira: "The Kingdom of Beny . . . is usually at war with its neighbors and takes many captives, whom we buy at twelve or fifteen brass bracelets each, or for copper bracelets, which they prize more."[18] Esigie bartered for modern guns to use in his wars. Non-Edo territories within the kingdom paid the Oba tribute, provided military support, and facilitated exchange with Benin merchants, but otherwise governed themselves. The Oba provided their rulers with their regalia as a sign of both his appreciation and his authority, underscoring their feudal relationship. Finally, there were the religious ceremonies and festivals established by Esigie to perpetuate the memory of his military struggles as great victories, which helped elevate the Oba to a superhuman level.

Benin City and the Royal Palace

Oba Ewuare took the throne following a bitter dispute with his brother over the succession, during which fire destroyed the old capital. He is credited with both the basic plan of the rebuilt Benin City and the complex administrative bureaucracy contained there (Fig. 8.3). He is said to have constructed the inner wall and ditch, a defensive earthwork six miles in circumference that surrounds the heart of the capital; under each of its nine gates he placed magical charms to protect the kingdom from its enemies. A wide street running northwest to southeast divides the enwalled space into two unequal parts. The larger precinct northeast of the street, called the Ore Nokhua, is organized into wards to accommodate the Town

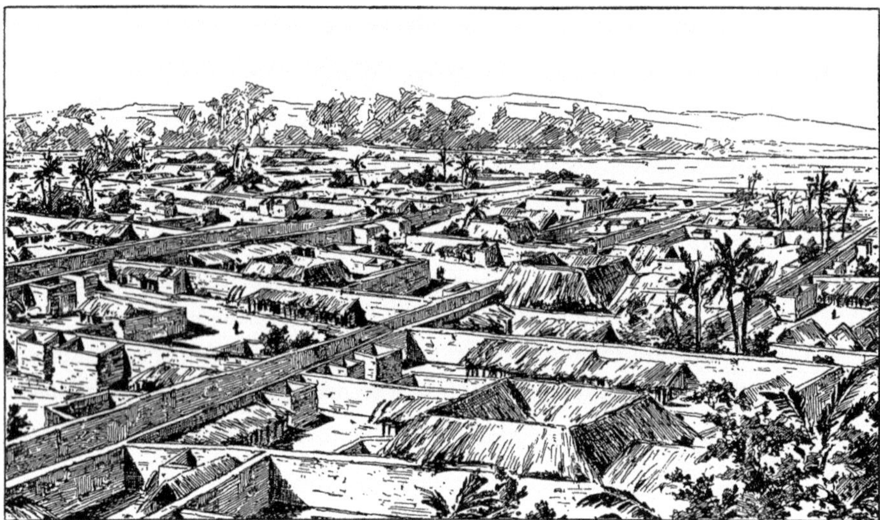

Fig. 8.3 Drawing of Benin City made by an English officer in 1897. From Henry Ling Roth, *Great Benin: Its Customs, Art and Horrors* (1903)

Chiefs and the dozens of specialists who owed their particular craft or ritual service to the Oba. Organized into guilds, their occupations ranged from leopard hunters to musicians, astrologers, and land purifiers; they also included the craftsmen who shaped brass, ivory, and wood sculpture, embroidered cloth, and made leather fans for the Oba and, with his consent, for the chiefs and priests in Benin City and the rest of the kingdom.[19] The royal brass casters guild, the Igun Eronmwon, is located in a quarter close to the palace with that name under the hereditary leadership of the Ineh n'Igun.[20] The smaller area to the southwest, known as Ogbe, comprises the Royal Palace, the various palace associations, and the residences of the Palace Chiefs. The palace was built on a large scale has remained ever since the spiritual and political hub of the nation.

The historical anthropology of Benin City, a site built and maintained by communities of makers within the royal court across the centuries, reveals the intricate political and cosmological significance of such enclosures beyond their defensive function.[21] The capital city and Royal Palace adapted the Yoruba town-plan that physically distinguished sacred and natural spaces to represent a powerful artefact that could be activated through sacrifice and ritual. Visitors remarked that it contained ruins, most likely the result of burials beneath the floor of a house, with objects placed there that the deceased used and valued during life, which was then allowed to fall into ruin. Derelict buildings containing human remains as well as artworks functioned as a form of royal and sacred memorialization in the city. Accordingly, when these places were burned and looted in 1897, it represented a deliberate despoilation of sacred mortuary monuments.[22]

An audience hall located deep within the palace, designed to communicate the power and majesty of the king, was the principal venue for the court's elaborate ceremonial life.[23] It was the site of production and display for royal ancestral altars and for hundreds of rectangular brass plaques stacked one atop another to sheath the pillars lining the courtyard; their relief imagery charted centuries of royal Edo lineage and historical events that animated the court. Wooden pillars supported the roof of a veranda with built-in seating that bordered a large open-air courtyard.

A Dutch writer, Olfert Dapper, described the compound in his 1668 book *Description of Africa*:

> The king's palace or court is a square, and stands at the right-hand side when entering the town by the gate of Gotton [Ughoton], and is certainly as large as the town of Haarlem, and entirely surrounded by a special wall, like that which encircles the town. It is divided into many magnificent palaces, houses, and apartment of the courtiers, and comprises beautiful and long square galleries, about as large as the Exchange at Amsterdam, but one larger than the other, resting on wooden pillars, from top to bottom covered with cast copper, on which are engraved the pictures of their war exploits and battles, and are kept very clean. Most palaces and houses of the king are covered with palm leaves instead of square pieces of wood, and every roof is decorated with a small turret ending in a point, on which birds are standing, birds cast in copper with outspread wings, cleverly made after living models.[24]

Some sixty years later, another Dutch visitor, David van Nyandael, saw the same complex. Although he does not mention either the "copper" birds or plaques, he does describe cast snakes affixed to the turrets:[25]

> On top of the last [gate] is a wooden turret, like a chimney, about sixty or seventy foot height. A large copper snake is attached to its top, its head dangling downwards. This snake is so neatly cast with all its curves and everything that I can say that this is the finest thing I have seen in Benin . . . [In another gallery] one sees behind a white carpet eleven human heads cast in copper; upon each of these is an elephant's tooth, these being some of the King's gods.[26]

Scholars disagree over whether the differences between the descriptions by Dapper and van Nyandael are due to omissions in reporting, changes in artistic practice, or perhaps the removal of the plaques due to some internecine stress.[27]

A plaque in the British Museum provides important visual evidence for the ornamentation of the palace (Fig. 8.4).[28] It shows four young men flanking an entrance to the Royal Palace or a courtyard within it. Two are soldiers standing guard, armed with shields and spears; their coral neckbands, beaded anklets, and elaborate hairstyles with agate decorations indicate high rank. To their sides two attendants (*emada*, recognizable by their nudity), wearing a single strand of beads around their necks, carry fans made of leopard skin.[29] Their steady gazes capture that of the viewer. One of the turrets described by van Nyandael, ornamented by a cast snake,

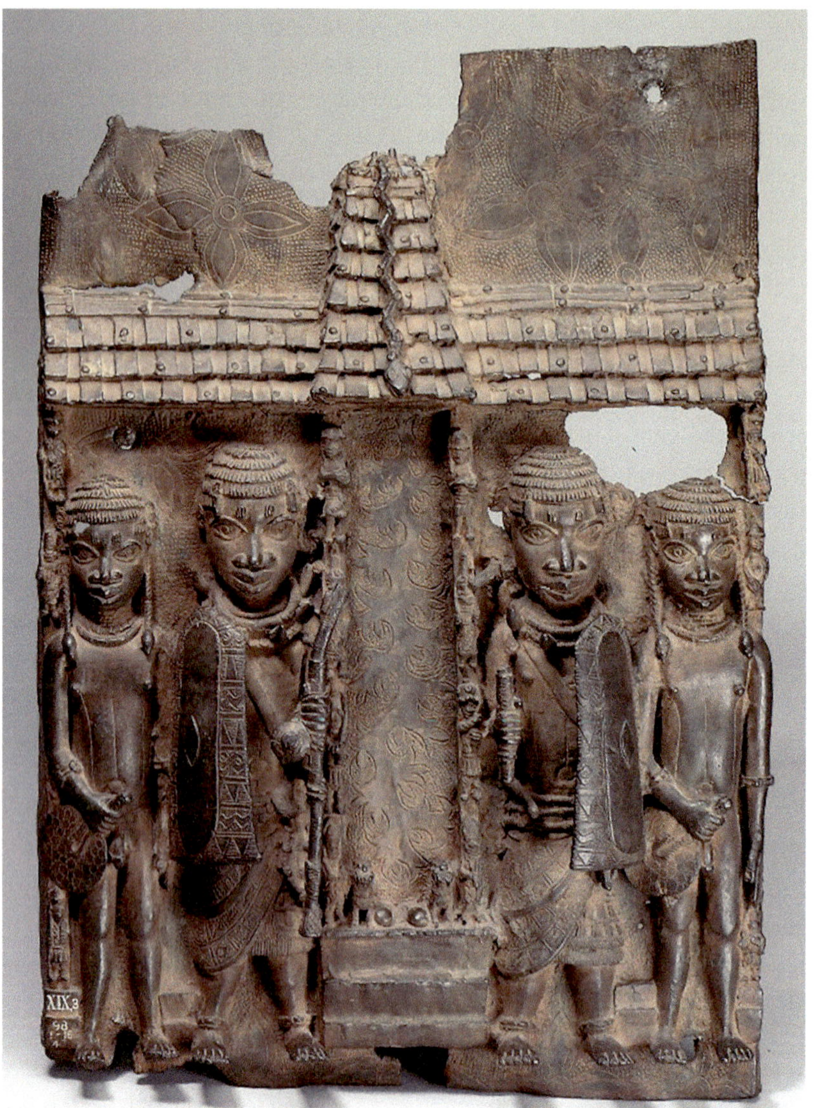

Fig. 8.4 Plaque representing a turreted gateway inside the Royal Palace decorated with other plaques. London, British Museum, Af189,0115.46. Photo: British Museum

projects high above the verandah roof; they marked the gates to the palace and passages from one courtyard to another. (Dapper illustrated such towers in his account: Fig. 8.5.) Each of the supporting pillars carries four narrow plaques showing courtiers and warriors whose carefully depicted costumes and regalia imitate those represented on other, full-size plaques. The two thunderbolts or stone axes that lie in the doorway between two leopards may indicate an altar.[30] The artists' specificity in recording different patterns in these plaques suggests that recognizable programs were installed at the audience hall. The plaques portrayed the king's soldiers and

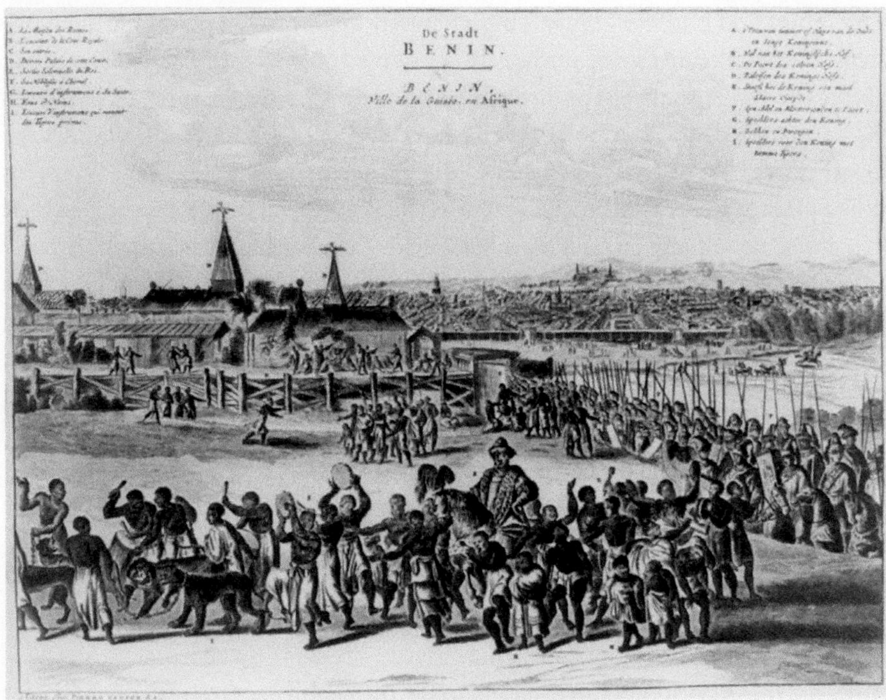

Fig. 8.5 Engraving illustrating the Oba in procession on horseback with attendants. From Olfert Dapper, *Beschreibung von Afrika* (1680)

loyal courtiers to all who visited, especially to any who might challenge his authority. Decorative imagery associated with Olokun indicated the Oba's control of all overseas trade and signified his power and wealth; moreover, attaching plaques on all sides of the pillars created the impression that they were made of solid brass—a principal currency in Benin at that time.[31] These programs provided a tangible record of his accomplishments, a visual propaganda that joined the public performance of religious and memorial festivals in the Oba's efforts to control his image.[32]

Metallurgy and Brass Casting in Benin

According to some traditions, terracotta heads were the dominant commemorative artform for cult sites and the ancestral altars of the Ogiso kings.[33] When a king died, his heir would command that a head be made of his predecessor. The Obas introduced commemorative heads in brass as their own distinctive shrine decoration to break with earlier rulers. Like most West African "bronzes," analysis has shown the works are actually made of brass of inconsistent composition, usually an alloy of copper, zinc, and lead in varying proportions. (The misidentification of bronze was first made when the looted objects made their way to Europe, since bronze had been the leading tradition in European sculpture going back to ancient

Greece.) In Edo tradition, brass is a particularly appropriate symbol for the monarchy. Its red color and shiny surface are considered both beautiful and threatening, having the power to repel evil forces; since it never corrodes or rusts, brass evokes the permanence and continuity of kingship.[34] Dapper's account indicates that the royal brasses were once kept polished to a high sheen.

The plaques were cast using the lost-wax technique, with details carefully incised in the wax mold. Early plaques are all cast in low relief, meaning that they are fairly flat, without many details that rise above the surface. In the later series of plaques, however, artists refined their practice until they were able to cast high reliefs having greater depth, featuring roughly shaped cavities behind the figures, ensuring that the metal is of regular thickness of as little as an eighth-of-an-inch throughout, exceeding the virtuosity of Renaissance masters in Europe.[35] The development of high relief forms may have been in response to how the completed plaques looked once installed on the pillars. The human figures filling the entire surface of later compositions create stronger contrasts between light and metal, perhaps making them more visible from across the large courtyard.

In another revelation of Eurocentric bias, Western scholars wrongly concluded that knowledge of metallurgy was introduced to Benin by Portuguese traders. However, the excavation of sites dating to the thirteenth century make it clear that early brass objects in Benin—bracelets, rings, and the like—were made by an indigenous culture. We do not know, however, when casting was first practiced in Benin. Scholars disagree as to whether those early bracelets and rings were made by forging or by lost-wax casting.[36] According to one tradition, the son of the Oni of Ife taught Benin metal workers the lost-wax casting technique during the thirteenth century.[37] When Portuguese navigators began to explore the West African coast in the second half of the fifteenth century, they found Benin a hub of African civilization with which they were able to establish diplomatic and trade relations.[38] In the seventeenth and eighteenth centuries the Dutch, English, and French supplanted the Portuguese and established the triangular trade with Africa and the Americas. By then the image of the Portuguese in sixteenth-century attire had become an essential element of a Benin visual expression of power and wealth. A plaque in the Metropolitan Museum depicts two rows of oversized manillas that dwarf two bearded figures, whose triangular-shaped button caps, doublets with tight-fitting patterned sleeves, and sleeveless jerkins worn over the doublets like vests are characteristic of early sixteenth-century Portuguese dress (Fig. 8.6).[39] The extraordinary number and scale of the manillas underscores their importance as a symbol of the prestigious overseas trade in court art.

There is no single word in the Edo language that corresponds with all that we consider to be "art," but there are ways of designating creative people, and the expertise of skilled weavers, potters, and carvers is esteemed. Regardless the medium, the possession of a body of forms and patterns defines an artist. According to Paula Ben-Amos, "The importance of these designs for artistic self-identity can be seen in the invocation that members of the carvers' guild make to their patron deity, Ugbe

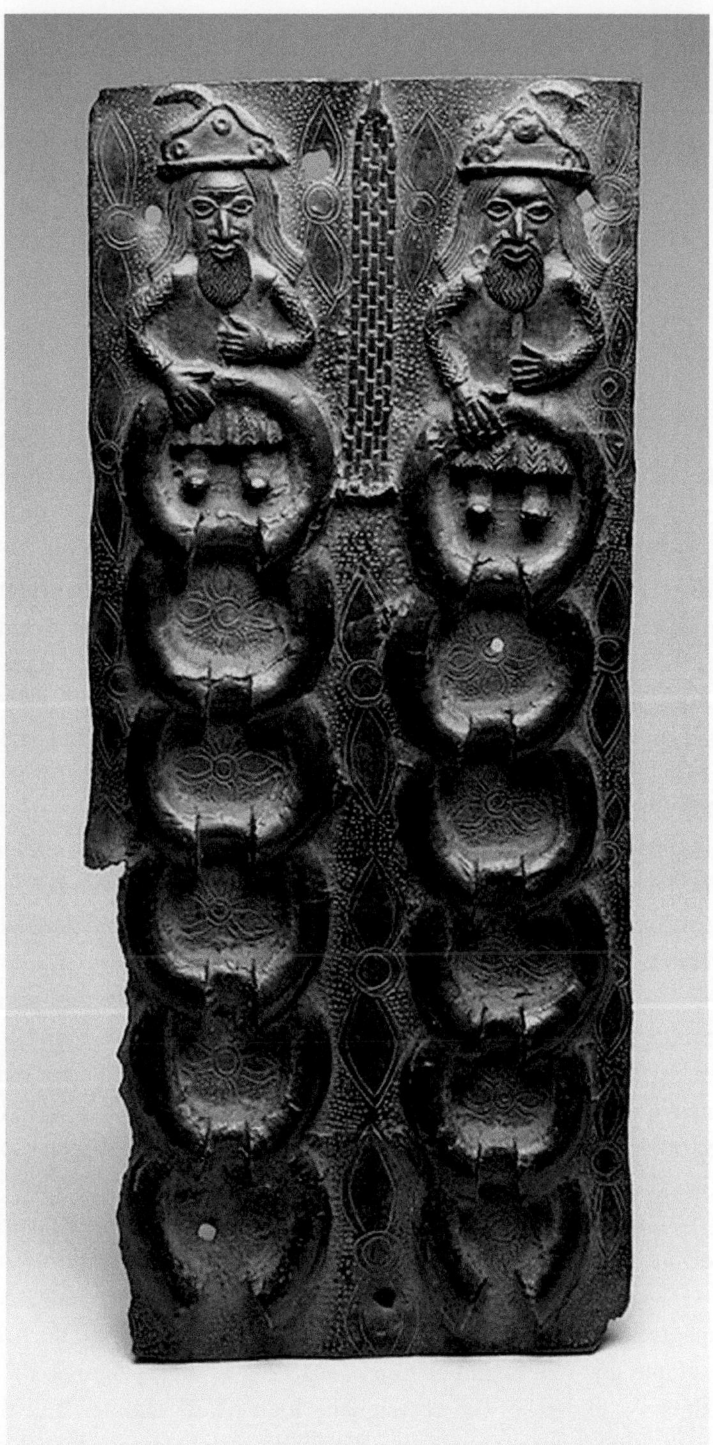

Fig. 8.6 Plaque representing two Portuguese traders with manillas. New York, Metropolitan Museum of Art, 1991.17.13. Photo: Metropolitan Museum of Art

n'Owewe, upon commencing carving: 'Ugbe n'Owewe, ancestors, let us prosper. Don't let us forget the patterns that we make. Don't let our children forget them.' "[40] These patterns are still seen as part of the guild heritage, handed down from generation to generation. Ben-Amos also relates that their products are described as *mosee*, which can mean "beautiful," but also has the connotations of "proportionate," "appropriate," and "morally good."[41]

Programs of Commemoration

The origin of the plaque form itself is controversial. William Fagg and Philp Dark suggest that their rectangular format and relief technique reveal European influence.[42] Items carried by the Portuguese—illuminated books, small ivory boxes with carved lids, and miniature paintings from India—might have inspired the format; even the river-leaf pattern may have originated in European or Islamic art.[43] Perhaps, but even if inspired by foreign sources the Benin artists created their own characteristic aesthetical forms endowed with specifically local meanings and functions.[44] The Nigerian art historian Babatunde Lawal argues that the plaques are truly indigenous, and cites examples of wooden doors, drums, and boxes, which might have suggested the idea for relief decoration on the pillars.[45] The background designs certainly contain specifically Benin references, if closely related to the Portuguese period.

Fagg used the oral tradition recorded by Rouppell to determine the mid-sixteenth century as the *terminus post quem* for plaque production and the end of the seventeenth century as the *terminus ante quem*, due to the absence after that date of any references to the plaques in European descriptions of the palace (such as that of van Nyandael). Ben-Amos suggests, based on the decorative motifs in the backgrounds and corners referring to Olokun and the arrival of the Portuguese, a strong correlation between plaque production, the Portuguese presence, and the reign of Esigie.[46] Dark concurs, further suggesting that plaque production ceased about 1640, when according to oral traditions Oba Ahenzae squandered the royal treasury, depleting the supplies of brass needed to make them.[47]

Kathryn Gunsch proposes a tighter chronology of about 30–45 years in the middle of the sixteenth century, conforming with the reigns of Oba Esigie and his son Orhogbua.[48] She proposes a chronology that incorporates technical developments in casting to determine three consecutive groupings: the first group displays simple low-relief compositions consisting of single figures, the second group exhibits a mid-relief (or occasionally high-relief) manner, and the third features high-relief figures of near three-dimensional representations with complex multifigure compositions. It is a convincing scheme that fits with current metals analyses, but much of the evidence is contingent and therefore controvertible.

The plaques were made to glorify the divine Oba and his imperial power; they also convey the categories of the chiefs, priests, court officials, titleholders, and attendants who constitute Benin's traditional administrative and ritual hierarchy and reinforce their roles in contemporary court life. Both oral traditions and descriptions by visitors indicate that the installation of the plaques as an assemblage allowed them to function as a record of the kingdom's history, portraying bygone figures and alluding to past events that promoted Benin's wealth, power, and spiritual greatness. Benin nobles today maintain that the plaques depict major events in their history. Significantly, in the Edo language, the literal translation of the verb *sa-e-y-ama* is "to cast a motif in bronze," but more generally means "to remember," the act of casting thus constitutes a form of recollection.[49]

When the British seized the Royal Palace the plaques were not on display, but were then stored in the part of the palace overseen by the Iwebo, the palace society that comprises the guilds who make the regalia and its keepers (Fig. 8.7).[50] An elder chief who served as a palace attendant recalled that they were "kept like a card index up to the time of the Punitive Expedition, and referred to when there was a dispute about courtly etiquette."[51] How the plaques were assembled on the pillars in the Oba's palace—or even in the storeroom where they were found in 1897—is now lost but we do know that they were not viewed as discrete objects; rather, proper interpretation largely depends on their relationships to each other, much as how on Trajan's Column whether a scene of sacrifice comes before or after a battle affects its significance. The regalia worn by individual figures on different occasions identify the context in which they are depicted, further distinguished through the arrangement of the plaques. Unfortunately, looting destroyed those arrangements, and our interpretations of individual plaques are necessarily provisional.

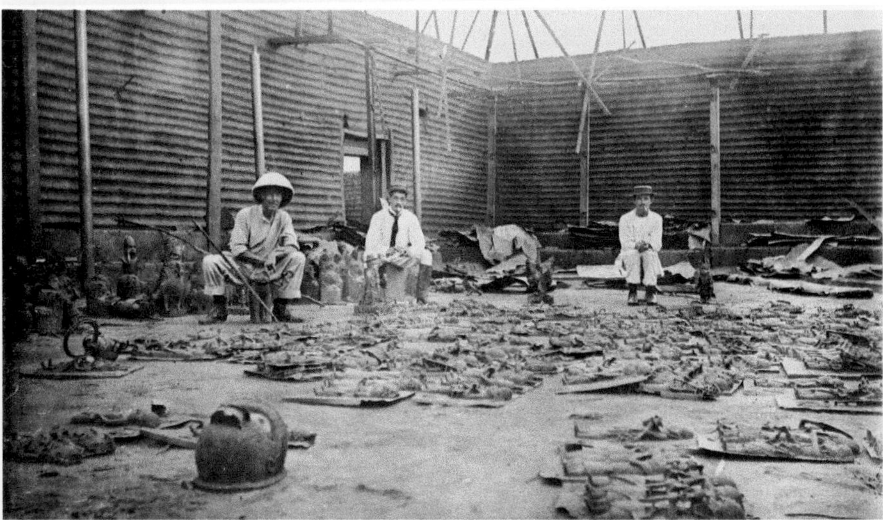

Fig. 8.7 Interior of the Royal Palace during the looting, February 1897. Photo: Pitt Rivers Museum, accession number 1998.208.15.11

Furthermore, the plaques lack the narrative specificity found in other historical artworks in this study. Gunsch argues that Euro-American scholars are misguided when they try to identify the moment or meaning expressed in each individual work, which can result in contradictory conclusions, because Benin's oral history is a form of contingent address.[52] It is recited at a particular moment as a way of transmitting tradition, bolstering argument, or explaining an immediately relevant idea to the audience. Taking the form of personal address, it is a fluid medium. She therefore suggests that the plaques were designed with a narrative strategy that invites multiple readings based on their installation context, and that when assembled, the corpus was never intended to capture a rigidly fixed, linear past but rather a narrative tradition that embraces polysemy, one that permits undercurrents of meaning to connect with the experiences and knowledge of oral interpreters and individual viewers.[53]

Thus the depiction of the tower gate is specific, and would have been recognizable to contemporary viewers, but the event commemorated is not. The image conveys a detailed ambiguity that allows it to be suitable to illustrate more than one particular event. Within a particular telling, neighboring plaques could lend temporal specificity to this scene, while the palace representation could establish a court setting in the overarching narrative formed by the installed group. In this system, the context of the surrounding plaques and each incidence of commentary or discussion at court shades the meaning of the individual compositions. According to Gunsch, "The plaque is therefore omnivalent, meaning that it could participate in a nearly limitless series of historical narratives."[54] Although one tradition holds that the battle plaque in Leipzig represents Oba Esigie's struggle against the Igala people in the north, it could just as easily be used to illustrate later wars.

There is no setting to convey where the Oba is riding in the New York plaque, whether into battle, returning in triumph, or in a religious ritual in Benin City. Although the paucity of weapons carried by the Oba or his attendants suggests it most likely represents Ugie Oro, the commemorative festival established immediately after Esigie's victory over Idah, it is not certain. Titleholders and bronze casters today explain such ambiguities and slippages as the telescoping of multiple events in one composition: it can be both Esigie's victory and his commemoration of it in Ugie Oro. These shifting layers of meaning do not negate the historical import of any plaque; instead "they multiply the historical moments referenced in one work . . . Viewed on its own, the artists' careful exclusion of temporal and spatial details allows the work to become part of many discourses."[55]

In an account of about 1540, a Portuguese pilot described divine kingship in Benin and neighboring monarchies on the west coast of Africa:

> The kings are worshipped by their subjects, who believe that they come from heaven, and speak of them always with great reverence at a distance and on bended knees. Great ceremony surrounds them, and many of these kings never

allow themselves to be seen eating, so as not to destroy the belief of their subjects that they can live without food.[56]

The Oba's separateness signals his immense religious power.[57] The plaques feature iconographic formulas that, like the preset iconic images repeated in most Egyptian monuments, are not restricted to any particular, unique historical event (cf. Fig. 2.2). Once he ascended the throne, the Oba had no true rivals at court to contend with. Like the pharaoh, the Oba operates in a mythic world removed from temporal restrictions. In contrast to the way *The Battle of San Romano* panels functioned in a Florentine palazzo, the specifics of any single battle were unimportant here; rather, the imagery propagated messages of unassailable power, which underscored a sense of permanence and continuity among Edo viewers and forewarning to visitors to the court. Regardless of the narrative Ihogbe priests read from any plaque(s) to visiting ambassadors or traders, the primary audience was always the court itself. When viewing the plaques closely, members of the various guilds, palace societies, title holders, and attendants would recognize their counterparts through visual signs such as distinctive clothing and regalia, scale (including relief height on the later plaques), and proximity to other figures that corresponded with their responsibilities and position within Benin City as first laid out by Oba Ewuare. To see themselves represented in brass reinforced their identities within both the court hierarchy and Benin's enduring history.

Destruction, Restoration, and Restitution

The seventeenth century was a period of great dynastic turmoil in Benin. While oral traditions relate the exploits of the fifteenth- and sixteenth-century warrior kings in great detail, little is recounted of their successors; similarly, art historical traditions are also scarce. Different factions struggled for the kingship following the death of Ehengbuda, weakening it seriously and allowing independent chiefs to establish private power bases and even select kings from among their ranks. In the eighteenth century, however, Oba Akenzua I and his son Eresoyen strengthened the kingship through a combination of political, economic (through increased trade with the Dutch), and ritual means. They subdued mutinous chiefs and reestablished the monarch's power and legitimacy. Alan Ryder, however, described fundamental changes brought to the kingship: "The revival could not carry the monarch and government back to the forms of the sixteenth century. Akenzua and his successors confined themselves within the palace . . . and maintained their authority . . . by an increasing emphasis upon their ritual function as guardians of the nation's prosperity and security."[58] Artisans emulated works from earlier reigns to evoke a time when the kingdom was at its height and led by a successful monarch of undeniably legitimate ancestry.

By the late nineteenth century, renewed conflicts weakened Benin's political and economic hold on its northern and eastern tributaries, while the British, who viewed Benin as an obstacle to their expansion, made incursions from the coast. Unlike the earlier settler colonialism pursued in the Pacific and North America, European colonialism in West Africa employed military power to extract natural resources for commercial interests. In 1897, after a British envoy to Oba Ovonramwen was ambushed and killed (he pressed forward after having been denied permission to enter Benin City due to religious ceremonies in progress), the British launched their Punitive Expedition against the kingdom. They set fire to the residences of the Queen Mother and important chiefs; much of the city was destroyed by the spreading conflagration. The bombardment of towns and civilian targets and the resulting scale of the killing and destruction prefigured the industrialized warfare of the twentieth century. Thousands of brass artworks and other objects of royal and religious significance were looted by the marines and Protectorate forces, many subsequently sold to museums and private collectors to offset expeditionary costs.[59]

Even today some scholars perpetuate the Victorian rationalization that the attack was "retribution for the murder of members of the British mission."[60] Dan Hicks, however, has definitively documented how the violence actually emerged from imperialist policies of gunboat politics and capitalist colonial rule. The capture of Benin City and subsequent exile of Oba Ovonramwen to Calabar marked the end of Benin as an independent kingdom; its incorporation into the British Protectorate commenced a new political and social—and thus artistic—era. A distinct colonial thinking about British West Africa emerged, grounded in a model of cultural imbalance, of inferiority.[61] The new fields of anthropology and ethnography set up "primitive" African art as a foil to European civilization, reducing a powerful kingdom to a temporally ancient and geographically distant culture that intruded into the modern world.[62] The inability to interpret the messages communicated by the plaques to their original viewers with the same specificity given to other artworks in this study demonstrates how effectively Benin's cultural memory—Dalton's "new 'Codex Africanus'"—was dismantled. Instead, the dual schemes of the museum and art market transformed sacred and royal material culture into objects that, rather than commemorating events in Benin's history, now memorialize colonial violence and cultural destruction.

Following the death of Oba Ovonramwen in 1914, his son Eweka II became Oba and in the 1920s began the process of reconstructing the Royal Palace, at reduced scale. Carvers and casters used traditional methods to fabricate replacements for objects taken during the Expedition. While artists continued to produce religious and prestige objects for the royal court, restrictions limiting the arts to the king and nobility were lifted allowing them to fashion new forms for a wider base of consumption, including colonial officers, tourists, and a Western-educated Nigerian elite. Today Benin City is a thriving metropolis and capital of the Edo State of Nigeria under Oba Ewuare II, the thirty-ninth in his line. Some artists now work independently, pursuing a Western entrepreneurial model, while others still actively produce forms rooted in the precolonial period, but which have been reformulated to meet new situations.[63] Thus, for example, Ekpo masqueraders, who once danced solely to combat disease, now travel to Benin City airport to greet high-ranking visitors. Western museums are beginning to reassess art in their collections that was seized under the auspices of colonial rule; an Edo Museum of West African Art, adjacent to the Royal Palace and designed by Ghanaian architect David Adjay, is planned for works repatriated to Benin.

9

The *Hünernāme*

Shaping Identity and Ensuring Legacy at the Ottoman Court

Highly competitive royal courts and burgeoning educational institutions promoted a dynamic book culture in the Islamic world during the sixteenth and early seventeenth centuries. Decidedly sophisticated Arab, Persian, and Ottoman elites employed teams of scribes and painters to produce exquisite illustrated manuscripts (Fig. 9.1).[1] Among the finest of these were the illustrated histories (*şehnāmes*) commissioned at the Ottoman court to chronicle its past achievements and celebrate contemporary accomplishments. In a world of shifting political currents, savvy patrons deployed these pictured annals as instruments to promote personal and partisan agendas, and to influence the views of current and even future members of the ruling elite. Analysis of their texts and images reveals that they reflected and also helped shape life at the imperial court; studying their availability and dissemination establishes their importance in fashioning courtly identity.

At the end of the sixteenth century, two men, the grand vizier Sokollu Mehmed Pasha and the court historian Seyyid Lokman, presided over scribes and illustrators who are commonly credited with shaping the canonical Ottoman historical record. Although the creation of a rhetoric of power through oral, literary, and artistic messaging is not unique to the Ottoman elite—its ubiquity has been demonstrated here with the Bayeux Embroidery, Japanese *gunki monogatari*, and Benin Plaques—reconstructing these processes in the Ottoman world enhances our understanding of the links between history writing and image formation in early modern courtly societies.

The Rise of Sokollu Mehmed Pasha

Sokollu Mehmed Pasha was born to a minor noble family in a Serbian village in Bosnia and in his teens entered Ottoman service during the early years of Süleyman the Magnificent's reign (r. 1520–1566). His progress through the ranks of the Ottoman imperial household became a paradigm for what was possible for someone with talent and ambition. He was educated in the Edirne Palace at the old Ottoman capital of Adrianople as part of the *devşirme* (recruiting) system for trainees. Sokollu

Power, Image, and Memory. Peter J. Holliday, Oxford University Press. © Oxford University Press 2024.
DOI: 10.1093/oso/9780190901080.003.0010

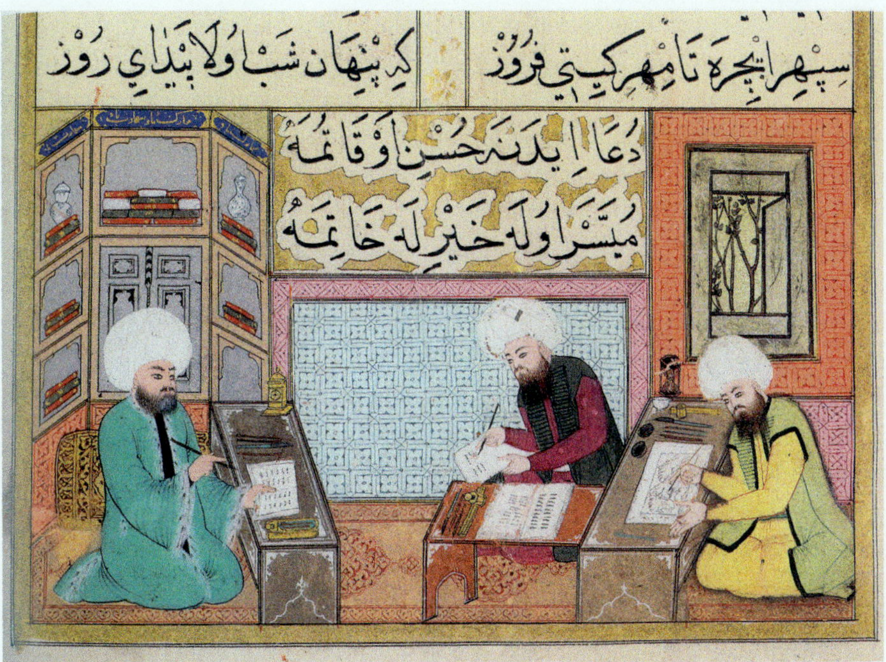

Fig. 9.1 *Şehnāme-I Mehmed Hān* of Talikizade, scribes at work. Istanbul, Topkapi Palace Museum, H.1609, fol. 74a. Photo: © The Presidency of the Republic of Turkey, The Directorate of National Palaces Administration

rose through the privy chamber as groom, valet-de-chambre, sword-bearer, chief taster, and finally gatekeeper, carefully making valuable alliances as he ascended. In 1549 he became governor-general of Rumelia, and in 1554, as a result of his military prowess and effective command of those forces, he was appointed by Süleyman to the Imperial Council as third vizier.

Sokollu quickly advanced to second vizier, and in 1562 he married Ismihan Sultan, the daughter of the sultan's son Selim. He became grand vizier under Süleyman in 1565, and after Süleyman's death served his immediate successors, Selim II (r. 1566–1574) and Murad III (r. 1574–1595), in the same position until 1579, when he was mortally wounded at his council by a petitioner dressed as a Bosnian Hamzawi dervish (a persecuted order). Süleyman had a number of sons who were equally capable of ruling the empire; Selim's ultimate designation as crown prince had never been certain. Sokollu orchestrated Selim's victory over the only remaining rival, his brother Bayezid, at the Battle of Konya in 1559, the last episode in a dramatic series of struggles among Süleyman's sons. According to the sixteenth-century historian Mustafa Âli, Sokollu Mehmed Pasha administered as the "virtual sultan" (*padişāh-i mā'nevī*) during the reign of his father-in-law, Selim II.[2]

Sokollu Mehmed Pasha was among the first—and undoubtedly most refined—of Ottoman nobles to use illustrated histories to fashion his image and ensure his legacy within the court. While his successors would go on to commission explicit accounts celebrating their own exploits, Sokollu inserted himself into the narrative of the Ottoman dynasty with great subtlety. The earliest manuscript that highlights Sokollu's involvement in events is the *Futūhāt-i jamīla* (Admirable Conquests) of about 1557–1558, which describes an important series of battles in 1551 against the Habsburgs in Transylvania. The manuscript has thirty-one folios and six illustrations, one of which spreads across two facing pages. The text praises Sokollu's bravery and military prowess; four of its illustrations represent him as an effective manager, leading the attack on the castles of Pecs and Lipva or sitting in council before his camp tent, collecting reports from subordinates or receiving Habsburg envoys imploring for peace.

The illustration of the siege of Pecs Castle is instructive. It shows Ottoman canon in the middle ground aimed at the fortress over its protective moat, its shimmering water portrayed in silver, which has now turned black (Fig. 9.2).[3] Sokollu rides on horseback at the base of the page, conspicuous against a green field and trotting slightly ahead of the other riders. His white turban makes him appear somewhat larger than the troops (whose helmets create a repetitive pattern) under his command. This decorous scene contrasts with the violent turmoil of the siege shown at the top, where the besiegers heave defeated soldiers from the castle walls. Sokollu's calm and controlled demeanor recalls that of Trajan, who fought in these same lands centuries before. Midway through the campaign, Kara Ahmed Pasha replaced Sokollu in command, and the single double-page illustration in the manuscript represents Kara Ahmed Pasha leading the Ottoman army in the taking of Timisoara. The final painting in the *Futūhāt-i jamīla*, however, shows Sokollu again at the head of the triumphant army. Although Kara Ahmed Pasha is honored with the only double-page illustration, collectively the images leave the wholly inaccurate impression that he was only involved at Timisoara. The cumulative narrative and illuminations thereby deftly casts Sokollu Mehmed Pasha as the architect of the victorious Transylvanian campaigns, a skilled leader who was ready to shoulder even greater responsibility.

When the *Nüzhetü'l-ahbar der sefer-i Sīgetvār* (The Joyful Chronicle of the Szigetvár Campaign) appeared in 1569, Sokollu Mehmed Pasha was already a member of the royal family through his marriage to Selim's daughter and had risen to the office of grand vizier. Süleyman had mounted an unsuccessful siege of Vienna in 1529. In May 1566, the sultan, who was then seventy-two years old and had ruled the Ottoman Empire for forty-six years, left Constantinople at the head of an enormous force (some accounts say more than 150,000 soldiers) to make another attempt. The fortified town of Szigetvár, defended with only 2,300 men under Nicholas IV Zrínyi, the former Ban (Viceroy) of Croatia, blocked his line of advance. The siege of Szigetvár was to be Süleyman's last campaign. Feridun Ahmed Beg, an imperial council secretary and close confidant of Sokollu Mehmed Pasha, wrote the prose account of the campaign. It discloses to the reader that the sultan died in his tent the night before the final assault of Szigetvár, which began on the morning of September 7. Sokollu sent word informing Prince Selim of his father's

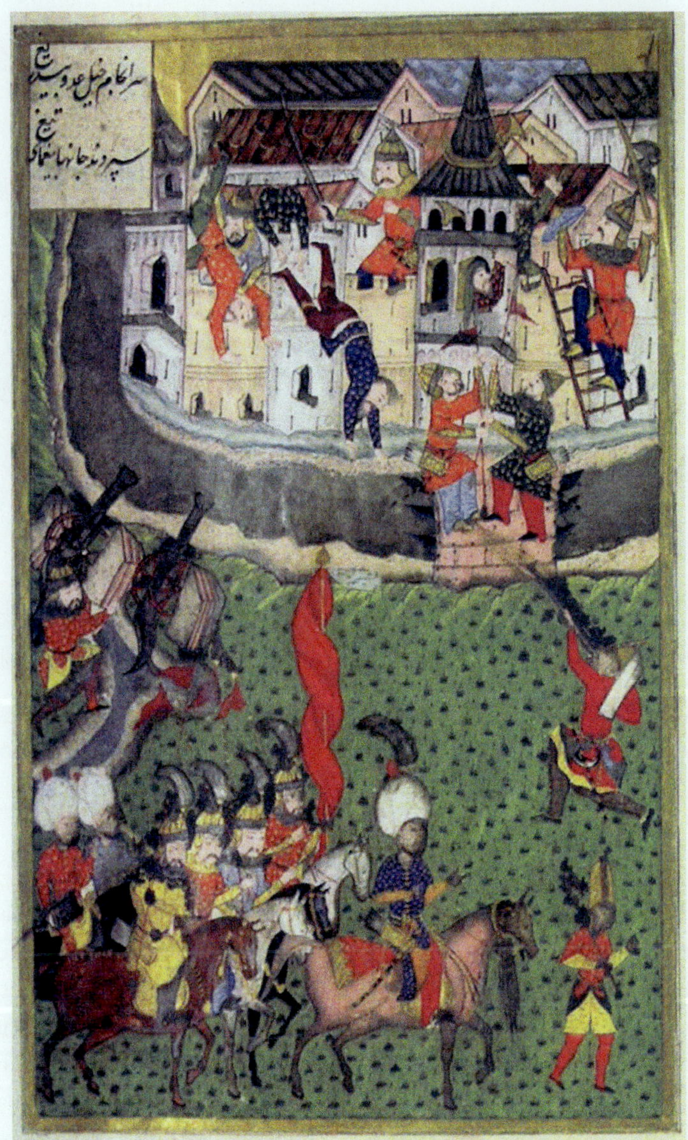

Fig. 9.2 *Futūhāt-i jamīla* of Arifi, conquest of Pecs Castle. Istanbul, Topkapi Palace Museum, H. 1592, fol. 5a. Photo: © The Presidency of the Republic of Turkey, The Directorate of National Palaces Administration

death, but with the assistance of two other courtiers he managed to keep the news from the army, a stratagem Sokollu devised to keep the situation from becoming chaotic. By revealing the sultan's death to the soldiers only after they began the march home, he ensured both a victorious outcome for the campaign and a smooth transfer of power from Süleyman to his father-in-law Selim.[4]

The beginning of that transfer is represented on a double-page depiction of the departure of Süleyman's carriage from the imperial tent (Fig. 9.3). The image invites

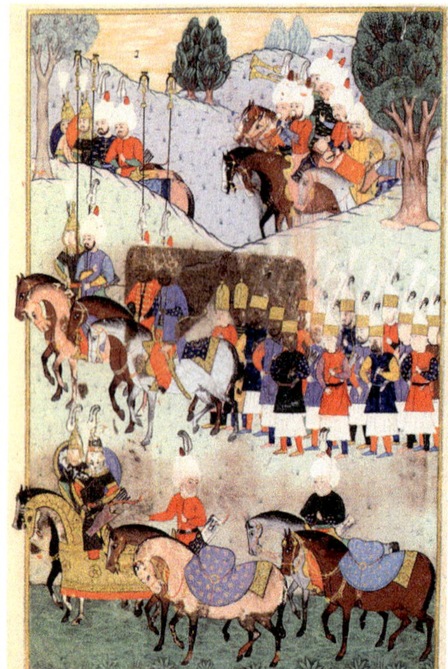
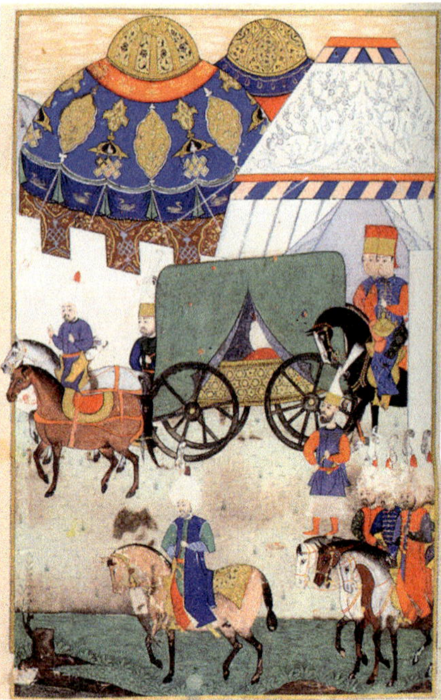

Fig. 9.3 *Nüzhetü'l-ahbar der sefer-i Sīgetvār*, Sultan Süleyman's carriage leaving the imperial tent. Istanbul, Topkapi Palace Museum, H. 1339, fols. 103b-104a. Photo: © The Presidency of the Republic of Turkey, The Directorate of National Palaces Administration

divergent readings of two conflicting—or even superimposed—realities. The text tells the reader that Sokollu approached the carriage and appeared to read various papers to the sultan so that the soldiers would not suspect anything was amiss. But here the parted curtains of the carriage reveal to the viewer a coffin crowned with the sultan's turban. Thus, the text gives us a sense of what was understood by the army at that time, whereas the image depicts what the reader knows now to have been the actual state of affairs. As the cortege departs the Ottoman compound Sokollu Mehmed Pasha rides a horse with richly embroidered equipage and he wears subdued green and blue garb, attire appropriate for mourning at the Ottoman court. Emıne Fetvaci points out how he rides below the sultan at the bottom of the page, "as his shadow and deputy, in the same position in which he would be seated in the imperial council chamber."[5] The positioning of the four mounted viziers who follow, the guards flanking the carriage, and other figures are just as they would be placed around the living sultan, carefully replicating the social hierarchy of the court. The composition of the illustration not only underscores the structure of the Ottoman court itself, but at the same time, by portraying so accurately the daily lived experience of the contemporary reader, it substantiates the authenticity of everything else represented.

Beginning with the reign of Süleyman and continuing under Selim, Ottoman political analysis shifted emphasis from the personality of the ruler to the institutions and systems of government. The sultan was increasingly regarded as a distant but legitimating figure for the dynasty while the grand vizier assumed the central position of actual power. These changes were not without tension, and during Selim's reign some of the new sultan's companions and advisors resisted Sokollu Mehmed Pasha's maneuvering. Although the manuscript's title gives prominence to the siege of Szigetvár, only the first 55 folios involve the actual campaign; the subsequent 250 folios focus on the ascension of Selim II. By commissioning this book Sokollu reminded readers of his pivotal role in Ottoman history—in particular his responsibility in assuring the peaceful transfer of power to Selim—by ingeniously inserting himself into the writing of a history that celebrates the order and unity of the realm.[6] The images portray Sokollu Mehmed Pasha as commander and servant to the sultan simultaneously, while Selim II was undoubtedly receptive to having himself portrayed as the dominant figure in the narrative.[7]

Sokollu Mehmed Pasha's illustrated books trace the transformation of the grand vizier from an assistant to the sultan to an executive administrator, as the position's governmental functions became more important than his personal service to the sultan.[8] Recording these events from his life would ensure that Sokollu would be remembered; the illustrations function as specific glosses on texts that are open to multiple interpretations to fashion an image of the grand vizier that captured the imagination of the Ottoman elite. Sokollu's successful use of imagery inspired later courtiers to imitate both his patronage and his specifically political use of illustrated histories.[9] None of his successors, however, had the advantage of as perfect a collaborator as did Sokollu Mehmed Pasha.

The *Şehnāmeci* Lokman

Originally from Urmiye in Azerbaijan, Seyyid Lokman served for time as a provincial judge and eventually became the private secretary for Sokollu Mehmed Pasha. In 1569 during the reign of Selim II, with Sokollu's influence and patronage Lokman became the third *şehnāmeci* (court historian), a position he held until 1596–1597.[10] Süleyman himself created the post of *şehnāmeci* as the genre rose in popularity. As *şehnāmeci*, Lokman served both a creative and managerial role: he was charged with composing the text for projects approved by the sultan and also coordinating their production. The original *Şehnāme* (or *Shāhnāma*, literally, Book of Kings) is an epic poem recounting the history and legendary achievements of Persian kings written by the Persian poet Firdawsi. The Ottomans adapted the *şehnāme* genre in order to associate (and ideally surpass) their early military victories to those in the revered *Şehnāme* and in so doing link the sultan with storied Persian heroes. As the genre's style and composition developed under subsequent sultans, its subjects turned increasingly to contemporary events rather than myth or distant history. Lokman was renowned for his ability to compose rhymed Persian couplets in the *mesnevi* style that became the principal language of the *şehnāmes*.[11]

Among the most celebrated works Lokman turned out were the *Suleymānnāma* (Book of Süleyman), *Shāhnāma-i Salīm Khān* (Book of Kings of Sultan Selim), *Hünernāme* (Book of Skills), *Zubtedu't tevarih* (The Cream of Histories), and *Kiyafetu'l-ins aniye fi sema'il-u'l-Osmaniye* (Human Physiognomy and the Disposition of the Ottomans). Early in his career, Lokman worked with intellectuals and literati who had close relationships with Sokollu Mehmed Pasha, and the first texts he wrote had to be approved by the most revered scholars of the empire (with whom Sokollu Mehmed Pasha had also established alliances). The *Zafarnāma* (Book of Victory), also known as *Tārīkh-i Sultān Sulaymān* (History of the Sultan Süleyman) of 1579, is Lokman's earliest work. It is a supplement or sequel to the account of Süleyman's reign begun in the *Suleymānnāma*, which covers 1520 to 1555. Late sixteenth-century Ottoman histories tend to emphasize the reign of Süleyman because he was seen as the great architect who defined the very nature of the empire. Süleyman's death and the transfer of power to his son Selim II take on significance as characterizing the connection between the revered Süleymanic past and the contemporary world in which the histories were written and first read.[12] Large parts of the *Zafarnāma* appear to versify and translate the earlier *Nüzhetü'l-ahbar der sefer-i Sīgetvār* into Persian, transforming Feridun Ahmed's straightforward historical account of the Szigetvár campaign into a *şehnāme* with the use of the same language, meter, and rhyme scheme as the Persian model of the genre, Firdawsi's *Shāhnāma*. The details in the new account, however, remained unchanged from those found in the *Nüzhetü'l-ahbar*.[13]

By the morning of September 7, powerful artillery had largely reduced the walls of Szigetvár to rubble. Before leading his remaining six hundred soldiers in a final charge against the attackers, Zrínyi commanded that a fuse be lit to the powder magazine of the inner fortress. When the Ottoman besiegers penetrated its remains, they also entered into the trap, and thousands were killed in the ensuing blast (Fig. 9.4).[14] The illustration represents the four castles of Szigetvár from a bird's-eye view. Following the page's vertical format, the composition moves up the page, revealing the first two castles to be ruined but firmly under Ottoman control, the third being contained, while the fourth is destroyed by the violent explosions within the magazine. The lustrous gold used in the pictorial border also marks the flames. (Unlike silver, the gold used in the manuscripts has retained its luster.) Although most of the defenders were slain, the Janissaries spared a few in honor of their courage.[15] The violence depicted here is horrific, but the underlying message remains clear: Ottoman order will prevail.

A double-page illustration of the procession after the siege of Szigetvár (Fig. 9.5) reproduces motifs from the *Nüzhetü'l-ahbar* (such as the parted curtains of the sultan's carriage revealing his coffin, cf. Fig. 9.3). Here additional groundlines define hills that partially conceal groups of soldiers, vividly conveying the massive Ottoman army that commands the terrain. Sokollu Mehmed Pasha now rides before the carriage at the center of the army, in the position that would have been taken by the sultan, suggesting that the troops have been informed of the sultan's

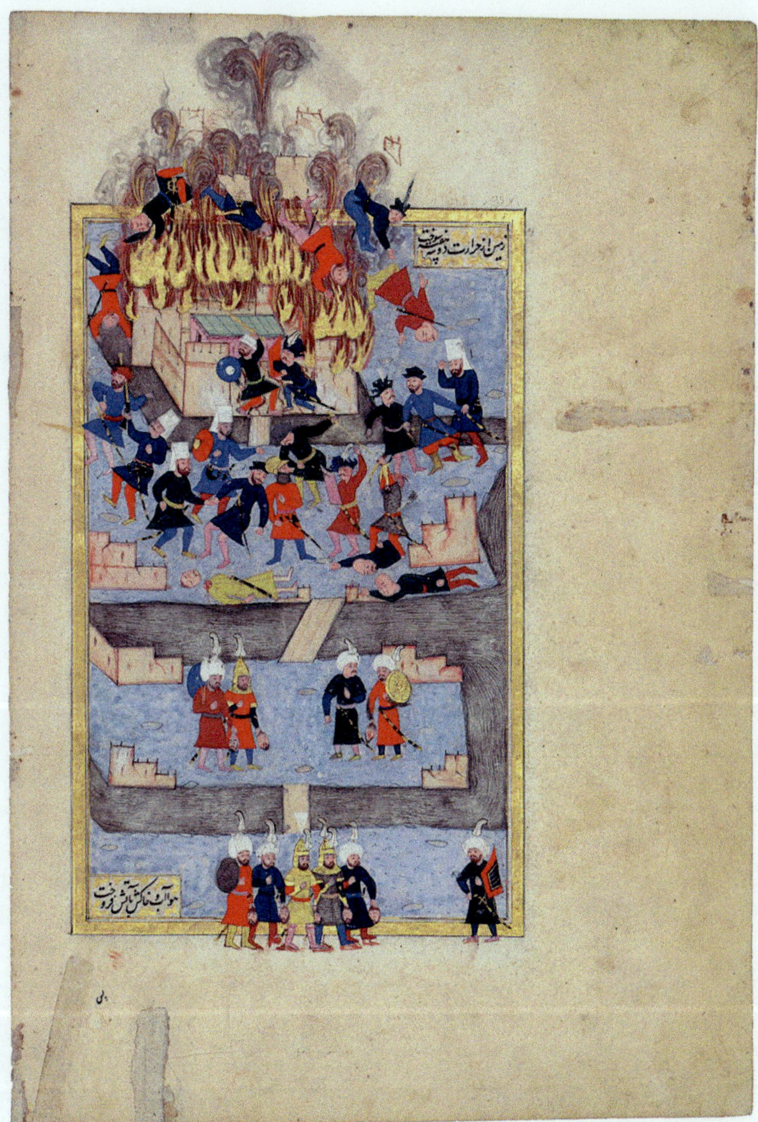

Fig. 9.4 *Zafarnāma* of Lokman, explosions at the fortress of Szigetvár. Dublin, Chester Beatty Library, T 413 f. 95. Photo: © The Trustees of the Chester Beatty Library, Dublin

death. Lokman probably began the *Zafarnāma* hoping to advance both his patron's fortunes and his own by exalting Sokollu, but he was unable to complete the project as originally envisioned; he instead had to defer to the requirements of new competitors in the arena of power.

The altered political realities of the 1570s become manifest in the *Shāhnāma-i Salīm Khān* (Book of Kings of Sultan Selim).[16] Early drafts in the Topkapi Palace Library and the British Library indicate that Lokman initially opened his account with Sokollu Mehmed Pasha's great military achievement, the Szigetvár campaign,

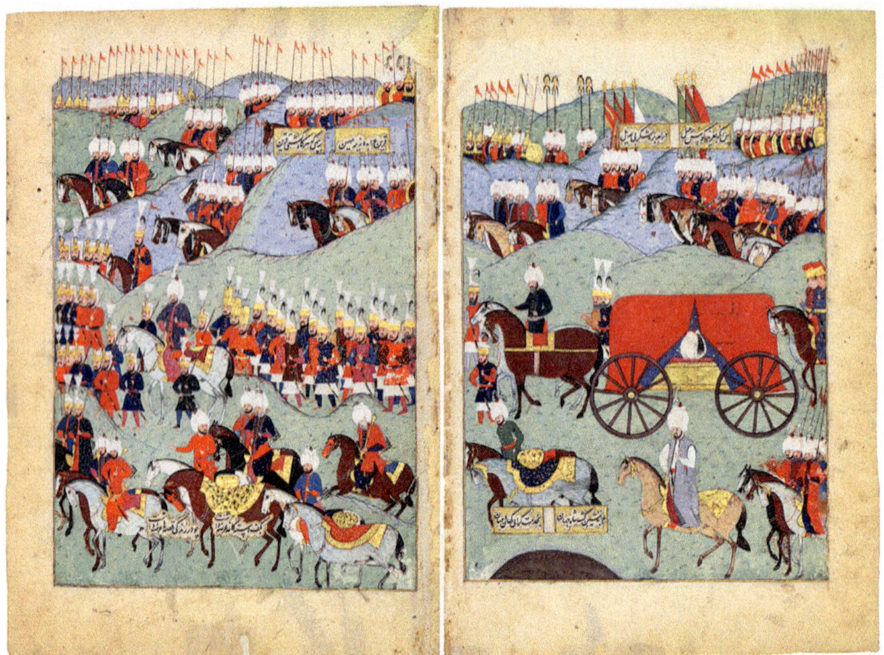

Fig. 9.5 *Zafarnāma* of Lokman, funeral procession of Sultan Süleyman. Dublin, Chester Beatty Library, T 413.113v and T 413.114r. Photo: © The Trustees of the Chester Beatty Library, Dublin

but Selim II's associates, which included many who were antagonistic toward the grand vizier and his elevated stature, were not pleased with this structure.[17] It was therefore revised to open with Selim II's ascension, which actually occurred at the end of the campaign. Nevertheless, the verbal and visual treatment of the aftermath of the Szigetvár campaign still makes clear that Sokollu Mehmed Pasha upheld the legacy of Süleyman and fulfilled his official functions with diligence; the emphasis now, however, pivoted to portray the collectivity of the Ottoman court with Sokollu's position subsumed into its overall harmony.[18]

The *Hünernāme*

The *Hünernāme* (Book of Skills) manuscripts are among the most refined of all Ottoman illustrated histories. Lokman's two predecessors began writing the *Hünernāme* during the reign of Süleyman. Originally four volumes were envisioned. The initial volume covers the accomplishments of the first nine Ottoman sultans, the second volume is devoted exclusively to the reign of Süleyman, but the last two volumes, focusing on Selim II and Murad III, had not yet been completed. Both the text and the fifty-two illustrations of the second volume depict Süleyman as an embodiment of the Sufi notion of the perfect human being and as an ideal ruler by drawing attention to his superior character with such examples as his prowess in hunting and astute strategies in warfare, but also his morality, liberality, and piety. At the same time the volume accentuates Sokollu Mehmed Pasha's role in preserving Süleymanic practices; and although he is portrayed as an essential part of the smoothly functioning of the state, he is pointedly only one of a number of important figures.

The depiction of Süleyman's final campaign illustrates the ideal ruler's reliance on the perfect vizier. Sokollu's support of Süleyman—or perhaps more accurately, the old sultan's dependence on his grand vizier—is intimated in an image that reproduces an illustration from the *Zafarnāma* depicting the ailing sultan leaning on Sokollu as he rides to Szigetvár (Fig. 9.6). The sultan's superior status is indicated by portraying him riding on horseback, with Sokollu walking beside him, but Süleyman's left arm rests on Sokollu's shoulder for support. Both figures are larger than the surrounding soldiers, and are centrally placed, although the vizier's form overlaps the sultan and his horse. (The carriage that will later hide the sultan's coffin is at the bottom left.) This illustration is followed by a two-page representation of Süleyman's arrival in Szigetvár (Fig. 9.7). The left-hand page again portrays the sultan astride his horse, positioned at the center of the page and shown to advantage by his white robes and turban. Just right of center at the bottom of the right-hand page Sokollu, also on horseback but set apart, enters the tents of the Ottoman compound to prepare the way for the sultan, exemplifying his role as perfect servant. The compound was erected on the Similehov hill to afford the ailing Süleyman an unobstructed view of the siege. At the top of the page are the campaign's objective—the four mighty castles of Szigetvár. The bird's-eye view allowing us to see the inside their massive walls contrast with the ruined fortifications depicted in the *Zafarnāma* (cf. Fig. 9.4).

Sokollu Mehmed Pasha participates in a war council, probably occurring while the news of the sultan's passing is still kept from the Ottoman army (Fig. 9.8). At the top of the image are the four castles of Szigetvár, rendered in vivid colors. Here and in the preceding illustration the silver used to represent the shimmering water of the moats has oxidized (cf. also Fig. 9.2). Just below against a pink ground is a line of the Ottoman cannon that will pummel the castle walls. A series of groundlines separate differently colored hills; orderly rows of soldiers set among them demonstrate that the Ottoman army commands the field. At the lower right of the page we see inside the grand vizier's tent situated within the Ottoman compound. Although the primacy of the protagonist is usually indicated by his privileged position within both the compositional format and the depicted space, his relatively larger scale, and his more elaborate regalia, here Sokollu is carefully incorporated into the crowd of secretaries, commanders, and petitioners performing their diverse functions inside the tent while many more await outside. He is portrayed as being instrumental in events from two complementary spheres of his duties, as military commander who will take the nearby castles and administrator at the court who oversees a smooth transition in power, but in a manner closer to that

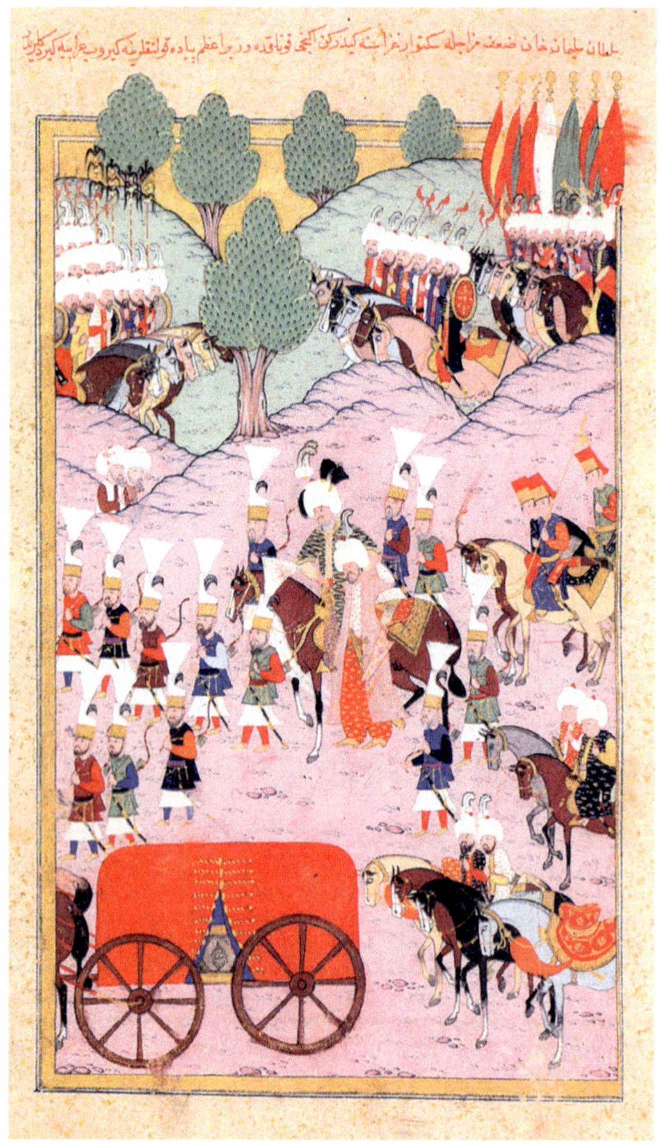

Fig. 9.6 *Hünernāme* of Lokman, vol. 2, Sokollu Mehmed Pasha supporting the ailing Sultan Süleyman. Istanbul, Topkapi Palace Museum, H. 1524, fol. 276a. Photo: © The Presidency of the Republic of Turkey, The Directorate of National Palaces Administration

shown in the *Shāhnāma-i Salīm Khān*: as the dutiful servant fulfilling his role in the well-organized Ottoman system.[19]

The *Hünernāme* epitomizes the high Ottoman style. There is a distinct move away from Persian prototypes: Lokman's text is now in Ottoman Turkish prose, or the *mülemma'* form,[20] and the paintings, while vivid and powerful, are also carefully ordered and majestic, signifying visually the stability and splendor of

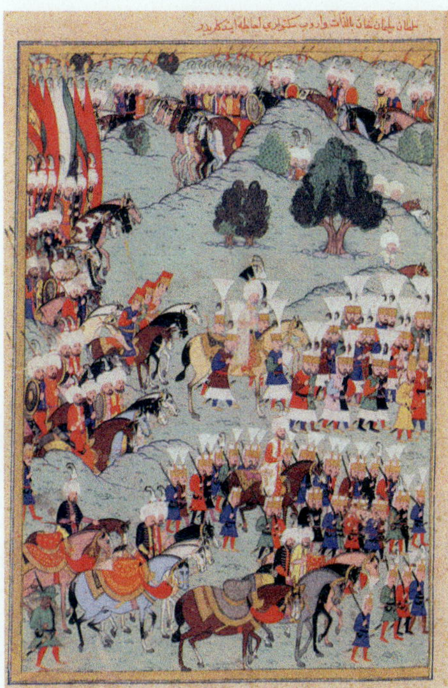
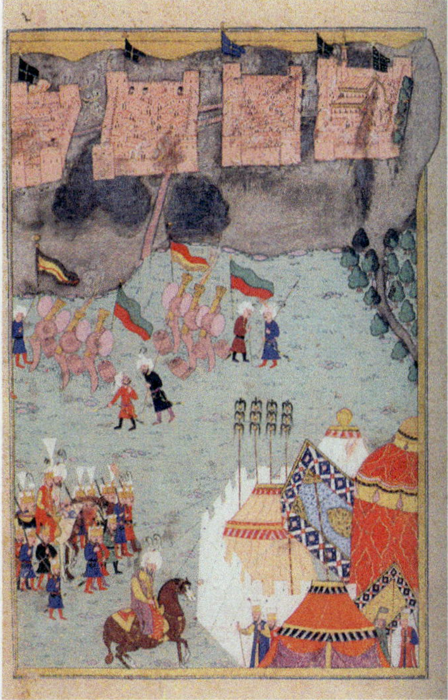

Fig. 9.7 *Hünernāme* of Lokman, vol. 2., Süleyman's arrival in Szigetvár. Istanbul, Topkapi Palace Museum, H. 1524, fols. 277b-278a. Photo: © The Presidency of the Republic of Turkey, The Directorate of National Palaces Administration

the empire. In contrast to the illustrations found in Safavid manuscripts, whose hectic compositions feature multiple focal points and include figures or anecdotal vignettes that do not contribute to the dominant narrative, the aesthetic properties of Ottoman historical manuscripts increasingly emphasize order and structure over playfulness; these characteristics suggest a more tendentious function for illustrated histories in the Ottoman court that contributes to their authoritative nature. Fetvaci observes that "the divergence of the two neighboring painting traditions was connected as much to the nature of the texts being illustrated as to a desire to create independent and distinct aesthetic systems. The most popular texts illustrated for the Safavids were literary works including heroic tales and romances, whereas the Ottoman manuscripts the differing 'Ottoman' aesthetic are primarily works of contemporary history."[21] The multiple audiences at the court for Ottoman illustrated histories required that a suitable style be developed, one that would contribute to their comprehensibility. The vivid colors and careful rendering of intricate details invite communities of users to study closely—and remember—the images and the events they illustrate, reminiscent of the spell cast by Japanese *gunki monogatari*.

Ottoman historical illustrations are highly subjective, either showing in what manner events ought to have taken place or representing the past in the most strategic way to be remembered. (For example, the walls of Szigetvár would have been

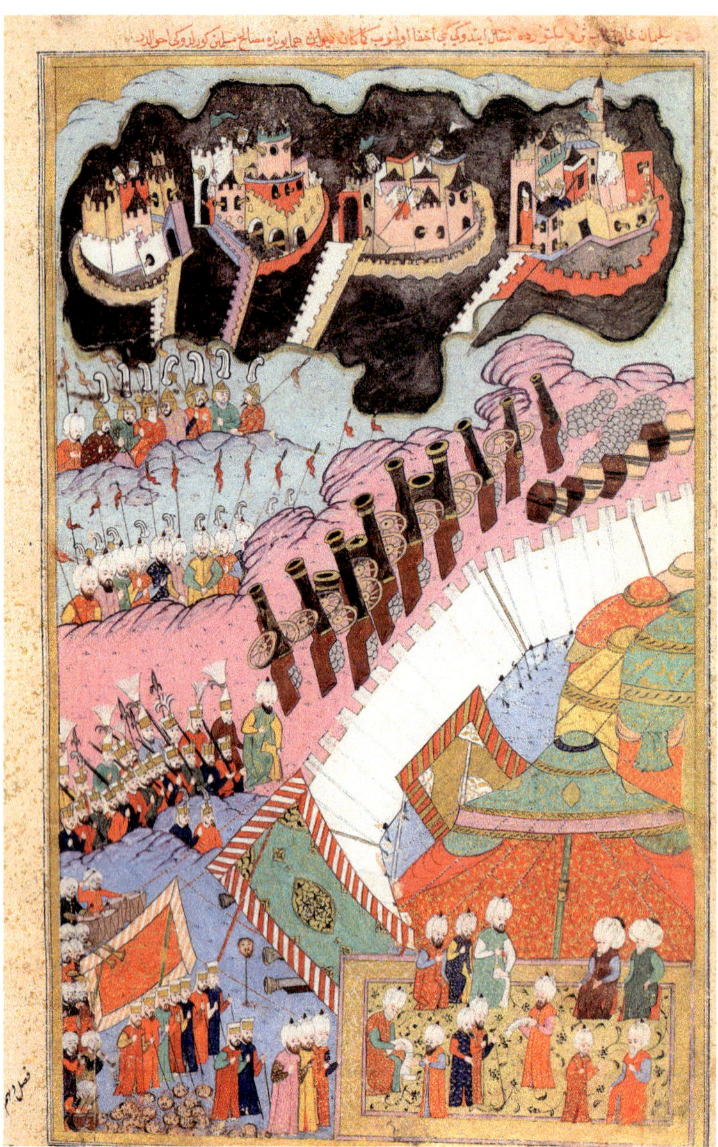

Fig. 9.8 *Hünernāme* of Lokman, vol. 2, Sokollu Mehmed Pasha's war council. Istanbul, Topkapi Palace Museum, H. 1524, fol. 279b. Photo: © The Presidency of the Republic of Turkey, The Directorate of National Palaces Administration

largely demolished by the time of the council depicted in Fig. 9.8.) Sokollu Mehmed Pasha's enduring reputation as an admirable grand vizier who brought stability to the empire and guaranteed the continuity of Süleyman's legacy rests chiefly on the way he is portrayed in the manuscripts produced under his patronage.[22] They advanced the Sokollu Mehmed Pasha's cause by creating a constructive image of him for posterity, and did so while at the same time enhancing the Ottoman court's self-definition by contributing to a growing body of literature that recorded its history, thereby countering the efforts of the grand vizier's opponents around Selim II and his later rocky relationship with Murad III.

Earlier works like the *Futūhāt-i jamīla*, the *Nüzhetü'l-ahbar der sefer-i Sīgetvār*, and the *Zafarnāma* took great liberties by portraying Sokollu Mehmed Pasha (who was only the third vizier at the time) as the principal engineer and hero of the Habsburg wars, and once he became the grand vizier as a personage almost eclipsing the sultan. The later *Shāhnāma-i Salīm Khān* and *Hünernāme*, in contrast, more prudently incorporate the grand vizier into the larger hierarchy of the Ottoman court. The representation of the grand vizier reverting from virtual sultan back to perfect servant reflects the realities of Sokollu Mehmed Pasha's changing fortunes late in life and his need to curry favor with Murad III.[23]

Fashioning an Ottoman Identity

The Ottoman Empire competed vigorously with the Safavid Empire of Iran (1501–1722) for political and religious supremacy, and strategically deployed the visual arts to distinguish their imperial traditions from each other. Thus, despite the initial adaptation of the distinctively Persian *şehnāme*, under Ottoman patronage the genre was transformed to commemorate contemporary accomplishments. The construction of a specifically Ottoman image in illustrated manuscripts parallels the increasingly prescribed nature of court ceremonial at this time. The groundbreaking work of Gülru Necipoglu has shown how the emergence of an Ottoman style in the visual arts, also discernible in portable objects and architecture, corresponds to similar developments in the Safavid Empire.[24] The two Islamic empires competed to express their distinct identities through the production of material culture, including artforms that ultimately extended beyond the confines of elite patrons.

During Süleyman's reign, the Ottoman Empire set about the redefinition and institutionalization of, in the words of Cornell Fleischer, the "ideals, identity, and practice of the dynastic state, particularly in matters of ideological representation, elite reproduction, and distribution of resources."[25] Political theories and practices related to the state were increasingly integrated at this time, and continued to be refined under Süleyman's immediate successors. Further conquests and territorial expansion during in the late sixteenth and early seventeenth century intensified the need to define the character of the new, enlarged Ottoman Empire.[26] Although many inhabitants of its central lands called themselves *Rumi*, the term was not one devised by or for the Ottoman state. Cemal Kafadar distinguishes from *Rumi* identity a smaller group within the empire: those who identified as *Osmanli*, or Ottoman. The latter, he maintains, implied those who identified with the institutions and conventions formed around the House of Osman.[27] In addition to their more general *Rumi* identity, the figures discussed here would have been distinguished among their contemporaries as *Osmanli*.

The Ottomans developed the *devşirme* system specifically to acculturate trainees of diverse ethnic and religious backgrounds to Ottoman practices and prepare them to join the Ottoman ruling elite. This system recruited children from families (including non-Muslims) living in conquered Ottoman lands and educated them in the Topkapi and other imperial palaces, training them for positions in the state bureaucracy or army according to the diverse talents they demonstrated.[28] According to Kafadar, they were drawn from the vast cultural geography of "the lands of Rum": they belonged to a larger social segment that spoke Turkish, "preferably a refined kind of Turkish (but not necessarily as their mother tongue) and acquired their social identity within or in some proximity to urban settings, professions, institutions, education and cultural preferences."[29] The prolonged period of acculturation in the elite centers created a cohort whose members, regardless of their background, shared a common court culture and whose personal indebtedness to the sultan guaranteed their loyalty.

Modern scholarship in Ottoman cultural studies has demonstrated that Ottoman identity developed in tandem with cultural production in the late sixteenth and early seventeenth centuries.[30] As shown in Fig. 9.1, a surge in the production of manuscripts and a growing number of patrons for them coincided with the swelling Ottoman bureaucracy's increasing demand for state-issued documents and the creation of networks of archives of guilds and professional organizations, Sufi associations, and madrasas that all sought to position themselves in the empire through writing their histories.[31] As the need to address the various members of the bureaucratic-military class within and beyond the imperial household—and potentially influence their opinions—became an integral part of the political process, even private individuals sought to record their achievements. Accordingly, at the Ottoman court manuscript patronage became an act of self-fashioning that propagated among its diverse constituents specific messages about one's self and the shared society of the court.[32]

Among Ottoman elites the ownership of books was a mark of distinction, an outward sign of prosperity and cultural refinement, and also one by which courtiers represented themselves as participating in both specifically Ottoman courtly sophistication and in the wider Islamic cultural sphere. Illustrated histories played a key role in this activity. As courtiers and palace trainees read and viewed these books, they confronted idealized images of their society.[33] A characteristic feature of the histories is the repetition of standardized compositions of court formalities. Their illustrations carefully mirrored the protocols of the Ottoman court in depictions of state ceremonies through their settings and details of different costumes and regalia. Manuscripts thereby reinforced courtiers' awareness of their own places within social hierarchies and instructed palace trainees about the unfamiliar world they had entered. It should be noted that since the illustrations in these manuscripts emphasize public ceremonial and rarely represent private lives, depictions of contemporary women are extremely rare: their actions as important patrons of art and architecture and as political actors at court most often took place behind the scenes or through agents.[34]

Book Production and Circulation

Patrons (sultans, viziers, high officials, and eunuchs), the comprehensive category comprising authors, and artists (painters, calligraphers, and illuminators) all took part in the making of books.[35] Patrons, of course, had much to say about what would be written. At the Ottoman court patronage also encompassed layers of intermediaries through whom sultans and others who commissioned books operated; as was demonstrated by the changes demanded in the narrative of the *Shāhnāma-i Salīm Khān*, these agents could influence the finished product. The production process began with a commission to an author. Authorship in the Ottoman milieu, however, is a fairly supple concept. While the texts and inscriptions in manuscripts and albums from elsewhere in the Islamic world sometimes assert collaborative production, the Ottoman examples are unique in the extent to which the text results from a process involving multiple authorial voices—a work of collective authorship, even if claimed or attributed to a single author in the preface.[36]

In the 1550s, the salaried position of the *şehnāmeci* was created. Christine Woodhead identifies the *şehnāmeci*'s responsibility as "compos[ing] literary accounts of contemporary or near-contemporary Ottoman history."[37] These accounts were carefully crafted to glorify the entire court, not simply the sultan, and were sensitive to the fluid power dynamics and personal relationships at the palace. The close involvement of Ottoman patrons throughout the production process means that the histories also contain traces of varying individual perspectives and motivations and of factional politics, but the histories invariably project fashioned identities of members of the court in ways that they preferred.

After the text was composed, the services of a scribe, an illuminator, and a binder were secured to fabricate the book. As with other Islamic dynasties, the Ottomans enlisted a corps of artisans attached to the royal household, known as the "community of craftsmen" (*ehl-i hiref*). During the reigns of Bayezid II and Selim I the *ehl-i hiref* working on books became a well-defined group, and had almost doubled in size to 636 by the end of Süleyman's reign in 1566–1567.[38] While earlier in the sixteenth century the *ehl-i hiref* was populated by artisans from conquered cities such as Cairo and Tabriz, by the end of Süleyman's reign artisans recruited through the *devşirme* system at a young age and trained in the palace came to prominence. According to Necipoğlu, "It was when apprentices of the *devşirme* origin became masters of the royal workshop that the classical Ottoman synthesis emerged."[39] It is this community of artists that was responsible for the eventual creation of a high Ottoman style exemplified by the *Hünernāme*.

Present knowledge of manuscript production in this period places a royal manuscript studio (*hāṣṣa nakkāşhānesi*) just outside the grounds of the Topkapi Palace. That studio, however, was not expressly linked to the office of the court historian; rather, the historian would engage artisans from the *ehl-i hiref* as they were needed.[40] According to Woodhead, "the number of specialist staff employed in the *şehnāmeci*'s office presumably varied with the volume of work to be carried out."[41] Their names and affiliations appear in archival documents, listed as painters (for example, Osman, Ali, Lüftü, and Velican), scribes (Haydar and Sinan), and illuminators (Mus and Ahmed) who collaborated for specific commissions on a temporary basis as the project demanded it.[42] Hence the number comprising Lokman's crews fluctuated, ranging from five artisans working on the *Shāhnāma-i Salīm Khān* to almost thirty working on the *Hünernāme*. In the office of the *şehnāmeci*, however, image was always subservient to text.

The circulation of books was closely connected to the various tasks and responsibilities of the Ottoman court. The Topkapi was a rigidly organized, hierarchical institution, home to the sultan and his family, but also an administrative hub employing bureaucrats, scholars, imperial household servants (mostly slaves), a military command center with ranks of soldiers, and male and female trainees enlisted as part of the *devşirme* system. Books were the ideal vehicles for training the young residents of the palace in the proper speech and protocols of the imperial court. Once established in the state bureaucracy or army, former trainees themselves commissioned books like those they had previously read at court, thereby perpetuating the courtly model.[43]

Consequently, book culture was not exclusive to only the highest members of the Ottoman elite. The most precious books were kept in the treasury, but many in the larger courtly community could borrow from it; in addition, smaller libraries throughout the palace also lent books.[44] In addition, silent reading was less common at the court than public recitations or reading aloud in groups, undoubtedly followed by discussion. The prominence of these oral rehersals is confirmed by the court historian's official title, referred to interchangeably as *şehnāmehān* (reader of the *şehnāme*); *şehnāmeguy* (the sayer/performer of the *şehnāme*); or *şehnāmeci* (maker or writer of the *şehnāme*).[45] Inclusive circulation and performance gave illustrated histories powerful agency in the formation of Ottoman courtly identity and rendered their contents significant.

Sokollu's architectural commissions emphasize the same themes found in the illustrated histories: his close association with Süleyman, the celebration of his role in the Szigetvár campaign, and later, his desire to remind Murad III of his many years of service to the court.[46] Although his support of scholarship was not limited to commissioning manuscripts that promoted his interests, he paid particular attention to history and historians. By "blurring the boundary between private and state patronage,"[47] Sokollu Mehmed Pasha's literary and architectural projects fashioned the courtly role by which he is remembered, be it as perfect vizier or merely perfect servant.

10

The Surrender of Breda

Public Gesture and Private Memory in Baroque Spain

Seventeenth-century Europe was wreaked by upheaval. Wars of religion were waged against the background of the rise of modern nation-states. "Propaganda" was given its modern name as popes and monarchs, who claimed to rule by divine right, undertook massive building projects and public art programs to advance personal and ideological agendas on a scale not seen since imperial Rome.[1] Commemorations of historical events in the imposing Baroque style secured reputations, sometimes by magnifying mundane incidents into something epic and even recasting troublesome negatives into flattering and memorable positives.[2] As in ancient Rome, artists deployed parallel allegorical and more documentary modes of representation. Allegories still depended on sophisticated viewers who knew how to interpret an often complex and arcane symbolic language in order to understand their significance; in fact, that language was sometimes purposely abstruse, obfuscating problematic narratives while conferring distinction upon those able to decipher them.

Fashioning a Queen's Image

As the Queen Mother of France and Regent of Louis XIII, Marie de' Medici, daughter of the Grand Duke of Tuscany and widow of Henry IV, pursued power relentlessly, made formidable enemies, alienated her son and potential allies, and suffered banishment for her efforts.[3] With the mediation of Cardinal Richelieu she managed to regain favor at court (reconciliation being a political expedient) and endeavored to promote her position. In 1621 Marie commissioned twenty-four paintings by Peter Paul Rubens for the Luxembourg Palace, her new Paris residence.[4] There courtiers, ambassadors, and the king himself would see and construe a wholly self-serving rewriting of history. With Rubens the Queen secured the services of an artist celebrated in Northern Europe for his monumental altarpieces and other religious works; doubtless Rubens welcomed the ambitious secular program as an opportunity to advance his reputation among an elite international audience.

Fashioning a literal depiction of Marie's life would be problematic for the artist: although lacking in the triumphant victories of her late husband, it did offer

Power, Image, and Memory. Peter J. Holliday, Oxford University Press. © Oxford University Press 2024.
DOI: 10.1093/oso/9780190901080.003.0011

plenty of scandal. Furthermore, he dared not offend the reigning French monarch in the process of promoting the Queen Mother. And because the paintings were commissioned by and represented a woman, Rubens had to adjust the traditional iconography of male authority. He therefore marshaled his extraordinary knowledge of biblical and classical literature in service to contemporary politics and created extravagant images of the Queen surrounded by ancient gods, personifications, and emblematic references that glorify mundane activities and unheroic events and portray unsavory and less favorable aspects of her tumultuous life in a tactful manner. The commission represents a selective approach to "historical truth," an imaginative transformation of the facts that appears to generate a highly ambiguous, if not plainly false, take on reality.

The War of the Jülich Succession (1609–1614) was one of the innumerable military conflicts during the Eighty Years' War that consumed Europe's Protestant and Catholic powers. The town of Jülich (the French Juliers) spanned the Ruhr River, making it of great strategic importance to France. Her struggle for position on the international stage caused Catholic Marie to support the Protestant cause against the Catholic forces.[5] *The Victory at Jülich* depicts the return of the city to the Protestants (Fig. 10.1). The only military event that the Queen encountered during her regency, it would have to serve to demonstrate that like her departed husband, the Queen Mother could also triumph over rivals in war. To render Marie heroic, Rubens adopted the European tradition of representing monarchs as contemporary exemplars of ancient virtues attributed to "good" Roman emperors like Augustus and Trajan—*virtus*, *pietas*, *clementia*—but filtered through Christian morality.[6] His composition emulates the trappings of equestrian portraits traditionally reserved for male leaders. Bathed in bright light, the dynamically yet elegantly posed figure of Marie rides sidesaddle on a glorious white steed. She wears the war helmet of the goddess Minerva and carries a marshal's baton of command in her right hand.[7] She is the center of the pictorial composition and the focus of attention of other figures in the painting. At the upper right, an adoring Victory crowns Marie with a conqueror's wreath of laurel leaves. Beside her Fame blows a trumpet so forcefully that a burst of smoke emerges. In the distant sky weaker birds flee from an imperial eagle, another symbol of victory.[8] Magnanimity or Generosity with her tamed lion trails behind Marie; the riches in her left palm include the Queen's treasured strand of pearls.[9] Representing her towering form physically distant from all other mortals normalizes the absolutist ideology of the age.

The formal accord between the two warring armies following the collapse of fortified Jülich takes place in the middle distance. Rubens appears to credit Marie for this glorious achievement, whereas she actually played no significant role in the outcome, having arrived too late to participate in the battle but in time to affect the aura of triumph.[10] Rubens eschews accuracy in favor of a largely fictious rendering of the event in the service of Marie's political agenda. Many who had participated

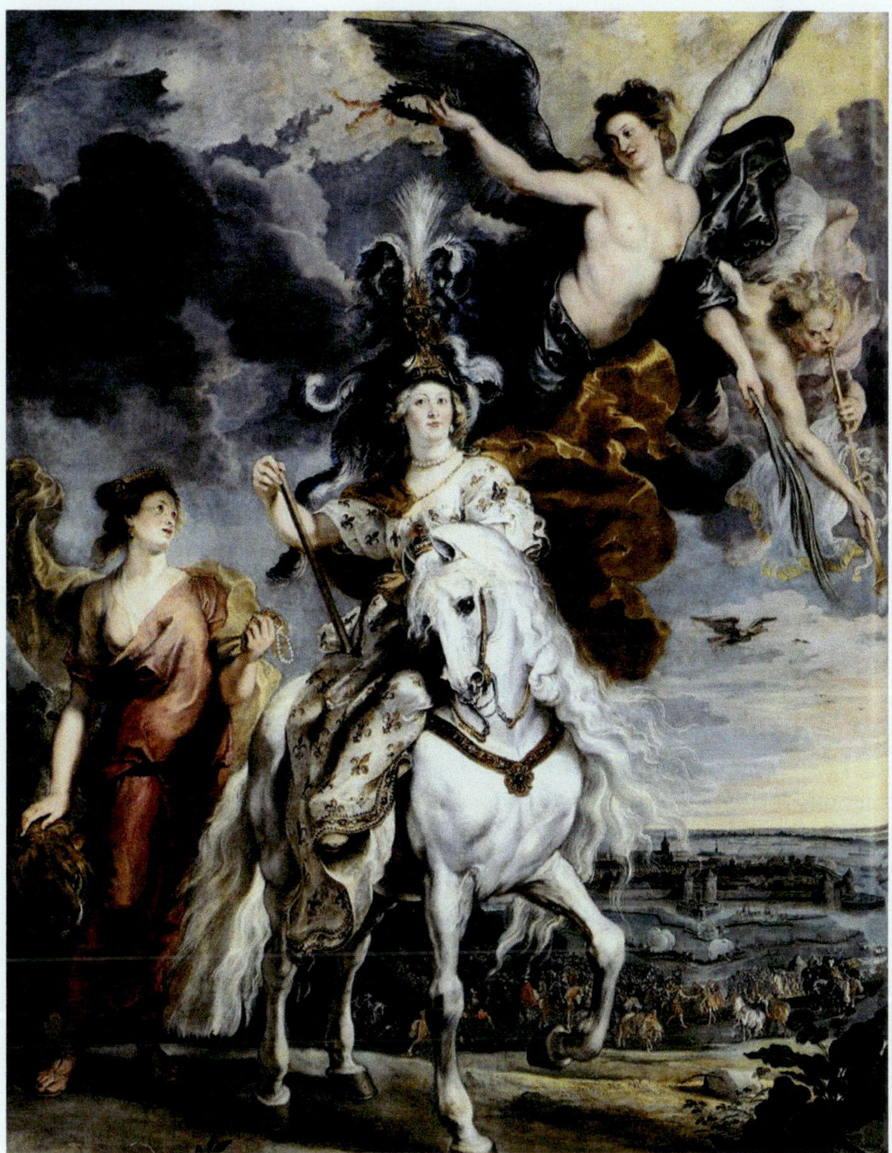

Fig. 10.1 Peter Paul Rubens: *The Victory at Jülich* (1625). Paris, Musée du Louvre. Photo: Wikimedia Commons

in the battle were still alive and knew what transpired, but with his strategic deployment of allegorical flourishes Rubens fashioned a tribute akin to a masque or other court celebration; the allegorical mode also helped render the Queen's usurpation of a masculine role palatable to contemporary viewers. Rubens's superlative artistic skill and reputation lend the representation authority, an informed viewer gives it coherence, and striking imagery makes the narrative image memorable: the ultimate goal of historical commemorations.

The Buen Retiro of Philip IV

The richest and most commanding of the great seventeenth-century European powers was Spain, whose *Siglo de Oro* (Golden Age) coincided with the rise of the Spanish Habsburg dynasty.[11] Philip IV (r. 1621–1665) commissioned the construction of the Buen Retiro just outside Madrid as a refuge from the immense dark fortification that was the Alcázar.[12] Its most sumptuous room was the grand Salón de Reinos (Hall of Realms), originally planned as a place from which the king could observe and assist in theatrical presentations in the courtyard; when Philip decided to turn the retreat into a full palace it was transformed into the principal stateroom, ornately decorated to glorify Philip and his empire (Fig. 10.2). Paintings representing the coats of arms of the twenty-four kingdoms that then formed Spain gave the salon its name; on its north and south walls twelve other paintings (one is now lost) celebrated major battles won by Philip's armies in his never-ending wars.[13] These all follow the same conventional pattern: they are life-size and relegate war itself to the background in order to celebrate victorious commanders, surrogates for Philip, full-length in the foreground. (Many dynasties share the practice of decorating extravagant reception spaces with repetitive images of triumphant kings, including the Obas of Benin.) Between them were ten allegorical paintings by Francisco de Zurbarán showing the labors of Hercules, likening the exploits of the hero (then put forward as an ancestor of the Habsburgs) with those of the king. The designer of the room's program is unknown, although ultimate responsibility belonged to Gaspar de Guzmán, the Count-Duke de Olivares, along with Jerónimo de Villanueva, the intellectual advice of Francisco de Rioja, and Juan Bautista Maíno and Diego Velázquez: two painters valued by Philip and Olivares. Appropriately for its era, the Salón de Reinos best exemplifies the strict meaning of propaganda: it was officially devised, centrally orchestrated, and methodically propagated imagery utterly favorable to the ruling power. Still, designed as an emblem of Habsburg supremacy, in reality the ruinously sumptuous palace instead masked Spain's decline as a world power.

The Wars of Religion and the Siege of Breda

The revolt of the Seventeen Provinces in what are today the Netherlands, Belgium, and Luxembourg against the political and religious domination by Philip II of Spain, the ruler of Habsburg Netherlands, initiated the Eighty Years' War (also known as the Dutch War of Independence), which lasted from 1568 to 1648. It was a sporadic conflict along the border separating the northern Dutch from the southern Spanish territories. Both nations claimed biblical prerogative: the kings of Spain claimed to rule in direct succession to the kings of Israel, and the princes of Orange maintained their descent from the House of Judah.[14] In 1581 the Habsburg

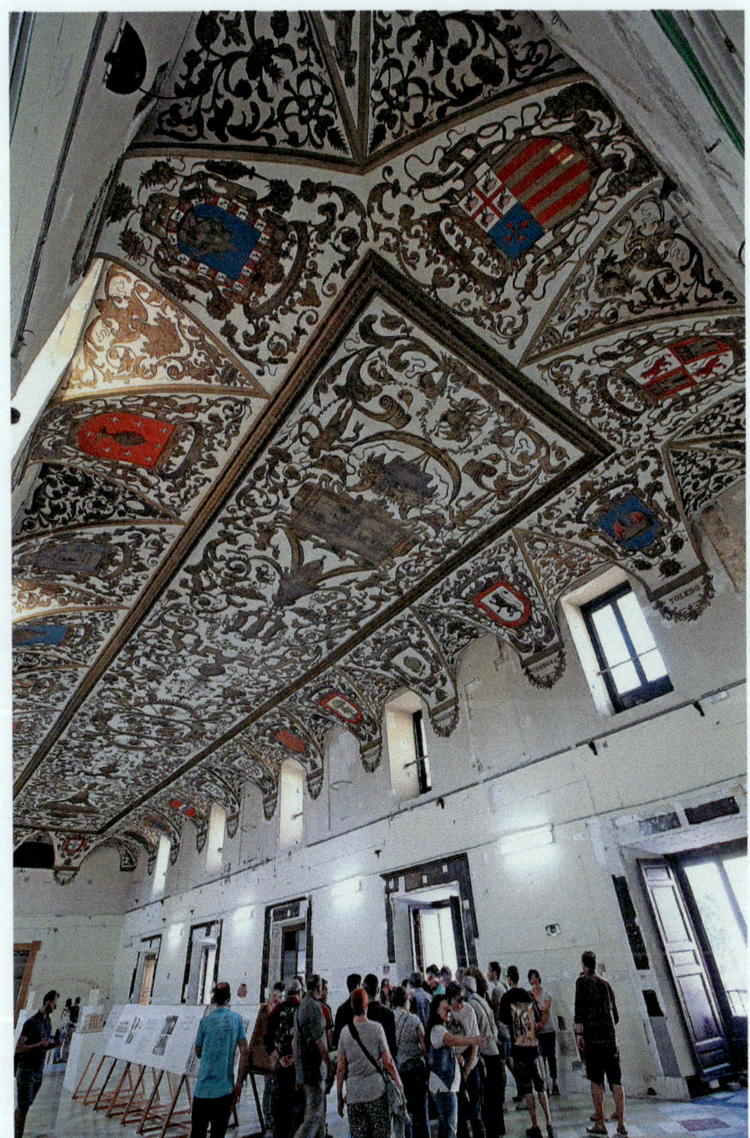

Fig. 10.2 Hall of Realms at the Buen Retiro (1630–1635). Madrid. Photo: Luis Garcia on Wikimedia Commons

armies were ousted, and the Republic of the Seven United Netherlands was established, which finally achieved de facto recognition by the Spanish Crown and other European powers with the Twelve Years' Truce in 1609. Hostilities broke out again in 1619, which generally coincided with the Thirty Years' War, a series of conflicts in Central Europe between 1618 and 1648, one of the longest, most destructive, and costly religious wars in European history, resulting in eight million casualties. This concluded with the Peace of Münster, a treaty under the Peace of Westphalia, which ended the European wars of religion.

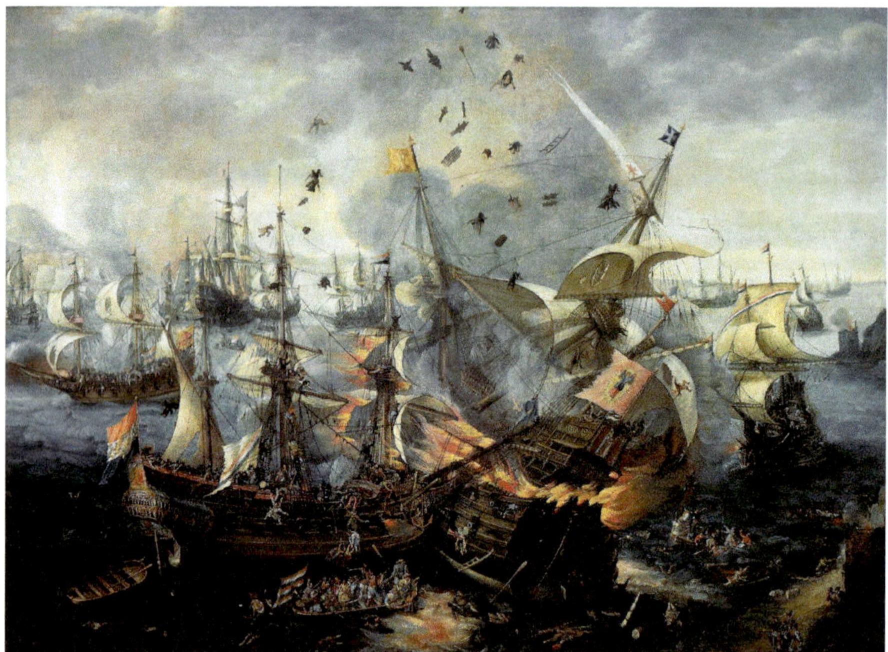

Fig. 10.3 Cornelis Claesz van Wieringen, *Battle of Gibraltar* (1621). Amsterdam, Rijksmuseum Amsterdam. Photo: Wikimedia Commons

Most paintings of the era that commemorate military victory depict the spectacle of battle with all the excitement and violence the artist could muster. Cornelis Claesz van Wieringen's *Battle of Gibraltar* represents the first sea battle the Dutch fought against the Spanish beyond their own waters during the Eighty Years' War (Fig. 10.3). On April 25, 1607, Jacob van Heemskerk led a Dutch fleet of 26 ships in a surprise attack on a Spanish fleet of 21 ships, including 10 galleons, under the command of Don Juan Álvarez de Avila anchored at the Bay of Gibraltar. Van Heemskerk positioned some of his ships at the mouth of the bay to prevent any Spanish escape and, over the next four hours of fighting, destroyed most of Spanish fleet. The Dutch lost a hundred men, including van Heemskerk. In revenge, the Dutch deployed small boats and killed hundreds of Spanish sailors swimming to escape. Between 350 and 4,000 Spaniards were killed or captured (depending on the source); Álvarez de Avila was also amongst the dead. Van Wieringen represented a small Dutch warship ramming the grand Spanish flagship longitudinally. It explodes when its powder magazine is breached, catapulting Spanish soldiers into the air to drown in the sea. His painting celebrates the astonishing Dutch victory that led to the recognition of the Dutch Republic with the Twelve Years' Truce.

The most important city in the southern Netherlands was Breda in Brabant near the frontier of Holland proper at the confluence of the rivers Mark and Aa.[15] It had been acquired through marriage by the House of Nassau, making it a center of Dutch political and social life. It was also a *residentiestad* (residence city): the presence of the Orange-Nassau family drew other nobles, who built grand houses in old quarters of the fortified city. Breda was captured by surprise in July 1581 by troops led by Claudius van Barlaymont, a Flemish military commander in Spain's Army of Flanders commonly called "Haultpenne."[16] Although the conditions of surrender stipulated that the city would not be plundered, the Spanish troops vented their rage upon the inhabitants. Over five hundred citizens were killed in the resulting mayhem, known as Haultpenne's Fury. On March 4, 1590, Maurice of Nassau, Prince of Orange recaptured Breda for the Dutch after men hidden inside a river-barge hauling peat penetrated the castle watergate and opened the city's northwest gate. The barge was later dragged onto the castle quay and for the next thirty-five years was featured in civic commemorations every March 4.

During the unfolding Thirty Years' War, Spain determined that besieging the tenaciously garrisoned towns of the Dutch Republic was too costly, instead concentrated on an economic blockade, and diverted the majority of its forces to central Europe. In 1624, however, the end of conflict in Germany allowed Spain to amass its forces against the Netherlands. Philip IV's best commander in the Thirty Years' War was the brilliant Genoese aristocrat Don Ambrogio Spinola Doria, commonly referred to as Ambrogio Spinola. Spinola recognized Breda's strategic significance and determined to advance on the city, accompanied by the Marquis de Leganés and Carlos Coloma. The opposing commander, Justinus van Nassau, was another military man famous throughout Europe.[17] The siege of Breda was not just another battle between the Netherlands and Spain, but a pivotal meeting of two renowned generals whose reputations were at stake. Contemporary observers were certain that the outcome would determine the future position of Spain as a world power.

Spinola decided to surround the city with four miles of ramparts. Surrendering Dutch soldiers were sent back to maintain pressure on the city's dwindling provisions. Combat was primarily limited to rebuffing Dutch and English attempts at relief. After a ten-month siege, an intercepted letter the new captain-general prince Frederick Henry had sent Justin alerted Spinola that the Dutch were perilously short of food and materiel. Rather than continue the bloodshed, Spinola proposed that the Dutch surrender, which was accepted June 5, 1626, when Justin ceded the city to Spinola. (According to Herman Hugo, Spinola's chaplain, by the end Breda had lost of third of its 15,000 citizens, mostly to disease and malnutrition.) The terms were remarkably ethical and lenient for the time. Spinola allowed Justin's forces to leave Breda for Leiden in military formation and bearing their ensigns; he forbade his soldiers to taunt or otherwise insult the defeated Dutch, and according to one contemporary account, he himself saluted Justin.

Frederick Henry would recapture Breda in 1637 after a four-month siege, and in 1648 the Peace of Westphalia finally ceded it to the Dutch.

"The Valor of the Vanquished Confers Honor on the Victor"

The taking of Breda was celebrated throughout Spain. Herman Hugo wrote an account, *Obsidio Bredana*, which was published in Latin, English, and French editions. Under the auspices of Olivares, Pedro Calderón de la Barca wrote a

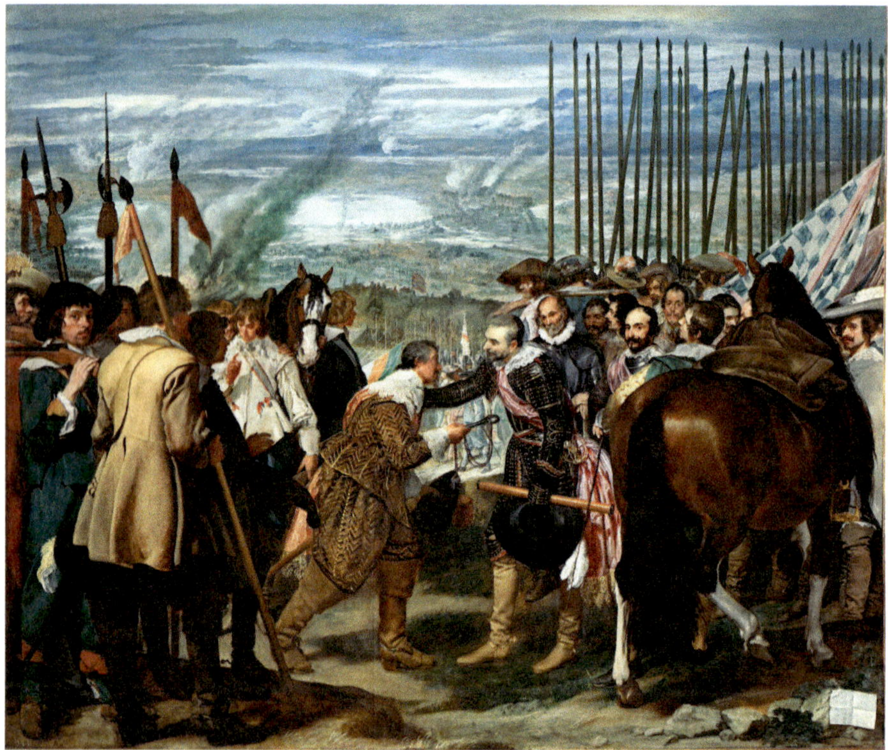

Fig. 10.4 Diego Velázquez, *The Surrender of Breda* (1634–1635). Madrid, Museo del Prado. Photo: Wikimedia Commons

masquelike play, *El Sitio de Breda*, performed at the Buen Retiro.[18] Based on what can be reconstructed, it was more a pageant weaving together a series of mannered *tableaux vivants* featuring stilted dialogue rather than a dramatic narrative. These and other productions commemorated the Spanish success in the distant Netherlands at the court (and for readers throughout Europe), but it would be Velázquez's painting that rendered the last great Spanish victory of the Dutch Rebellion truly memorable (Fig. 10.4).

He achieves this by translating a conventional martial theme into a highly personal testament. Both epic and intimate, *The Surrender of Breda* famously centers on a simple gesture of kindness. According to an eyewitness account, "Both commanders had dismounted from their horses and Spinola awaited the arrival of Nassau surrounded by a 'crown' of princes and officers of high birth. The governor then presented himself with his family, kinsfolk, and distinguished students of the military academy, who had been shut up in the city during the siege. Spinola greeted and embraced his vanquished opponents with a kindly expression and still more kindly words, in which he praised the courage and endurance of the protracted defense."[19]

Velázquez developed a composition in which eloquent gesture and meaningful facial expression tell this story of shared respect and dignity; he also employs them to convey diverse responses among witnesses as the narrative unfolds. Dismounting from his horse, Spinola meets the Dutch commander on—quite literally—an equal footing, side by side with his enemy. Justin bows, extends the key to the city, and raising his head to meet the eyes of Spinola is surprised as Spinola places his hand on Justin's shoulder to stop him mid-way in the act of kneeling. This courteous gesture, the offering of consolation from one soldier to another, distinguishes *The Surrender of Breda* from conventional submission scenes. Velázquez placed the key Justin tenders to Spinola at the exact center of the painting. He encloses it in a dynamic parallelogram at the hub of the entire composition; according to my ancient class notes, Howard Hibbard described it as the key that locks all the painting's components into place (Fig. 10.5). Although Spinola's compassion at

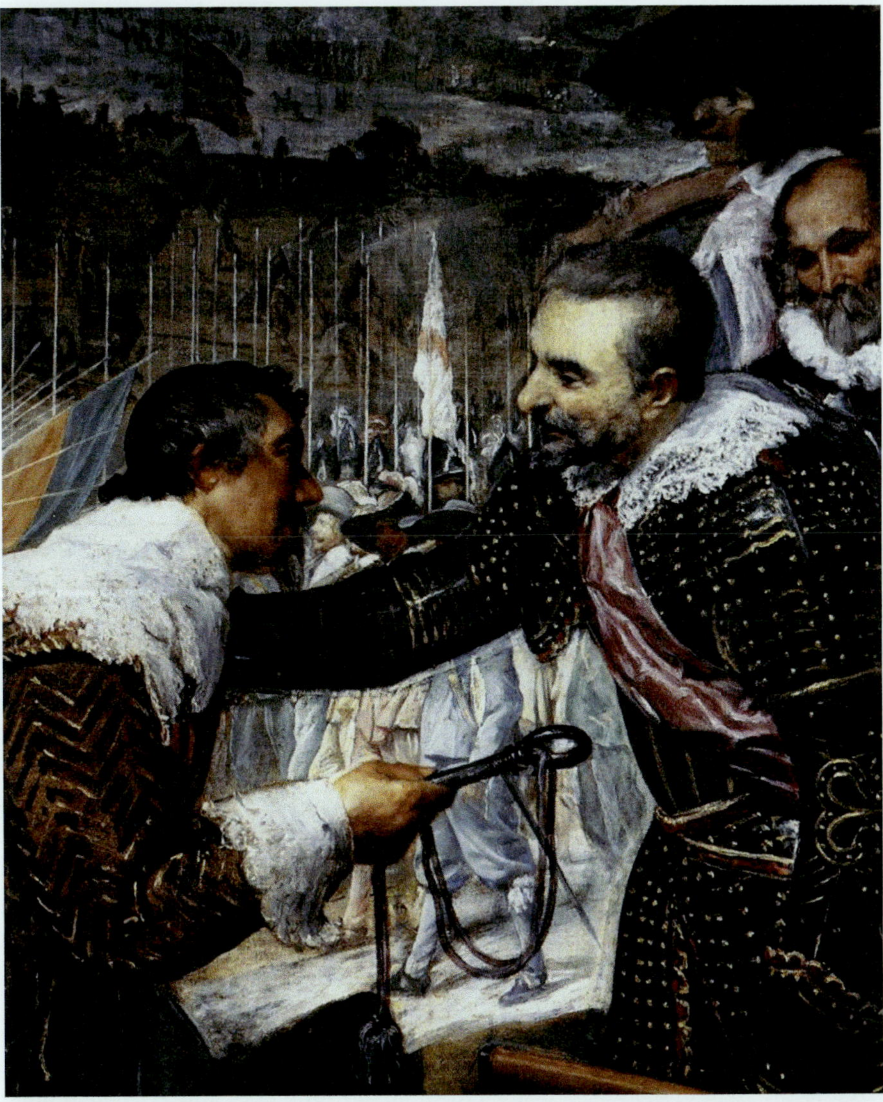

Fig. 10.5 Diego Velázquez, *The Surrender of Breda*, detail of the exchange of the key. Madrid, Museo del Prado. Photo: Wikimedia Commons

the surrender is well documented, the actual transfer of the key is not. A common motif, Velázquez may have taken it from prints or another painting.[20] It featured in Calderón's play, which has Spinola say, "the valor of the vanquished confers honor on the victor."[21] In contrast to the allegorical personifications attending Marie de' Medici, here Spinola himself embodies magnanimity.

Groups of men watch or glance away, distracted. Velázquez distinguished the two armies by showing the few remaining Dutch, on the left, as disorganized and disheveled. In contrast the Spanish officers on the right, depicted as unflagging, disciplined, and bareheaded for the solemn ceremony, convey similar messages to those coded within the Roman army on the Column of Trajan. An orderly assembly of twenty-six erect lances emphasizes the military proficiency of the Spanish troops; they are echoed by numerous other spears in the dim middle distance, just before the sprawling city and its glistening waters, creating the impression that there are more Spanish troops than we can actually see.[22] The numerous spears rising over the horizon give the painting its popular name, *Las lanzas* (*The Lances*). Lances had been a cavalry weapon for centuries, wielded by Alexander mounted on Bucephalus, the Roman equestrian at Adamclisi, and the horsemen at the Battle of San Romano; in contrast the two shorter Dutch pikes are defensive arms. The arquebus shouldered by a Dutch soldier at the far left is a predecessor of the musket, indicating the kind of weaponry that would supplant the lance and play a decisive role in Europe's imperial enterprise.[23]

What appears to be a white sheet of paper at the bottom right-hand corner may allude to the intercepted letter that precipitated the surrender. Above, the rump of Spinola's splendidly foreshortened horse looms large; its form leads us into the illusion of space in a manner that recalls the Persian charger in the Alexander Mosaic (yet to be unearthed). Beyond Spinola's arm banners and pikes indicate the Dutch garrison marching forth, allowed to leave the city with honor intact. Aerial perspective relegates the siege to the background, where columns of smoke suggest the destruction of war without showing it graphically. One of those columns may rise from the fire ordered by the Spanish to destroy the revered river-barge, as though to expunge their earlier loss from memory.

Velázquez also broke the fourth wall by including subjects that look directly out at the viewer to grab and hold our attention. The most prominent is the youthful Dutch soldier carrying the arquebus at the picture's left edge. Alberti advocated such interlocutors: "In an *istoria* I like to see someone who admonishes and points out to us what is happening there; or beckons with his hands to see; or menaces with an angry face or flashing eyes, so that no one should come near; or shows some danger or marvelous things there; or invites us to weep or to laugh together with them."[24] Counterbalancing at the right the faces of three Spanish soldiers also gaze out at us, their bodies obscured by overlapping men. One, crammed in and sequestered to the right of the horse, bears a distinctively long nose and W-shaped mustache which gave rise to the idea that he might be a self-portrait of the artist. All these figures conform to the traditional placement of *repoussoir* figures in painting to heighten the illusion of depth by leading the viewer's eye into the composition.[25] The organizational tactic helps draw attention to the main subject by framing the edge; the figures' gazes also engage the viewer.

The Surrender of Breda stands out among the military paintings completed for the Salón de Reinos. Baroque artists generally represented the triumphant commander elevated on horseback (like Marie de' Medici) or on a throne, while the surrendering leader knelt on the ground, debased and humiliated. Typical is Jusepe Leonardo's *The Surrender of Jülich* (1634–1635), also for the Salón de Reinos, which commemorates Spinola's retaking the Rhenish city from the Dutch in 1622 at the beginning of the Thirty Years' War (Fig. 10.6). On a rise in the foreground a mounted Spinola looms triumphantly over the kneeling Dutch commander, Frederick Pytham, rendering surrender as a clear act of submission. Leonardo depicts the battlefield and city in a much smaller scale, with no aerial blending of the foreground and background, the conventional manner of emphasizing the main scene while also including details crucial to the narrative. A page standing behind another Spanish general looks out at the viewer and proudly points to the capitulation; in contrast, two Dutch soldiers shown beside Pytham's horse express distress and shame at the scene. Although *The Surrender of Breda* keeps with the room's thematic program, Velázquez's rendering of surrender as reconciliation breaks

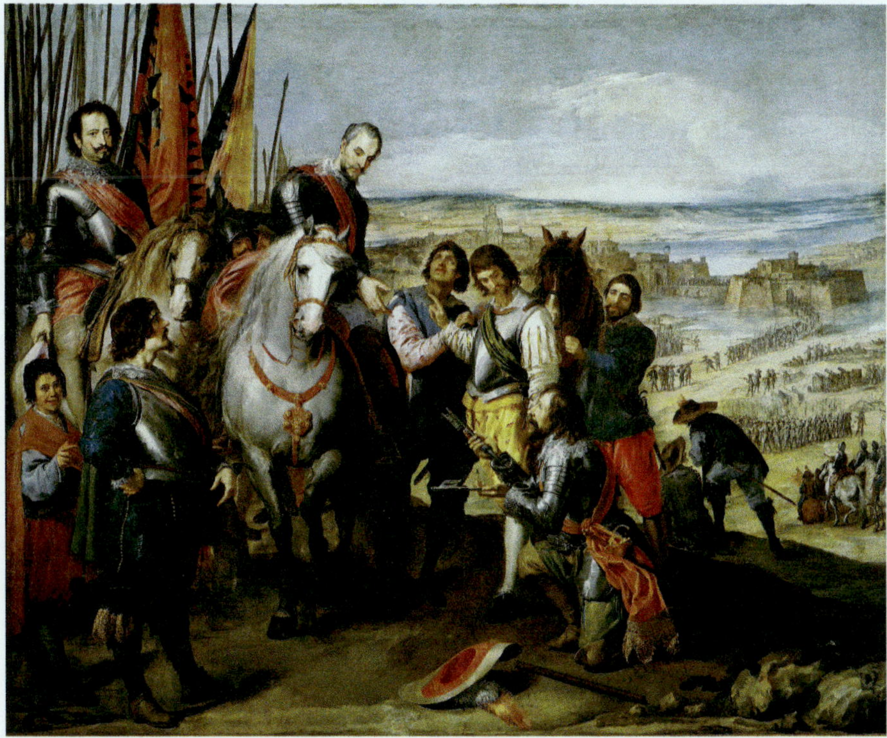

Fig. 10.6 Jusepe Leonardo, *The Surrender of Jülich* (1634–1635). Madrid, Museo del Prado. Photo: Wikimedia Commons

radically with this formula. By concentrating on the extraordinary consideration Spinola showed Nassau and the defeated Dutch army he celebrates the glimpses of humanity and dignity that can be revealed even in war.

A Special Friendship

Born a prodigy in cosmopolitan Seville, Diego Velázquez would prove himself the equal in talent of any contemporary painter, including Rubens. Social connections with the alarmingly shrewd Count-Duke of Olivares—the power behind the Spanish throne—facilitated Velázquez's advancement in Madrid, where, in 1623, at the age of twenty-four, he rose to become court painter; he remained attached to the court for the rest of his life. There he studied the Italian and Northern Baroque masters, and was especially moved by the naturalism of Caravaggio.

Ambrogio Spinola was considered as one of the greatest military commanders of his time and in the entire history of Spain. The wealth and power of his family made them rivals with the Doria family for authority in the Republic of Genoa which, in the sixteenth century, was effectively a protectorate of the Spanish Empire; the Genoese, in turn, were the bankers of the Spanish government and controlled its finances. Seeking to advance his family's position by serving the Spanish crown, in 1602 Spinola entered an agreement with the Spanish crown—a *condotta* on the ancient Italian model—and marched overland to Flanders with nine thousand Lombard mercenaries he had raised. In 1604, Ostend fell to him. For this victory he was awarded the Golden Fleece and appointed commander-in-chief of the Spanish forces in the Low Countries. He won renown through the number of his victories in spite of the tough resistance waged by Maurice of Nassau. In 1606 he returned to Spain and was received with much honor. However, he did not receive his desired Spanish grandeeship (or peerage) and was obliged to pledge his family's entire great fortune as security for military expenses before bankers would advance additional funds to the Spanish government. Spain never repaid its debt to him.

Spinola continued to lead Spain's armies successfully until the signing of the Twelve Years' Truce in 1609, after which he not only retained his post but assumed other duties, including negotiating with France. Although he obtained the desired *Grandeza*, Spinola's financial downfall was complete. After the Thirty Years' War began, he campaigned vigorously in the Lower Palatinate, and was rewarded with the grade of Captain-General for his achievements. When war in the Low Countries was renewed in 1621, his military career culminated with the taking of Breda. Frederick Henry of Nassau, however, took Groll (Groenlo) in 1627, a suitable trade for Breda. Spinola left for Spain in January 1628. There the jealous Olivares blamed him for the loss of Groll. Spinola refused to take command again in Flanders unless he received a guarantee for the support of his army, but the utter want of money paralyzed the Spanish government.

Meanwhile, Philip augmented Spain's burdens with a war over the succession to the Duchy of Mantua. The bellicose Olivares thwarted Spinola's attempts at diplomacy in the Netherlands, where military prospects darkened, and posted him to another quagmire: the defense against partisan uprisings and French advances in northern Italy. Spinola was appointed as plenipotentiary (i.e., with full powers as prerogative) and general. He sailed to Genoa in September 1629. At the suggestion of Rubens, Velázquez sailed with him to study the famous artworks in Italy.[26] The two men forged a deep friendship. In addition to his own vivid memories, Velázquez may have sketched Spinola on that trip and used the drawings subsequently for *The Surrender of Breda*.[27]

Velázquez headed straight for Venice, where he deepened his understanding of such masters as Titian, Tintoretto, and Veronese, whom he had first encountered in the collections assembled by Philip II. There and in Rome he procured antiquities and additional paintings for Philip IV. During his year in Rome, Velázquez probably met Bernini, and also the French artists Poussin and Lorrain, under whose influence he lightened his palette. Studying Michelangelo helped him master anatomy, complementing his facility with faces. (When goaded by the king that his critics claimed he could paint only heads, Velázquez is reported to have answered: "Sire, they favor me greatly, for I don't know anyone who can paint a head.")[28]

The animosity of Olivares dogged Spinola in Italy, where the Count-Duke's father, Don Enrique de Guzmán y Ribera, was the Spanish ambassador to Rome and caused Spinola's powers as plenipotentiary to be withdrawn. Already sixty-one years old and barely a year into his foredoomed mission, Spinola's health broke down and he died on September 25, 1630, at the Siege of Casale, muttering the words "honor" and "reputation." The title of Marquis of Los Balbases, still borne by his descendants in Spain, was all that he received for the vast fortune his family expended in the service of Philip III and Philip IV. Olivares expressed irritation at Spinola's poorly timed death, and Spain's circumstances in the Low Countries deteriorated rapidly. Velázquez's biographer Carl Justi observed, "The artist must have been more deeply affected by the tragic result of the siege of Casale, which occurred soon after the voyage—Spinola was shamefully sacrificed; and how, mortified at the slur cast on his military honor, he soon sank with gloomy thoughts into the grave."[29] Velázquez painted his tribute five years after Spinola's death.

Truth and Honor

Within the context of the Salón de Reinos, *The Surrender of Breda* represents one of a dozen triumphs for the Spanish crown. The paintings function as a group to assert the invincibility of Spain and the Catholic Church. In fact, there is little to distinguish this victory from the others represented. Its significance lies in how the artist characterized the event.

In contrast to Rubens' use of myth and allegory to embellish and glorify Marie de' Medici, Velázquez reconstructed the historical event to emphasize its human reality.[30] Nevertheless, it is highly unlikely that the personal encounter between the two commanders transpired exactly as represented. Velázquez's astonishing skill is revealed in his ability to transform viewers into observers of a seemingly impromptu encounter. Not present at either the siege or the surrender himself, Velázquez consulted eyewitness accounts and maps and engravings of the city and battlefield.[31] His naturalistic style—especially apparent in the muted earth tones and soft light—can mislead us into believing that the painting is an entirely faithful reproduction of the event rather than the artist's imaginative reenactment. His main demonstrable invention is placing the surrender on a hill affording a panoramic view with Breda in the distance, where in reality the terrain is low and watery. Accounts verify that the remaining Dutch garrison marshaled an impressive show before the fairly disheveled victors; but to serve Philip's propagandistic program, Velázquez reversed their states, portraying the Dutch as shabby and the Spanish as smart.

Spinola is depicted accurately as far as his portrait is concerned. Velázquez emphasized the general with attributes like his splendid armor, commander's baton, and a bright magenta sash reminiscent of the vividly colored costumes in Uccello's *The Battle of San Romano*, but his figure is not represented as of unusually large stature, nor as an image of special strength and prowess—the standard trappings of military commemorations. Velázquez instead enhanced Spinola's character by showing his leadership defined by his generous demeanor. The artist's relationship with Spinola bestows the painting with another dimension of historical accuracy. Spinola's memories of the battle, shared with the artist during their travels, contributed to the empathy Velázquez brought to the painting; his intimate knowledge of Spinola's role in the siege makes it an especially important commentary. Velázquez was deeply affected by Spinola's death and sought to restore his late friend's reputation. He "desired in his modest way to raise a monument to one of the most humane captains of the day, by giving permanence to his true figure in a manner of which he alone had the secret."[32]

That Velázquez was able to break so clearly from the recurring pattern of the other battle scenes in the Salón de Reinos and, quite possibly, overcome objections from Olivares, speaks to the esteem in which he was held at court and his own powers of persuasion. He chose the event commemorated in *The Surrender of Breda* to tell the story of a compassionate meeting in the midst of the chaos and brutality of war. Velázquez demonstrates how a truly great leader emphasizes grace and magnanimity in victory rather than mere ferocity in combat. Spinola, the Spanish troops, and by extension Philip IV, are all epitomized as both powerful and admirable. In its original setting the painting was a rhetorical acclamation of Spanish national identity, a celebration of Philip IV and his army, but also an homage to Spinola, a personal friend of Velázquez who had died just a few years before its commission. Even today its representation of compassion evokes empathy in viewers differing from any response induced by the other paintings.

Rather than sustaining Spain's armies abroad, much of the nation's taxes were disbursed to give the impression that the Spanish empire was conquering its enemies on all fronts and that the forces of Catholicism were triumphing over heretical Protestants, and to reinforce the impression that everything *va bien* at home. Within a generation the claims would prove false, while impoverished Spain persisted in living in the memory of its *Siglo de Oro*. In the end, it would be the style of Rubens—especially when made academically "correct" through the application of the purist rigor of Poussin and artistic theory derived from Alberti—that directed the development of the genre of history painting throughout the century, most likely because that style was also applicable to representing religious subjects in the service of the other great patron of the age.

11

The Death of General Wolfe

Fashioning Imperial and Colonial Identities in the Americas

Conflicts over religion and succession continued into the eighteenth century as Spain's glory faded and the English, Dutch, and French vied to establish their colonial empires. During the Seven Years' War (the North American campaign is known as the French and Indian War) the struggle between France and Britain for dominance in North America led the French army, accompanied by First Peoples allies, to make forays into territories claimed by both powers. In bold response British Secretary of State William Pitt the Elder decided to send Major-General James Wolfe to take Québec in New France (now Québec province), the easternmost stronghold defending the St. Lawrence River, the gate to extensive interior waterways. No battle of the war was more important than the Battle of the Plains of Abraham, where Wolfe lost his life but won for Britain dominion over the vast interior of North America. The exploitation of new lands and their resources gave rise to new fortunes, hastening power shifts that gave groups other than crown and clergy a say in what subjects were worthy of remembrance, and how. Benjamin West's commemoration of Wolfe's death demonstrates how those groups employed historical subjects to promote modern colonial and imperial ideologies (Fig. 11.1).

The Siege of Québec

Wolfe assembled his army In Nova Scotia. He expected to lead a promised force of 12,000 men, but was given only 400 officers, 7,000 regular troops, and 300 gunners.[1] After numerous delays, Wolfe finally made his way up the St. Lawrence with only part of his force, leaving orders for the rest to follow later. He arrived at Québec in June 1759 and laid siege to the city. Throughout the summer the French forces refused to engage the British. As autumn approached, Wolfe grew impatient, recognizing that he had to take Québec before the St. Lawrence froze and trapped his men with their ice-bound ships. General Amherst's slow advance toward Montreal ruled out any prospect Wolfe had of receiving aid from him. The French prepared to defend Québec from the south and east, believing that the St. Lawrence would prove impassable and prevent a British approach from any other direction. Wolfe devised a daring plan: he would send a force upriver to the less protected

Power, Image, and Memory. Peter J. Holliday, Oxford University Press. © Oxford University Press 2024.
DOI: 10.1093/oso/9780190901080.003.0012

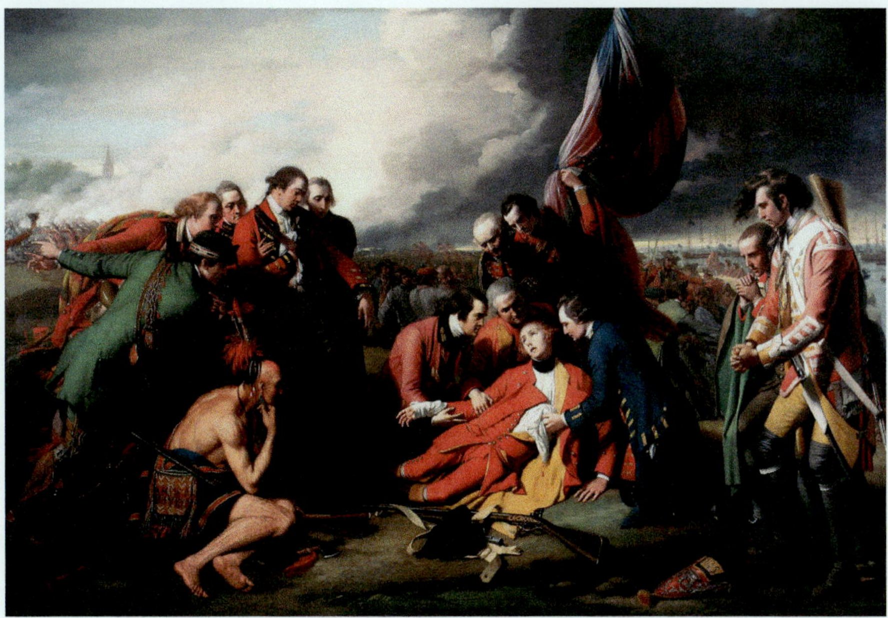

Fig. 11.1 Benjamin West, *The Death of General Wolfe* (1770). Ottawa, National Gallery of Canada. Photo: Wikimedia Commons

western side of the city and, in the dark of night, climb the sheer cliffs to attack the exposed French defenders. On the morning of September 13, 4,400 men in small boats landed at the base of the cliffs and successfully scaled them, hauling two small cannons. Fearing that the British would haul up more cannons and destroy the city's remaining defenses, the French commander, the Marquis de Montcalm, engaged the British outside the city on the Plains of Abraham where Wolfe had massed seven battalions. When Wolfe began to advance, he received musket-ball wounds in the arm, in the shoulder, and mortally in the chest. Within fifteen minutes the battle was over.

Francis Parkman described the death of Wolfe in *Montcalm and Wolfe*, the sixth volume of his monumental seven-volume *France and England in North America* (itself an expression of imperialism):

> They asked him [Wolfe] if he would have a surgeon; but he shook his head, and answered that all was over with him. His eyes closed with the torpor of approaching death, and those around sustained his fainting form. Yet they could not withhold their gaze from the wild turmoil before them, and the charging ranks of their companions rushing through the line of fire and smoke.
>
> "See how they run," one of the officers exclaimed, as the French fled in confusion before the leveled bayonets.
>
> "Who run?" demanded Wolfe, opening his eyes like a man aroused from sleep.
>
> "The enemy, sir," was the reply; "they give way everywhere."

> "Then," said the dying general, "tell Colonel River to cut off their retreat from the bridge. Now, God be praised, I die contented," he murmured; and, turning on his side, he calmly breathed his last breath.[2]

Montcalm died from wounds the next day, and the city, with only three days' provisions left, surrendered on September 17.

Wolfe's audacious triumph at Québec enabled Amherst's decisive assault on Montreal the following September, ending French control in North America outside of Louisiana and the small islands of Saint-Pierre and Miquelon. When news of the victory at Québec reached England it sparked a period of fervid nationalism. Popular sentiment, fed by the London press, demanded that Wolfe's heroism be commemorated with a monument in Westminster Abbey; King George II offered to pay for it, but signaling the era's changing power structures, Pitt promptly declared that Parliament would finance the memorial for the British people.[3] Yet it was Benjamin West's rendering of Wolfe's triumph that became iconic. Working within—and, at least by his own account, against—longstanding artistic conventions, it brought the painter fame and put North America on the artistic map.

The "American Raphael"

Benjamin West was born a colonial subject near Springfield, Pennsylvania. At seventy-eight he collaborated with John Galt—tellingly, a novelist—on a memoir, *The Life and Studies of Benjamin West*.[4] West dictated a series of interesting but questionable anecdotes to Galt, such as how First Peoples showed an adolescent West how to make paint by mixing riverbank clay with bear grease in a pot. (This yarn would not be the last time West played to Europeans' fascination with First Peoples.) Supporting himself painting portraits for Pennsylvania sitters, he worked from an engraving illustrating Charles Rollin's *Ancient History* to paint a history painting, the *Death of Socrates* (1756), which has been declared "the most ambitious and interesting painting produced in colonial America."[5] The work's renown facilitated introductions to prominent Philadelphians, including John Wollaston and Benjamin Franklin; Franklin stood as the godfather of West's second son, Franklin.

In 1760, through the assistance of wealthy Philadelphia patrons, West undertook a Grand Tour of Italy. In Rome he met the international group of Neoclassical painters—the style that began to dominate artistic practice—in the circle of the J. J. Winckelmann, which included fellow-German Anton Rafael Mengs, the Scott Gavin Hamilton, and the Austrian Angelica Kauffmann.[6] Responding to a beauty he found both physical and moral, Winckelmann argued that society should return to the values of classical art, asserting: "The only way for us to become great, perhaps inimitable, is by imitating the ancient."[7] His theory of a nonpareil Greek art nurtured by freedom of thought profoundly influenced contemporary Enlightenment views.

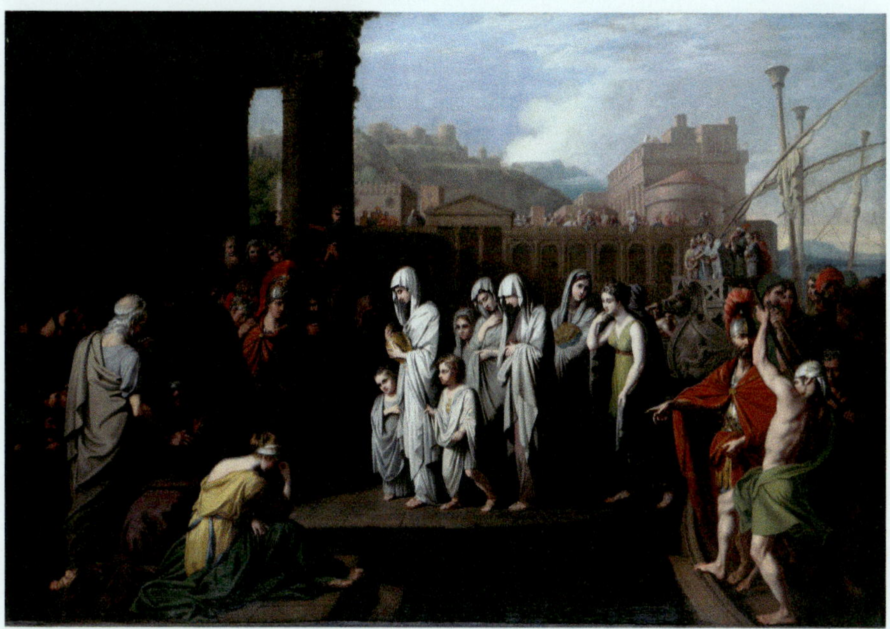

Fig. 11.2 Benjamin West, *Agrippina Landing at Brundisium with the Ashes of Germanicus* (1768). New Haven, CT, Yale University Art Gallery. Photo: Wikimedia Commons

In 1763, West reached London just when many of his American friends and financial sponsors arrived, and soon gained widespread popularity there as a portraitist.

West secured his reputation in 1768 with *Agrippina Landing at Brundisium with the Ashes of Germanicus* (Fig. 11.2) His depiction of an ancient *exemplum* for modern emulation follows Winckelmann's prescription to the letter. The painting's moralizing narrative operates on multiple levels. There is the backstory of a Roman hero who sacrificed his life for his country, treacherously assassinated by a jealous rival, and more immediately the representation of his widow's courageous display of stoic dignity in the face of tragedy as she carries her husband's ashes in a cinerary urn accompanied by her grieving children.[8] West's theatrical arrangement echoes Baroque practice, with light from outside the frame raking across the primary figures at center stage bordered by supporting players. That frieze-like group reproduces the planar layout of classicizing painters like Poussin, but West enhanced the scene's authenticity by basing the figures on a published detail of the imperial family from the *Ara Pacis Augustae*, emphasizing his classical source through its monochromatic tonality.[9] The arcade in the background derives from Robert Adam's illustrated *Ruins of the Palace of the Emperor Diocletian at Spalato* (1764), and the triangularly composed grieving group on the left is reminiscent of classical pedimental sculpture.[10] Jules Prown claims West's *Agrippina* "prefigures French Neoclassicism, notably the paintings of Jacques-Louis David, in the political implication of its call for a change in the values and standards of contemporary society, in its concern for historical accuracy and realism, and in the new classicism of its sculptural, coloristically muted style."[11]

An autodidact, West was highly aware of academic teaching and knew Jonathan Richardson's *An Essay on the Theory of Painting*, the first major work of art theory in English, which argued that the painter who aspired to paint history well must command the subject as completely as the historian, and know "the habits, customs, buildings, etc. of the age and country in which the thing was transacted more exactly than the other needs to know 'em."[12] Even before executing the first sketch, an artist should prepare by writing down the story "and give it all the beauty of description with an account of what is said and whatever else he would relate were he only to make a written history."[13] *Agrippina* shows how West had grasped all the factual details of the event he depicts—including supplementary information regarding dress, architecture, and embellishments—that Richardson argues makes any historical representation faithful to its era, whether ancient or modern. West also embraced Richardson's second imperative: the artist must "consider how to improve [the painted subject] keeping within the bounds of probability."[14]

West deployed compositional schemes disclosing expressive figures and colors in what he called "epic representation." His assimilation of classical sculpture elevated Agrippina and her family above the mundane and rendered the scene more substantial to contemporary viewers. Sir Joshua Reynolds would describe such practice in his *Discourses* as the "Great Style" where "invention, strictly speaking, is little more than a new combination of those images which have been previously gathered and deposited in the memory. Nothing can come of nothing."[15] West became an intimate of Reynolds, and in 1768 helped him convince George II to establish a Royal Academy based on French and Italian models.[16] He later gained the friendship and patronage of George III, who in 1772 appointed West historical painter to the court. England hailed West as the "American Raphael."

A Secular Lamentation

With *The Death of General Wolfe* (1770), West again conducted the painstaking research and careful planning urged by Richardson to compose a convincing account of the battle, a remarkable continuous narrative within in a single frame focusing on the death of Wolfe as the climactic moment (Fig. 11.1). For the setting West referred to sketches of Québec prepared by draftsmen and engineers within the corps of British field officers, echoing the designer of Trajan's Column and Velázquez; contemporary Britons were thereby apprised of the distant lands now under their control. At the same time, his representation had to be more than a mere transcription of details. According to West, "It must exhibit the event in a way to excite awe & veneration & that which may be required to give superior interest to the representation must be introduced, all that can show the importance of the Hero. Wolfe must not die like a common soldier under a Bush . . . To move the mind there should be a spectacle presented to raise & warm the mind & all should be proportioned to the highest idea conceived of the Hero. A mere matter of fact will never produce this effect."[17] West wanted to fashion a kind of historical fiction that mixed fact and fabrication; not accurate, perhaps, but plausible and eloquent.

His study of old masters taught West how to edit, tighten, and clarify his compositions to tell a story cogently. He again arranges the figures theatrically, with the main drama at the center stage flanked by supporting players. He mastered figural anatomy and expression, and how to use body language—*attitudes*, in eighteenth-century parlance—that are readily understood (instructions from Alberti that were central to academic practice). To heighten its dramatic impact, West suffused the painting with visual references that thrilled knowledgeable eighteenth-century viewers. The figures appropriate the stances of classical heroes and Christian saints from older, well-known works; yet they also express individuality and genuine feeling of personal distress, thereby adding something fresh to artistic tradition. Although all this may strike us today as artificial, at that time "artificiality" had positive connotations, artifice denoting that something was artfully made, not literal but ingenious, pleasing, and effective.

West staged the event as a secular Lamentation scene. Wolfe takes on the pose of the dying Christ, the body elegantly swerved, the draped flag behind him recalling numerous compositions of the descent from the cross. He famously went into battle armed as his men were, and here wears a fairly simple red coat, waistcoat, and breeches and a modest white shirt; before him on the ground lie his musket, cartridge box, and bayonet. In a detail recalling Baroque conventions, Wolfe raises his eyes heavenward, the source of salvation. The canvas strikes the viewer initially as a monoscenic composition focused on the Wolfe's gripping death, but upon closer inspection one discerns that within the fog of war from which that central tableaux emerges West has managed to compress all the major events of the day. The battle itself is pushed to the background, as in *The Surrender of Breda*. At the right several warships anchor on the river while the troops they carried ascend the cliffs. To the left of the central group an advancing runner waves his hat to attract their attention and carries a captured flag to reveal the French defeat to the dying Wolfe. Québec lies in the distance, with columns of smoke rising from fires scattered about the landscape. The dissolving smoke allows a heavenly light that unifies the composition by illuminating the temporal martyr yet also revealing a steeple: the symbol of both Wolfe's salvation and the righteousness of the British cause.[18] The painting suggests how notions of divine right were passing from the person of the king to the body of the nation.

Although imposing religious subjects had not figured in the cultural memory of Protestant England or America, during the eighteenth century devotional artworks poured into England as a result of Grand Tourists and wealthy connoisseurs acquiring works of Italian masters as well as classical antiquities with a zeal equaling that of ancient Romans' desire for Greek art.[19] Moreover, Enlightenment viewers did not need to share the beliefs contained in a work's religious imagery to appreciate its significance. The grand manner was an art *about* art that augmented the enjoyment of a picture for knowledgeable viewers who were able to discern the sacred subtext within the contemporary text, a strategy that enhanced the telling of a story by deepening its meaning. This method not only provided aesthetic pleasure but also raised the contemporary subject to the level of classical art without recourse to the inflated rhetoric of Baroque allegory.[20] Viewers steeped in the classicism of the age might have seen West as embodying explicitly Virgilian virtues of duty and sacrifice, transforming Wolfe's death from a mere casualty of war into a heroic sacrifice for the British cause.

Like the Chorus of a Greek tragedy, the mourners' expressions of pain and sorrow comment on and amplify the action and prompt the viewer how to respond to the hero's sacrifice. There is nothing excessive or self-indulgent in their noble attitudes; rather, they demonstrate the self-mastery commended by Winckelmann. They are named warriors like the heroes in the *Iliad* who sought glory at far-off Troy. Brigadier General Robert Monckton, Wolfe's deputy, was severely wounded in the battle.[21] The curious rendering of his limp left arm, which hangs loosely over the arm of the figure supporting him, evokes a fainting Mary Magdalen.[22] Dr. Thomas Hinde, the kneeling figure in the blue jacket, attempts to staunch the bleeding from Wolfe's wounds; Captain Hervey Smith holds Wolfe's right arm;[23] Robert Rogers wears green;[24] and Simon Fraser of Lovat, Lieutenant Colonel of the 78th Fraser Highlanders, is dressed in the Fraser tartan worn by officers in that regiment.[25] The grenadier at the right foreground represents the mourning of the common soldier, wringing his hands like St. John the Evangelist. West modeled his facial expression, down to the inclination of the head and the cascading hair, after the type for "compassion" in Charles le Brun's treatise.[26]

His regiment played a crucial role throughout Wolfe's campaigns, but Fraser, recovering from wounds received earlier, was not present at the battle. In fact, no evidence supports the presence of any of the other prominent figures portrayed surrounding Wolfe; since they were all senior military officials they would have been engaged elsewhere during the siege. Even more problematic is the contemplative Indigenous warrior. None fought with the British forces at Québec, a fact West acknowledged soon after completing the painting. Artistically, the figure demonstrates West's iconographical finesse by placing the scene in the New World (new to Europeans) to thrill contemporary English viewers with what they would have perceived as an exotic element of local color, while also evoking another type for the mourning St. John. Although the crowded foreground was roundly decried for its historical inaccuracy, the modifications clearly demonstrate West's aspiration to achieve a more perfect truth by blending the literal and ideal in his art. Representing these figures together suggests the diversity and geographic breadth of the emerging British Empire.

West depicts the nearly nude warrior with anthropological precision: he is identified as an Iroquois by his distinctive trade blanket, hunting pouch, and body paint.[27] His torsional pose—kneeling with his chin on his fist, gazing at Wolfe—derives from the *Belvedere Torso*, one of the most esteemed antiquities in art history (Fig. 11.3).[28] The artistic convention of touching one's face with one's hand

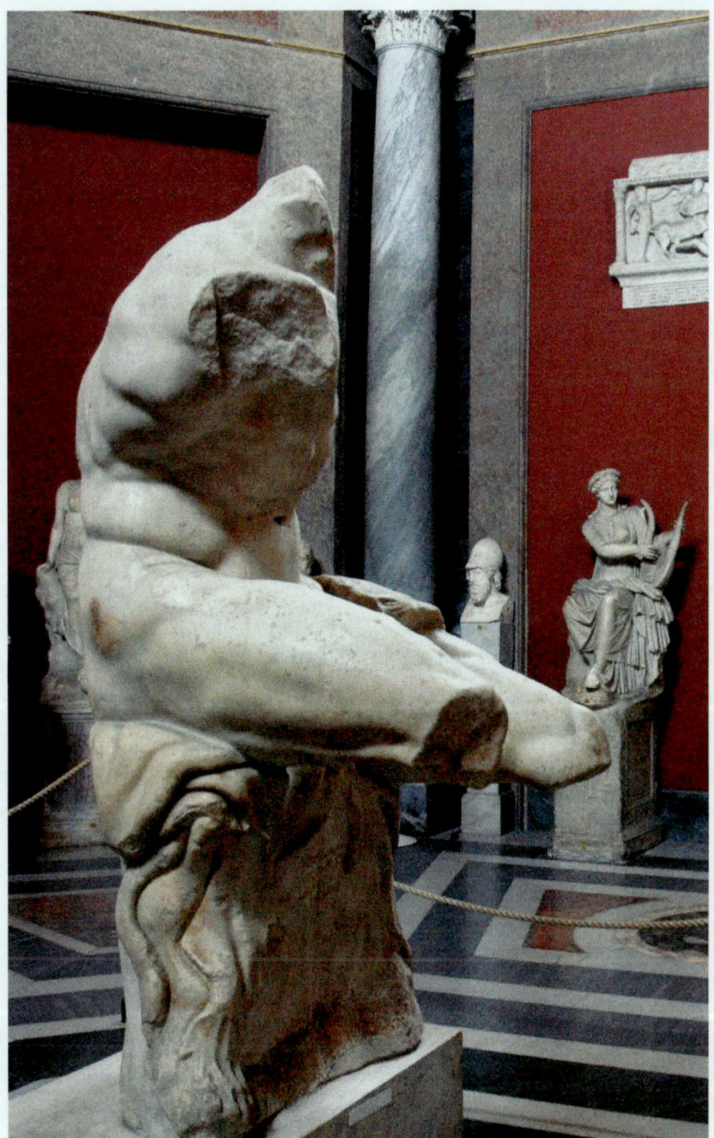

Fig. 11.3 Apollonius of Athens, *Belvedere Torso* (first century BCE or AD copy of an early second-century BCE original). Vatican, Pio-Clementino Museum. Photo: author

traditionally connotes deep thought and intelligence, traits emphasizing the figure's nobility and suggesting that he embodies the "noble savage."[29] In his pamphlet, *Remarks Concerning the Savages of North America* (1784), West's American compatriot and fellow Quaker Benjamin Franklin (who negotiated with the First Peoples during the French and Indian War), deplored the use of the term: "Savages we call them, because their manners differ from ours, which we think the perfection of civility; they think the same of theirs."[30] When during his Roman sojourn West's was shown the famous *Apollo* also in the Belvedere courtyard, he exclaimed: "My God, how like it is to a young Mohawk warrior."[31] Here West again reveals that Winckelmann's classical ideal flourished in the perceived rudeness of North America.

Yet however progressive according to the conventions of eighteenth-century discourse, these appraisals are less than satisfactory for viewers today, who cannot help but read the display of the nearly naked body opposed to the clothed Europeans through the lens of postcolonialism and find them simplistic and reductive. Vivian Fryd observes that in contrast to the action and commitment demonstrated by the British soldiers, both the Indigenous warrior and Wolfe are inactive and thus passive, "qualities that are coded as feminine."[32] Whereas Wolfe is "unmanned" by his impending death, posing the warrior seated on the ground disrupts the masculine potential of his body and places him in a secondary position, subservient to British dominance. In fact, West's allusions to classical antiquity can be seen as a strategy that however well-intentioned, annihilates the warrior's authentic identity. Colonial stability required the cultural subordination of the nonwhite Other for transformation into the subaltern native.[33] Although he is not degraded like the nude barbarians depicted on the Stele of Naram-Sîn or Trajanic monuments, he is nevertheless represented as deserving of being dominated, effectively inviting the colonizer to civilize—educate, convert, and otherwise culturally assimilate—him into the empire. Represented as a British ally, he facilitates his new identity as a colonial subject, displaced to the periphery of imperialism's geopolitical enterprise, an undertaking that not incidentally demanded the willing if occasional sacrifice of its perpetrators. At least, that is how a modern viewer might interpret him through our current ideological lenses.

"A Revolution in the Art"?

West claimed to break with contemporary academic conventions when he chose not to portray the event allegorically with the grandeur of a classical setting amidst gods and personifications, and that he was pressured by Reynolds and others to dress his figures in classical Roman clothing.[34] In Galt's biography, West purports to have responded: "The event intended to be commemorated took place on the 13th of September, 1758 [*sic*] in a region of the world unknown to the Greeks and Romans, and at a period of time when no such nations, nor heroes in their costume, any longer existed. The subject I have to represent is the conquest of a great province of America by the British troops. It is a topic that history will proudly record, and the same truth that guides the pen of the historian should govern the pencil of the artist. I consider myself as undertaking to tell this great event to the eye of the world; but if, instead of the facts of the transaction, I represent classical fictions, how shall I be understood by posterity!"[35] When Reynolds inspected the completed painting, Galt quotes West as saying that Reynolds exclaimed: "I foresee that this picture will not only become one of the most popular, but occasion a revolution in the art."

Whether Reynolds really ever said it would stimulate a "revolution in the art," the controversy West stirred generated publicity. Rather than transforming the practice of history painting, the work actually evidences changes already under way. Whereas nonreligious narrative paintings were overwhelmingly of classical subjects, like West's own *Agrippina*, painting postclassical history, particularly recent battle scenes, was by no means unusual, and frequently depicted dress contemporary to the event.[36] In fact, West was not the first to portray Wolfe in contemporary dress: several years earlier both George Romney and Edward Penny had publicly exhibited paintings portraying the same subject in a realistic style.[37] However, although the earlier representations had proved popular, West also wanted *official* recognition, exhibiting his painting at the recently founded Royal Academy in London. George III refused to purchase it, supposedly because the contemporary clothing was thought to compromise the dignity of the event.[38] In reality, by domesticating the classical and religious trappings of his hero, West ensured the success of his work by mediating between academic doctrines and popular taste.[39]

The Death of General Wolfe thereby became a national icon and created such a stir that five full-sized copies of it were eventually authorized.[40] West's mastery of the grand manner appealed to the cognoscenti, while his outwardly realistic commemoration of a modest man's heroism attracted a popular audience caught up in the enthusiasm for Britain's imperial agenda, which works like this helped generate. Cynthia Roman observes, "Resourceful artists adjusted to a shift from the patronage of great men and public institutions of government or religion to the patronage of anonymous customers, dealers, and publishers following the general commercial character of English culture."[41] A forerunner in the new consumer society of eighteenth-century Britain, West himself directed the production of an engraving after the painting by William Woollett, the most talented printmaker of the time. The result was a great commercial success and rendered West's painting one of the most popular images in England. With its dissemination the British public literally brought home an emblem of their proud new identity as citizens of a burgeoning military and economic empire.[42]

An American Contribution

Though loyal to America, West never returned. Gilbert Stuart and John Trumbull both worked in his London studio, ensuring that West exerted considerable influence on the development of art in America during the first decades of the nineteenth century. John Singleton Copley especially was impressed by West's realism. He arrived in England in 1774, aspiring like West before him to go beyond portraiture and become a history painter. Copley initially won recognition with his exhibition of *Watson and the Shark* at the Royal Academy in 1778 (Fig. 11.4).[43] The painting represents the extraordinary maiming of Brook Watson, a fourteen-year-old midshipman aboard one of his uncle's merchant ships. In 1749, while the vessel

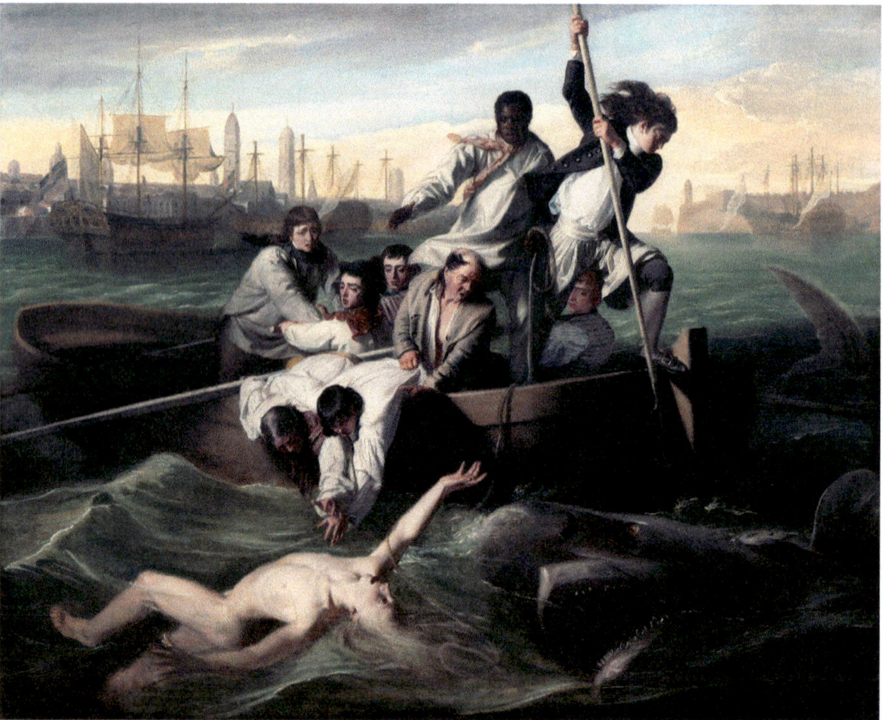

Fig. 11.4 John Singleton Copley, *Watson and the Shark* (1778). Washington, DC, National Gallery of Art. Photo: Wikimedia Commons

was anchored in Havana harbor, Watson went swimming and was attacked by a shark. On its first strike the shark removed the flesh from Watson's right leg below the calf; it then returned and bit off his right foot at the ankle. His shipmates rescued him, although his leg had to be amputated below the knee. Nevertheless, Watson persevered, prospered in colonial America and became a successful shipper himself and Lord Mayor of London.[44] He commissioned Copley to commemorate this harrowing event from his youth.[45]

Like West's *The Death of General Wolfe*, Copley portrayed a recent event set in the Americas. He incorporated such identifiable landmarks (known through engravings) as Morro Castle, the cathedral, and a convent's towers to provide an accurate view of Havana harbor. The figures represent diverse types—young and old, some simply dressed sailors, others more affluently (as implied by the metal buckles on the leather shoes of the harpooner)—to form a cross section of social ranks united in a common endeavor. Copley drew on all he had assimilated on his own Grand Tour. The composition binding the figures' frenzied activity recalls Raphael's cartoon for the *Miraculous Draught of Fishes* (Fig. 11.5), a touchstone in Reynolds's *Discourses*, and Rubens's rendering of the same theme (which echoes Raphael).[46] Rather than martyrdom, Copley's allusions to Christian art cast Watson's rescue as a contemporary tale of salvation. The harpooner recalls images of Saint George fighting the dragon or Saint Michael banishing Satan from heaven; the shark

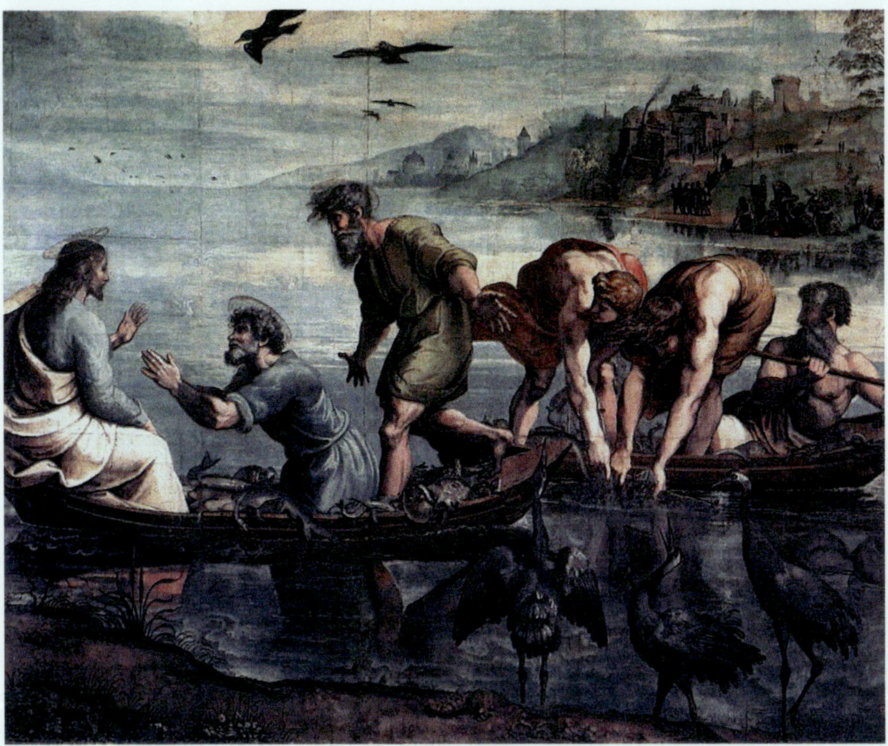

Fig. 11.5 Raphael, cartoon for *The Miraculous Draught of Fishes* (1515–1516). London, Victoria and Albert Museum. Photo: Wikimedia Commons

rising from the murky depths conjures evil incarnate, its open jaws analogous to the gaping mouth of hell. The figure of Watson copies the *Borghese Gladiator*, an esteemed antiquity that evoked the pitting of man against beast (Fig. 11.6).[47] These quotations from famous artworks cast an event otherwise deemed too personal and contemporary into a subject worthy of commemoration; at the same time, the sensationalism of Copley's subject and its sense of pending but uncertain impact reflect an eighteenth-century fascination with the exotic and the sublime that anticipate Romanticism's sensibilities.

Copley also enhanced the drama of his scene by referencing Le Brun's treatise on using the facial expressions to portray inner states, including dread (the sailor at the far left), astonishment (the older, balding sailor), and contempt (the harpooner aiming at the shark). Most striking, however, is the representation of a West African, who is given the expression Le Brun identifies as compassion; infrared analysis shows that this figure was initially painted as a white man with long, flowing hair.[48] He wears a red neck scarf and white, silky uniform that suggest that he may be in service to a nearby merchant. Standing near the center of the group on the rescue boat, he completes a compositional triangle with Watson and the shark; he is the only person who holds the towline that links the victim to the boat, giving him the main role in the rescue operation. It is a sympathetic portrayal: compared with

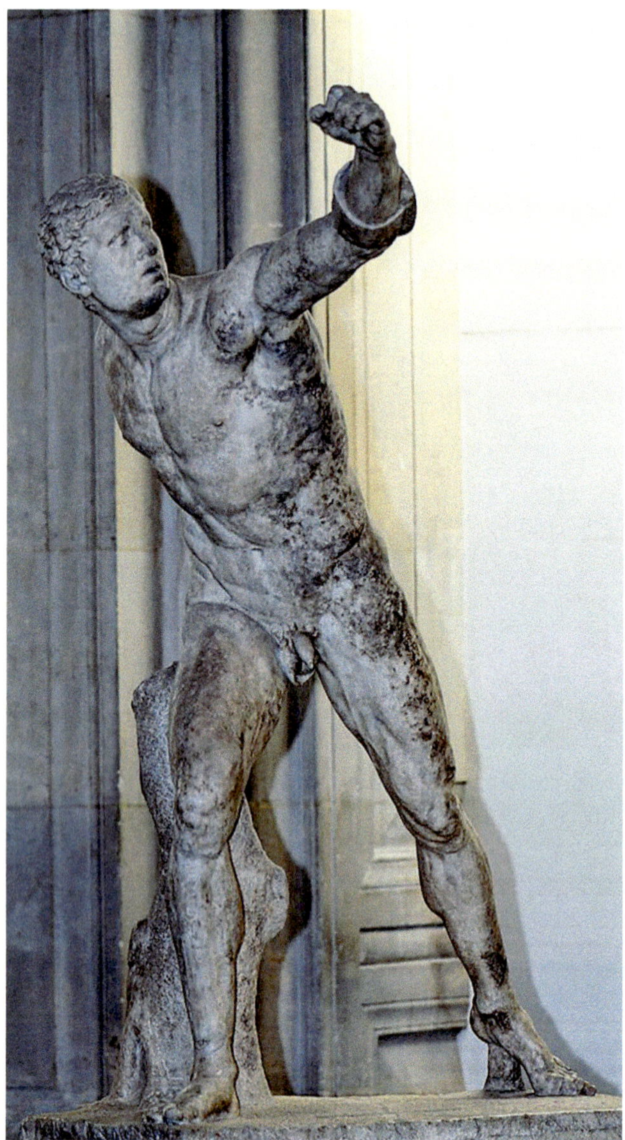

Fig. 11.6 Agasias of Ephesos, *Borghese Gladiator* (ca. 100 BCE). Paris, Musée du Louvre. Photo: author

other eighteenth-century and even many nineteenth-century images of Africans, he is both direct and dignified.

European exploitation of colonial resources included people and their labor; in reaction to these injustices of imperialism, the British abolitionist movement began about this time.[49] West enlarged the meaning of *The Death of General Wolfe* with the prominent depiction of a Indigenous warrior, and here Copley portrays a Black man as the pivotal figure in the scene; but whereas West had worked as an independent entrepreneur, Copley painted on commission from Watson, who certainly prompted how he represented the event. Watson may have had the figure of a Black man included to indicate his own abolitionist sympathies, and Copley's portrayal of the harpooner next to him as a secular saint vanquishing evil might underscore Watson's conviction in slavery's immorality. Watson left the painting to Christ's Hospital, a London school for disadvantaged youth, where Copley's unambiguous visual record of a physically disabled orphan who bore tragedy to become a man of wealth and political significance would offer "a most usefull [sic] Lesson to Youth";[50] its counsel about the injustice of slavery was no less edifying.[51]

Both West and Copley commemorate recent events to offer moral instruction in the service of the social order. Wolfe's sacrifice in the service of empire with stoic dignity and courage demonstrated how contemporary Britons could channel those ancient virtues.[52] Copley's portrayal of ordinary men in the midst of extraordinary circumstances showed how salvation can be found even in the pursuit of colonial enterprise. Their American origins may have made West and Copley react more sensitively and decisively to the emerging modern sensibilities of a flourishing middleclass that began to displace aristocratic patronage (even if artists hungered for its recognition), and their initial status as provincials may have made them more responsive to new modes of art-viewing and the changed character of its public. For all the conventional references to European artistic tradition, Jules Prown maintains that their innovative realism constitutes the first American contribution to Western art.[53] Perhaps, but the matter-of-factness of their representations also enhanced the perceived authenticity of the images, and thus their authority, complementing their ultimate commemorative purpose.

12

Guernica

Modernism and Picasso's Blasted Allegory

Following the close relationship in France between Napoleon and artists celebrating his exploits, the academy's grip on artistic practice loosened through the course of the nineteenth century. Challenging the bias of the annual salon (while at the same time craving inclusion in it), artists increasingly found support from the burgeoning middle class rather than aristocratic and institutional patronage. Changes in exhibition practices linked to a flourishing art market and the rise of avant-garde movements contributed to a general loss of interest in the previously dominant genre of history painting. The relevance of historical subjects in art did not, however, vanish entirely; rather, artists increasingly focused on issues of social justice linked with contemporary events. Those concerns frequently ran counter to the interests of dominant power structures, and the ensuing artworks performed as vehicles of criticism and protest rather than celebratory propaganda.

Protesting Imperial Adventures

The Greek War of Independence (1821–1829) stirred the sympathies of European and American artists and intellectuals much as the Spanish Civil War would a century later.[1] They were appalled by the 1822 Ottoman offensive against the island of Chios, which resulted in the deaths of 20,000 Greeks and the enslavement of the 70,000 survivors. Eugène Delacroix represented this horrific event to arouse fellow citizens and, hopefully, advance his career. *The Massacre at Chios* (1824) portrays the plight of ordinary people caught up in extraordinary events (Fig. 12.1). Delacroix's visual language puts across his message clearly and forcefully. He began with a powerful structure: Delacroix arranged his figures—thirteen men, women, and children assembled for either slaughter or enslavement—in two triangles to the left and right of the canvas, a seemingly incongruous layout of which he wrote: "One must fill up; if it is less natural, it will be more beautiful and *fécond*. Would that everything should hold together!"[2] His color and brushwork complement the subject matter.[3] Delacroix's figures lack the muscular anatomy of academically conceived bodies, but they stand out from the mass, their gestures broad and easy to read.[4] The disparate displays of exotic and colorful costumes, suffering and disease, terror and

Power, Image, and Memory. Peter J. Holliday, Oxford University Press. © Oxford University Press 2024.
DOI: 10.1093/oso/9780190901080.003.0013

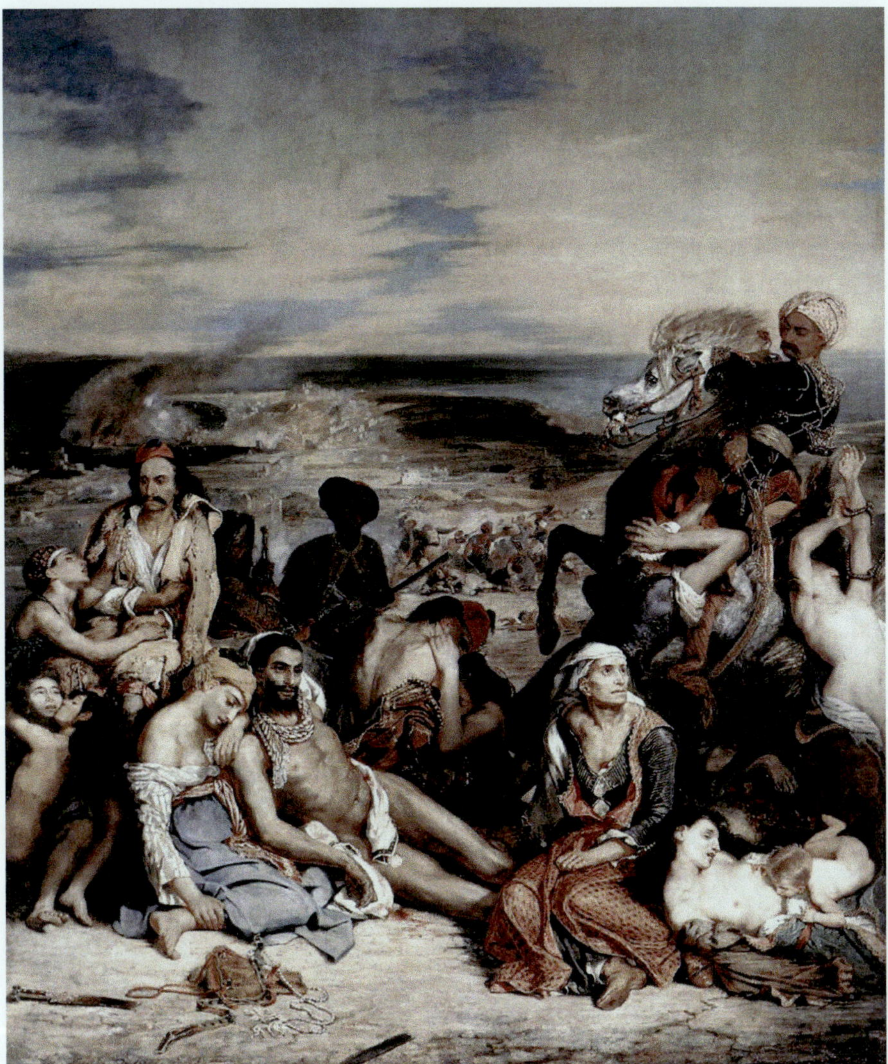

Fig. 12.1 Eugène Delacroix: *Massacre at Chios* (1824). Paris, Musée du Louvre. Photo: Wikimedia Commons

death all appealed to the Romantic sensibility, and also contested the traditional role historical subjects had played in supporting the powerful. The anonymous victims cut across class and other lines. There is no hope, no hero or charismatic leader depicted, only the plight of civilians facing the horrors of wartime destruction. War is shown as failure, the consequence of hubris, not a glorious triumph of state policy.

Although Romantic artists like Delacroix continued to regard history painting as the epitome for their most ambitious works, its practice underwent profound changes. The Enlightenment had undermined the Catholic Church's claim to moral authority, greatly reducing its demand for large group scenes from the Bible and other traditional religious paintings, and revolutionary ideologies challenged the political authority of *anciens régimes*. Free citizens were less inclined (consciously) to have their identities shaped than obedient subjects had been. Now the powerful appeared (and often were) incompetent and oppressive, and war often seemed senseless. But representations of historical events that attacked the established order or exhibited radical departures in style were as threatening to bourgeois as they were to elite sensibilities. There was a growing preference for narrative subjects drawn from historical literature and events from distant lands rather than themes celebrating the dubious achievements of contemporary leaders. Such scenes were expected to be as carefully researched as earlier history paintings had been, using the work of historians of architecture, costume, and other elements of décor to produce convincing scenes.[5] Artists like Paul Delaroche, José Moreno Carbonero, and Richard Parkes Bonington practiced what became known as *genre historique* or *peinture anecdotique*.

After French intervention in Mexico led to the unseating of President Benito Juárez, Napoleon III convinced Maximilian, an Austrian aristocrat, to head the short-lived Second Mexican Empire (1861–1867). Maximilian reached Mexico in 1864 but was immediately opposed by forces loyal to Juárez. The Empire collapsed when Napoleon withdrew French troops in 1866. After his capture in 1867, Maximilian was tried and executed by firing squad together with two trusted generals. Evidently an honorable man, his execution stirred up European—and even Mexican—emotions favorable to Maximilian and hostility toward an unethical French government.[6] Édouard Manet shared the general outrage, and despite the threat of government censorship, he proceeded to paint three large canvases capturing the *Execution of Maximilian* (Fig. 12.2).[7] Each painting represents the firing squad at the moment of discharge. Manet researched a number of different sources: early newspaper stories, photographs, and finally authoritative eyewitness accounts provided by artists and officers returned from Mexico. Yet details are arrayed to reinforce potential political significance as much as appeal to authenticity: in the Boston version Juarista soldiers wear the clothes and sombrero of the Mexican Republicans to whom Manet was sympathetic; in the final version in Mannheim, they wear nineteenth-century field dress, so widespread among contemporary armies that the soldiers could easily be mistaken for being French, an ambiguity with obvious partisan implications.[8] Manet also draws on earlier works of art, emphasizing Maximillian's martyrdom by positioning him between the two generals like Christ between the two thieves. He clearly evokes the composition of Goya's *Third of May, 1808* (Fig. 12.3); however, Manet's paintings eschew Goya's passion and terror in favor of a more straightforward portrayal, a chilling detachment that speaks to Napoleon's abandonment of Maximilian and underscores the French government's treachery and deception. In Stephen Bann's assessment, "In commemorating the fall of one emperor Manet was covertly castigating the policies of the other."[9] The compressed rendering of pictorial space in all three versions is unreal; it creates a focus on perception that represents a

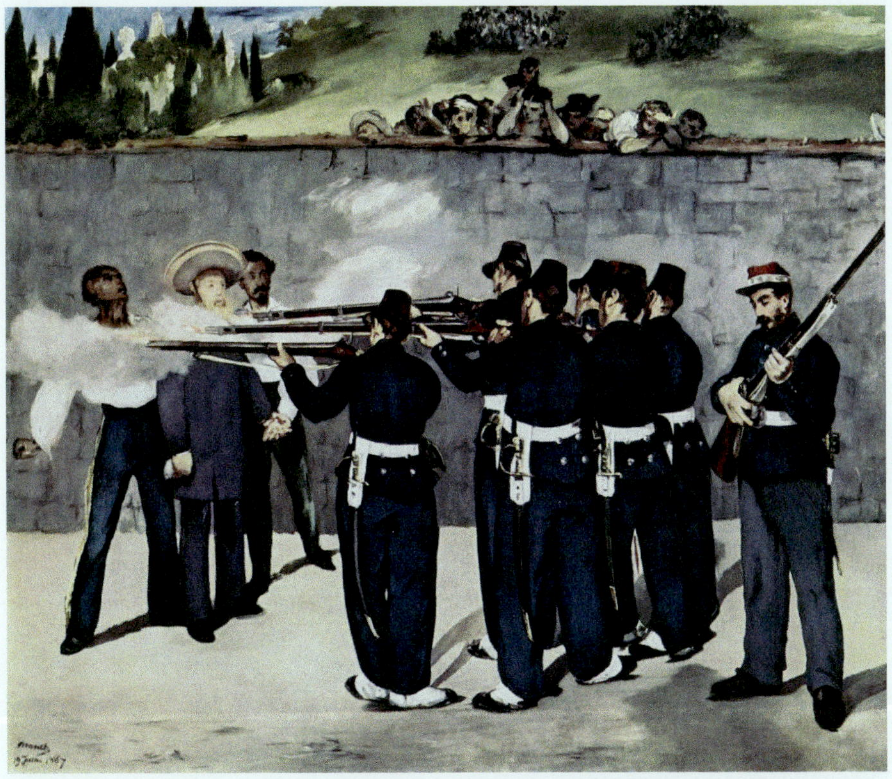

Fig. 12.2 Edouard Manet: *The Execution of Emperor Maximilian* (1868–1869). Kunsthalle Mannheim. Photo: Wikimedia Commons

modernity that leaves traditional narrative behind in the search for a new way of picturing the present.

Ruling elites—the primary patrons for the historical subjects examined in this study—continued to commission historical commemorations in the hope of legitimating their authority and validating their policies;[10] overwhelmingly conservative, they tended to prefer objective imagery to persuade citizens and to counter subversive narratives like Manet's. Nevertheless, historical subjects ceased to be the dominant artistic theme they had once been, and henceforth few important examples were produced. Perhaps the last great realistic picture of war is John Singer Sargent's stunning *Gassed* (Fig. 12.4) The British War Memorials Committee commissioned Sargent to create a heroic war painting, but he was unable to find anything heroic—at least as traditionally understood—to paint.[11] He wrote to Evan Charteris:

> The Ministry of Information expects an epic—and how can one do an epic without masses of men? Excepting at night I have only seen three fine subjects with masses of men—one a harrowing sight, a field full of gassed and blindfolded men—another a train of trucks packed with "*chair à cannon*"—and another frequent

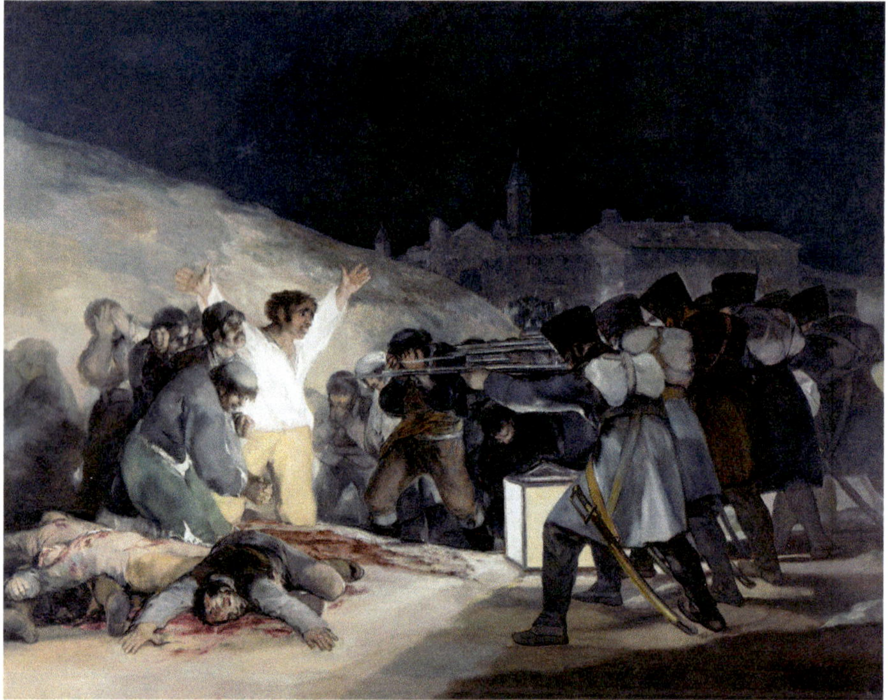

Fig. 12.3 Francisco Goya, *The Third of May, 1808*. Madrid, Museo del Prado. Photo: Wikimedia Commons

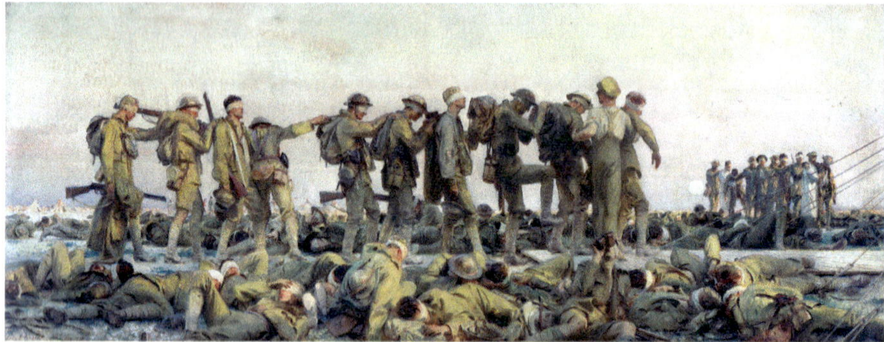

Fig. 12.4 John Singer Sargent, *Gassed* (1918–1919). London, Imperial War Museum. Photo: Wikimedia Commons

> sight a big road encumbered with troops and traffic, I daresay the latter, combining English and Americans, is the best thing to do, if it can be prevented from looking like going to the Derby.[12]

It was on an excursion near Arras in 1918 that Sargent caught sight of the column of soldiers blinded by mustard gas fumbling toward a dressing station, the subject he ultimately chose.[13] He depicted a horizontal queue of eleven nearly life-size anonymous soldiers, the wounded assisted by orderlies, walking along a duck-board toward a dressing station; a similar group advances in the background. There is nothing to distinguish the barren landscape, which has been wiped out by the weapons of mechanized war more thoroughly than Darius's orders to clear the plain at Gaugamela. At nine feet high and twenty feet long, its large scale—which evokes Uccello's *The Battle of San Romano* triptych—and lack of centralized subject make the sightlines fragment, thwarting the viewer from taking it all in at once. The composition makes reference to Pieter Bruegel's *Parable of the Blind Leading the Blind* (1568), which draws on Christ's admonition, "If the blind lead the blind, both shall fall into the ditch" (Matthew 15:14). Formally, however, it recalls ancient Greek temple friezes; David Lubin describes how its understated treatment of the victims with unsentimental compassion "smacks of Greek tragedy, where men suffer blindness, madness, and agonizing death at the whim of indifferent gods."[14] Sargent's portrayal of the hopeless desolation of World War I was Picture of the Year at the Royal Academy in 1919.

Kurt Schwitters responded to the war by making assemblages: nonobjective works made of fragments; he felt there was no possibility of a meaningful pictorial narrative in response to the stupidity of war. Marcel Duchamp played chess. Marsden Hartley painted personal memorials to a soldier who died for Germany. In Paris, Pablo Picasso was still working out his private revolution in painting. After a visit to Spain in 1934 he never returned. Nevertheless, the Prado Museum named him honorary director-in-exile. In January 1937, the Spanish Republican government commissioned him to paint a large work for the Spanish Pavilion at the Paris International Exposition. He chose to depict his recurrent theme of the artist's studio and worked on the commission disinterestedly from January until late April.[15]

"Completely Destroyed"

The Spanish Civil War (1936–1939) was fought between the Republican forces and General Francisco Franco's Nationalists, who were supported by Nazi Germany. The Nationalists sought to return Spain to a pre-Republican state of "law and order" founded on traditional Catholic values. The Basque town of Guernica, the northern bastion of Republican resistance, stood at a major juncture just 6 miles (10 km) from the front lines. Most of the town's men had left to fight, leaving behind mostly women and children.[16] The German guideline for tactical bombing deemed all routes for transporting troop and materiel to be legitimate military targets; being a hub of Basque culture increased Guernica's importance as an attractive Nationalist target.

At approximately 4:30 p.m. on Monday, April 26, 1937, German military planes commanded by Colonel Wolfram von Richthofen bombed Guernica, supposedly to halt and disrupt the Republican retreat toward Bilbao, but which never passed through the town. In Hitler's *Blitzkrieg* plan of "total war" there were no civilians; the purpose of the attack, therefore, was entirely one of terrorization. For April 30, 1937, Richthofen wrote: "When the first Junkers squadron arrived, there was smoke already everywhere . . . nobody could identify the targets of roads, bridge, and suburb, and so they just dropped everything right into the center. The 250s toppled a number of houses and destroyed the water mains. The incendiaries now could spread and become effective. The materials of the houses: tile roofs, wooden porches, and half-timbering resulted in complete annihilation."[17] Accounts of survivors describe how people had gathered in the town center for market day, and once the bombing began found they could not escape as rubble filled the roads and the bridges leading out of town were demolished. The bombing lasted for almost two hours.

On April 28, the Republican sympathizer George Steer brought the event to the world's attention with his eyewitness account:

> Guernica, the most ancient town of the Basques and the centre of their cultural tradition, was completely destroyed yesterday afternoon by insurgent air raiders. The bombardment of this open town far behind the lines occupied precisely three hours and a quarter, during which a powerful fleet of aeroplanes consisting of three types of German types, Junkers and Heinkel bombers, did not cease unloading on the town bombs weighing from 1,000 lbs. downwards and, it is calculated, more than 3,000 two-pounder aluminium incendiary projectiles. The fighters, meanwhile, plunged low from above the centre of the town to machinegun those of the civilian population who had taken refuge in the fields. The whole town of Guernica was soon in flames, except the historic Casa de Juntas, with its rich archives of the Basque race, where the ancient Basque Parliament used to sit. The famous oak of Guernica, the dried stump of 600 years and the new shoots of this century, was also untouched. Here the kings of Spain used to take the oath to respect the democratic rights (*fueros*) of Vizcaya and in return received a promise of allegiance as suzerains with the democratic title of *Señor*, not *Rey Vizcaya*.[18]

When he first learned of the bombing, the Spanish poet Juan Larrea—a native of Bilbao—sought out Picasso in his studio to urge his fellow exile to make the assault the subject of his pavilion mural.[19] On April 29, Picasso read George Steer's report of the bombing in *L'Humanité*, which was headlined: "*MILLE BOMBES INCENDAIRES lances par les avions de Hitler et Mussolini*," accompanied by explicit photographs of the ravaged town and civilian casualties. According to the *Times*, "In the form of its execution and the scale of the destruction it wrought, no less than the selection of its objective, the raid on Guernica is unparalleled in military history."[20]

On May 1, Picasso abandoned his initial project and in a burst of creative energy started sketching a preliminary drawing for *Guernica*, his representation of the

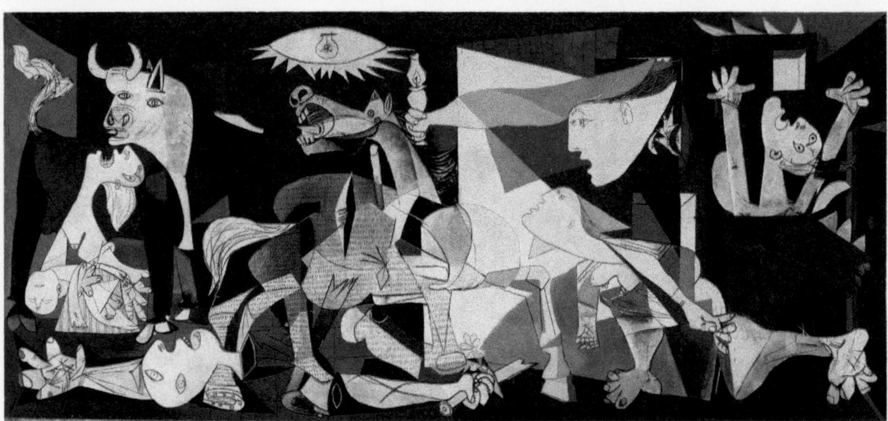

Fig. 12.5 Pablo Picasso, *Guernica* (1937). Madrid, Museo Reina Sofia. Photo: Wikimedia Commons

horrific slaughter in Spain that became an enduring indictment of fascism and the senselessness of war (Fig. 12.5).

Picasso's Process

The six weeks Picasso spent in preparing and executing *Guernica* are among the most rigorously documented for any commission in art history. Filled with a sense of urgency, Picasso produced numerous studies preceding and accompanying the mural, recording its evolution as he worked. Of the forty-five studies for the *Guernica* still preserved, all but one is dated to a particular day, and those generated in a single day are numbered in their order of creation, allowing us to track Picasso's creative process with precision. They are in different media, in diverse styles, and range from rough and uncertain to highly finished. About halfway through Picasso began work on the mural itself, but he continued to search for solutions through the unfolding studies.

Twenty-eight photographs by Dora Maar, who had worked with Picasso since earlier that year, record seven distinct phases *Guernica* went through, probably at Picasso's suggestion. He had previously written: "it would be very interesting to preserve photographically, not the stages, but the metamorphoses of a picture. Possibly one might then discover the path followed by the brain in materializing a dream."[21] Maar's photographs show that the final mural does not follow any of the studies exactly and includes elements that are in none of them; they make clear that Picasso's ideas evolved from a bluntly "militant vocabulary to the universal image of suffering."[22] Realistic, illustrative details were added as the work progressed, but they only serve symbolic rather than direct narrative value.

According to Picasso biographer John Richardson, in addition to their documentary importance, Maar's images also "helped Picasso to eschew color and give the work the black-and-white immediacy of a photograph."[23] He suggests that Picasso may have allowed Maar to photograph the progress of the painting for the publicity it might generate for the Republican cause. Breaking further with his normal practice, Picasso admitted influential visitors to his studio to view him at work, believing that might also help the antifascists. "The Spanish struggle is the fight of reaction against the people, against freedom," he observed. "My whole life as an artist has been nothing more than a continuous struggle against reaction and the death of art. How could anybody think for a moment that I could be in agreement with reaction and death? . . . In the panel on which I am working, which I shall call *Guernica*, and in all my recent works of art, I clearly express my abhorrence of the military caste which has sunk Spain in an ocean of pain and death."[24]

Picasso finished the painting on June 4, 1937, after thirty-five days of work.

A "Blasted Allegory"

For all the documentation of *Guernica*'s creation, its imagery and meaning remain provocatively elusive. Alfred Barr provided a succinct description of the mural:

> Briefly, one sees: at the right a woman with arms raised falling from a burning house, another rushing in toward the center of the picture; at the left a mother with a dead child, and on the ground the hollow fragments of a warrior's figure, one hand clutching a broken sword near which a flower is growing. At the center of the canvas is a dying horse pierced by a spear hurled or dropped from above; at the left a bull stands surveying the scene in apparent triumph. Between the heads of the bull and the horse is a bird with upraised beak. Above, to the right of the center a figure leans from a window holding a lamp which throws an ineluctable light upon the carnage. And over all shines the radiant eye of night with an electric bulb for a pupil.[25]

Otto Brendel amended: "The woman on the right seems to be hurling herself down on the street in flames, and that the explanation of the electric lamp as 'the radiant eye of night' is apparently conjectural and quite uncertain."[26] Thus the artist's idiosyncratic and highly personal treatment of details, which might normally help explain an artwork's meaning, here invites conflicting readings. Experts even disagree over whether the scene is set within a room or outdoors in a public square.[27] Two dominant motifs—the bull and the horse—have also generated entirely contradictory interpretations.

The mural's classical references in form and iconography mark the end of the explorations into neoclassicism that characterized Picasso's work from 1917 to 1937. In discussing the composition, Barr describes how Picasso divided the composition in half; two diagonals slice through the two halves to come together to form a gable-shaped triangle whose apex is the lamp held at the center, a triangle that recalls the pedimental form of a Greek temple.[28] Three figures—the fallen warrior, the rearing horse, and the kneeling woman spreading her arms—fill out the structure of the triangle whose harmonic symmetry does what it can to bring stability and order to their frenzy.[29] Anatomical extremities—hooves, knees, hands, and feet—form its base (or the cornice for the imagined temple). To the left and right of the triangle, the bereaved mother and the lighted portion of the burning woman are like acroteria on either side of a pediment. As Brendel observes, "the effect is static monumentality seemingly in contradiction to the vehement movements in which it becomes established, thereby creating a strong feeling of formal tension."[30] Singly the figures thrash about, but collectively they establish a still symmetry of Attic rigor.[31]

The woman's arm holding the lamp intrudes into the structure and breaks the classical mold, and yet it is the light from her lamp that defines the triangle of the pediment. The terrified horse pushes his head outside of the triangle's strict confines to counterbalance the arm. The elements that define a two-dimensional triangle, organizing the surface of the painting, also establish a pyramidal form behind it. The cornerstones include the warrior's hands and kneeling woman's left foot (her torso diminishes upward along one slope); the tiny hand clutching the lamp are at the apex. The horse's hooves are turned forward along the base, their underside forced upward and visible in the animal's drastic tilting, as it were, from the angle of vision of the fallen warrior. Rearing backward from its hooves to its head, the horse is planted as a smaller pyramid within a pyramid.

Be it inside a building or (more likely) in the town plaza, the unfolding massacre emerges in what Simon Schama describes as a "claustrophobic Cubist space" that provokes an intense feeling of oppression.[32] Yet under the screen of Cubism, perhaps the most analytical of modern styles, *Guernica* conveys a last great surge of Romanticism. Picasso's pedimental form echoes both the pyramid of agony piled above a death-strewn foreground in Théodore Géricault's *Raft of the Medusa* and the dead across the base of Eugène Delacroix's *Liberty Leading the People* (Fig. 12.6); the woman's lamp thrust forward is a descendant of Liberty's *tricolor* held aloft in the midst of smoke and fearlessness. Whereas West's *The Death of General Wolfe* had brought the grand manner down to earth, Delacroix democratically rendered figures drawn from every class in an epic manner. Here Picasso's historical layering, echoes of past art in dialogue with the present, contains no glorious heroism, and there is no way out of its nightmarish landscape. As Sargent understood, the heroics of war had been blown up on the industrialized fields of Verdun and Arras. Picasso disposed the bodies to express revulsion. The collapsing walls of the burning buildings convey the destruction of Guernica specifically and the destructive power of war generally. Picasso brings forward the unbearable violence suffered by civilians many other works kept in the discreet distance.

Anthony Blunt observes: "Picasso was both a revolutionary and a great traditionalist: methods of works and thought conform far more than might be imagined to those of the great masters of the past."[33] He thoroughly absorbed the vocabulary of

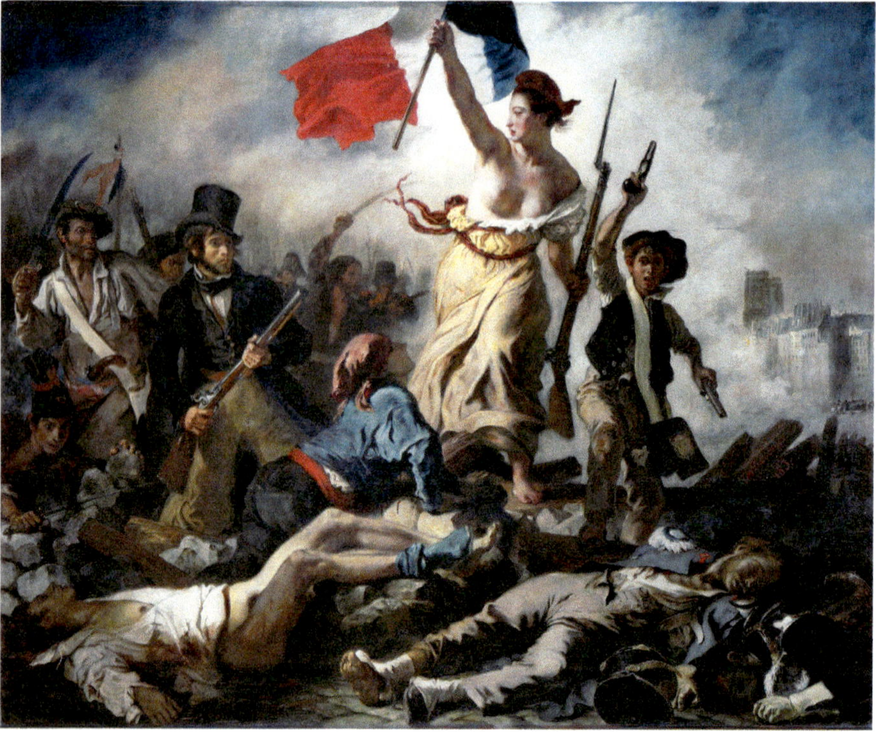

Fig. 12.6 Eugène Delacroix, *Liberty Leading the People* (1830). Paris, Musée du Louvre. Photo: Wikimedia Commons

traditional painting and appropriated motifs to his particular needs. The mother with her head thrown back in anguish draws from both the raving maenads of Dionysiac reliefs and the Magdalenes of Christian iconography.[34] We cannot determine specific prototypes for his forms, however: no *Belvedere Torso*, *Borghese Gladiator*, or *Miraculous Draught of Fishes*.

Despite the lessons he drew from art history, Picasso did not deploy traditional schema to lend hierarchical importance to the motifs. Light reinforces the painting's structure, but it does not focus our attention on any image more than another; nor does scale give prominence to any single motif. Nevertheless, the symbolism of each of the images, human and animal, has a long and dense history in both European art of earlier periods and the work of Picasso himself. For example, Barr discerns the symbolism of the bullring in *The Dream of Franco*,[35] and the shrieking horse in his bullfight series of 1933–1935; the *Crucifixion* (1930) is "comparable in its iconographic complexity and certain details," while the *Minotauromachy* "anticipates in the important dramatic relationship between the bull and the woman holding the lamp over the dying horse."[36] The woman with the lamp, her eyes filled with anguish, her face a tragic mask expressing horror and outrage, fulfills the same function as the onlooker in earlier compositions. According to Brendel, "She takes the part of the Chorus in a Greek tragedy, who can by the same token be described as an onlooker. It is an interesting fact that for this one face, Picasso chose the grand and, to our contemporary world, alien manner of a classic style."[37] The crucifixion, along with the goring of the picador's horse, evoke Picasso's upbringing in Catholic Spain, while the monstrous bull-man relies on classical allusions. All conjure the sacrifice of innocent victims.

The fallen warrior's broken sword recalls the sword of the matador and the pike of the picador, vestiges of premodern warfare. His sacrifice invokes Christ, but crucified upside down like St. Peter, all this in a figure commemorating the deaths of soldiers fighting for the Republican cause. His fallen body shatters into three large fragments: the left arm with open palm, sculptural head, and severed from both, the right arm clasping the sword. They suggest the plaster casts of academic artistic traditions Picasso had seemingly smashed. The broken warrior also conveys the absence of heroes, the fragile plaster the insubstantiality of their archaic memorials. His form expresses a specific classical coolness related to the lack of gore throughout the mural. When he saw it, Edvard Munch remarked: "The painting is not cruel at all—imagine how Goya would have done it—and yet it represents war. It's good that pictures running with blood are no longer painted."[38]

For all the sophisticated compositional structuring, the sifting images in *Guernica* do not cohere to form a naturalistic narrative: they are startling and inexplicable but do not have the kind of conscious meaning usually evaluated by Panofsky; rather, they trigger in the viewer a series of unconscious symbols and associations like those identified by Freud in his *Interpretation of Dreams* (1899). It is a broken narrative, but the avant-garde movements to which Picasso had already contributed gave him the instruments to piece it together. The shattering of images mirrors the shattering of our world, but Cubism allowed him to reassemble and organize the fragments in an orderly and ingenious fashion,[39] while Surrealism permitted him to excavate dreamlike and deeply personal symbolism.[40] Brendel recognized that with his "symbolic selection of images, suggesting possible rather than actual meanings," Picasso is able to place them into a "purely compositional context" that gives "the images their peculiar strength."[41] He understood that the test of the truth of the images is the degree to which they become memorable, again as in a dream—or perhaps more properly a nightmare. Picasso created a modern allegory or, to appropriate John Baldessari's apposite phrase, a "blasted allegory."[42]

In trying to construe the imagery and composition we also try to make sense of the event. It ultimately becomes meditative, like a religious painting of sacrifice. Like the crucifixion, it is an event from the past, but through reflection it is made present, transcending time. Artists like West and David drew on the traditions of religious imagery to elevate the representation of an historical event to the realm of heroic tragedy; in contrast, Picasso incorporated that imagery to commemorate the anonymous players on the world stage.

We recognize each image for itself, but how they all relate together is difficult to determine. Together they do not represent an episode of war—the destruction of a Basque town—as in the manner of the journalistic accounts Picasso read, but something less unified and far more problematic. With the newsprint used in the mural the monochromatic palette of blacks, white, and greys indicates how Picasso learned of the carnage and suggests that his painting will become the primary document by which the atrocity will be remembered. Photography had invaded the territory of historical representations, but at the same time liberated artists from the burden of mere literal depiction. Whereas historical commemorations usually achieve their efficacy through their specificity, in *Guernica* Picasso deployed a highly personal and idiosyncratic iconography, and by refusing to explicate its significance, he paradoxically rendered his work universal. It is less about the factual details—the Basque town or German bombers—and more about the human cost of war: the screaming woman, the dead baby, and the impaled horse. The episodes are not exclusive to the Spanish Civil War, but rather they are ancient and eternal, from biblical and Homeric accounts to contemporary bulletins from the Near East. It is powerful because it is so highly personal, like Velázquez.

Exhibition and Reception

The struggling Republican government financed the Spanish Pavilion primarily to publicize their social and political goals and to expose the suffering imposed by the civil war, notwithstanding the exposition's dominant theme: the celebration of the advances of modern technology. A huge photomural at its entrance showed Republican soldiers with the slogan: "We are fighting for the essential unity of Spain. We are fighting for the integrity of Spanish soil. We are fighting for the independence of our country and for the right of the Spanish people to determine their own destiny." Rather than being sited near the Eiffel Tower among France's allies, the pavilion stood some distance away on the right bank of the Seine with the pavilions of smaller and less significant nations.[43] It opened seven weeks after the official inauguration of the exposition, and therefore it did not benefit from the publicity generated by the opening ceremonies, nor was it shown on official maps or mentioned in most illustrated magazines and souvenir programs. *L'Humanité* published a brief notice about its opening and illustrated Picasso's mural three weeks later.

Conservative critics denounced the work's modernist style and wanted it replaced with something more traditional. Communist journalists objected to what they perceived as a lack of partisan fidelity and for not showing the promise of a better future. But Max Aub, one of the officials responsible for the Spanish Pavilion, defended the work, and the art critic Jean Cassou and the poet José Bergamin admired the mural, both praising it as truly Spanish. Michel Leiris identified it as a foreshadowing: "On a black and white canvas that depicts ancient tragedy . . . Picasso also writes our letter of doom: all that we love is going to be lost."[44] And the artists and writers associated with the *Cahiers d'Art* defended both *Guernica* and the cause of the Spanish Pavilion, publishing Picasso's sketches and preliminary studies for the work as well as Maar's photographs.[45]

Although the exposition provided an international audience, it was confined to those who traveled to Paris. Paul Rosenberg arranged to have Picasso lend *Guernica* to a significant exhibition of four artists—Henri Matisse, Georges Braque, Henri Laurens, and Picasso—that toured Norway, Denmark, and Sweden in 1938. Later that year Picasso had it shipped to London where, under the auspices of the National Joint Committee for Spanish Relief, it was shown at the New Burlington Galleries off Regent Street, then at the Whitechapel Art Gallery in the East End, and in February 1939 in a rented automobile showroom Manchester.[46] The second venue received strong support from the Labour party and its leader, Clement Attlee; David Hockney relates that his father remembered the price of admission was a pair of reusable boots to be repaired and shipped to the Republican troops.[47] The painting went largely unremarked in Scandinavia, but attracted wide public attention in England and evoked controversy among critics, who discussed it in terms of the civil war, fulfilling Picasso's goals perfectly.[48]

Picasso then shipped *Guernica* to New York for an exhibition sponsored by the Spanish Refugee Relief Campaign to raise funds for evacuees then flooding into France from Catalonia.[49] It drew about two thousand visitors during its three-week run at the Valentine Gallery on East 57th Street, where the "dual attraction of a world-renowned painting and a benefit for war refugees drew a distinguished audience from the world of art, politics, and society."[50] A subsequent nationwide tour included showings at the Stendahl Art Galleries in Los Angeles, the San Francisco Museum of Art, and the Arts Club of Chicago.[51] As in Britain, the painting was attacked by conservative critics and artists. Certainly, politics and aesthetics overlapped and intertwined, but increasingly the political potential of *Guernic*a as a public statement against Fascist aggression came to be valued.[52] Touring and press coverage amplified the mural's propaganda value for the Republican cause.

On November 15, 1939, *Guernica* returned to New York to join Barr's great retrospective at the Museum of Modern Art, *Picasso: Forty Years of His Art*. By that time Britain and France were at war with Germany and the Spanish Civil War was relegated to history. That exhibition was the first time the painting was seen and discussed not only as a document of political strife and war but also as an important stage in the development of Picasso's art.[53] At Picasso's request it stayed at MoMA where it came to signify New York's artistic ascendence as a center of a modernism saturated with machismo; today that history is being reassessed. Picasso died in 1972, and Franco in 1975. After Spain was transformed into a democratic monarchy in 1978, MoMA ceded the painting to Spain, where it was welcomed in 1981.

Conclusions and Coda

Art into History

The artworks featuring historical subjects explored in the preceding chapters not only affirm ideas about power relationships and social hierarchy their makers wanted to broadcast, they also exercise power themselves over the minds of receptive viewers. This is achieved by appearing to substantiate claims to superiority by elites through the veracity of their narratives, and sometimes by their very materiality. Changed contexts, however, can change their meaning profoundly.

Most of the artworks here were produced by cultures that emphasized personal and dynastic power. Each viewing of a monument revivifies the memory of exceptional leaders and their achievements. Representations of warfare portray victors as heroic, formidable, sometimes charismatic or even erotic, whereas their vanquished enemies appear worthy of being defeated, occasionally even as something quite "other" (especially in images celebrating imperial expansion). In contrast, liberal societies that embrace egalitarian or democratic ideals seem to eschew historical subjects celebrating "great men," suggesting why the practice of historical subjects in the history of art is somewhat intermittent. Fifth-century Athens only experimented with historical subjects, and in the modern West they have generally fallen out of favor.

The Visual Authority of Historical Representations

Throughout this study we have seen that makers of historical representations deploy numerous techniques to emphasize the veracity of their narratives and thereby enhance their propagandistic usefulness. Although modern viewers are sometimes tempted to perceive the works as documenting historical events, their function was primarily commemorative. Inscriptions give specificity to conventional imagery to identify significant figures, locations, and events; they even give voice to persons portrayed visually who are otherwise mute: Ramses gives a first-person account of what the viewer sees. The texts in Japanese *gunki monogatari* and Ottoman *şehnāme* provide contextual information—origins and antecedents, anecdotal material, and more—that amplify the meaning of the images they accompany.

Power, Image, and Memory. Peter J. Holliday, Oxford University Press. © Oxford University Press 2024.
DOI: 10.1093/oso/9780190901080.003.0014

Detailed depictions of topography, costume, and weaponry characterize events and lend the narrative specificity; they give viewers distant in space or time a vivid sense of an occasion. The inclusion of such details to heighten a commemoration's propaganda value by convincing a contemporary audience of its accuracy can sometimes render monuments historical records in their own right, which are then valued by later viewers for the information they contain. Zainab Bahrani writes about Babylonian scribes who systematically catalogued public monuments from earlier kingdoms, including those going back to the Akkadian dynasty of nearly five centuries before. They carefully described the ancient statues and steles and faithfully recorded the wording and placement of their inscribed texts, antiquarian practices that presage modern art historical practice.[1] Egyptian scholars in the Ptolemaic period used evidence carved on temple walls to compile such histories as Manetho's *Aegyptiaca*, as did the later savants who accompanied Napoleon to prepare the *Description de l'Égypt* (1809–1821).[2] Scholars turn to *Night Attack on the Sanjō Palace* for information about Kamakura-period armor. Andrea Mantegna drew on surviving antiquities like Trajan's Column to recreate ancient Rome in his *Triumph of Caesar* (begun in 1486), and West's use of the Ara Pacis for the grieving cortege in his *Agrippina Landing at Brundisium with the Ashes of Germanicus* enhanced the iconographic and stylistic authenticity of his own composition. But that documentary quality can be misleading.

Francis Haskell recounts how Montfaucon and Lancelot studied the Bayeux Embroidery for antiquarian information about medieval customs and artefacts.[3] Based on its style and details, they determined that the embroidery dated to the period of the Conquest itself; since both those who directed and embroidered the work were "*témoins oculaires des évènemens qui sont rapportez*" (eyewitnesses to the events it reports), they further concluded that the record it provided must be accurate.[4] They meticulously applied their antiquarian knowledge to decipher the story, for unlike Trajan's Dacian campaigns, the facts surrounding the Norman Conquest were still highly debated. They pointed to details illustrated in the embroidery that were not mentioned in the written accounts.[5] The implications of this method were remarkable. As Haskell recounts, for the first time visual evidence took precedence over literary sources in reconstructing an historical event. Neither savant considered that just like written narratives, images might be contrived as propaganda to persuade.

In 1767, Lord Lyttelton rejected Montfaucon's claim that the embroidery had been commissioned by "Matilda, wife of William the Conqueror, and [was] therefore . . . an authentic evidence of the facts therein represented." He argued that the portrayal of events not recorded in written sources proved the embroidery could only have been made much later on the basis of "vulgar tradition" and was not at all reliable. "Tapestry-makers are bad historians: and it is a common fault in antiquaries to lay more stress upon a discovery of this kind than is really due to it, as Montfaucon seems to have done in the present instance."[6]

Even when artists draw upon contemporary sources to confirm the accuracy of their representations, the desire for authenticity does not guarantee an exact transcription of events. Facts are modified and detailed evidence manipulated to meet the directives of patrons and to achieve aesthetic or expressive purposes. West depicted General Wolfe surrounded by his officers to ennoble the scene. Manet altered details in the Mexican firing squad's uniforms and arms in order give his representation a decidedly subversive spin. Contemporary viewers may be aware of such divergences from the facts, but they will fit disparate bits of information into coherent patterns and then-present ideological constructs, just as later audiences use details depicted in the artwork to substantiate their own cultural models.

The Material Significance of Historical Representations

The physicality of monuments can enhance the persuasive power of their narratives. Materials and methods of making were part of their power and meaning. The provenance of the pink limestone used for Naram-Sîn's commemorative stele literally embodies the land he conquered, while the lustrous red of polished brass signified the enduring power of the Oba and wealth of Benin. The *Opus Anglicanum* workmanship of the Bayeux Embroidery gave its predominantly Norman bias an authority it might otherwise lack among William's new subjects. Textiles were still so highly esteemed in Renaissance Florence that Uccello emulated their appearance and placement for the San Romano paintings. His application of gold and silver leaf for arms and armor captures the attention of the viewer; the development of linear perspective creates the illusion of three-dimensional space, inviting the viewer to enter the world depicted and heightening the impression of its reality. In addition to identifiable protagonists, witness figures sometimes draw the viewer into the scene. The Alexander Mosaic accentuates such visual effects as foreshortening and depicting reflections to draw attention to the skill of the artist and concomitantly to the authority of the artwork, rendering the image and the event it celebrates memorable for contemporary and future viewers alike.

After their rediscovery, the consistency of the details of the Kadesh reliefs at Abu Simbel with those at other Egyptian sites, compounded by their scale and sacred context, ensured the immortality of Ramses's account; even after the discovery the Hittite tablets, Ramses remains better known than Muwatalli. Although Duke William was not necessarily a magnanimous hero whose kindness to Harold was repaid by betrayal, the Bayeux Embroidery guarantees that that is the story preserved in popular culture. Akira Kurosawa drew heavily on *gunki monogatari*—along with diverse Western sources—for his epics of medieval Japan. His translation of those tales into film broadcasts those characters and their achievements to audiences previously ignorant of their stories, and careful reference to the detailed imagery of *emakimono* scrolls lends them authenticity, just as it did to the original scrolls. Cemal Kafadar observes that "the Ottoman enterprise was successful in turning itself into an imperial state in part because it was able to erase or marginalize other narratives of conquest and settlement, competing memories of accomplishments that were once attributed to others."[7] Seyyid Lokman's *Hünernāme* enshrined Sokollu Mehmed Pasha's role in that enterprise. The endurance of monuments not only promises that viewers will continue to see those narratives, but in modern times reproductive processes help popularize their imagery and ensure *that* memory of the event.

Even if the ideological intent of a particular commemoration fails to gain traction, its physical form may exert enduring influence in other ways. Although the tendentious narratives of Rubens's Marie de' Medici paintings were instantly contested by her powerful rivals, contemporary viewers admired the artist's ingenious allegories while not acknowledging their significance; today we still admire Rubens's striking images for their aesthetic value and art-historical importance, divorced from their primary propagandistic function.

Rulers sometimes emulate (not merely imitate) earlier monuments to collapse time and connect themselves with a long and illustrious history. Despite Naram-Sîn's vilification in the Mesopotamian cultural memory, later rulers appropriated the powerful visual statement of conquest represented in his Victory Stele. Rock reliefs at Sar-i Pul and Darband-i Gawr in the Zagros Mountains in Iraqi Kurdistan, probably dating to the end of the third or the beginning of the second millennium, show local rulers victorious over their fallen enemies in images strikingly similar to the Akkadian type (Fig. C.1).[8] Significantly, although they show the king trampling over dead enemies as he ascends the mountain to his victory, his helmet does not boast horns with their problematic pretensions to divinity.

Exceptionally successful monuments, like the Column of Trajan, have been widely emulated. Derivative commemorations in the Roman world include the Column of Marcus Aurelius (ca. 193), as well as monuments like the now-lost Column of Arcadius (ca. 401) and the Column of Justinian at Constantinople (ca. 543). The column dedicated to Napoleon I in the Place Vendôme (Fig. C.2) and the Washington Monument at Baltimore (1829) were both directly inspired by Trajan's Column. Nelson's Column in Trafalgar Square (1843) draws on this larger tradition while also directly addressing its Napoleonic predecessor.

The act of commemoration can amplify the significance of both event and monument. Long after the original participants are gone, an event can attain greater significance because of an artwork commemorating it while the artwork can earn consequence because of what it represents, a phenomenon that can intensify over generations. The circle of Kimon sought to convince Athenians to continue war with Persia by displaying the *Marathon Painting* on a wall of the Stoa Poikile, while decades later the designers of the Nike temple frieze may have depicted the same hallowed victory to rally a city recently devastated by Sparta. When Alberti wrote that the subject matter of paintings should provide *exempla* to help regulate

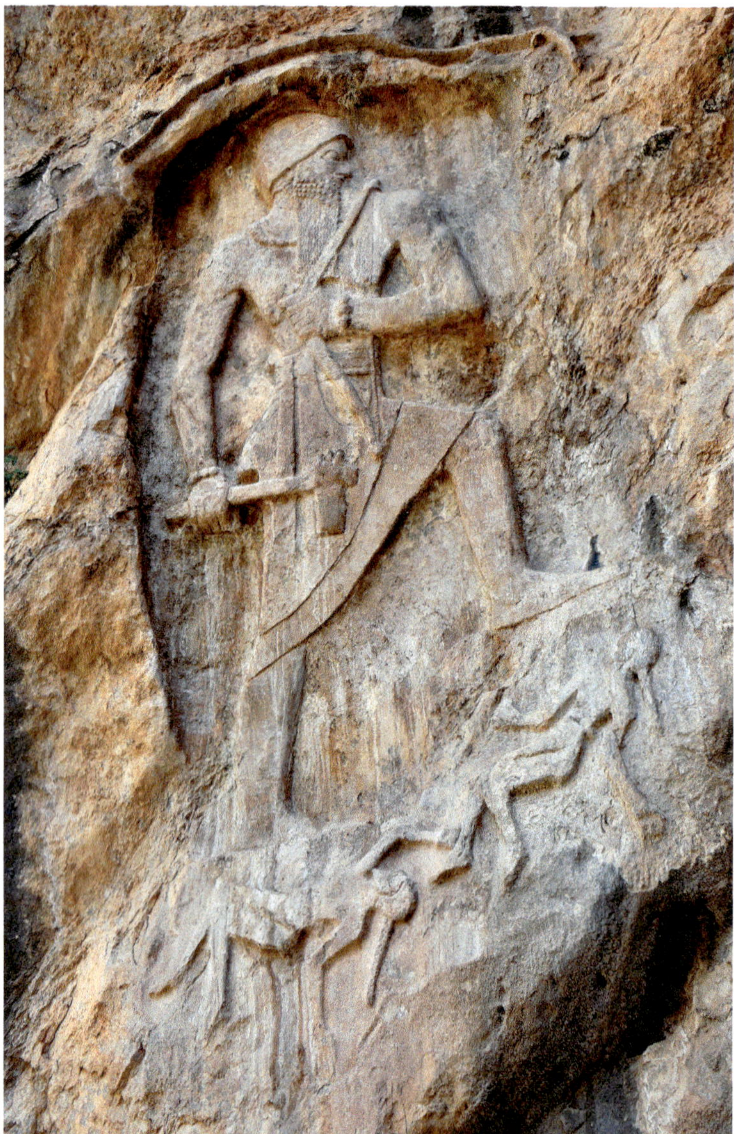

Fig. C.1 Rock relief at Darband-i Gawr (end of the third or the beginning of the second millennium). Darband-i Gawr, Iran. Photo: Osama Shukir Muhammed Amin on Wikimedia Commons

the social mores of civil society, he acknowledged how public monuments transform private and internalized responses into a collective moral purpose, insofar as it is shared communally. Even smaller works designed for private delectation like Japanese *gunki monogatari* and Ottoman *şehnāme* shaped the viewer's perception of history and pointed to proper conduct in the present. (And we should not forget that initially embedded texts from these two traditions were also given public recitations.)

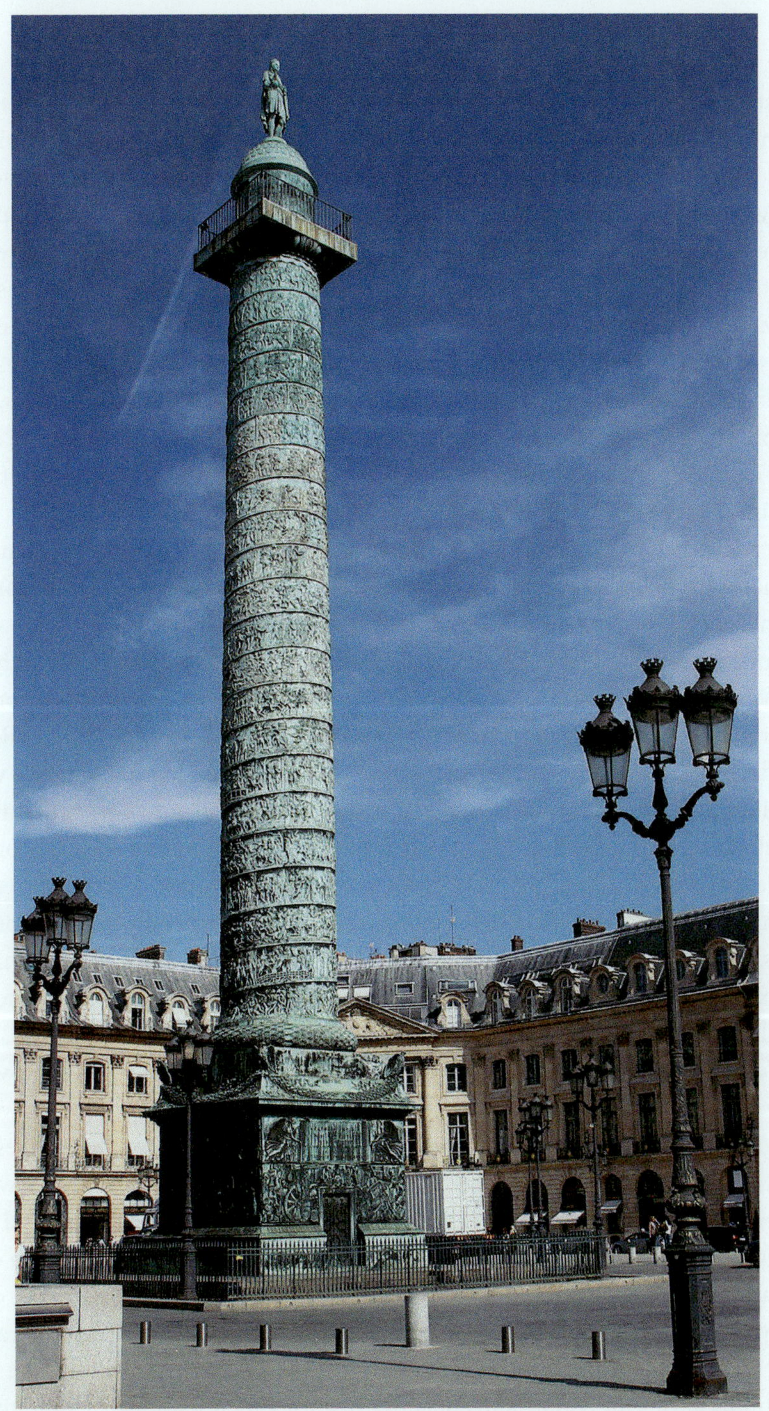

Fig. C.2 Vendôme Column (1806–1810; re-erected 1874). Paris, Place Vendôme. Photo: author

Changed Contexts and Meanings

This study has explored the way meaning appears as a projection of the intention of communities of makers—artists and patrons—as comprehended by the viewer. It has been demonstrated that the spaces containing artworks play an active role in how viewers experience them. Those spaces—temple, reception room, public square—are where the historical subjects—persons and events—are represented, and strongly affect how viewers construe their meaning. Although the focus here has been on individual works, it is understood that plaques, reliefs, and paintings were sometimes conceived as part of a larger ensemble designed to impress the viewer. Works of art, as factors of social agency between makers and viewers, have the ability to modify their contextual conditions, which are both a premise and a result of cultural practice. Not only did the spaces containing artworks affect their meaning, but the works affected how viewers reacted to those spaces.

My reconstructions of how viewers might have experienced works of art in their original cultural context are necessarily conjectural. Interpretations of the conceptual meaning of works beyond their identifiable subjects are bound by what we are able to reconstruct of the *habitus* of the originating society. Recent cultural theory, however, gives images and other meaningful objects in social practice an autonomy that transcends the intentions and interests of those makers and viewers. Rather than fixed ciphers of set meanings, artworks are understood to hold multiple visual meanings, and possess conceptual meanings not essentially inherent in that image but intentionally ascribed to it by viewers outside its originating cultural context. Accidents of survival, rediscovery, and restoration of artworks necessarily recontextualize them and also affect the meaning they convey, especially commemorative works. Monuments discussed in the preceding chapters, distinguished by having had extraordinary histories or afterlives following their original creation and display, illuminate this phenomenon.[9]

Since ancient Mesopotamia, the purpose of war—the dominant theme of works discussed here—usually centers on the pursuit of political and economic power: to seize control of land and its resources, including its people, through conquest (cf. Fig. 1.4). Historically, victors remove artworks as booty—either for material wealth or prestige (symbolic power)—or to disrupt the bonds between a people and their identity. The pillaging of Benin City in 1897 and the destruction of Guernica demonstrate how the destruction of the architecture and public monuments of an enemy city, even if it has little military importance, is believed to serve strategic objectives. The destruction of those material objects that shape cultural memory profoundly affects individual and collective histories and identities. In antiquity religious and royal images were thought to hold true power whose removal or destruction could adversely affect the state.[10] Frequently, armies simply left them in place, but defaced and fragmentary: what we call iconoclasm.[11] In other cases the control of monuments was an integral act of war. Their removal was understood "as a form of banishment or exile that had profound repercussions for the entire land."[12] This elaborate and complex practice was deployed in the ancient Near East and classical antiquity and more recently by the armies of Napoleon, the British Empire, and the Third Reich.

Historical commemorations are especially prized as booty due to their crucial role in defining national identity. The Victory Stele of Naram-Sîn still stood in the sacred temple courtyard at Sippar a thousand years after its dedication when Shutruk-Nahhunte invaded Akkad and removed numerous Mesopotamian dedications to the Elamite capital at Susa; when the French archaeologists discovered the stele in 1898 it was intermingled with other booty, including a series of Kassite *kudurrus* (boundary stones) and the famous Babylonian *Stele of Hammurabi*.[13] Many had their original inscriptions chipped away or abraded, and highly skilled stone carvers added new inscriptions with dedications to Elamite gods. Its new explanatory inscription repositions the Victory Stele, which is identified specifically with Naram-Sin, as a proclamation of Shutruk-Nahhunte's military and political prowess.

When Xerxes removed the *Tyrannicides* to Persepolis it was emblematic of taking Greece captive. According to Arrian's *The Campaigns of Alexander* (3.14), after Alexander conquered the Persian Empire in 330 BCE, he had the group returned to Athens, where it stood side-by-side with the replacement sculptures by Kritios and Nesiotes.[14] For such a famous Greek work, there are surprisingly few Roman copies in marble of that replacement group. It may be that the theme was too bluntly "democratic" for the imperial Roman regime. Filippo Coarelli, however, proposed that the torso and head in the Conservatori Museum belong to a marble copy erected on the Capitoline hill under the consulship of Metellus Scipio in 52 BCE to commemorate the assassination of Tiberius Gracchus in 133 BCE.[15] If this is true, then the group would have continued to signify decisive political action, but now transposed to celebrate a different deed in a different nation five centuries later. When his forebear, the Roman general Q. Caecilius Metellus Macedonicus, removed Lysippos's Granikos Group in 146 BCE, the monument's display in a new portico in Rome transformed its meaning from one of Macedonian victory to one of Roman triumph. Both Roman viewers and foreigners visiting the *caput mundi* could now wonder at how the greatest general in history had come to be literally confined within Rome.

Since the discovery of the Alexander Mosaic in 1831, art historians have had to reckon with how its imagery functioned in two very different contexts: first as a fourth-century Greek painting and then as a first-century Roman mosaic. A painting celebrating a Macedonian victory meant something quite distinct when originally displayed in a Hellenistic palace than when it was possibly displayed as war booty in a Roman temple, and the mosaic copy in a Roman private house would carry still different significance. The patron who commissioned the mosaic copy belonged to the new Roman ruling class, which appropriated older Greek artworks, the fruits of their conquest, to express social status. It was prominently featured in a luxury dwelling, of a type also of Greek origin, whose colonnaded courtyards and receptions rooms were sumptuously decorated with other paintings and sculptures meant to impress visitors. Its Roman owner may even have appreciated the Alexander Mosaic as a "work of art": an image divorced from its original context by its new role in a Roman social performance.

Heinrich Fuhrmann first suggested that the Roman patron had participated in the Macedonian Wars, and that this mosaic copy of a spoil of war functioned as both a sign of his admiration for the "greatest" general and perpetuated the memory of his own role in overthrowing the dynasty that Alexander founded.[16] A Roman viewer might have imagined a broader reenactment of the paradigmatic conflict between East and West, a conflict he may have participated in or merely appreciated through the lens of Roman ideology. Given the Roman taste for the allusive, a history become anachronistic could have been appropriated and meaningfully reused through a cognitive metaphor whereby in place of Alexander's empire Roman viewers could have understood their own (since Rome had conquered the territories formerly occupied by Macedonia). Roman sources repeatedly compare Roman campaigns on the eastern frontier with earlier Greek struggles.[17] Since Parthia, which had fought on the Persian side against Alexander (Arrian 3.11–4; Curtius 4.12.11), was now Rome's enemy in the east and Alexander's legacy was now Roman, a Roman viewer could have easily identified with the Greeks. Differing motivations were again in evidence after the mosaic's discovery in the nineteenth century when various European leaders such as the Prussian King Fredrick Wilhelm IV ordered copies of the copy: Was the desire for prestige achieved through association with the art of antiquity or with the political symbolism of the historical subject that inspired the modern commissions?

During the French Revolution the Bayeux Embroidery's royal and religious associations caused it to be confiscated to cover military wagons.[18] After the Terror the Fine Arts Commission, set up to protect national treasures, removed the newly appreciated textile to Paris for exhibition at the new Musée Napoléon where it caused a sensation, even inspiring a popular musical, *La Tapisserie de la Reine Mathilde* (assuming the then traditional association with Queen Matilda). Napoleon exploited the embroidery's popularity to whip up public enthusiasm for a second conquest of England; it may be at this time that the possibly spurious titulus *Et fuga verterunt Angli* was added to stir anti-English sentiment. After Napoleon canceled his planned invasion its modern propaganda significance diminished, and the embroidery was returned to Bayeux.[19]

We are left to ponder whether a contemporary viewer really would have interpreted the Bayeux Embroidery differently in a cathedral than in the great hall of a noble residence, yet modern scholars posit one setting or the other as evidence to determine who was responsible for its creation. The meaning of Uccello's San Romano panels, however, changed very little after they were transferred from Lionardo Bartolini Salimbeni's Camera Grande to the Palazzo Medici: in either setting they would celebrate both the condottieri and the Medici faction that wisely hired them to ensure Florence's victory. Similarly, it is doubtful that *Night Attack on the Sanjō Palace* scroll changed its meaning when passed down from one member of the Honda family to another: it still recalled a worthy instance of the warrior ethos to inspire each successive generation. Today, however, these works are all in art museums, which necessarily changes their meaning. Most of the brass plaques, which had formed the bedrock of the cultural identity and history of Benin, are also in museums;[20] those plaques that made their way to the art market and thence to private collections now signify the wealth and sophisticated tastes of their owners, much as Greek artworks did for Roman collectors.

This study has demonstrated how artworks were once integrated into the spaces and practices of public and private life. Artworks had functions in social practice—here predominantly commemorative functions—and their meanings within specific contexts of social spaces and situations. Exhibited in modern museums (those thoroughly modern institutions created for aesthetic pleasure or learned study) and recontextualized as "art," works are divorced from their original religious and political contexts, neutralizing both their power and that of their makers. The Uccello panel at the Louvre now joins collections that include former royal treasures, Napoleonic spoils, and archaeological materials including the Mesopotamian artifacts brought back from Iraq. The modern universal or encyclopedic art museum thus represents a strategic deployment of cultural property to construct a visual narrative serving an elite that justifies its domination with scientific knowledge and economic power. What is meant by universal or encyclopedic, however, is mostly a projection of one's own cultural assumptions, and can quickly betray a slippage in language from narratives setting forth universal values to those of other globalist ideologies.[21]

By no means is this a blanket indictment of modern museums; in fact, their ability to recontextualize objects can have positive value. The removal to museums and open-air parks of monuments to the "workers' paradise" in the former Soviet Union and Eastern Bloc nations has proved an effective strategy. The recent restoration of the Atlanta Cyclorama repositions it as a multilayered artifact that presents a metanarrative about how successive elites endeavored to shape how people remembered the Civil War. Exhibits that now accompany it detail myths and truths about that war, including the role popular entertainment has played in shaping perceptions of it; a new didactic film suggests how memories of the Civil War have less to do with what actually happened than with the political agenda of the people remembering it. The installation demonstrates how recontextualization of Confederate monuments might let us articulate their story, rather than having them recount our history to us.

The Rise of Modernism and the Decline of Historical Subjects in Art

When the Enlightenment challenged the authority of absolute monarchies and religious doctrine in the West, it prompted profound transformations that affected historical commemorations. Artists and critics began to disassociate images from their original political and religious significance and instead sought other qualities in them, prompting art production itself to change. In *The Death of General Wolfe*, West overhauled inherited conventions to create what he felt was a more effective historical commemoration. Academicians considered his break with traditional practice an affront, but it eventually won Reynolds's approval and became a popular success. The painting's dissemination through prints and other reproductions facilitated the construction of Britain's imperial identity, but such imagery could equally raise doubts about the state's authority.

Powerful cohorts continued to commission historical subjects; but as artists began to work independently, they sought out subjects, including historical subjects, conforming with their own beliefs for their own purposes. As noted in the introduction, the genre of history painting—a species of narrative painting prefigured in antiquity, defined in Renaissance, and later considered the highest form of art—was developed to play a didactic role, to show people what was sacred and what their duties were to society. The *exempla* extolled by Alberti and his successors were contrived for an age of princes; in the modern era the hold of academic theory declined as economic and social patterns changed.[22] History painting lost its place in the hierarchy because the hierarchy itself was overthrown. Progressive artists might still work with historical subjects, but now more often to celebrate the common man or antihero.[23]

Modernism appeared to rebuff the world and turn into itself while rejecting subject matter and narrative altogether, or at least the *importance* of subject matter, since much modern art still used such traditional themes as nudes and still lifes. Viewers were encouraged to look *through* that content to artistic form to distinguish the new ways artists rendered how these things looked. Viewers grasped how Cézanne reconceived his subjects. Like Uccello, he drew attention to his artifice to show that he was creating a new formal code, one that engages the viewer in actively working to reassemble painting's formal elements. In the twentieth century, the triumph of abstraction further dispensed with subject and narrative, which seem essential for the commemorative function of historical subjects. Art was looked at predominantly for its formal qualities—its design, shapes, colors, and relationships (the elements Kandinsky called nonobjective)—that communicate with the viewer directly. It is a learned mode of looking that allows viewers to deny the significance of political ideology or religious doctrine they do not share in order to appreciate a work, to suspend, if only momentarily, the recognition of objectionable subject matter to admire the artist's skill and inventiveness in representing it.[24] (Being products of modernism ourselves may explain why we respond more deeply to the personal statements of Manet and Picasso, and even of Velázquez, than those works in which the patrons seem to have dictated the content more fully.) Nevertheless, those aesthetic qualities had been developed to put across the stories artists portrayed. They were not the ends, but rather the means to represent historical episodes and commemorate persons and their achievements; they were among the artistic practices deployed by communities of makers.

Coda: The Limitations of New Media

Today film, video art, comics, and graphic novels dominate the world of storytelling, and the representation of historical subjects has largely been transferred to photographic reporting.[25] The very coincidence of an event and its recording bestow the photograph an immediacy that we perceive as authentic, one of the essential objectives of historical representations. That accuracy encourages us to consider photographs as evidence or documentation, as in forensic photographs or photojournalism. But as Susan Sontag observed, "photographs are as much an interpretation of the world as paintings and drawings are."[26] Photography's concern with angles, framing, and lighting echoes the compositional structure and expression of feeling academic theoreticians emphasized for rendering effective representations in painting and sculpture.

Early photographers embraced the deceptive possibilities of this supposedly empirical medium as an attribute rather than a liability. The Civil War was one of the first conflicts to be portrayed by photography. Americans embraced the new technology to promote their cause and memorialize their loved ones. Although the action of battle itself took place too rapidly for contemporary exposure times, its aftermath was captured. The Battle of Gettysburg produced the greatest number of casualties of the war. Alexander Gardner's *Home of a Rebel Sharpshooter* shows a lone dead soldier lying inside what he called a "sharpshooter's den" (Fig. C.3). Analysis indicates Gardner staged the scene by moving the soldier's body and bracing his head to face the camera.[27] He carefully set his own rifle beside the corpse, thereby calling attention to the soldier's prone position and the cause of his death. Although violating present-day ethics, at that time there was no sharp divide between a photograph's artistic and reportorial functions. Gardner aestheticized the scene and heightened its emotional impact, arguably the acts that make photography an art form. The image remains a tragic icon of that war, as moving as any painting of similar subjects.

Almost a century later, nearly seven thousand Americans were killed when, on February 19, 1945, the US Marines invaded Iwo Jima—a small island roughly midway between Guam and the Japanese home island—hoping to neutralize its airfield. On the fourth day of the campaign, they took Mt. Suribachi, the island's highest point, and Marines raised a small flag at the summit; later in the day, they raised a larger one. Joe Rosenthal of the Associated Press arrived just as it was being raised and swiftly snapped a picture (Fig. C.4). The Pulitzer Prize-winning photo became the subject of sculptor Felix de Weldon's Marine Corps War Memorial at Arlington National Cemetery (Fig. C.5), underscoring the enduring commemorative power of war photography. Yet the image is cloaked in controversy. Because of confusion over the earlier flag raising and the identity of the men shown, Rosenthal was accused of staging the shot. One of the participants, Pfc. Rene Gagnon, identified one of the six men as John Bradley, a Navy hospital corpsman. In June 2016 the US Marine Corps officially announced that Bradley was not in the photo,

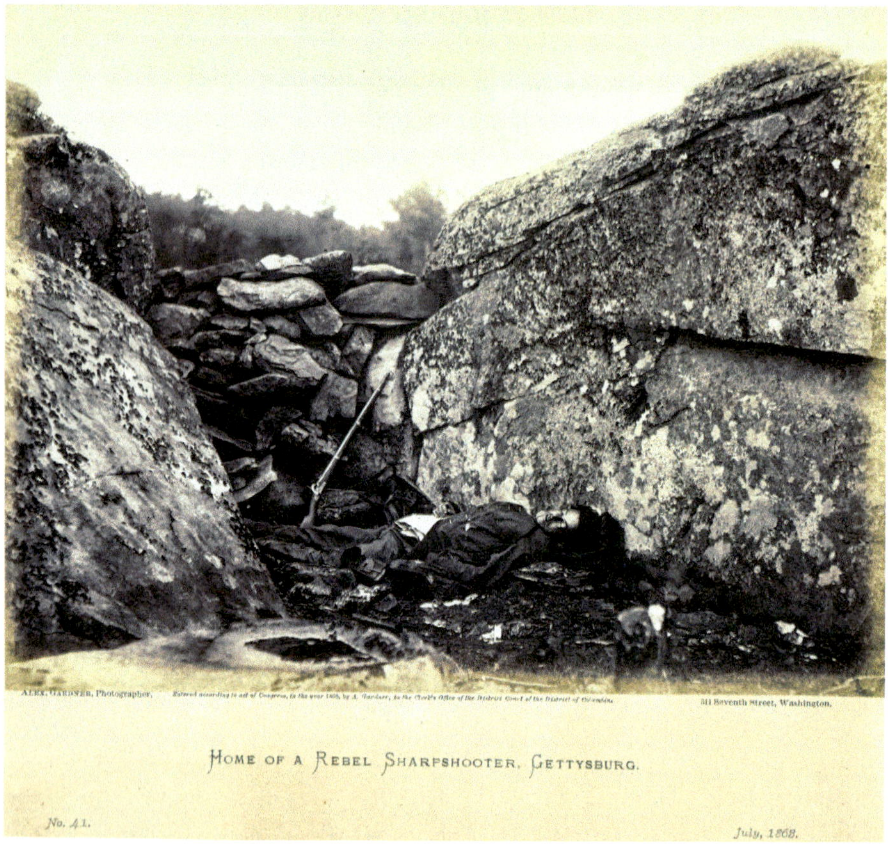

Fig. C.3 Alexander Gardner, *Home of a Rebel Sharpshooter* (1863). Photo: J. Paul Getty Museum

but that another man, Marine Pfc. Harold Schultz, was. Bradley had taken part in the first flag-raising earlier that day. The careful examination of details like a strap hanging from Schultz's helmet and the sling improperly attached on his rifle—details not visible in the photograph but evident in film footage that was shot at the same time—aided historian Eric Krelle in matching Schultz to other pictures taken there that day.[28]

Photography, therefore, is not innately more authentic, and the substitution of digital technologies for film has multiplied the myriad ways to disseminate and manipulate images that surpass our capacity for detecting deception. Only after careful examination of the video, recorded expressly for broadcast to an international audience, did experts determine that jihadists smashed plaster copies as well as authentic artifacts during their 2015 rampage at the Mosul Museum. People are rightly distrustful of the supposed veracity of pictures, which has helped generate conspiracy theories regarding the "staging" of the flag raising at Iwo Jima or even the moon landing. Franz Kafka warned, "Nothing can be so deceiving as a photograph. Truth, after all, is an affair of the heart. One can get at it only through art."[29]

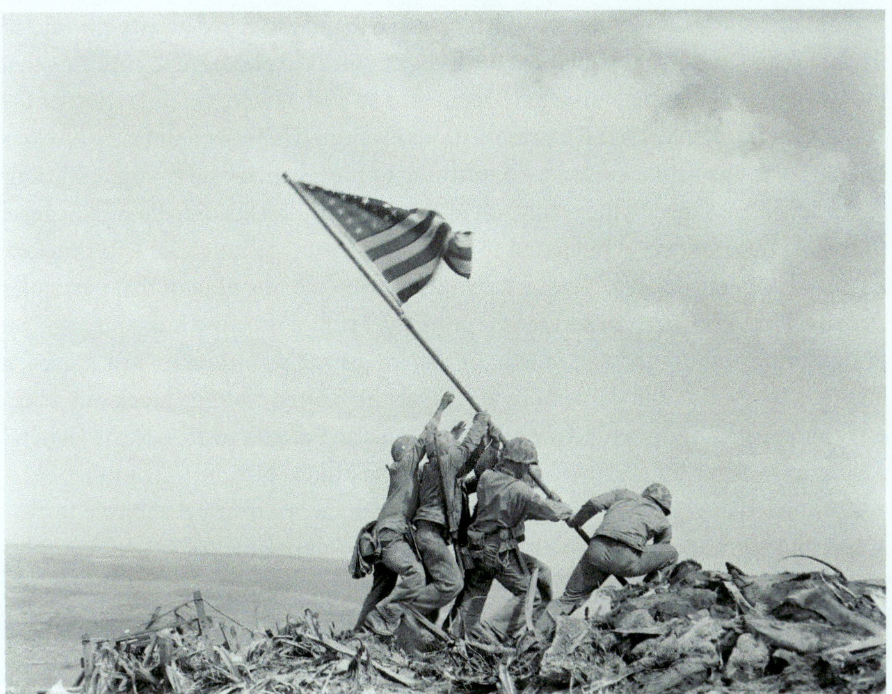

Fig. C.4 Joe Rosenthal, *Raising the Flag on Iwo Jima* (February 22, 1945). Photo: Joe Rosenthal for the Associated Press

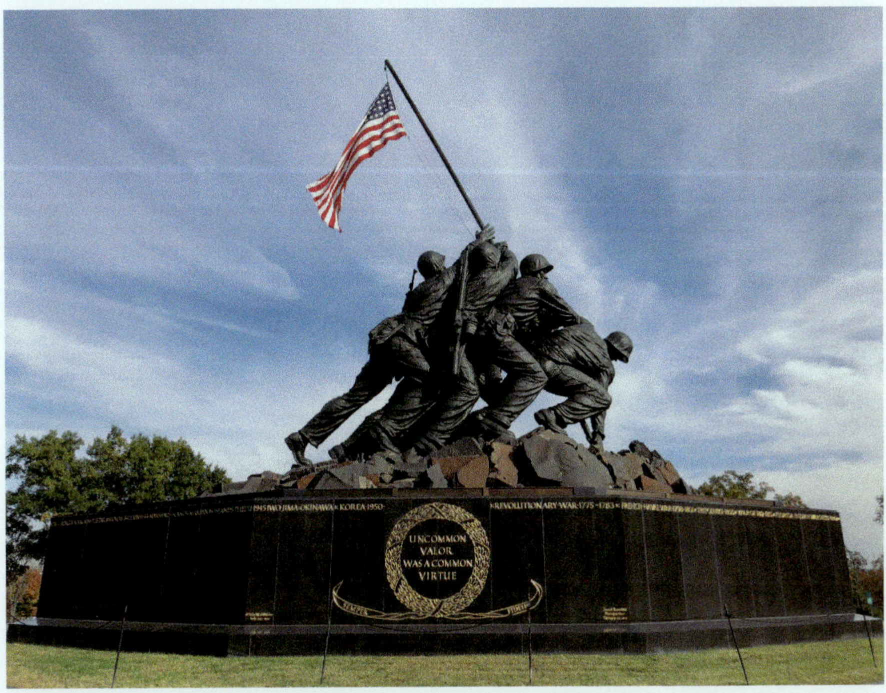

Fig. C.5 Felix de Weldon, *Marine Corps War Memorial* (1954). Arlington County, VA. Photo: Famartin on Wikimedia Commons

Contemporary newspaper accounts, newsreels, and radio broadcasts chronicled the attack on Guernica. The black and white references to photography indicate that Picasso conceived of his mural as a document as well as a commemoration of the event. Unlike other historical representations examined here, it contains no obvious references to the actual episode: no portraits of protagonists, no topographical or other details that specify the when and where. Rather than limiting its significance, this generalization has contributed to making its message universal and timeless. As Kafka understood, it took an artist to transcribe the meaning of that particular atrocity. Picasso's *Guernica* serves as a powerful symbol warning humanity against the suffering and devastation of war, but its imagery also intimates, just maybe, a hope for renewal.[30] The demand in 2003 that the United Nations block out a tapestry after the painting behind the rostrum for Colin Powell's address to the General Assembly to argue for the invasion of Iraq demonstrates its enduring power.[31]

Authoritarian regimes still deploy representations of historical subjects to persuade, but to modern eyes the results can appear ominous, sometimes even ludicrous or kitsch.[32] The concrete and documentary can appear too literal and confining, unlike the menacing figures of Leon Golub, the bleak landscapes of Anselm Kiefer, or the ambiguous testimonies of Gerhard Richter, whose allusive imagery haunts our imagination.[33] Because some conservative commentators objected to Maya Lin's austere Vietnam Veterans Memorial (Fig. C.6), Frederick

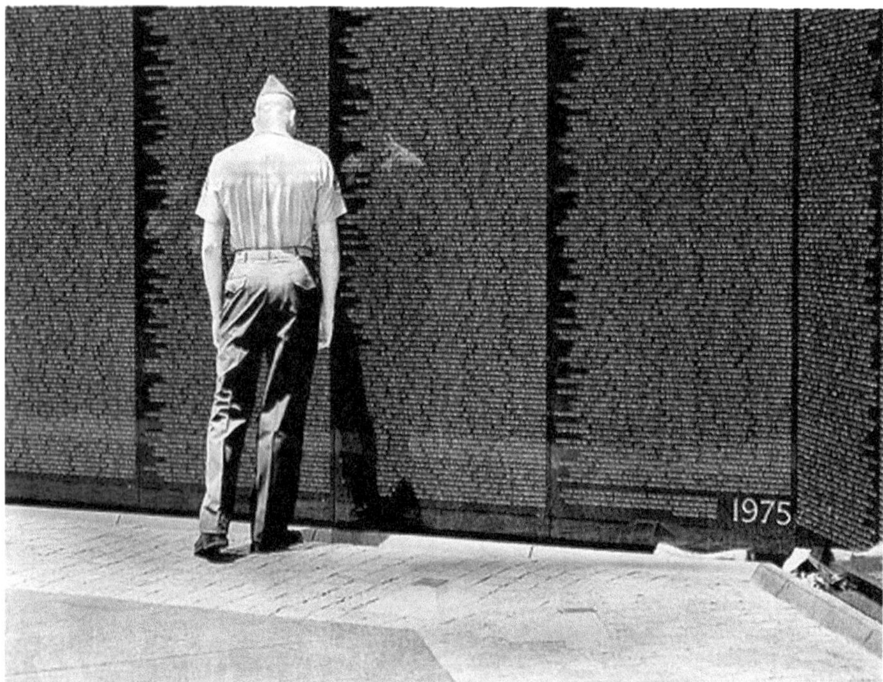

Fig. C.6 Maya Lin, *Vietnam Veterans Memorial* (dedicated November 1982). Washington, DC. Photo: Meutia Chaerani on Wikimedia Commons

Hart's *Three Servicemen*, a figural group in the heroic tradition, was incorporated into the site. Today the abstract wall defines a hallowed space where private and collective rituals of remembrance are enacted. It is ranks tenth on the American Institute of Architecture's list of America's Favorite Architecture, while the figural sculpture is fairly ignored.[34] Viewers in liberal societies have come to look to art to transform and clarify the world, and seek works—of any time or place—that are channels of communication that explain, challenge, and at their best produce greater understanding.

Notes

Introduction

1. It is worth noting at the outset that monument derives from the Latin *monumentum*, itself derived from the verb *moneo*, which means to remind or to tell about. A monument, therefore, is something that stimulates the remembrance of a person or event.
2. Hitt (2018): 67. Kevin Stayton first recommended that Confederate monuments might effectively introduce issues examined in this study; an anonymous reader suggested the Atlanta Cyclorama.
3. "Panorama" was patented by British artist Robert Barker in 1787; by 1793 he had built "The Panorama" rotunda in London's Leicester Square where audiences viewed his vistas of London and Edinburgh; see Comment (2004): 23–28. Further technical innovations to remove errors in perspective and heighten the illusion increased their popularity.
4. Entrepreneurs commissioned panoramas showing the Battle of Gettysburg, Chattanooga, and the naval encounter between the Merrimac and Monitor, among others.
5. Janney: (2013): 4.
6. Heine thanked him by portraying him on horseback just behind a covered-wagon ambulance.
7. These include Generals James Morgan, Joseph Lightburn, James McPherson (lying in the ambulance, where he died of his wound), and Captain Francis DeGress; William Tecumseh Sherman observes maneuvers on a far hill. Most prominent was Logan, whose postwar popularity led James Blaine to choose him as his vice-presidential nominee in 1884.
8. Hitt (2018): 69.
9. They illustrate one of Foucault's (1982): 221 later paradigms of power exercised by those not *in power*: "Power is less a confrontation between two adversaries or the linking of one to the other than a question of government. The word must be allowed a very broad meaning . . . [designating] the way in which the conduct of individuals or groups might be directed . . . more or less considered and calculated, which were destined to act upon the possibilities of action of other people . . . To govern, in this sense, is to structure the possible field of action of others."
10. The United Confederate Veterans and *Confederate Veteran Magazine* joined in arguing that Southern resistance to Northern aggression was just and moral, and sought to ensure that Southern whites remembered the "true" Civil War narrative to justify white supremacist policies. Among the recent literature especially pertinent to this study, see Blight (2001), Janney (2013), and Domby (2020).
11. Mills and Simpson (2003): 209. A resurgence of memorial construction in the 1950s corresponded with the rise of the civil rights era.
12. Atlanta Constitution (February 28, 1892), quoted in Judt (2017): 27; see Hitt (2018): 72.
13. Judt (2017): 34.
14. Part of the 1934–1936 restoration, those exhibits included the *Texas*, a steam locomotive that pursued the captured train the *General*, the raid depicted in the 1927 Buster Keaton film *The General* and later again in the 1968 Disney film *The Great Locomotive Chase*.
15. Judt (2017): 34.
16. Quoted in Hitt (2018): 74.

17. Judt (2019).
18. Halbwachs (1992): 34.
19. In this Halbwachs differed from the approach of his teacher, Émile Durkheim, often cited with Max Weber as the founder of modern social science.
20. Rieff (2016): 8–9. Rieff argues that true implementation of many theoretical constructs of remembrance may actually be less beneficial to societies than is usually believed.
21. Assman (2010) emphasizes the importance of Warburg's study of the *Nachleben* (afterlife) of classical antiquity in Western culture, which he called Mnemosyne (Greek for memory and the mother of the nine Muses) in studies connecting culture and memory; see also Harth (2010). Gombrich (1986) discusses the implications of Warburg's study of *Bildgedächtnis* (iconic memory) as a mode of cultural memory for wider reception studies of symbolic forms.
22. Young (1993). More crucial for this study, research in the neuroscience of memory points to (multi)sensory experiences effecting strong impressions on the mind: see Stock et al. (2016).
23. Geary (2000): 17. Although Geary was referring to written texts, the statement is applicable to visual images as well.
24. The word is derived from the Counter-Reformatory *Congregatio de Propaganda Fide* (Congregation for Propagating the Faith) founded by in 1622 by Pope Gregory XV. Most of the term's negative associations come from the experiences of the twentieth century, particularly under the Third Reich.
25. Modern study of this subject can be traced back to such foundational texts as Courbaud (1899). Brendel (1979) analyzed diverse contributions to the theme through the middle of the last century. Exemplary of more recent contributions to the ongoing study of *Historiendarstellungen* are Zanker (1988) and Hölscher (2004).
26. See Giglio (2018).
27. Reynolds, Discourse IV (1959): 59–60: "How much the great style exacts from its professors to conceive and represent their subjects in a poetical manner, not confined to mere matter of fact, may be seen in the cartoons of Raffaelle . . . Alexander is said to have been of a low stature: a painter ought not so to represent him. Agesilaus was low, lame, and of a mean appearance. None of these defects ought to appear in a piece of which he is the hero. In conformity to custom, I call this part of the art *history painting*; it ought to be called *poetical*, as in reality it is." On Reynolds's pragmatism, see Phillips (2019): 69–70.
28. Grafton (1999). An Italian translation, *Della pittura*, was published in 1436. Written as a practical handbook for artists, the treatise followed in the tradition of medieval works such as Cennino Cennini's 1390 *Il libro dell'arte* (The Book of Art) and surveys of all the techniques and painting theories then known. Book One provides the first account of linear geometric perspective, which Alberti credits to Brunelleschi and to whom he dedicated the 1436 edition. Alberti commends *istoria* in Books Two and Three. See Edgerton (2009): 117–25.
29. Blunt (1940): 11–12.
30. Le Brun also exercised influence with the publication of his treatise *Conférence de M. Le Brun sur l'expression generale et particulière* (1698); see Gareau (1992). For a recent examination of the shifting power dynamics within the French Academy and the larger political sphere, see Michel (2020). The Getty Research Institute is engaged in an initiative to make the academic literature accessible to modern readers; titles thus far include Spaniard Jusepe Martínez's discourse of 1673–1675 (2017) and Samuel van Hoogstaten's Dutch treatise of 1678 (2021).
31. Nationalism as an ideology is distinguished by the advancement of the interests of a particular nation in order to gain and maintain its control over its homeland; it seeks to fashion and uphold a national identity based on shared societal traits such as ethnicity, language, creed, politics, and recognition of a shared history. See Anderson (1983) and Triandafyllidou

(1998). For critiques of the term identity, which is sometimes burdened with anachronistic associations, see Brubaker and Cooper (2000).

32. Alberti (1966): 77.
33. White (1981): 6.
34. Some scholars also refer to these types as narrative modes or styles, the latter a word so freighted with other meanings in art historical discourse that I will avoid its use here. For evolving approaches to visual narratives, with semiotics playing an increasing role, see Alpers (1976), Grabar (1979), Marin (1980), Searle (1980), Bakhtin (1981), Brilliant (1984), Kessler and Simpson (1985), Holliday (1993), Bal (1997) and Hölscher (2004).
35. This can cause the sequence of events to be ambiguous within the narrative. Although a synoptic narrative usually offers visual signs to articulate its sequence, those unfamiliar with the story may have difficulty interpreting it.
36. Bellosi (1999).
37. White (1978): 47.
38. In this sense, Barthes (1977) heralded "the death of the author," intending thereby the notion of a creative genius as the exclusive authority of a work's meaning.
39. Becker (1982): 1.
40. Becker (1982): 29.
41. See Gell (1998): 24.
42. Gell (1998): 7; see also Appadurai (1986).
43. Gombrich (1960).
44. Gombrich's dialectic of making and matching, schema and correction, was an attempt to understand how artists "see": "I believe it is only by considering these psychological aspects of image making and image reading that we may come closer to an understanding of the central problem of the history of art . . . that is, why representation should have a history; why it should have taken mankind so long to arrive at a plausible rendering of visual effects that create the illusion of life-likeness," Gombrich (1960): 291.
45. Mamassian (2008) provides a critical survey of more recent research on this topic, although always mindful of Gombrich's contributions.
46. Bourdieu (1990): 54. Although distinct, some scholars currently refer to a society's collective understanding of their world derived from those cultural expressions (books, movies, television, etc.) through which a group identifies itself *as* that group as the "imaginary," a term I prefer to confine to a society's collective fantasy.
47. In a previous study (2002), I organized chapters thematically to examine artistic practices that informed Roman historical commemorations in the republican period.
48. In chapters examining the Alexander Mosaic and Bayeux Embroidery, however, I also look at how scholars study the works to determine information about the historical events themselves.
49. An anonymous reader fittingly compared this to Van Wyck Brooks's exploration of a "usable past," in which Brooks argued that the past "has no objective reality; it yields only what we are able to look for in it": cf. Brooks (1918): 338.
50. The classic statement is Panofsky (1939).
51. Reconstructing how viewers from the past might have experienced works of art is a highly speculative matter. Diverse filters of life experience (including age, gender, nationality, and more) affect their reading, sometimes causing individual reactions to deviate from the intentions of the makers. Consequently, what can be investigated are the collective cultural possibilities within which "normal" viewers would have perceived, understood, and reacted to specific images. Never uniform within a given society, this calls for circumspection.
52. Among the vast literature see Barthes (1964), Holly (1984), Mitchell (1986), Bal and Bryson (1991), and Hölscher (2004).

53. Among the classic studies that examine specific historical periods are Courbaud (1899), Locquin (1912), Wind (1938), Lee (1940), Hamberg (1945), Groenewegen-Frankfort (1951), and Moscati (1961).

Chapter 1

1. Although the Persians arose on the Iranian plateau east of Mesopotamia proper, their inclusion is logical, given the conquests of Cyrus the Great, who claimed the historical royal titles used by Mesopotamian rulers: King of Sumer and Akkad, and King of Babylon.
2. Schmandt-Besserat (1992) demonstrates how the archaic Sumerian counting system and pictographs drawn into moist clay slabs with a pointed stylus evolved into a writing system—cuneiform—composed of phonograms (symbols representing syllable sounds). These were adopted for the grammatical forms of the Akkadians and successive Near Eastern peoples for administrative purposes; however, many people would continue to use Sumerian for literary, scholarly, and religious texts, resulting in an essentially bilingual culture. This phenomenon in cultural production, sometimes denoted by terms such as *appropriation* and *accommodation*, evokes Homi Bhabha's notion of cultural hybridity (1996) and will recur throughout this study.
3. The development is an important part of what archaeologists have come to describe as an "urban revolution," which began in ancient Sumer when Mesopotamians consciously staged their cities in meaningful ways to transform and improve on nature; see Leick (2003); Cruickshank (2015).
4. Religious and commemorative rituals brought large groups of people together that framed and extended the legitimacy of power structures, while creating a sense of belonging to a larger cultural and political community. Historical commemorations would also play a role in framing and validating those constructs.
5. Bahrani (2017): 46.
6. Their prolific iconographies traveled throughout the ancient world. For example, the Narmer palette (discussed in the next chapter) exhibits a famous case of Mesopotamian imagery—the dragons forming the edges of the circular hollow on the verso face—making its way as far as Egypt.
7. Significant examples are found at the foremost Assyrian palaces (e.g., the Northwest Palace of Assurnasirpal II at Nimrud, the Central Palace of Tiglath-Pileser II Nimrud, the Palace of Sargon II at Khorsabad, the Southwest Palace of Sennacherib at Nineveh, and the North Palace of Assurbanipal at Nineveh), where walls were lined with stone reliefs representing the king's activities (hunting, battle, religious ritual, and banqueting).
8. Frankfort (1970): 34. This would be especially appropriate during the period when cities were being founded, placing special emphasis on shaping a communal identity.
9. Bahrani (2017): 51. She observes that by retaining the natural form of the rock, the stele emphasizes rather than diminishes its medium of representation.
10. Winter (1985): 21–23; Ariane (2020).
11. The world's oldest epic (written about 4,700 years ago), the *Epic of Gilgamesh* is a 3,000-line poem describing the adventures of the semidivine Gilgamesh, who braves danger on his heroic quest to find meaning in human existence and ponder the nature of immortality.
12. The idea was long-lived. For example, bricks stamped with name of Nebuchadnezzar II (r. 605–562 BCE) have been found at Babylon.
13. Schmandt-Besserat (2007) demonstrates how the inclusion of inscriptions on funerary and votive art objects emancipated writing from its original accounting function and allowed it to evolve to replicate speech.

14. Bahrani (2017): 83–84.
15. This is confirmed by examples in which flanges of undressed stone at the sides of the square are clearly intended to be covered by the surrounding plaster: Lloyd (1978): 114.
16. Winter (1985). Fragments of comparable steles found elsewhere are too small to allow their designs to be reconstructed.
17. Bahrani (2017): 103.
18. The discoveries in the royal burials at Ur initially garnered attention because of the association of this ancient site with the biblical patriarch Abraham, but soon the impressive finds themselves became the focus of attention.
19. Winter (1985): 19–21.
20. Hansen (2003). Bahrani (2017): 115 describes how Akkadian military expansion allowed the acquisition of valuable materials from distant lands to celebrate the dynasty. Akkadian rulers came to favor diorite in most monumental sculpture and it "continued to be associated with royal monuments in successive eras into the second millennium BCE."
21. Harper and Amiet (1992): 162–64; Nigro (1998).
22. Compare this to the cloak (*chlamys*) worn over the shoulders or wrapped around the arms of some Lapith warriors on the Parthenon metopes, or on the figure of Aristogeiton in the second Tyrannicides group (discussed in Chapter 3).
23. Bahrani (2017): 115, 125. This contrasts to later Greek art, where nudity could denote heroism.
24. Nigro (1998): 85.
25. Amiet (1976): 10; Nigro (1998): 93–96. Elsewhere Nigro points out that the bound captives not only serve as a symbol of victory, but as future slave labor provide "a rich visual message addressed to that social group upon which Sargon founded his power" (98).
26. Amiet (1976); Aruz and Wallenfels (2003); Bahrani (2017): 114–15, 120.
27. Winter (1985): 20.
28. In utilizing the composite view, artists generally show heads in profile, clearly capturing the nose, forehead, and chin, while rendering the eyes frontally, their most distinguishable and meaningful viewpoint. Hips, legs, and feet are also in profile, whereas the torso is fully frontal.
29. Winter (1996): 15 observes that the crown worn by Naram-Sîn does not have the multiple tiers of horns that distinguish the high gods of the Mesopotamian pantheon, but rather a single tier of horns often worn by the lesser gods on seals, "a detail that would have permitted the contemporary viewer to read simultaneously the king's divine standing and yet his relatively lower status with respect to the high gods." Furthermore, Nissen (1988): 139–40 argues that rather than promoting himself at the level of the major gods of the pantheon, Naram-Sîn portrayed himself specifically as a city-god. Nissen sees continual tension in third-millennium Mesopotamia between the local interests (exemplified by the city-god's temple) and the centralized interests of the king.
30. Eppihimer (2019): 74 notes that at the time this garment was an attribute of the so-called figure with mace, who may represent a god, a king, a divine or heroic king, or the personification of kingship.
31. Winter (1996).
32. Both the careful shaping of the stele to echo the shape of the mountain and the depiction of a naturalized landscape contrast with the purposely unfinished character of the earlier Warka lion-hunt, yet both play upon the viewer's recognition of natural forms.
33. The fusion of the hero and ruler into a new royal body to elevate the king to divine status is also apparent in Akkadian inscriptions: both Naram-Sîn and his son precede their names with the divine rather than mortal determinative, and adopt certain epithets in their titularies, such as "god {not king} of Agade." Nissen (1988): 173–74 describes how the dedicatory inscription of the Bassetki statue preserves Naram-Sîn's name with the determinative for a god and recounts

how the people of the city of Akkad constructed an urban temple for him, making Naram-Sin a city-god. With this action, he lays claim to the temple's property (as a city-god) and embodies the centralized state, thereby attempting to resolve the conflict between the temples and the territorial state.

34. The Elamite homeland was on the Iranian plateau (now in southwestern Iran). Shutruk-Nahhunte ruled from about 1184 to 1155 BCE. Like other kingdoms in the region, Elam was a secondary power throughout the Late Bronze Age, although it was linked through marriage to some of the important nations. In a letter written to the Kassite court (found at Babylon by German excavators), Shutruk-Nahhunte asserts that his mother was a Kassite princess, and that he was married to the daughter of a Kassite Babylonian king, just as many of his predecessors had been: see Cline (2014): 123.
35. Heim (1992): 125; Feldman (2007).
36. *The Curse of Agade* is an example of a Mesopotamian literary genre known as naru literature, which presents a celebrated historical figure (typically a king) as the protagonist in a moralizing story that most frequently addresses humanity's relationship with the gods; see Westenholz (1997); Eppihimer (2019): 66–67.
37. Nissen (1988): 174. Not all societies reject the idea of divine kingship. The divinity of the pharaoh was central to Egyptian belief for 3,000 years (Chapter 2), and the African kingdom of Benin still honors its semidivine king (Chapter 8).
38. Another example of the appropriation is mentioned above in the first note; see also Burke (2009): 45–55. Achaemenid elaborations included special characteristics inseparable from the religious nature and symbolism of Iranian traditions.
39. Polastron (2007): 2–3. Discovered at the archaeological site of Kouyunjik in northern Iraq by Austen Henry Layard in 1849, most of the tablets were taken to England and are now kept at the British Museum.

Chapter 2

1. Writing starts with stylized pictures. The Egyptians developed the hieroglyphic writing system around 3000 BCE, about the same time the Mesopotamians invented cuneiform. The Greeks apprehended the symbols as sacred carvings, and their name for them, derived from the Greek words *hieros* (sacred) and *gluphein* (to carve), has endured.
2. For example, the dominant image of Narmer about to dispatch the kneeling enemy on the recto face becomes the typical smiting icon of Egyptian monarchs (cf. Fig. 2.5).
3. Robins (1997): 14–18. We know primarily about Egypt's kings and elite scribal classes, and despite new archaeological finds, what we know of the bulk of the population beneath them primarily comes from what the elite chose to record.
4. For millennia, Egyptian artists followed this practice for representing the human figure as a conceptual composite of individual parts from multiple viewpoints when depicting royalty and other dignitaries, although persons of lesser social rank might be represented in ways that appear more lifelike to us.
5. The pylon can be construed as the mountains on the horizon between which the sun (Aten) rises and sets, a symbolism integrating the pylon into the king's duty of preserving *Ma'at*; see Arnold (1997): 2.
6. Robins (1997): 25.
7. Documents from Deir el-Medina, a village for workmen who built the royal tombs in the Valley of the Kings, indicate that sculptors' workshops and other types of production worked in teams; see Robins (1997): 29.
8. Haeny (1997): 110–12.

9. A lower register on the north exterior wall shows Seti on his Libyan campaign, and in an upper register he sacks the Hittite city of Kadesh.
10. Robins (1997): 178.
11. Not satisfied with that, Ramses (r. 1279–1213 BCE) also appropriated the works of predecessors by superimposing his name onto a work or by reworking its imagery to represent him (e.g., statues of Senusret II and Amenhotep II).
12. Haeny (1997): 115–18 discusses Ramses's various claims to divinity at Abu Simbel.
13. Freed (1987): 65. The Egyptians began cutting tombs into the cliffs facing the Nile in the Middle Kingdom. In the Nubian temples the hypostyle hall was often cut into the face of the cliff, and the holy of holies (the sanctuary housing the cult statues of the temple's resident gods) was carved deeper into the mountain.
14. Also colossal in scale, the Small Temple in honor of Nefertari and Hathor stood about 500 feet away. When extended forward, the central axes of the temples intersected in the Nile's life-giving waters, their positions thereby expressing a generative power embodied in the royal couple. This association was dissolved when, in the 1960s, engineers relocated the temple of Ramses upward nearly 700 feet to raise it above flood levels resulting from the construction of the Aswan Dam; on that UNESCO operation, see Säve-Söderbergh (1987): 98–126.
15. Habachi (1969): 8–10.
16. Arnold (1997): 2.
17. Freed (1987): 66. These represent the main cult deities at that time, whose primary cult centers were at Heliopolis (Ra-Horakhty), Thebes (Amun Ra), and Memphis (Ptah).
18. Wilkinson (2000): 225–27.
19. Inscriptions on Karnak's temple walls record the details of his campaigns in Canaan and Syria; see Murnane (1985).
20. "No battle fought in antiquity is so well-documented as the clash between the Egyptians and the Hittites before the city of Kadesh on the Orontes in 1275 B.C.": Ockinga (1987): 38; see also Ralby (2013).
21. Some scholars argue that the *Poem*, known from eight copies (including fragmentary papyri), is not actual verse, as opposed to a written account similar to what other pharaohs recorded; cf. Gardiner (1960): 2–4, and in contrast Lichtheim (1978): 58. The *Bulletin*, which survives in seven copies, is the extensive description accompanying the pictorial reliefs depicting the battle; more than a mere caption, it is a verbal rendition of those scenes. In addition to these lengthy inscriptions, numerous small captions draw attention to various details in the reliefs.
22. The temple at Luxor and the Temple of Ramesses II at Abydos also contain reliefs that are nearly identical to those at Abu Simbel. In those two cases, however, the reliefs are on the exterior, public walls of the temples, where the masses would have the ability to see them.
23. Although written as a grammar text, Van den Hout (2011) contains an account of the discovery of the tablets and other cultural and historical background. Most tablets are written in the Hittite language, but some feature Hurria, Hattic, Akkadian, and Assyrian texts. With funding from the German Research Foundation, scholars at the universities of Mainz, Marburg, and Würzburg are now making the 30,000 tablets and fragments available online.
24. Bryce (1998) 257, citing Kadesh Inscription P40–53. These would have included regular Hittite troops, troops from a wide range of vassal states, and large numbers of mercenaries. The numbers of chariots deployed by both sides made this one of the largest engagements in chariot warfare.
25. According to Freed (1987): 41, the Egyptians traveled an estimated two miles per hour, or 15 miles on a good day.
26. Kadesh Inscription B8-18, adapted by Bryce (1998): 258 from a translation by Gardiner (1960).
27. Gardiner (1960): 29.

28. Adapted from the *Poem* by Faulkner (1958): 101.
29. Many scholars believe that the Hittites could have won the battle had Muwatalli deployed all his forces; cf. MacQuitty (1965): 117.
30. Recent events (e.g., Attorney General William Barr's March 2019 mischaracterization of the Mueller Report) demonstrate how the first telling not only affects individuals' initial comprehension of a story but also their long-term interpretation of it, regardless of any additional or contradictory information publicized later.
31. The opposite wall to the south commemorates Rameses's Syrian, Libyan, and Nubian wars; see Wilkinson (2000): 226.
32. Gaballa (1976): 119 observes that "when artists came to translate these events into reliefs they met with a certain amount of difficulty resulting on the one hand from the difference in nature of expression between art and literature, and on the other from the conventional methods of Egyptian art in particular."
33. Adapted from the *Poem* by Faulkner (1958): 104.
34. Spalinger (2011): 205: "Topographic localities serve as readily identifiable markers, topoi, to which the viewer was directed and concerning which specific identities of time and place could be readily ascertained."
35. Bryce (1998): 261.
36. Due to the purposeful destruction of his capital city of Amarna, little physical evidence remained of the reign of Amenhotep IV (r. ca. 1353–1336 BCE), who assumed the name Akhenaten and imposed monotheism on Egypt. Even less was known of the shaky reign of his successor, Tutankhamen, until the discovery of his tomb in 1922.
37. Lists of Hittite officers slain in the battle appear on the walls of the Ramesseum, and some of the names are also present in the temples at Abydos and Abu Simbel. There is no reason to doubt the accuracy of these specific details; see Healy (2001) and Bryce (2003): 89–90.
38. Bryce (2004): 103 notes: "A strong, permanent military and political presence in this region was vital to Hatti's status as one of the great international powers of the Late Bronze Age."
39. Not surprisingly, according to Hittite accounts, Ramses approached Hattusilis.
40. Two clay tablets discovered at Hattusas preserve the Hittite version of the treaty. The Egyptian version is carved on temple walls at Karnak, the Ramesseum near the Valley of the Kings, and at Abu Simbel.
41. The peace was further strengthened by the marriage of Ramses to Hattusilis III's oldest daughter, an event commemorated on a stele at the southern end of the exterior terrace; Wilkinson (2000): 225.

Chapter 3

1. J. J. Pollitt (1972): 23–24 vividly describes how both playwright (Aeschylus) and historian (Herodotus) contemplated the question of how *hybris* ("arrogance, unbridled ambition without restraint") gave rise to *ate* (folly) and finally *nemesis* (retribution) in the lives of men and nations. Reading that book in Richard Brilliant's class inspired me to study with him later.
2. The series of conflicts between the Greek city-states and the Achaemenid Empire was initiated when Cyrus the Great conquered the Greek region of Ionia (the western coast of modern Turkey) in 547 BCE. It persisted from 499 BCE, when the Ionians revolted against Persia, through two invasions of Greece (490 and then 480–479 BCE), to a putative peace treaty in 449 BCE.
3. Stewart (2008): 70–73 gives a careful account of this complex transformation. Contemporary drinking songs came to credit the assassins with making the Athenians *isonomoi* (equal) under the law.

4. Thucydides, *Peloponnesian War* (6.55–59) and Herodotus, *Histories* (5.55–57). Many other ancient writers document the story, and like historians today frequently criticize the work of their colleagues. Thus Plutarch, in his "More on the Malice of Herodotus" in the *Moralia*, criticized his predecessors for prejudice and misrepresentation. *The Constitution of the Athenians* (17.3–19.1), attributed to Aristotle or his school, offers details not found in other sources. None of these accounts mentions either statue group.
5. In Athens only male citizens eighteen years or older could participate at the assembly (elected magistrates and jurors were restricted to those over 30), thereby excluding women, slaves, and *metoikoi* (resident foreigners) from civic life. Steinbock (2013): 70–83 emphasizes that these constitute different memory communities, which might preserve versions of the past not otherwise attested or conflicting with the *polis* tradition. At the same time, they may well have exercised a similar "soft" power to that of the Ladies' Memorial Associations in the American South, a "threat" unpacked in Aristophanes's *Lysistrata*.
6. Although Camp (2010) favors a location east of the Stoa Basileios and the Stoa of Zeus, Azoulay (2014), revising Travlos, places the group just east of the temple of Ares and north of the later Odeion of Agrippa.
7. Similarly, Lendon (2005): 37 identifies reverence for epic—along with competitiveness—as a central Greek cultural value affecting the evolution of their battle tactics: "The heroes of epic always sat invisible upon the shoulders of the Greeks, whispering their counsel."
8. The issue of male nudity in Greek art is controversial: Andrew Stewart (1997): 24–42 and Jeffrey Hurwit (2007) offer critical reviews of conflicting interpretations.
9. Edmonds (1931) vol. 2: 377.
10. Again, this discussion privileges Athenian citizens. Shear (2021): 253–313 discusses how other residents in the city developed identities in relation to its religious festivals.
11. Azoulay (2014), however, prefers to date Antenor's group after Marathon, too, rather than immediately after Cleisthenes' reforms.
12. As Stewart (2008): 73 observes, "the group puts their homoerotic bond at the core of Athenian political freedom," indicating another appropriation of aristocratic structures to serve the democratic polity. Stewart cites Plato (*Symposium* 182A): "If we go on to consider decorum in love affairs among men, we shall find that whereas in other cities principles are laid down in black and white and thus are easily comprehensible, ours are more complicated . . . The Persians condemn such love because of their empire's absolutism; it doesn't suit the interest of the state that a generous spirit and strong friendships and attachments should spring up among its subjects—effects that this love has a special tendency to produce. The truth of all this was actually experienced by our tyrants at Athens: it was the love of Aristogeiton and Harmodios that destroyed their power."
13. The innovative lunging poses became iconic for later Greek representations of combat. Although the importance of the commemorative subject is fundamental, echoes of the composition in completely different contexts suggests that the figures were also valued by artists for their formal qualities; see Ridgway (1970): 81.
14. Alcock's 2002 study explains how for generations the ancient Greeks discerned their history in their landscape.
15. See Pollitt (1990): 141–45 and Camp (2001): 68–69. Stoicism takes its name from this building where Zeno of Citium first expounded its philosophical tenets.
16. The otherwise anonymous vase painter received his name from the scene on the other side of the vase representing the slaying of Niobe's children by Apollo and Artemis.
17. The painting emphasizes Athens' role in the Persian War. See Yates (2019): 29–98, who argues that the Greeks recalled the conflict as members of their respective *poleis*, differing in terms of contemporary interests, real experiences, and preexisting social memories, rather than as a panhellenic experience.

18. These were probably identified by inscriptions; otherwise, the painting would probably not have escaped the generalizing quality of Greek art at that time: see Cohen (1997): 26–27.
19. There may even have been a personification of the battle itself. The Greeks, who so proficiently anthropomorphized their gods, are also credited with devising personifications: the representation in human form of places and even abstract concepts that will endure throughout Western art; see Shapiro (1993).
20. An allegory is metaphor that combines symbolic figures (such as divinities and personifications of places and abstract concepts) with imagery that can include actual persons to convey complex moral, political, or religious meanings. This mode of communication is often used to deliver a broader message about real-world issues and events than is possible with a factual depiction.
21. In his funeral oration commemorating the war dead, Pericles does not distinguish individual warriors, but rather eulogizes shared Athenian virtues and accomplishments (Thucydides, *Peloponnesian War*, Book 2). Although Steinbock (2013): 48–99 defines funeral orations as the most powerful means of consolidating a shared image of the past to construct the identity of the *polis*, he also includes tragedies, festivals, rituals, assemblies, and legal proceedings as instruments for transmitting memory.
22. This would especially be true if, as Pausanias (1.28.2) asserts, Pheidias's earlier creation, the 30-foot-tall bronze Athena Promachos (ca. 456 BCE), really was financed from the spoils of Marathon.
23. Yates (2019) discusses Alexander's coin issues with relevant iconography (215–17) and dedications of booty at meaningful locations, effectively refounding Platea as a panhellenic "Persian-War theme park" (228). He expands Steinbock's (2013) exploration of how the memory of events distant in time implies a degree of complication different from those more recent; see also Flower (2000). Successor kings (including newly ascendent powers who had not fought in the fifth century and cities that fought but were no longer major powers) used the strategy successfully for their own purposes.
24. Velleius Paterculus (*Historia Romana* 1.11.3–4) writes that Lysippos produced a "likeness" (*similitudo*) of each figure, while Pliny (*Naturalis historia* 34.61) states that the portraits were done with "utmost likeness" (*summa . . . similitudine*). Although Velleius is the only authority that portrays Alexander inserted (*interponeret*) among the Companions, his description reads like an eyewitness account.
25. Significantly, Greek experiments in realistic portraiture appeared first in Asia Minor, ruled by Persian satraps, though initially restricted to philosophers, poets, and playwrights; cf. Boardman (2000): 174–78.
26. Stewart (1993): 128 estimates that the cost for 26 horsemen would have been 390,000 drachmas or 65 talents: "To put this in perspective, we know from Aristoboulos that the king's entire war chest on landing in Asia was exactly 70 talents."
27. Stewart (1993): 129.
28. All the sources agree that Lysippos was the sculptor, but based on datable signed bases, he would have been quite old at that time; Stewart (1993): 129 suggests that the *shop* of Lysippos was entrusted with the commission. The images may have merely incorporated realistic details to confer them with portrait-like qualities. Although descriptions of the monument do not correspond with any account of the battle itself (Alexander did not fight among those Companions when they fell), it undoubtedly affected how viewers remembered the event.
29. It was damaged in the earthquake that struck in AD 62, and was patchily restored before the eruption of Vesuvius in 79. Donderer (1990) has advanced the thesis that the mosaic was originally laid somewhere in the East, and lifted and shipped in sections to Italy, thus explaining some of its illogical passages.

30. This proposition, first advanced by Rumpf (1962), suggests the way details of the pictorial narrative can be construed for an historical interpretation.
31. Here Darius recalls the depiction of Muwatalli at Abu Simbel: both are shown in their chariots elevated above the fray monitoring the action and directing their forces, but both end up as passive observers of their defeat.
32. Polybius (29.21.3–6) reflected on the Macedonian defeat of Persia. On the obsession with Fortune in the Hellenistic age, see Pollitt (1986): 1–4.
33. Hölscher (1973): 152.
34. Although Greek authors from Homer to Herodotus do not necessarily consider barbarian enemies as inferior and often portray them in sympathetic and even valorizing terms, like all peoples they remain subject to Fortune; see Ford (2020).
35. Stewart (1993): 142.
36. Plutarch (ca. 46–120) and Diodorus (ca. 90–30 BCE) were also of Greek extraction. Other ancient sources include works by Justin and Curtius Rufus. Scholars attempt to determine what passages in these accounts might derive from more reliable, but now lost, contemporary accounts, such as the *Journals* kept by Alexander's secretary, or the memoirs written by his general Ptolemy. But even if testimony is contemporary, that does not guarantee its reliability, as demonstrated by the account of Kadesh perpetrated by Ramses.
37. For the most thorough analysis of the three battles in reference to the mosaic, see Stewart (1993): 130–38.
38. Stewart (1993): 134–40.
39. Cohen (1997): 138, argues that the mosaic "combines an absence of specific referents on the one hand and, on the other, an intense entanglement with general historicity, if history be understood as a discourse on events and facts rather than a transcription of absolute ontological truth."
40. Several compositional and iconographic lapses (such as the incoherent chariot and confusing helmeted head to the left of Darius's outstretched hand) suggest that the Roman mosaicists misunderstood or radically abbreviated their model. See again Donderer (1990).
41. Stewart (2008): 291. Compare them with the repoussoir figures that engage the viewer in Velázquez's *The Surrender of Breda* (Chapter 10).
42. For Philoxenos: Pliny *Naturalis historia* 35.110, Plutarch *de mul. virt.* praef.; for Aristides: Pliny *Naturalis historia* 35.98; for Helen of Alexandria: Ptolemaeus Hephaistion ap. Photium Bibl. 482. Vespasian eventually exhibited Helen's painting in the Temple of Peace at Rome.
43. Plautus's *Mostellaria* ("Haunted House") was written about 150 years after Alexander's death. While he probably didn't invent the title, it may well have been of Roman coinage.
44. Stewart (2008): 291. As pharaoh, Alexander might be understood as divine by his Egyptian subjects, but not by Greeks or Macedonians.
45. When Pompey "the Great" celebrated his eastern victories in 61 BCE, he mounted a triumph modeled on those used to celebrate Alexander, most notably the great festival in Alexandria in the 270s.

Chapter 4

1. Similarly, although Etruscan art does not lack realistic representations, especially in funerary works, it exhibits little interest in historical commemoration before the early Hellenistic age.
2. In his analysis of the Roman use of these two "modes of representation," Per Gustav Hamberg (1945): 15–45 determined that the allegorical is a classicizing style derived from Greek art that favors representation approximating the natural, more visual experience of space, whereas the documentary mode prefers more symbolical renditions of space that

appear unnaturalistic and nonclassical. Although the combination of different perspectival conventions on the column backs up his assessment for Roman art, this does not necessarily hold for works produced by other cultures examined in this study.

3. An addendum to Liverani et al. (2018): 90–97 suggests that the most likely display context for the relief panels was an arch-like monument.
4. Fasces are a bound bundle of wooden rods, sometimes with an axe blade appearing, that symbolized a magistrate's executive authority.
5. Since many Romans believed in and worshipped those ancient gods, it is problematic to apprehend such works as allegorical in the same way as those Rubens devised for Marie de' Medici discussed in Chapter 10. Rather, it may be more suitable to understand them as explicit metaphors for Roman *imperium*; see Burke (1992): 197.
6. Langer and Pfanner in Liverani et al. (2018): 80–84. Recarvings such as this were not all that common, but they did occur. Some instances may strike the modern audience as rather bizarre, as when Augustus had the head of Alexander the Great replaced with his own portrait on a famous painting by Apelles displayed in the Forum of Augustus.
7. In reality, conquering Dacia had been on the Roman agenda since the Roman army suffered a defeat at the Battle of Histria in 62–61 BCE. Then in 85 the Dacians crossed the Danube, pillaged Moesia, and defeated a Roman army sent by Domitian. Some scholars believe the unfavorable truce Domitian established after a Roman defeat at the Battle of Tapae in 88 may have led to the unpopular emperor's assassination in September 96.
8. Vestiges of the mining activities are still visible at sites like at Rosia Montana.
9. He also built roads, gates, and an immense bath complex to improve Rome's infrastructure, and outside the city he created a new harbor at Ostia and built other roads and bridges, strengthening the empire as a whole.
10. Bennett (1997): 158. According to Jones (1993): 31–32, the stairs make a full turn every 14 steps, a layout that entailed a more complex geometry than the more typical choice of 12 or 16.
11. That statue vanished in the Middle Ages, but on December 4, 1587, Pope Pius V installed the bronze figure of St. Peter still present today: see Paoletti and Radke (2005): 541.
12. Lancaster (1999): 419.
13. Jones (1993): 34–36; Lancaster (1999): 426–28.
14. Among the earliest at Rome is the now-lost rostrate column (*column rostrate*) erected in honor of a naval victory celebrated by Caius Dulius after the battle of Mylae in 260 BCE.
15. There were Roman columns with ornamental motifs that spiraled around the shaft, such as that depicted on the first-century relief from the Tomb of the Haterii, or columns with horizontal rings of figural relief, such as the so-called Jupiter Column at Mainz (ancient Mogontiacum) erected in honor of the emperor Nero, but nothing that prepares us for Trajan's monument.
16. Becatti (1960): 11. See also Lehman-Hartleben (1926): 3, Hamberg (1945): 120, and Dillon (2006): 244–71.
17. Bianchi Bandinelli (1950); Gauer (1977): 76; Bruno and Bianchi (2006).
18. *Disciplina* as well as *virtus* feature prominently in Roman war discourse, with military loyalty to the commander receiving special emphasis: see Lendon (2006): 163–71; Vijgen (2020).
19. These were all organized and carefully analyzed by Karl Lehman: Lehman-Hartleben (1926).
20. Lehmann-Hartleben (1926): 88.
21. Classics once dominated elite curriculum, particularly in Britain during the late eighteenth and nineteenth centuries, a period of colonial expansion. On the voyage out, Macaulay famously read Livy to prepare himself to govern India for the British Empire. Related attitudes have affected modern scholarship, which customarily assessed the history of Roman art through the lens of self-justifying imperialism. See also the references cited in note 41 below.
22. Wickhoff (1900): 111–15.

23. Varying treatments of Trajan's hair, eyes, and facial proportions indicate that a number of different sculptors were responsible for rendering the emperor.
24. Of the six times Trajan is shown participating in a sacrifice, three of those times his head is veiled (*velato capite*), indicating that he is officiating.
25. In this particular regard, however, the execution seems to have been somewhat haphazard. Some figures have tools and weapons carved in stone, the hands of others are empty but have small holes drilled for metal attachments, while still others are empty without even holes provided.
26. Some seventy years later, the designer of the reliefs on the Column of Marcus Aurelius increased the height of the spiral band and cut into the stone more deeply to make the figures more visible.
27. For example, see Rockwell (1985), who argues that the column was carved upward from the bottom.
28. Brilliant (1984): 90–94.
29. Apollodorus likely also drew on the innovative combinations of perspectival conventions found in Roman tradition of triumphal paintings made by artists who accompanied Roman generals on their campaigns to record battles and the exotic locales in which they took place. These spectacular paintings, all of which are now lost, were carried in triumphal processions and later displayed in temples and public buildings; see Holliday (2002).
30. Some have even proposed that the sculpted reliefs truly represent a scroll: Birt (1907): 269; Bethe (1945): 80–83; Hamberg (1945): 111; Becatti (1960): 21. Japanese painted scrolls also display a fusion of perspectival strategies; see Chapter 6.
31. Only a single sentence from the work survives. The fragments of Cassius Dio's reports, first written some seventy or eighty years after Trajan's death, can be added to this.
32. Although Weitzmann (1947 and 1948; see also Bober 1948) claimed that continuously illustrated scrolls were probably not disseminated at that time, Florescu (1969) argues that illustrations could have been interspersed with Trajan's text.
33. As in the Augustan programs that served as his model, the discourse of victory is coupled with the bounty of peace; cf. Vijgen (2020): 365–434.
34. Rossi (1971): 13.
35. The dedicatory inscription above the entrance in the column's base corroborates this: "The Senate and People of Rome [give or dedicate this] to the emperor . . . to demonstrate of what great height the hill [was] and [what area of] ground was removed for such mighty works."
36. According to Davies (1997) 47–48, from its inception the column was designed to function as Trajan's tomb. The golden urns that held the ashes of Trajan and his wife, Plotina, later disappeared from the monument.
37. Davies (1997): 49.
38. The Mausoleum, in turn, recalled such monuments as the tumulus popularly known as the Heroon of Aeneas at ancient Lavinium and numerous Etruscan and republican era tombs in central Italy.
39. The Temple of Mars Ultor (2 BCE) was built to celebrate Augustus's victory over the assassins of Julius Caesar, which also culminated in the east (at the Battle of Philippi in 42 BCE). This revenge would be for earlier losses under Domitian.
40. Rossi (1972); Ferris (2003).
41. Current postcolonial approaches to archaeology stress non-Roman elements in provincial art rather than merely looking at the elites attested in literary sources. Ferris (2003), Johns (2003), Scott (2003), and the articles edited by Alcock, Egri, and Frakes (2016) challenge long-held assumptions about provincial deviation from metropolitan models.
42. Brilliant (1988): 110.
43. Representations of bound captives on the monument's crenellations significantly include German and Sarmatian allies of the Dacians.

Chapter 5

1. Literary sources describe numerous lost subjects like the sixth-century mosaics depicting the expeditions of Belisarius to North Africa and Italy and his triumphal parade, once in the Chalke of the Palace of Justinian in Constantinople; and scenes from the life of the Lombard queen Theodolinda in her chapel at the Cathedral in Monza (replaced by other pictures in the fifteenth century). Such subjects as Charlemagne's campaigns in Spain and Saxony once decorated his palaces at Aachen and Ingelheim in the ninth century. Later representations do survive that held particular importance as historical sources for contemporary contests between pope and emperor: these include the mosaic of Leo III and Charlemagne in the triclinium of the Lateran Palace in Rome showing both as vassals of St. Peter, and four mosaics from 1122 in the Lateran depicting Calixtus II, the struggle over investiture, and the Concordat of Worms.
2. Richly illuminated manuscripts competed with textiles in prestige, but these small and private items were not as accessible to as extensive and diverse an audience as were the Ottoman books discussed in Chapter 9.
3. Of Norman birth and Duke William's chaplain, his ca. 1071 commentary *Gesta Willelmi ducis Normannorum et regis Anglorum* (The Deeds of William, Duke of Normandy and King of England) was written to justify William's claim to the English throne. See also Oderic Vitalis, *Historia Ecclesiastica* (ca. 1123–1131).
4. Baswell (1999) examines the Norman literary manipulation of the past in order to foster a sense of continuity and smooth the rupture arising from the introduction of their rule and thereby gain acceptance among their new subjects; see also Thomas (2008): 43.
5. For example, the *Historia novorum in Anglia* written by the English theologian and historian Eadmer (ca. 1060–ca. 1126), which deals with the history of England between 1066 and 1122.
6. Any echoes of the conflict between Alexander and Darius are not accidental. The literary tradition known as the *Alexander Romance* was so popular in the Middle Ages that Chaucer referred to it in his *Canterbury Tales*; see Stoneman (2008).
7. These were commonly added in classical and medieval art. Whereas the terse commentary provides invaluable information to some scenes, in others the very concision inhibits interpretation. There is a growing consensus that a high percentage of nobles had at least basic literacy, and viewers without would have had others present to read, or even translate, for them. Here the artisans usually used a dark blue—almost black—wool yarn, although toward the end of the work other colors were used, occasionally for each word or for each letter; see Lemagnen (2011): 40.
8. Musset (2005): 174 argues that his presence could be interpreted as a pro-Norman attempt to undercut Harold's coronation.
9. Observed and recorded since at least 240 BCE by Chinese, Babylonian, and early medieval chroniclers, the comet's appearances were not recognized as reappearances of the same object until its periodicity was determined by Halley in 1705. This appearance of the comet is probably that of April 24, 1066, nearly four months after Harold's coronation.
10. William landed unopposed, as Harold had been drawn north to York to deal with an uprising led by his brother, Tostig Godwinson, with support from a Norwegian force led by King Harald Hardrada. Harold's victory at the Battle of Stamford Bridge signaled the end of the Viking Age.
11. Military historians suggest that Harold's army was exhausted by the forced march south to Hastings, where the Normans not only occupied the high ground, but were aided by such technological advances as a kind of stirrup that helped them fight on horseback; see Bloch (2006).

12. Medieval heroic narratives feature a good number of fighting higher clergy, most famously archbishop Turpin in the Charlemagne stories. Hollywood gave lowly Friar Tuck a similar task to comic effect in *The Adventures of Robin Hood* (1938).
13. We have here a case in which, given a lack in the reliable literary sources, the visual record of the embroidery has affected the traditional recounting of events; see Foys (2009): 158–75.
14. These are the careful drawings published in 1729 by Montfaucon discussed below. On Montfaucon's publication, see Pastan (2014b): 60–64.
15. The beginning section also shows some evidence of restoration.
16. Hicks (2006): 47–53, argues for only one additional panel. Among other restorations are the linen backing cloth added in 1724. Around 1800, large numerals were inked on the backing roughly enumerating each scene that are still frequently used for reference (as in the captions here): see Fig. 5.5.
17. For example, warriors are depicted fighting barehanded, although contemporary accounts suggest the use of gloves in battle and hunting was customary; knights carry shields.
18. The inscription on the Stele of the Vultures (cf. Fig. 1.3) citing the swearing of an oath of the nets of the gods demonstrates just how venerable this concept is.
19. In contrast, the Norman kings of Sicily and Castile self-crowned without the mediation of ecclesiastics. A twelfth-century mosaic prominently visible in the Church of Martorana, Palermo, shows Roger II receiving the crown directly from Jesus Christ, which may be evidence of Mediterranean encounters with more ancient Islamic traditions of sacred kingship, in addition to reflecting hostility to any papal interference. Similarly, whether or not the banner depicting a cross flying from the masthead of one of William's ships (scene 43) represents a papal insignia (as argued by some scholars), it signals that William's claim was divinely anointed and legitimate according to the traditions of medieval kingship: while making no claim to be a god like Naram-Sîn, William would nevertheless rule by the grace of God.
20. Contemporary scholars have not settled the controversy, although they generally agree that Ealdred performed the coronation. William was crowned following English ritual and even using Edward's regalia to lend authority to his reign; see Baswell (1999): 128.
21. The *Domesday Book* was the "Great Survey" of greater England and Wales ordered by William to establish what taxes had been owed during the reign of Edward the Confessor and to facilitate his reassertion of the rights of the Crown, including a wholesale redistribution of land. The title is Middle English for *Doomsday Book*, a popular designation due to the fact that "its decision, like those of the Last Judgment, are unalterable": Richard FitzNeal, *Dialogues de Scaccario* (ca. 1179). Today the manuscript is housed at the National Archives at Kew.
22. Orderic Vitalis (1969–1980): vol. 4, 94–95. Having grown up in England the son of a Norman priest and an English mother, Orderic may have heard first-hand accounts, but they would have been subject to the tellers' memories.
23. Reilly (2020) expands upon Gameson (1997) in her arguments for this interpretation.
24. The legend endured long after specialists began to doubt it. Introducing some version of it to students allows art history teachers—including the author—to introduce the role of women as patrons and artists in their survey courses.
25. Earenfight (2013) classifies such diverse medieval queenly roles as co-ruler with her husband, dowager upon the death of her husband, queen mother, and regent ruling for her minor child. In addition, queens could exercise real political power through such functions as advisor, intercessor or negotiator, and representative of the Crown. See also Stafford (1997).
26. Martin (2013) argues that as patrons, aristocratic women should be considered "makers" of art just as much as the artisans who crafted their commissions. This is certainly the case for the textile hangings (sometimes cited as a precedent for the embroidery) described in the *Liber Eliensis* (an ecclesiastical text from Ely) "made" by AElfflaed to commemorate the deeds

of her husband Byrhtnoth, killed at the Battle of Maldon in 991: see Digby (1965): 37; Musset (2005): 19; Hicks (2006): 39. This situation compares with the implementation of the "soft" power exercised by the Ladies' Memorial Associations following the Civil War discussed in the introduction.

27. Proctor-Tiffany (2019): 5.
28. Hicks (2006): 30–39.
29. Taking the pro-Godwinson position, its tone is very unstable since it seems to have been started when Edward was still alive but altered and revised right up to 1067. It was edited and translated by Barlow (1992); see also Tyler (2017), which provides the most recent (and universally respected) account on the shifting position of Queen Edith and her artistic patronage.
30. Proctor-Tiffany (2019): 9–11, demonstrates how gift-giving established social ties, and through the expectations of reciprocity, further bound communities and individuals together over time. Later medieval didactic works, such as *De regimine principum* of Aegidius Romanus, aka Giles of Rome (ca. 1243–1316), were widely known and translated, and instructed that offering rich gifts could benefit royal people politically.
31. For attributing it to Odo, see: White (2014b): 89–94.
32. The earliest reference to the embroidery is an inventory from 1476 listing the treasures of Bayeux Cathedral where it was hung annually for the week of the Feast of St. John the Baptist.
33. Pastan and White (2014): 289.
34. White (2014a): 53.
35. Beech (2005): 79–83.
36. Digby (1965): 40. Grape (1994) has challenged the view that the technique is English, differentiating between English and other Northern European practices, but according to Coatsworth (2005): 26, "The attempt to distinguish Anglo-Saxon from other Northern European embroideries before 1100 on the grounds of technique cannot be upheld on the basis of present knowledge."
37. Quoted in Hicks (2006): 37.
38. Cited in Hicks (2006): 37.
39. For example, the inscriptions include the Old English word *ceastra*: see White (2014a): 39. In the section showing the death of Harold's brother Gyrth, the name is spelled with a barred letter D, the majuscule (capital) form of the Old English graph called "thorn," which is pronounced "th."
40. Owen-Crocker (2012); contra, see Pastan and White (2014): 290, who argue that it definitely was made there.
41. Clarke (2013); see also Pastan (2014b): 194–95. Scolland was sent as an ambassador to Rome in 1073 where he advocated for the role of Augustine's importance as an apostle to the English, which improved the case for Canterbury's primacy. Gameson (1997) argues that Scolland's presence at St. Augustine's helps explain the embroidery's prominent depiction of Mont-Saint-Michel.
42. Proctor-Tiffany (2019) demonstrates that many medieval luxury objects—including sculptures, jewels, and manuscripts in addition to textiles—were also functional articles that were essential markers of personal identity and therefore traveled with their owners.
43. Gameson (1997).
44. Reilly (2020): 192.
45. Reilly (2020): 17, 89, 193. Reilly corroborates this interpretation through her examination of the comparable way Norman patrons employed architectural commissions.
46. Bloch (2006): 202.
47. Haskell (1993): 137–44, provides a full account of the rediscovery.
48. Montfaucon, *Monuments* II, 2, cited in Haskell (1993): 138. Montfaucon and Lancelot collaborated on the extended commentary.

49. Montfaucon, *Monuments* II, 2.
50. Quoted in Hicks (2006): 134–35.
51. For example, the fragmentary *Nine Worthies* tapestries (1400–1410) at the Cloisters in New York combine portrayals of historical, scriptural, and legendary heroes such as Julius Caesar, Joshua, David, Hector of Troy, and King Arthur.

Chapter 6

1. A phonetic script (*katakana*) was abbreviated into a cursive alphabet (*hiragana*) with a distinctive writing method unique to Japan.
2. They are also known as *senki monogatari* ("battle tales") and *gunkimono* ("war tales" or "warrior tales").
3. Their texts also intermingle Japanese with Chinese phrases, as opposed to warrior tales of the mid-Heian period composed entirely in Chinese prose (*kanbun*). For examples of *waka* and critical commentary, see De Bary et al. (2001).
4. Brown and Ishida (1979): 385–86.
5. Thomas Michie first drew my attention to this scroll while we escaped a January blizzard at the MFA.
6. Japanese surnames come first and given names second. Fujiwara and Taira are surnames; "Minamoto" can be expressed by "Genji" and "Taira" by "Heike."
7. Reischauer and Yamagiwa (1951): 451–52.
8. Mason and Dinwiddie (2005): 183–85.
9. Murase (1996): 160. Akiyama Terukazu (1961): 95–98, describes it as "a masterpiece on the subject of the world's military."
10. Suzuki (1960): 211. For those who cannot read Japanese, Mason (1977): 181–85, summarizes many of his identifications.
11. Ikeda (2003): 36.
12. Currents in feminist art history have alerted scholars to the outsized number of female to male victims (20 female to 3 male), many of which are depicted with exposed breasts, suggesting that such scrolls represent a form of pornography to male viewers: see Ikeda (2003): 39.
13. Reischauer and Yamagiwa (1951): 453. Since another illustration showing the burning of Shinzei's house would normally have followed, and since the scroll is some nine feet shorter than the other two surviving original scrolls (which are about 32 feet in length), it is assumed that a second section of painting became separated from the scroll.
14. Brown and Ishida (1979): 388 and 391.
15. Brown and Ishida (1979): 392.
16. Aoyagi (1997): 560.
17. Tomita (1925): 54.
18. McCormick (2018): 2.
19. Although there is no historical connection between the two traditions, Roman artists also employed a multipoint linear perspective in narrative programs, as seen in, for example, the fresco cycle of scenes from the Odyssey excavated in the via Graciosa, now in the Vatican Museum.
20. Iwao and Iyanaga (2002) vol. 1, describe how this type was commonly applied in epic and historical chronicles.
21. Grilli (1959): 7–8. McCormick (2018): 3 emphasizes how the selection of scenes and textual passages "encapsulate the story in a compelling and meaningful way for the patron."
22. Grilli (1959): 7–8.
23. Saint-Marc (2001).

24. Murase (1996): 160.
25. Okudaira (1973): 67–70.
26. Saint-Marc (2001).
27. Although some manuscripts do not mention Yoritomo's death, Yasuaki Nagazumi (2002) claims that it is almost certain that the manuscripts belonging to Group One are the oldest. Ishii (2014) confirmed that the fragment of the oldest manuscript of the story was included in the article dated 1246 in *Shua shugetsu shoso* (a book written by Shoso); indicating that the work was completed by the mid-thirteenth century and widely known by the century's end.
28. Tomita (1925): 54. The master of this scroll was also once identified as Hamuro Tokinaga, but that attribution is highly uncertain, too; see McCormick (2018): 6. McCormick states that artworks before 1600 lack documentation, making it difficult to determine who produced them.
29. Seckel and Hasé (1959): 41–43.
30. Seckel and Hasé (1959): 39–41.
31. There is further comparison with how Greek Archaic elites fashioned themselves as heirs of a Homeric ideal, implementing a heroic—and poetic—past to bolster their claims to power.
32. Mason (1979): 186–89.
33. *Gunki monogatari* espouse Amida Buddhism, which allows even the most violent warriors to summon Amida's name in repentance and be resurrected in his Western Paradise.
34. Okudaira (1973): 32.
35. Although Murase (1996): 160 describes this synthesis as evidence for "the emergence of national taste," in conversation on October 16, 2021, Kendall Brown advised me that discussing "national taste" during a period of feudal division is an inaccurate projection of modern nationalism imposed on the past.
36. McCormick (2018): 6.
37. Varley (1994).
38. For example, in the *Heike monogatari* Takahashi, an older warrior, spares the life of the young Genji warrior Yushikige due to his youthful resemblance to his own son. Yushikige then attacks and kills Takahashi. While pity for a younger adversary due to paternal regard is a frequent theme in the plot of *gunki monogatari*, Yushikige's determined loyalty to his faction to the exclusion of compassion exemplifies the rigid model of honor promoted by the warrior class.
39. Tomita (1925): 55 describes how they became a part of the so-called *E-awasé* (literally "picture contest") among refined aristocrats who demanded unusual pictures of fine workmanship.
40. When Emperor Meiji abolished the feudal system and samurai class in 1868, Edo-period literature perpetuated the warrior ethos. Thus, Nitobe Inazo's *Bushido: The Soul of Japan* (1899) idealized the warrior ethos as the epitome of all that was most admired in traditional Japanese culture and society.
41. In 1868, samurai clans brought Japan's feudal period to a violent end and installed the young emperor Meiji into a new role as the figurehead of a modern nation.
42. Many spectacular works left Japan during the period. The collecting activities of Fenollosa and Weld and their affiliations with the Boston Museum of Fine Arts are brilliantly explored in Reed (2017).

Chapter 7

1. Machiavelli, Chapter 12 (1981): 41.
2. The fresco was detached and relocated twice in modern times; today it is on the cathedral's north wall, flanked by a similar fresco monument by Andrea del Castagno to fellow mercenary

Niccolò da Tolentino (1456). The triumphal image of the leader on horseback—derived from ancient types like the equestrian statue of Marcus Aurelius in Rome—was revived in the Quattrocento: cf. Donatello's Gattamelata in Padua (1447–1453). Later modifications to the Hawkwood fresco's iconography reveal the ideological role such commissions played in Renaissance Italy's internal politics, here between the Albizzi and Medici factions in Florence.

3. Caferro (2006): 9.
4. Alberti (1966): 63. In the same passage he also notes that the dialogue between artwork and viewer promises "great admiration for the painter."
5. Griffiths (1978).
6. The Florentine chronicler Giovanni Cavalcanti described Niccolò as a selfish and reckless man who put himself and the army in a compromising position. According to Neri di Gino Capponi, a mediator between the Medici and Albizzi families, Niccolò used this opportunity to pressure the Sienese troops, which began to recede before Michelotto arrived. But according to Cavalcanti, Niccolò, feeling defeated and almost in tears, was relieved when Michelotto arrived and snatched victory from defeat. The accounts differ on who deserved more credit for the victory, Tolentino or Attendolo.
7. Quoted in Griffiths (1978): 314.
8. Born Paolo di Dono in Pratovecchio (1397–1475) in Tuscany, Vasari (1991): 77 claims he was named *Uccello*, Italian for "bird," because of his love of birds.
9. This symbol securely distinguishes the leader as Tolentino since it also appears in Castagno's *Equestrian Monument for Niccolò Tolentino*. The same symbol shown on a standard held aloft by a Florentine soldier in the London painting probably indicates the city's final victory.
10. Hudson (2008): 163.
11. Hudson (2008): 166.
12. Not only do written sources identify Michelotto as the other principal Florentine condottiere at the battle, but here his banner bears heraldic emblems similar to those of his relative Cardinal Ascanio Sforza in the church of Santa Maria del Popolo in Rome: see Hudson (2008): 164.
13. Rubin (2007): 255.
14. Pope-Hennessy (1969): 19.
15. Hudson (2008): 162 argues that the considerable differences in the handling of the landscape among the three paintings may indicate that the painting of the commission took so long that Uccello's style evolved while completing them.
16. This is especially evident when one considers the increasing naturalism shown in *cassone* painting that followed.
17. Cf. Rubin (2007): 214, 232. As Pope-Hennessey (1969): 21 observed, "the crossbows held by foot-soldiers and the polychrome *mazzocchi* are treated as objects of beauty in themselves; black, red, and yellow lances appear to have no other function than that of establishing fantastic linear patterns against the dark-green trees."
18. Starn and Partridge (1984): 42–43; Minardi (2017): 216–17.
19. According to Pope-Hennessy (1969): 20, "Like the horse of the 'Hawkwood,' the horses in 'The Rout of San Romano' are constructed round a framework of geometry . . . 'The Rout of San Romano,' possibly in conjunction with Alberti's treatise on the horse, depicts the full repertoire of postures of what, after the human figure, was the canonical subject of Renaissance artists." In correspondence on July 5, 2020, however, Patricia Rubin informed me she doubts that Uccello had access to Alberti's treatise, and believes rather that the panels indicate that he had sculptural models to study and turn in various directions.
20. Ghiberti's unfinished *Commentarii* (ca. 1447) outline the development of art from Cimabue through his own work and may represent the earliest known surviving autobiography of an artist, providing a major source for Vasari's *Vite*. Smith (2001) suggests that Ghiberti's "Third

Commentary" may have helped disseminate among his Italian contemporaries the eleventh-century Arab polymath Alhazen's writings about the optical basis of perspective. It may have been in Ghiberti's studio that Uccello began his lifelong friendship with Donatello.

21. Vasari (1991): 79, 83. On Uccello's perspective studies, see Minardi (2017): 224–27.
22. Pope-Hennessy (1969): 19 compares the careful placement of these details to how Uccello had used the depiction of ladders and other properties to create orthogonals in his earlier *The Flood*.
23. Rubin (2007): 232. Elsewhere (133) she astutely describes the compositions of fifteenth-century Florentine artists as "figurative arguments addressed to the sense of sight."
24. Alberti (1966): 43; see Rubin (2007): 229.
25. Rubin (2000): 68.
26. Brucker (1977).
27. For example, Leonardo Bruni and Alberti cited the ancient Greek philosopher Aristotle in support of such costly display. Aristotle's theory that *megaloprepaeia* (magnificence) is a pre-requisite of *megalopsuchos* (magnanimity) in the public arena (cf. *Nicomachean Ethics* IV.2–3) had been revived in the early fourteenth century as a part of political ideology and continued to inform such treatises as Giovanni Pontano's *De Magnificentia* (1486).
28. Popular subjects included biblical stories, episodes from romances, and hunts and battles. Iconographic links often makes it difficult to distinguish clearly between representations of sacred and secular history, and these representations continued to follow parallel conventions up to the seventeenth century. Isolated instances of authentic historical subjects are usually related to military, political, and religious crises.
29. For a recent assessment of the evidence, see Minardi (2017): 177–94.
30. The nine members of the Signoria, the government of medieval and Renaissance Florence, were elected to serve two-month terms. Members of the "Ten of War" were elected as the need arose.
31. Caglioti (2001): 49–50; see Hudson (2008): 163–65.
32. Rubin (2007): 238.
33. Caglioti (2001): 47.
34. According to Vasari, the Bartolini family commissioned other representations of military leaders from Uccello. He describes works in the Palazzo Bartolini Valfonda in the sixteenth century including "horses and armed men in the apparel of the time. Among the men are portraits of Paolo Orsino, Ottobuono da Parma, Luca da Canale, and Carlo Malatesta Lord of Rimini . . . all commanders of those times"; Vasari (1991): 84.
35. See Rubin (2007): 235–38. The Renaissance display of such items was undoubtedly directly connected to the ancient Roman practice of exhibiting ancestral portraits, *stemma* (family trees), war spoils, and other commemorative items alongside artworks—including Greek originals or copies—in aristocratic houses such as that in Pompeii housing the Alexander Mosaic.
36. A representation survives on the floor of their family chapel in Santa Trinita: Hudson (2008): 169.
37. Cox-Rearick (1984): 48.
38. Rubin (2007): 16 notes that this was even true of such artifacts as ancient coins and gems.
39. Caglioti dates the episode to sometime between 1479 and 1486. The report was made on July 30, 1495. Caglioti (2001); Dobson (2001): 38; cf. Rubin (2007): 275, n. 33.
40. Cox-Rearick (1984): 48. The reddish sour orange (*citrus aurantium*) that grew in Tuscany was called *mala medica*, offering a pun on the name Medici that permitted the family to make a visual equation between the red *palle* of their *stemma* and the fruit. As Cox-Rearick further notes, the allusion: "may have been all the more compelling because the *mala medica*, in turn, which was identified with the golden fruit of the Garden of the Hesperides (*mala aurea*) and

with the Golden Age." The idea of the immortal tree was a logical choice for Cosimo's promulgation of the ideology of dynastic succession.

41. Rubin (2000): 69.
42. Caglioti (2001): 37–38; see Hudson (2008): 163–65.
43. The Albizzi were duly punished for breaking the terms of their 1434 banishment: they left their place of exile, came within 100 miles of Florence, and allied with Piccinino, the duke of Milan's condottiere, to fight against the Florentine forces. In 1440, Bartolommeo de' Burelli da Cesena, a member of the Dieci di Balìa and *capitano del popolo*, directed that portraits of the rebels be painted on the façade of the Palazzo del Bargello, hanging upside down as though executed and dead, a commission awarded to Castagno: see Hudson (2008): 164.
44. After the expulsion of the Medici, the Council Hall was newly constructed by the Republican regime as the gathering place of franchised citizens. Michelangelo, who had just completed his *David*, was chosen to commemorate the Battle of Cascina on the opposite wall; although a preparatory drawing survives, he did not remain in Florence long enough to finish the commission.
45. Rubens's work was traditionally thought to be based on engraving of 1553 by Lorenzo Zacchia, which was either executed after the painting itself or perhaps a cartoon by Leonardo; recently, however, Wood (2011) suggests that Rubens was actually reworking an extant painting. In 2012 it was announced that a team had found evidence for Leonardo's painting on a concealed inner wall behind a cavity, underneath a section of a fresco by Vasari thought to cover the painting, but nothing seems to have come of that discovery.
46. Although Alberti's *Della pittura* captures ideas that were in wide circulation among artists and humanists, they have a much more complicated development than mere dependence on his treatise. Patricia Rubin advises me that the influence of the original Italian version of his treatise quickly disappeared, only to gain authority with the sixteenth-century translation from the Latin edition, which was embraced by academicians.
47. Kemp (2004): 184, 200–202.
48. Compare them with the Ottoman *Hünernāme* (Chapter 9), where battles, sieges, and the capture of cities are represented realistically yet restrained by a certain formalism.
49. Quoted in Griffiths (1978): 313.

Chapter 8

1. Not to be confused with the modern Republic of Benin, the former Dahomey, which has no historical relation to the Kingdom of Benin.
2. Plankensteiner (2010): 84; Hicks (2020): 139.
3. In discussing the various terms used to label the action, Layiwola (2007): 83, writes: "Within this logomachy for the truth of cultural rape, language yields the understanding that memory is not merely an instrument for probing the past, but also the theatre of the past."
4. Quoted in Hicks (2020): 139.
5. As Robert Farris Thompson used to teach about the Yoruba people, this is a culture whose ideals and tenets are expressed in art, music, and dance rather than text; see, inter alia, Thompson (1974).
6. Obas Ewuare the Great (r. ca. 1440), Ozolua (r. ca. 1480s-1517), Esigie (r. 1517–ca. 1550s), Orhogbua r. ca. 1550s-1570s), and Ehengbuda (r. ca. 1578–1608).
7. According to Layiwola (2007): 84, "Festivals reinforce the concept of remembering in Edo belief . . . [and are] an avenue for recalling reciting, remembering and refreshing various traditions on which the identity of the people is leaned heavily upon."
8. Inneh (2007): 103.
9. Read and Dalton (1899), quoted in Roth (1968): 229–30; see also Ezra (1992): 119.

10. Ben-Amos (1995): 25, 28.
11. Gunsch (2019): 48.
12. Seige (2007).
13. These may be what Dapper termed "engraved" pictures in his 1680 account (cited in note 24). Ben-Amos (1995): 40–41 notes that river leaves are also used by Olokun priestesses in healing rites. Their quadrivial patterns constitute a basic cosmological form in Benin thought: the four cardinal directions, the four days of the Edo week, and the unfolding of the day—morning, afternoon, evening, and night—at the time of creation.
14. The image of an equestrian figure expressed domination throughout West Africa in this period, and was an important component of the artistic vocabulary of warfare and triumph: Thompson (1974): 74–76; Ben-Amos (1999): 54–55.
15. Ezra (1992): 118–19; Blackmun (2007).
16. Coral was both an imported and a royal material. Coral neck rings were a sign of nobility whose use was granted exclusively by the Oba.
17. Initially intended as armlets or anklets, they soon became standardized units of exchange rather than jewelry.
18. Translated by Hodgkin (1960): 93.
19. Ben-Amos (1995): 14. Craftsmen in villages were not "servants of the king," as were their counterparts in the capital.
20. Ezra (1992): 47. According to Ben-Amos (1995): 17, religious strictures once prevented women from handling metal or metal tools, restricting their participation to the weavers' guild, although in recent years female members admitted to the brass casters' guild have begun making highly decorated ritual pots.
21. This is also the case with comparable earthworks at Saví in the Republic of Benin to the west; see Monroe (2010).
22. Hicks (2020): 133.
23. Edo (2007); see also Ezra (1992): 117. Accounts from European traders suggest that the courtyard was about 98.43 x 196.85 feet (30 x 60 m) and could hold 500 people.
24. Translation of Dapper's *Naukeurige Beschrijvingen der Afrikaensche gewesten* in Roth (1968): 74; see also Ezra (1992): 117.
25. On the significance of bird imagery on the Royal Palace, see Blier (1998): 55–58.
26. Translated by A. van Dantig, quoted in Ben-Amos (1995): 42.
27. Fagg (1963): 33 suggests that the absence of reference to the brass plaques in van Nyandael's account indicates that they were no longer being made by that time.
28. A nearly identical plaque is in the Berlin Ethnologisches Museum. According Gunsch (2018): 140–42, it is earlier than that in London. It shows pillars carrying plaques representing Portuguese men.
29. Gunsch (2018): 62.
30. Willett (1999): 202, no. 32.
31. Ezra (1992): 128.
32. Gunsch (2018): 40. Gunsch also notes that although the strategic use of art as a method of propaganda is frequently recognized in the art historical literature on European courts, similar discussions of African commissions are rare.
33. Ancestral altars were another site for the fashioning of memory, which "not only embody but shape the memories of the deceased, conveying his great success in life and relegating to an 'off-stage existence' any failures or flaws": Ben-Amos (1999): 131.
34. Ben-Amos (1995): 25, 88.
35. Ezra (1992): 129 suggests that the influx of manillas from Portuguese trade caused the increase and improvement of Benin casting techniques in the early sixteenth century.
36. Connah (1975): 142–43 argued for forged, whereas Garrard (1983): 17–18 believes Benin may have produced simple castings in the thirteenth century, which would conform to oral

traditions claiming an autochthonous tradition of brass casting going back to Ogiso times. See also Inneh (2007): 103–105.

37. The Ineh n'Igun is a direct descendant of this man, known as Igueghae: Ezra (1992): 47.
38. According to Benin traditions, the monarch ruling at that time was either Oba Ọzolua or more probably Oba Esigie: Ben-Amos (1995): 35.
39. Ezra (1992): 129. Their exaggerated depiction evokes that they were perceived as remarkably exotic, implying a kind of "Occidentalism," even if not in the service of political or economic dominance as Said (1978) argued for the European collective fantasy of Orientalism.
40. Ben-Amos (1995): 17.
41. Ben-Amos (1995): 18.
42. Fagg (1963): 33; Dark (1973): 4.
43. Ben-Amos (1995): 39.
44. Plankensteiner (2007a): 59.
45. Lawal (1977): 121. Although Benin artists may have been influenced by European models (cf. Fagg (1963): 33, Dark (1973): 4), they created their own characteristic aesthetic forms with specific meanings and functions that depart from their sources. The process is sparsely documented and has been woven into colonial and postcolonial discourses strongly impregnated with ideology; see Eisenhofer (2007): 59.
46. Ben-Amos (1995): 37, 39–41.
47. Dark (1975): 58.
48. Gunsch (2018): 37–40. Among the technical distinctions considered are flanges and decorative patterns, which she also adduces to reconstruct the placement of the plaques.
49. Plankensteiner (2007b): 22.
50. Ezra (1992): 118.
51. Willett (1971): 105.
52. Gunsch (2018): 45–58. Finnegan's pioneering work (e.g., 2012) demonstrates that in African storytelling oral and written—and by extension visual—traditions can interpenetrate.
53. Gunsch (2018): 58.
54. Gunsch (2018): 63.
55. Gunsch (2018): 61–62. Gunsch was writing about a plaque with a similar scene in the British Museum, but her argument holds here, too.
56. First published in G. B. Ramusio's *Navigazioni e Viaggi* (1550), translated by Hodgkin (1960): 100–101.
57. Ben-Amos (1995): 11–12.
58. Ryder (1969): 20.
59. Hicks (2020): 114.
60. Plankensteiner (2007b): 25.
61. Hicks (2020): 188.
62. Hicks (2020): 190, n. 44.
63. Nevadomsky (1997).

Chapter 9

1. Learning how to make paper from the Chinese, and then refining the process, helped generate the golden age of Arab science. Papermaking eventually made its way westward, where printing accelerated Europe's scientific advancement, but since Arabic script did not lend itself to moveable type, the practice of written manuscripts remained the dominate book form in the Islamic world until the twentieth century.
2. Fetvaci (2013): 103. The seventeenth-century historian Peçevi declared that Sokollu exercised more power and freedom than any preceding grand vizier. Fetvaci's valuable publications,

particularly this one, have made the Ottoman illustrated histories accessible to anglophone students.

3. This tarnishing compares with the oxidized silver in Uccello's *The Battle of San Romano* Paris panel (cf. Fig. 7.4).
4. During this period, succession anxiety was a very real concern. Since neither the decisions nor appointments made by one sultan were binding on his successor, the death of a ruler was akin to the dissolution of the state, and the personal allegiances that kept the government functioning could easily unravel. Such turmoil decreased as the Ottoman state became more bureaucratic; see Darling (1994) for an analysis of a nearly contemporary British account.
5. Fetvaci (2013): 117.
6. Fetvaci (2013): 118–19 describes how other sources indicate that the succession was not as seamless as this particular history portrays it.
7. Fetvaci (2013): 122.
8. A brief etymology of the term vizier may be useful. In the Quran, Aaron is called the *wazir* or "helper" of Moses (from the Arabic *wazara*, "to bear a burden"; *wizr* = "burden"). The proto-Shi'a chiefs al-Mukhtar and Abu Salama adopted it as a title constructed as *wazīr āl Muhammad* ("Helper of the Family of Muhammad"). Under the Abbasid caliphs, it came to mean a "representative" or "deputy," but at the Ottoman court, the title always kept the connotation of "perfect helper."
9. Even when falling out of favor under Murad III, Sokollu presented books to the sultan that reminded him his successes as a commander and statesman and how instrumental he had been for his father and grandfather before him.
10. He was preceded by Arif Celebi (ca. 1550s–1563) and Eflatûn-ı Şirvan-ı (ca. 1562–1569).
11. This deference to Persian models seems contradictory to the desire to articulate a distinctive Ottoman culture; nevertheless, one may be reminded of the cultural bilingualism already present in the ancient Near East: cf. Chapter 1.
12. Fetvaci (2013): 109.
13. Fetvaci (2013): 123.
14. Nafziger and Walton (2003): 105 put the number at three thousand soldiers.
15. Many events about the campaign are highly contested. For diverging views, see Fodor (2019). Walton (2019) discusses the continuing significance the siege plays for different national and religious identities.
16. Fetvaci (2013): 132.
17. Among Selim II's most trusted advisors was the tutor Hoca Ataullah, in the forefront of the anti-Sokollu faction at court and resentful of the grand vizier's power and influence. See Fleischer (1986): 41–70.
18. The final draft was not completed until after Sokollu's death, and Lokman continued to alter the manuscript's contents to emphasize the positive contributions of other courtiers, such as Lala Mustafa Pasha and Koca Sinan Pasha, important figures in the court of Murad III; see Fetvaci (2013): 129.
19. Fetvaci (2013): 136.
20. Fetvaci (2013): 133.
21. Fetvaci (2013): 12.
22. Fleischer (1986): 52–53.
23. Fetvaci (2013): 146.
24. Necipoğlu (1991): 15–30. See also Krstic (2013) for how other kinds of palace manuscripts helped shape concepts of what constituted a good Muslim and a good subject of the House of Osman.
25. Fleischer (1994); quoted in Fetvaci (2013): 7.
26. Murphey (2008): 77–98, and more generally the essays in Veinstein (1992).

27. Kafadar (2007): 12; Fetvaci (2013): 7.
28. On the *devşirme* system and the palace school, see Necipoğlu (1991): 111–22; for how they influenced shared aesthetic tastes among the ruling elite, see Necipoğlu (1992).
29. Kafadar (2007): 11.
30. The work of Necipoğlu (1991; 1992) is especially prominent; see also Fleischer (1992).
31. Fetvaci (2013): 7, who also notes an increasing audience for political treatises on the nature of the sultanate and the role of government.
32. Fetvaci (2013): 5.
33. Comparisons with how courtiers at the Palace of the Oba in Benin confronted the brass plaques might prove instructive.
34. Fetvaci (2013): 8.
35. Pedersen (1984): 99–100. For specific case studies in later Ottoman times, see the essays in Çipa and Fetvaci (2013).
36. Pedersen (1984): 99–100, but N.B. the editor's notes; Fetvaci (2013): 65–70.
37. Woodhead (1983): 157.
38. Fetvaci (2013): 71.
39. Necipoğlu (1992): 205.
40. Fetvaci (2013): 74.
41. Woodhead (1983): 161.
42. Necipoğlu (2005): 274–75; Fetvaci (2013): 72.
43. Outside the Topkapi Palace, books were also prized by many who followed other educational tracks in the empire, such as the madrasas or provincial palaces. Provincial elites also owned and esteemed books, and private and public readings were popular.
44. For the most part palace trainees used religious manuals and language aids: see Fetvaci (2013): 30–31.
45. Fetvaci (2013): 26.
46. Necipoğlu (2005): 331–68; Fetvaci (2013): 145.
47. Necipoğlu (2005): 362.

Chapter 10

1. In 1622, Pope Gregory XV established in Rome the *Congregatio de Propaganda Fide* (Congregation for the Propagation of the Faith). A neologism, propaganda is the gerundive form of the Latin *propagare* (to spread or to propagate): thus, propaganda means that which is to be propagated.
2. The word baroque is tellingly derived from *barocco*, Spanish for an encrusted pearl.
3. Marie's ceaseless political intrigues began even before her coronation in 1610 as the second wife of Henry IV. She acted as regent until her son Louis came of age in 1617.
4. Rubens devised twenty-one paintings depicting events in Marie's life couched in allegorical terms; the remaining three are portraits of the Queen and her parents. His contract stipulated that the paintings be completed in two years and that he paint all the figures, presumably allowing him to employ assistants to paint backgrounds, drapery, and other details. Although not a male-line descendant of Lorenzo the Magnificent, Maria (1575–1642) was the daughter of Francesco I de' Medici, the "cadet" branch of the family. She did descend from Lorenzo in the female line, however, and she was also a Habsburg through her mother. On the decoration of the Luxembourg Palace, see Belkin (1998): 173–75.
5. The war over the right of succession to the United Duchies of Jülich-Cleves-Berg saw Catholic Archduke Leopold V battle the united forces of the Protestant Margaviate of Brandenburg and Palatinate-Neuburg, further complicated by the involvement of Spain and the Netherlands.

6. Saward (1982): 133.
7. Compare this with the same iconographical motif held by Niccolò Tolentino on the London *The Battle of San Romano* panel (Fig. 72.).
8. The personifications reveal Rubens's deep knowledge of classical art. The Victory is derived from Roman types similar to that on the Cancelleria *profectio* panel (Fig. 4.1), whereas a laurel wreath is depicted on *adventus* panel (Fig. 4.2). Imperial eagles appear on the base of the Column of Trajan (Fig. 4.4).
9. The figure was once thought to represent Fortitude, who also has a lion as an attribute; see Millen and Wolf (1989): 155.
10. It was actually Ambrogio Spinola and Maurice of Nassau who initiated the settlement of Cleves and Jülich on October 13, 1614.
11. Although other nations locate their own Golden Age in the seventeenth century, excesses associated their colonial pasts have complicated the phrase. In 2019, the Amsterdam Museum announced that it would change the name of its permanent exhibition "Hollanders of the Golden Age" to "Group Portraits of the 17th Century," recognizing that the term "does not cover the load of historical reality in this period" since it ignores "the many negative sides of the seventeenth century such as poverty, war, forced labor, and human trafficking." In contrast, the Rijksmuseum announced that it would retain the term.
12. On this commission, which cost 3 million ducats over nine years, see Brown (2004).
13. See the reconstruction in Brown (2004): 108.
14. Bailey (2011): 8.
15. The city's name derived from *brede Aa*: wide or broad Aa.
16. The name was derived from his title, lord of Haultpenne in Flémalle, a Walloon area in the bishopric of Liege.
17. Justin of Nassau (1559–1631), governor of Breda from 1601 to 1625, was the only extramarital child of William the Silent and Eva Elincx, his mistress between his first and second marriage. William of Orange recognized him and raised him with his other children. The Dutch head of state, Maurice of Nassau, died before the end of the siege and was succeeded by Prince Frederick Henry of Nassau.
18. Bailey (2011): 98–99, who notes that Calderón may have had personal experience as a soldier in the Netherlands.
19. As related by Justi (1889): 202.
20. The motif also features in the Bayeux Embroidery (Chapter 5) with Conan represented handing the keys to his castle at Dol de Bretagne to Duke William at Dinan.
21. Brown (1986): 119. According to Hugo's account (1627), Spinola held that they were "more wise who are more gentle in cruelty, and that the fame of clemency was to be preferred before the name of severity."
22. Compare this with similar effect of the diagonal line of Macedonian spears in the Alexander Mosaic (Fig. 3.6).
23. The lance was phased out in favor of the bayonet (depicted in *The Death of General Wolfe*, Fig. 11.2), which could be fastened to a rifle for close-quarters combat. Lances were last used during the First World War.
24. Alberti (1966): 78. As noted in Chapter 7, the sixteenth-century translation of the Latin edition of *De pictura* ensured Alberti's treatise became a principal source for art theory among academicians.
25. From the French *répousser*, meaning "to push back," the compositional tactic can be the depiction of a tree or building, but when a human figure it is usually shown from behind or shadowed to define the viewer's position outside the pictorial space. Caravaggio was a master of repoussoir and set the standard for later Baroque artists. Velázquez, however, may surpass even him in the way he uses the device to establish not only the illusion of depth but also

rich spatial and sophisticated psychological relationships among his figures, perhaps most famously in his *Las Meninas*.

26. Rubens had befriended the younger artist during a diplomatic mission to Madrid (1628–1629). This was the first of Velázquez's two protracted visits to Italy. On both trips he was directed to obtain works for the royal collections. His reputation for success in that endeavor was such that when owners of prized works learned he was coming they evaded his requests to see them or absented themselves altogether. In Rome, he painted the famous portrait and of Pope Innocent X, who was said to have remarked of the formidable likeness, "*È troppo vero!*" ("It's too true!"): Bailey (2011): 157.
27. He may also have seen other portraits of Spinola, such as those by van Dyck and Rubens. López-Rey (1968): 79 notes that since Velázquez never saw Justin of Nassau, he probably made use of other artists' works for this figure.
28. Antonio Palomino, a court painter in Madrid who was one of Velázquez's first biographers, recalled the occasion and credited Vincente Carducho, a Tuscan, with the jibe; cf. Harris (1982): 15.
29. Justi (1889): 203. Howard Hibbard led me to appreciate how even though Carl Justi's (1832–1912) "great men" biographical approach to art history is no longer fashionable, his multivolume lives of Winckelmann, Velázquez, and Michelangelo masterfully evoke the world in which his subjects lived, and for the sensitive reader, that of their author. David Rosand took a similar approach to his predecessors.
30. Harris (1982): 127.
31. Saxl (1957): 316 suggests that Velázquez knew the large engravings of the siege and surrender of Breda by Jacques Callot, who had visited the city in 1627, commissioned by the Infanta Isabel Clara Eugenia.
32. Justi (1889): 203.

Chapter 11

1. Admiral Charles Saunders provided support with a fleet of 49 ships and 140 smaller craft.
2. Parkman (1884): 296–97. Today Parkman's *France and England in North America* (published between 1865 and 1892) is considered a literary masterpiece, although its usefulness as an historical study is considered limited.
3. Dedicated in 1772, Joseph Wilton's marble monument in the north ambulatory of the Abbey cost 3,000 pounds.
4. Rather (2004).
5. Staley (1989): 28 makes this extravagant claim, with which many critics disagree. At that time prints helped spread pictorial ideas all over Europe, shrinking the Western world and engendering a shared visual culture much like photography and video do today.
6. The term "Neoclassical" was invented about a century later; artists contemporary with the movement called it "the true style," a paring down of Baroque bombast and jettisoning of Rococo superficiality to return art to what they considered art's essentials.
7. Winckelmann was the first scholar to chart the history and development of Greek and Roman art. His *Gedanken über Nachahmung der griechischen Werke in der Malerei und Bildhauerkunst* (1755) was translated by Henri Fuseli as *Reflections on Painting and Sculpture of the Greeks* (1765, reprinted with corrections in 1767).
8. Adopted by his paternal uncle, the emperor Tiberius, and married to Agrippina the Elder, the granddaughter of the late emperor Augustus, Germanicus was celebrated for his victories over Germanic tribes. While on a mission in the east, he clashed with the governor of Syria, Gnaeus Calpurnius Piso. When Germanicus became ill and died in Antioch in 19, it was

popularly believed that he was poisoned on Piso's orders. Due to his military prowess, dashing physique, virtuous character, and death in the East at a young age, Roman supporters fashioned him as a modern Alexander the Great.

9. Prown (1969): 39. At this time ever more antiquities were coming to light in Rome and Naples: statues and even entire buried cities with houses preserving vivid wall paintings from which artists drew inspiration.
10. Prown (1969): 39.
11. Prown (1969): 40. His later *Death on a Pale Horse* (1817) is often cited as a precedent for developments in French Romantic painting; in 1802 he visited Paris and exhibited his final sketch for the work.
12. Richardson (1715): 18, quoted in Montagna (1981): 85. According to Galt, West first read Richardson as a youth while still in America; Reynolds credited the *Essay* with inspiring him to paint and write. See Prown (1996): 30; Gibson-Wood (2000).
13. Richardson (1715): 68, quoted in Montagna (1981): 85.
14. Richardson (1715): 41, quoted in Montagna (1981): 86.
15. Reynolds, Discourse II (1959): 27.
16. Reynolds became its first president and West succeeded him on the death of Reynolds in 1792.
17. Quoted in Staley (1989): 54.
18. Busch (1992): 46.
19. Busch (1992): 56.
20. Already questioning traditional authority, sophisticated Enlightenment viewers identified the discrepancy between the conventional religious meanings of motifs and the contemporary action they expressed. Form and meaning drifted apart, with art well on its way to aesthetic autonomy; more generally, see Grossman (2015).
21. Monckton (1726–1782) took control of the south bank of the St. Lawrence River facing Québec and then commanded the artillery batteries trained on the city.
22. Busch (1992): 46.
23. In addition to being a British officer, Smith was also a topographical painter.
24. Initially a provincial company from the colony of New Hampshire, Rogers' Rangers was attached to the British army in the Seven Years' War.
25. The son of an infamous Jacobite clan chief, Fraser raised 800 men from his family's forfeited estate to fight against the French in Québec. He resisted attempts by his superiors to make the soldiers of his regiment discard their full Highland regalia for clothing thought more appropriate for the North American climate. Mackenzie (1896): 490, argued that in addition to their bravery and agility, "their dress contribute [*sic*] to adapt them to this climate, and render them formidable."
26. Mitchell (1944): 31. Even if one's French was poor, Le Brun's 1698 treatise was illustrated by a series of engravings; cf. the introduction.
27. The British Museum holds the original items that West drew from.
28. Pronounced by Winckelmann the "utmost perfection of ancient sculpture," the *Belvedere Torso* had also been admired by artists such as Raphael and Michelangelo, inspiring several of the latter's figures in the Sistine Chapel ceiling.
29. Fryd (1995): 75. The phrase "noble savage" first appeared in English in John Dryden's *The Conquest of Granada* (1672):

    I am as free as nature first made man,
    Ere the base laws of servitude began,
    When wild in woods the noble savage ran.

    The application of the term in the portrayal of First Peoples comes with Alexander Pope's "Essay on Man" (1734).
30. Reprinted in Levine (2017): 462.

31. Galt (1820): vol.1: 101, cf. 104. If the anecdote is true, one wonders if the young American might not have had a few such lines at the ready. The figure allowed West to transport Winckelmann's arguments for the superiority of the vanished world of the ancient Greeks—the idealized musculature developed by physical exertion in the open air and sunshine of a more salubrious life—to contemporary America; by extension, it follows that in fulfillment of Winckelmann's prescriptions a superior art would come from that realm, a construct that would promote West's own identity.
32. Fryd (1995): 83–84, a reading reinforced by "Wolfe's pale skin, wounded state, and expressive face."
33. Said (1993) provides a fundamental analysis demarcating the unequal relationships separating the "civilized" colonist from the "savage" colonized native—the Other—that transforms the latter into the colonial subaltern.
34. The classic essay on the impact of West's painting on the tradition of history painting remains Wind (1938–1939).
35. Galt (1820): vol. 2: 232. Giving the incorrect date for the battle makes one wonder what else may have been remembered and reported incorrectly—or improved—in this account.
36. For example, Pierre Lenfant's *The Battle of Fontenoy, 11 May 1745* (1747) and David Morier's *The Battle of Culloden* (1746) .
37. Romney's 1760 painting is now lost but is generally believed to have been a precedent for Penny's 1763 version. Although panned by conservative critics, the paintings (especially Romney's) enjoyed great popular success.
38. In contrast, Wilton's monument at Westminster Abbey conforms to standard conventions, including depicting the dying general heroically, even partially clothed in classical drapery; wolves' heads decorate his Roman epaulets, making a visual pun on his name.
39. Solkin (1993): 212–13.
40. For more on the painting's reception, see Abrams (1985) and Schama (1991). The original painting was presented to Canada in 1918 as a tribute for its assistance in World War I, further imbricating it in the British imperial project; it now hangs in the National Gallery of Canada at Ottawa. One replica is in the Royal Ontario Museum, another in the Clements Library at the University of Michigan, and a fourth version hangs at Ickworth House, Suffolk. Each version varies slightly in the portrayal of Wolfe's death. Regretting his initial rejection, George II commissioned a fifth autograph copy, now in the Royal Collection.
41. Roman (2019): 105.
42. McNamara (2012): 19–20. On the evolving role of history painting in creating in the people a sense of nationhood at this time, see Barrell (1986).
43. The original version was acquired in 1963 by the National Gallery of Art, Washington, DC, from Christ's Hospital, London. Copley also painted a second, full-size replica for himself (now in the Museum of Fine Arts, Boston) and a third, smaller version (now in the Detroit Institute of the Arts).
44. At one point he served as commissary under Robert Monckton at the Battle of Beauséjour and later under Wolfe at the Siege of Louisbourg. He was known as "the wooden-legged commissary."
45. Sources differ as to whether Watson and Copley traveled on the same ship from Boston to England or met once Copley arrived in London.
46. The Raphael cartoons were in London at that time (now in the Victoria and Albert Museum), and Copley owned an engraving after Rubens's version.
47. Copley saw the sculpture at the Louvre. The figure of Watson is also similar to Raphael's *Transfiguration* in the Vatican, which he described in a letter to his wife was "allowed to be the greatest picture in the world," a painting whose religious significance underscores

the meaning of Copley's imagery. Watson's head recalls the head of one of the sons in the Laocoön, another famous antiquity Copley saw at the Vatican.

48. The flowing hair also helps identify the grenadier with compassion in West's *The Death of General Wolfe*.
49. Britain had a near monopoly on the slave trade, and in the period depicted in the painting, when the young Watson participated in the mercantile affairs of Cuba, England operated a vast slave smuggling operation designed to avoid paying duties on imported Africans to the custom house in Cuba, perhaps the largest slave market in the Atlantic sphere; see Boime (2002): 171–72.
50. Watson's will, dated August 12, 1803, cited in Neff (2014): 198. The lesson was further disseminated through Valentine Green's 1779 engraving, *Youth rescued from a Shark*.
51. However, writing in another period of American political and cultural turmoil, Dunlap (1834): 1.133–34, described Copley as a traitor "in support of the trade in human flesh . . . To immortalize such a man was the pencil of Copley employed"; see Kamensky (2016): 282–89, 396. As noted by Rebora (1996): 20, even modern scholars of Copley "have employed various approaches, primarily grounded in social history, with provocative, informative, and sometimes contradictory results."
52. Prown (1969): 40.
53. Prown (1966): vol. 2: 267–74.

Chapter 12

1. As the Ottoman Empire declined in the eighteenth century, young Greeks came into contact with the radical ideas of the Enlightenment and nationalism. Their cause drew support in Western Europe, leading eventually to military intervention by the British, French, and Russian states. Philhellenism enabled a younger generation of artists and intellectuals to treat modern Greece as an extension of ancient Greece, fomenting the idea of a regeneration of the spirit of ancient Greece that linked Romantic ideals with Winckelmann's nostalgia.
2. Entry for May 9, 1824, in Joubin (1932) vol. 1: 96.
3. For a close analysis of Delacroix's painting of this work—of his color and *facture*—see MacNamidhe (2015): 67–89.
4. It is therefore all the more striking that in his later *Liberty Leading the People*, which commemorates the July Revolution of 1830, Delacroix revived the academic type of the personification for the figure of the eponymous Liberty. Nevertheless, even with her artful partial nudity, she is, as Alexandre Dumas observed, "not at all a classic Liberty; it is a young woman of the people"; quoted in Jobert (2018): 130.
5. Museums like London's Victoria and Albert were established to instruct both industrial designers and artists.
6. Wilson-Bareau (1992): 38, 48–51.
7. The final version is now held in Kunsthalle Mannheim. Fragments from an earlier and larger painting are held by the National Gallery in London, while a third, unfinished version is in the Museum of Fine Arts, Boston. The Ny Carlsberg Glyptotek in Copenhagen holds a smaller oil study for the Mannheim version. A lithograph after the painting was not printed until after Manet's death.
8. Wilson-Bareau (1992): 55–56. The anachronistic French-style spats and ceremonial swords in scabbards hanging from white belts (an accessory worn only by French *gendarmes*) led Manet's friend and supporter Émile Zola to write that it was "a cruel irony, France executing Maximilian"; see Rubin (2012): 119, 137 n.1.
9. Bann (1990): 178.

10. As shown, artists like West may have painted works without a specific commission, hoping to sell them later to the state.
11. The painting was to be part of a planned "Hall of Remembrance," but after that project was abandoned *Gassed* entered the Imperial War Museum. The Ministry of Information also commissioned British painters for the project, but as an American Sargent's work would be emblematic of Anglo-American cooperation.
12. September 11, 1918, quoted in Charteris (1927): 214. Stephen Crane, author of the very unheroic *The Red Badge of Courage*, described the gradual loathing for "the romantic distortions of generations of battle paintings"; quoted in Burke (2001): 149.
13. Lubin (2016): 152.
14. Lubin (2016): 154.
15. Cowling (2002): 575–77 asserts: "The studio subject was surely intended to constitute a life-affirming, anti-war statement—an injunction to make art, not war."
16. Preston (2007): 12–19.
17. Quoted in Oppler (1988): 166.
18. Steer's report was published in both *The Times* (London) and *The New York Times* on April 28, 1937, and in French translation in the Communist daily *L'Humanité* on April 29. See Preston (2007).
19. Larrea (1947).
20. Quoted in Tóibín (2006).
21. Quoted in Barr (1946): 200.
22. Utley (1999): 72.
23. Richardson (2016). Cowling (2002): 579, describes Picasso's motivation from having experienced the bombing through black and white photographs and films.
24. Quoted in Barr (1946): 202.
25. Barr (1946): 200.
26. Brendel (1955): 127.
27. Arnheim (1980): 19 identifies the setting as the interior of a room, whereas Blunt (1969): 13 writes that the summary drawing of buildings "show exterior walls, and the electric light could be a street lamp just as well as a hanging light in a bedroom." Barr (1946): 201 suggests that Picasso changed his conception from exterior to interior space as the painting progressed. Ray (2006) provides a survey of critical opinions.
28. Barr (1946): 201. See also Cowling (2002): 582–84, who discusses Picasso's allusions to ancient sarcophagi.
29. One thinks immediately of the violent figural groups held within a stabilizing triangular composition by such early classical vase painters as Exekias.
30. Brendel (1955): 154.
31. According to Elgar and Maillard (1956): 173, Picasso "solved what seemed an unanswerable problem, how to give classical form to a work which overflows the classical bounds through the violence of its effusiveness and forms."
32. Schama (2009).
33. Blunt (1969): 2. The Getty Research Institute's copy belonged to the rancorous critic Douglas Cooper, who made marginal notes questioning Blunt's assertions (sometimes citing his political leanings) that date prior to Blunt's exposure as the "Fourth Man."
34. Blunt (1969): 9. Cowling (2002): 593–601 connects Picasso's "weeping women" to Matthias Grünewald's *Isenheim Altarpiece* and Rogier van der Weyden's *Descent from the Cross*.
35. The sequential images of the *Sueño mentire De Franco*, etchings (January 8 and 9, 1937) run like the reliefs on the Column of Trajan or the Bayeux Embroidery (although the immediate inspiration was more likely contemporary comic strips) and have great force as political propaganda; see Barr (1946): 9–13.

36. Barr (1946): 201. In the last case, however, he notes that the symbols in the 1935 etching probably express more personal than public meaning.
37. Brendel (1955): 137. Brendel suggests that the figure might represent a kind of Nemesis, but also reflects that "classical" does not necessarily mean Greek.
38. Quoted by Boeck and Sabartés (1955): 232. The absence of gore also recalls Uccello's *The Battle of San Romano*, but without the pageantry of Renaissance spectacle.
39. The influence on the development of Cubism of Bergson's questioning of traditional concepts of order and disorder has long been recognized: cf. (1911): 186–271. Whereas Analytical Cubism focused on destruction in its breakdown of form and space-time, Synthetic Cubism was more reconstructive, reassembling the pieces in a new form of order, one that remains multiple and decentered.
40. Among the many psychoanalytic interpretations of the motifs, see Schneider (1947–1948). Brendel's 1955 essay demonstrates how one can appreciate such analyses without necessarily subscribing to any limiting explanation.
41. Brendel (1955): 154.
42. Baldessari appropriated the term from Nathaniel Hawthorne, who wrote in an 1854 letter, "Upon my honor, I am not quite sure that I entirely comprehend my own meaning in some of these blasted allegories, but I remember that I always had a meaning—or, at least, thought I had." Karen Kleinfelder (1996): 30, 32 cited this in her interpretation of Picasso's *Minotauromachy*, which she generously shared after reading a draft of this chapter.
43. Chipp (1988): 141.
44. Quoted in Martin (2003): 129.
45. Chipp (1988): 152.
46. Already in 1820, 40,000 people came to see the exhibition of Géricault's *Raft of the Medusa* in London, where even if the audience did not respond directly with the painting's French political implications, it did coincide with increasing antislavery agitation, ensuring a favorable reception: see Riding (2003): 71.
47. *Artnews* 82.1 (January 1983), cited in Chipp (1988): 156–58.
48. Chipp (1988): 156–69 provides a full itinerary.
49. Organized in 1936 by the Socialist and Protestant minister Herman Reissig, the Campaign's distinguished list of supporters included Harold Ickes, Malcolm Cowley, Theodore Dreiser, Albert Einstein, Lillian Hellman, Ernest Hemingway, Archibald MacLeish, Thomas Mann, Edna St. Vincent Millay, Robert Millikan, Lewis Mumford, Dorothy Parker, James Roosevelt, and others.
50. Chipp (1988): 161.
51. An elaborate preview in Los Angeles sponsored by the Motion Picture Artists' Committee for Spanish Orphans on August 10, drew most of the movie colony, where many attendees, including Fritz Lang, Galka Scheyer, George Balanchine, Ernst Lubitsch, and Luise Rainer were refugees themselves.
52. Utley (1999): 73.
53. Chipp (1988): 166.

Conclusions and Coda

1. Bahrani (2017): 194.
2. It was on this 1799 expedition that the Rosetta Stone was discovered, leading to the eventual transliteration of hieroglyphics by Jean-François Champollion. Once a French prize, it is now displayed at the British Museum and commemorates the British victory over the French in 1801.

3. Haskell (1993): 137–44.
4. Lancelot (1733): 605, cited in Haskell (1993): 142.
5. For example, writers disagreed whether Harold landed in Normandy because he had been accidentally shipwrecked there on a fishing expedition, because he had gone there to rescue his brother and nephew who were hostages of the duke (in this version he was shipwrecked in the wrong place), or because he had been sent specifically by Edward to assure William that he would be next in succession to the crown. Lancelot acknowledged that the embroidery's imagery does not settle the problem, but noting that in a scene showing Edward on his throne its arms end in dogheads (which were associated with England) and he appears to be giving an order to Harold and a courtier (cf. Fig 5.2), which suggested that the last of the above hypotheses was correct. Lancelot therefore proposed that the defective inscription REX RD be amended to read REX EDWARDUS MITTIT HAROLDUM AD WILLHELMUM.
6. Lyttelton (1769): I, 353–55, cited in Haskell (1993): 143. Lyttelton also dismissed Lancelot's arguments about the nature of Harold's mission to Duke William based on the first scene. For an assessment of more recent attempts to reconstruct historical events from the embroidery, see Burke (2001): 153–54.
7. Kafadar (2007): 12.
8. Bahrani (2017): 170–72. Eppihimer (2019): 57–69 concludes that although Naram-Sîn's stele was not the direct model for these reliefs, they invoked traditions "that responded to Akkadian images and memories of Akkadian kingship" (60).
9. Warburg termed the diffusion and recycling of Greco-Roman motifs in Christian imagery the *Nachleben der Antike* (Antiquity's afterlife). Whereas Warburg was concerned with how a visual motif (*Leitfossil*) recurs through art history—the image of the victorious king in Near Eastern art, or the dead Meleager on a Roman sarcophagus transformed into a Christian martyr and later into a British commander killed in North America—here I intend new meanings construed in specific artworks that were never intended or conceived by their makers or original viewers, exceptional moments in their "object biographies."
10. The famous bronze head identified as Sargon (2300–2200 BCE, Iraq Museum, Baghdad) shows traces of deliberate damage that selectively target the image of the king. Pritchard (1969): 340 cites an omen regarding a statue from the later Babylonian period that expresses this belief, which reads: If the image of the king of the country in question The image of his father, or the image of his grandfather Falls over and breaks, or if its shape warps, this means That the days of the king of that country will be few in number.
11. Iconoclasm is not relegated to the past, as demonstrated by the recent destruction of the Buddhas at Bamyan by the Taliban or that at Palmyra and the Mosul Museum perpetrated by the Islamic State. As I make final revisions to this text in the summer of 2022, we are learning about Russia's purposeful targeting of Ukraine's cultural heritage in an attempt to annihilate its national identity.
12. Bahrani (2017): 122. Bahrani describes how such a removal "was considered a terrible event, a form of occultation, when divine power and protection were removed from the city." Cult statues of gods and royal monuments were purposely appropriated, and wars were waged in order to recover images that had been looted by enemies.
13. Feldman (2007).
14. Alternatively, the Roman writer Valerius Maximus credits the return to Seleucus I, and Pausanias (1.8.5) to Antiochus.
15. Coarelli (1969).
16. Fuhrmann (1931). De Vos and de Vos (1982): 164 revised this proposal and suggest that the owner may have participated in a Roman war in the east and identified with Alexander. It should be noted, however, that there is no concrete evidence that the owner of the House of the Faun was a military man, or not.

17. Kennedy (2013): 267; see more generally Cohen (1997): 190.
18. Musset (2005). A local lawyer rescued it from a wagon and secured it in his house until order was restored, when he conveyed it to the Bayeux city administrators.
19. Hicks (2006) recounts further events in the embroidery's biography, including the clashes between Hermann Goering and Heinrich Himmler, both of whom coveted what they identified as a chronicle of the battles and victories of a "Germanic prince" (205–47).
20. Hicks (2020): 21: "The obligation in these objects is temporal. It is a deferral, a hesitation, and so a duration. As for the whole museum, so for each thing contained within it, each obligation constituted in material form, the knowledge involved is a kind of memory, a re-collection."
21. See Hicks (2020): 213.
22. Among the extensive studies on correlations among changes in public and patronage, style, and politics, Haskell's observations in his essay "Enemies of Modern Art" are particularly sensitive (1987): 205–21. More recent assessments are provided in several of the essays edited by Phillips and Bear (2019).
23. For a time, patrons might seek to instill national identity through artworks that celebrated—and romanticized—a distant past; hence the popularity of medieval subjects in the nineteenth century.
24. The subject matter of any number of traditionally canonical paintings—Rubens's *Rape of the Daughters of Leucippus*, for example—can, along with aspects of artists' biographies, render classroom discussion problematical.
25. Films have explored the lot of the common soldier from *The Big Parade* (1925) to *1917* (2019). When focusing on the famous, some films do not shy away from exposing their faults, occasionally resulting in ambiguity. Many critics saw *Patton* (1970) as an anti-war film, whereas Richard Nixon watched it twice before ordering the invasion of Cambodia. For film as historical evidence, see Burke (2001): 154–56 and as historical interpretation 159–62; more generally, see Lowry (2000).
26. Sontag (1977): 6.
27. Frassanito (1975): 186–92; Rosenheim (2013): 96–98. In 1861, Matthew Brady made Mary Todd Lincoln's hands daintier and trimmed a few inches off her waistline to allay her fears that she looked too matronly.
28. On June 23, 2016, news media covered the announcement of Marine Corps commandant General Robert Neller: "Although the Rosenthal image is iconic and significant, to Marines it's not about the individuals and never has been. Simply stated, our fighting spirit is captured in that frame, and it remains a symbol of the tremendous accomplishments of our Corps—what they did together and what they represent remains most important. That doesn't change."
29. Quoted in Janouch (1953): 87.
30. At least that is how I like to read the artist's stylistic allusions when viewed in light of what Panofsky and Saxl wrote just a few years earlier: "we can understand why, from the crisis of the Counter Reformation . . . down to the crisis of our own days, which, among other phenomena, has given rise to the classicism of Picasso, almost every artistic and cultural crisis has been overcome by that recourse to antiquity which we know as Classicism"; (1932–1933): 278.
31. Dowd (2003).
32. The London exhibition of Picasso's *Guernica* provoked a lively exchange between Anthony Blunt and Herbert Read that suggests what those works lack. Endorsing the Marxist idea that the primary duty of art is to serve a social or political movement, Blunt maintained that Picasso had ignored contemporary realities to produce a work too complex and esoteric for ordinary people to comprehend, whereas Read attacked Blunt for backing the dullness of the social realism promoted by totalitarian regimes like the Soviet Union, and argued that Picasso

embodied a modern spirit that was more universal and transcended schools and categories. See Chipp (1988): 158–59.

33. Green (2000).
34. In 1993, Glenna Goodacre's group of three uniformed nurses with a wounded soldier comprising the *Vietnam Women's Memorial* was added south of the Wall, thereby expanding the community of makers to address the needs as understood for wider communities of users.

References

Abrams, Ann Uhry. *The Valiant Hero: Benjamin West and Grand-Style History Painting*. Washington, DC: Smithsonian Institution Press, 1985.

Akiyama, Terukazu. *La Peinture japonaise, Les trésors de l'Asie*. Genève: Albert Skira, 1961.

Alberti, Leon Batista. *On Painting*. Translated with introduction and notes by John R. Spencer. New Haven, CT: Yale University Press, 1966.

Alcock, Susan E. *Archaeologies of the Greek Past: Landscape, Monuments, and Memories*. Cambridge: Cambridge University Press, 2002.

Alcock, Susan E., Mariana Egri, and James F. D. Frakes. *Beyond Boundaries: Connecting Visual Cultures in the Provinces of Ancient Rome*. Los Angeles: Getty Publications, 2016.

Alpers, Svetlana. "Describe or Narrate? A Problem in Realistic Representation." *New Literary History* 8, no. 1 (1976): 15–41.

Amiet, Pierre. *L'art d'Agadé au Musée du Louvre*. Paris: Éditions des Musées Nationaux, 1976.

Anderson, Benedict. *Imagined Communities: Reflections on the Origin and Spread of Nationalism*. London: Verso Editions, 1983.

Aoyagi Masanori. *Nihon bijutsukan* [= *The art museum of Japan*]. Tokyo: Shōgakkan, 1997.

Appadurai, Arjun. "Introduction: Commodities and the Politics of Value." In *The Social Life of Things: Commodities in Cultural Perspective*, edited by Arjun Appadurai, 3–63. Cambridge: Cambridge University Press, 1986.

Ariane, Thomas. "Votive Relief of Ur-Nanshe, King of Lagash, and His Sons." In *Mesopotamia: Civilization Begins*, edited by Thomas Ariane and Timothy Potts, 164. Los Angeles: Getty Publications, 2020.

Arnheim, Rudolf. *The Genesis of a Painting: Picasso's Guernica*. Berkeley: University of California Press, 1980.

Arnold, Dieter. *The Encyclopedia of Ancient Egyptian Architecture*. Translated by Sabine H. Gardiner and Helen Strudwick, edited by Nigel and Helen Strudwick. Princeton, NJ: Princeton University Press, 1997.

Aruz, Joan, and Ronald Wallenfels, eds. *Art of the First Cities: The Third Millennium B.C. from the Mediterranean to the Indus*. New Haven, CT: Yale University Press, 2003.

Assmann, Jan. "Communicative and Cultural Memory." In *A Companion to Cultural Memory Studies*, edited by Astrid Erll and Ansgar Nünning, 109–18. Berlin: Walter de Gruyter, 2010.

Azoulay, Vincent. *Les Tyrannicides d'Athens: vie et mort de deux statues*, L'Universe historique. Paris: Éditions Seuil, 2014.

Bahrani, Zainab. *Art of Mesopotamia*. New York: Thames & Hudson, 2017.

Bailey, Anthony. *Velázquez and* The Surrender of Breda: *The Making of a Masterpiece*. New York: Henry Holt, 2011.

Bakhtin, Mikhail M. *The Dialogic Imagination: Four Essays*. Edited by Michael Holquist, translated by Caryl Emerson and Michael Holquist. Austin: University of Texas Press, 1981.

Bal, Mieke. *Narratology: Introduction to the Theory of Narrative*, 2nd ed. Toronto: University of Toronto Press, 1997.

Bal, Mieke, and Norman Bryson. "Semiotics and Art History." *Art Bulletin* 73, no. 2 (1991): 174–208.

Bann, Stephen. *The Inventions of History: Essays on the Representation of the Past*. Manchester, UK: Manchester University Press, 1990.

Barlow, Frank. *The Life of King Edward, who rests at West-minster. Attributed to a monk of St. Bertin*. Edited and translated by Frank Barlow. Oxford: Clarendon Press, 1992.

Barr, Alfred H. Jr. *Picasso, Fifty Years of his Art*. New York: The Museum of Modern Art, 1946.
Barrell, John. *The Political Theory of Painting from Reynolds to Hazlitt: "The Body of the Public."* New Haven, CT: Yale University Press, 1986.
Barthes, Roland. "Élements de sémiologie." *Communications* 4 (1964): 91–135.
Barthes, Roland. "The Death of the Author." In *Image-Music-Text*, essays selected and translated by Stephen Heath, 142–48. New York: Hill and Wang, 1977.
Baswell, Christopher. "Latinitas." In *The Cambridge History of Medieval Literature*, edited by David Wallace, 122–51. Cambridge: Cambridge University Press, 1999.
Becatti, Giovanni. *La colonna coclide istoriata. Problemi storici, iconografici, stilistici*. Roma: "L'Erma" di Bretschneider, 1960.
Becker, Howard S. *Art Worlds*. Berkeley: University of California Press, 1982.
Beech, George. *Was the Bayeux Tapestry Made in France? The Case for St. Florent of Saumur*. New York: Palgrave Macmillan, 2005.
Belkin, Kristin Lohse. *Rubens*. London: Phaidon, 1998.
Bellosi, Luciano. *Duccio: The Maestà*. New York: Thames and Hudson, 1999.
Ben-Amos, Paula Girshick. *The Art of Benin*, rev. ed. Washington, DC: Smithsonian Institution Press, 1995.
Ben-Amos, Paula Girshick. *Art, Innovation, and Politics in Eighteenth-Century Benin*. Bloomington: Indiana University Press, 1999.
Ben-Amos, Paula, and Arnold Rubin, eds. *The Art of Power, The Power of Art: Studies in Benin Iconography*. Los Angeles: Museum of Cultural History, University of California, Los Angeles, 1983.
Bennett, Julian. *Trajan: Optimus Princeps: A Life and Times*. Bloomington: Indiana University Press, 1997.
Bergson, Henri. *Creative Evolution*. Translated by Arthur Mitchell. New York: Henry Holt, 1911.
Bethe, Erich. *Buch und Bild im Altertum*. Leipzig: O. Harrassowitz, 1945.
Bhabha, Homi. "Culture's In-Between." In *Questions of Cultural Identity*, edited by Stuart Hall and Paul Du Gay, 53–60. London: Sage, 1996.
Bianchi Bandinelli, Ranuccio. "Il 'Maestro delle Impresse di Traiano.'" In R. Bianchi Bandinelli, *Storicità dell'arte classica*, 2nd ed., 209–28. Florence: Electa, 1950.
Birt, Theodor. *Die Buchrolle in der Kunst*. Leipzig: B. G. Teubner, 1907.
Black, Jeremy A. *The Literature of Ancient Sumer*. New York: Oxford University Press, 2006.
Blackmun, Barbara W. "221. Relief Plaque: Oba Esigie on Horseback with Retainers." In *Benin Kings and Rituals: Court Arts from Nigeria*, edited by Barbara Plankensteiner, 441. Ghent: Snoek, 2007.
Blier, Suzanne Preston. *The Royal Arts of Africa: The Majesty of Form*. New York: Harry N. Abrams, 1998.
Blight, David W. *Race and Reunion: The Civil War in American Memory*. Cambridge, MA: Belknap Press of Harvard University Press, 2001.
Bloch, R. Howard. *A Needle in the Right Hand of God: The Norman Conquest of 1066 and the Making and Meaning of the Bayeux Tapestry*. New York: Random House, 2006.
Blunt, Anthony. *Artistic Theory in Italy, 1450–1660*. Oxford: Clarendon Press, 1940.
Blunt, Anthony. *Picasso's Guernica*. Oxford: Oxford University Press, 1969.
Boardman, John. *Persia and the West*. London: Thames and Hudson, 2000.
Bober, Harry. Review of Weitzman (1947). *Art Bulletin* 30, no. 4 (1948): 284–88.
Boeck, Wilhelm, and Jaíme Sabartés. *Picasso*. New York: Harry N. Abrams, 1955.
Boime, Albert. "Blacks in Shark-Infested Waters. Visual Encodings of Racism in Copley and Homer." In *Race-ing Art History: Critical Readings in Race and Art History*, edited by Kymberly N. Pinder, 169–89. New York: Routledge, 2002.
Bourdieu, Pierre. *The Logic of Practice*. Translated by Richard Nice. Stanford, CA: Stanford University Press, 1990.
Breasted, James Henry. *A History of the Ancient Egyptians*. New York: Charles Scribner's Sons, 1908.
Brendel, Otto. "Classic and Non-Classic Elements in Picasso's Guernica." In *From Sophocles to Picasso*, edited by Whitney Oats, 120–59. Bloomington: Indiana University Press, 1955.

Brendel, Otto. *Prolegomena to the Study of Roman Art*. Revised by Jerome J. Pollitt. New Haven, CT: Yale University Press, 1979.

Brewer, Douglas J. *The Archaeology of Egypt Beyond Pharaohs*. Cambridge: Cambridge University Press, 2012.

Brilliant, Richard. *Visual Narratives. Storytelling in Etruscan and Roman Art*. Ithaca, NY: Cornell University Press, 1984.

Brilliant, Richard. "Roman Art and Imperial Policy." *Journal of Roman Archaeology* 1 (1988): 110–14.

Brooks, Van Wyck. "On Creating a Usable Past." *The Dial* (April 11, 1918): 337–41.

Brown, Delmer M., and Ichiro Ishida. *The Future and the Past: A Translation and Study of the Gukanshō, An Interpretative History of Japan*. Berkeley: University of California Press, 1979.

Brown, Jonathan. *Velazquez: Painter and Courtier*. New Haven, CT: Yale University Press, 1986.

Brown, Jonathan, and John H. Eliot. *A Palace for a King: The Buen Retiro and the Court of Philip IV*, rev. and expanded ed. New Haven, CT: Yale University Press, 2004.

Brubaker, Rogers, and Frederick Cooper. "Beyond Identity." *Theory and Society* 29, no. 1 (2000): 1–47.

Brucker, Gene. *The Civic World of Early Renaissance Florence*. Princeton, NJ: Princeton University Press, 1977.

Bruno, Matthias, and Fulvia Bianchi. "La colonna di Traiano all luce delle recenti indagini." *Papers of the British School at Rome* 74 (2006): 293–322.

Bryce, Trevor. *The Kingdom of the Hittites*. New York: Oxford University Press, 1998.

Bryce, Trevor. *Letters of the Great Kings of the Ancient Near East: The Royal Correspondence of the Late Bronze Age*. London: Routledge, 2003.

Bryce, Trevor. *Life and Society in the Hittite World*. Oxford: Oxford University Press, 2004.

Burke, Peter. *The Fabrication of Louis XIV*. New Haven, CT: Yale University Press 1992.

Burke, Peter. *Eyewitnessing: The Uses of Images as Historical Evidence*. Ithaca, NY: Cornell University Press, 2001.

Burke, Peter. *Cultural Hybridity*. Cambridge: Polity Press, 2009.

Busch, Werner. "Copley, West, and the Tradition of European High Art." In *American Icons: Transatlantic Perspectives on Eighteenth- and Nineteenth-Century American Art*, edited by Thomas W. Gaehtgens and Heinz Ickstadt, 34–59. Santa Monica, CA: Getty Center for the History of Art and the Humanities, 1992.

Caferro, William. *John Hawkwood: An English Mercenary in Fourteenth Century Italy*. Baltimore: Johns Hopkins University Press, 2006.

Caglioti, F. "Nouveautés sur la *Bataille de San Romano* de Paolo Uccello." *Revue du Louvre* 51, no. 4 (2001): 37–54.

Camp, John McK. II. *The Archaeology of Athens*. New Haven, CT: Yale University Press, 2001.

Camp, John McK. II. *The Athenian Agora Site*, 5th ed. Princeton, NJ: Princeton University Press, 2010.

Chandler, Raymond. *The Little Sister*. Boston: Houghton Mifflin, 1949.

Charteris, Hon. Evan K. C. *John Singer Sargent: With Reproductions from His Paintings and Drawings*. New York: Charles Scribner's Sons, 1927.

Chipp, Herschel B. *Picasso's Guernica. History, Transformations, Meanings*. With a chapter by Javier Tusell. Berkeley: University of California Press, 1988.

Ciappelli, Giovanni, and Patricia Lee Rubin, eds. *Art, Memory, and Family in Renaissance Florence*. Cambridge: Cambridge University Press, 2000.

Cichorius, Conrad. *Die Reliefs der Traianssäule*. Berlin: G. Reimer, 1896.

Çipa, H. Erdem, and Emıne Fetvaci, eds. *Writing History at the Ottoman Court: Editing the Past, Fashioning the Future*. Bloomington: Indiana University Press, 2013.

Clarke, Howard B. "The Identity of the Designer of the Bayeux Tapestry." *Anglo-Norman Studies* 35 (2013): 120–39.

Cline, Eric H. *1177 B.C.: The Year Civilization Collapsed*. Princeton, NJ: Princeton University Press, 2014.

Coarelli, Filippo. "Le *tyrannoctone* du Capitole et la mort de Tiberius Gracchus." *Mélange de l'École Française de Rome: Antiquité* 81 (1969): 137–60.

Coarelli, Filippo, Paul Zanker, Bruno Brizzi, Cinzia Conti, Roberto Meneghini, and Paul Zanker. *The Column of Trajan*. Translated by Cynthia Rockwell. Rome: Colombo in collaboration with the Deutsches Archäologisches Institut, 2000.

Coatsworth, Elizabeth. "Stitches in Time: Establishing a History of Anglo-Saxon Embroidery." In *Medieval Clothing and Textiles* 1, edited by Robin Netherton and Gale R. Owen-Crocker, 1–27. Woodbridge, UK: The Boydell Press, 2005.

Cohen, Ada. *The Alexander Mosaic. Stories of Victory and Defeat*. New York: Cambridge University Press, 1997.

Comment, Bernard. *The Panorama*. London: Reaktion Books, 2004.

Connah, Graham. *The Archaeology of Benin*. Oxford: Clarendon Press, 1975.

Courbaud, Edmond. *Le bas-relief romain à représentations historiques: étude archéologique, historique, et littéraire*. Paris: A. Fontemoing, 1899.

Cowling, Elizabeth. *Picasso: Style and Meaning*. New York: Phaidon, 2002.

Cox-Rearick, Janet. *Dynasty and Destiny in Medici Art: Pontormo, Leo X, and the Two Cosimos*. Princeton, NJ: Princeton University Press, 1984.

Cruickshank, Dan. "The First Cities." In *Brick*, edited by William Hall, 8–13. London: Phaidon Press, 2015.

Cust, Edward. *Lives of the Warriors of the Seventeenth Century*, 3 vols. London: John Murray, 1865–1869.

Dapper, Olfert. *Beschreibung von Afrika*. New York: Johnson Reprint Corp., 1967 [first published in Amsterdam: Jacob van Meurs, 1680].

Darling, Linda T. "Ottoman Politics through British Eyes: Paul Rycaut's 'The Present State of the Ottoman Empire.'" *Journal of World History* 5, no. 1 (1994): 71–97.

Dark, Philip. *An Introduction to the Benin Art and Technology*. Oxford: Clarendon Press, 1973.

Dark, Philip. "Benin Bronze Heads: Styes and Chronology." In *African Images: Essays in African Iconology*, edited by Daniel F. McCall and Edna G. Bay, 25–103. New York: Africana Pub. Co., for the African Studies Center, Boston University, 1975.

Davies, Penelope J. E. "The Politics of Perpetuation: Trajan's Column and the Art of Commemoration." *American Journal of Archaeology* 101, no. 1 (1997): 41–65.

De Bary, William Theodore, Donald Keene, George Tanabe, and Paul Varley. *Sources of Japanese Tradition, Vol. 1, From Earliest Times to 1600*. New York, Columbia University Press, 2001.

De Vos, Arnold, and Mariette de Vos. *Pompei, Ercolano, Stabia*. Guide archeologiche Laterza. Rome: Laterza, 1982.

Didion, Joan. *Where I Was From*. New York: Knopf, 2003.

Digby, George. "Technique and Production." In *The Bayeux Tapestry. A Comprehensive Survey*, 2nd ed., edited by Frank M. Stenton, 37–55. London: Phaidon Press, 1965.

Dillon, Sheila. "Women on the Columns of Trajan and Marcus Aurelius and the Visual Language of Roman Victory." In *Representations of War in Ancient Rome*, edited by Sheila Dillon and Katherine E. Welch, 244–71. Cambridge: Cambridge University Press, 2006.

Dobson, Chris. *Paolo Uccello: San Romano, The Art of War*. Clare, UK: C. Dobson, 2001.

Domby, Adam H. *The False Cause: Fraud, Fabrication, and White Supremacy in Confederate Memory*. Charlottesville: University of Virginia Press, 2020.

Donderer, Michael. "Das pompejanische Alexandermosaik—Ein östliches Importstück?" In *Das antike Rom und der Osten. Festschrift für Klaus Parlasca zum 65. Geburtstag*, edited by Christoph Börker and Michael Donderer, 19–31. Erlingen: Universitätsbund Erlanden-Nürnberg: Auslieferung, Universitätsbibliothek Erlangen, 1990.

Dowd, Maureen. "Powell Without Picasso." *New York Times*, February 5, 2003.

Dunlap, William. *History of the Rise and Progress of the Arts of Design in the United States*, 2 vols. New York: G. P. Scott, 1834 [reprinted New York: Benjamin Blom, 1965].

Earenfight, Theresa. *Queenship in Medieval Europe*. New York: Palgrave Macmillan, 2013.

Edgerton, Samuel Y. *The Mirror, the Window, and the Telescope. How Renaissance Linear Perspective Changed Our Vision of the Universe*. Ithaca: Cornell University Press, 2009.

Edo, Victor Osaro. "Hierarchy and Organization of the Benin Kingdom and the Palace." In *Benin Kings and Rituals: Court Arts from Nigeria*, edited by Barbara Plankensteiner, 91–101. Ghent: Snoek, 2007.

Eisenhofer, Stefan. "Olokun's Messengers. The Portuguese and the Kingdom of Benin." In *Benin Kings and Rituals: Court Arts from Nigeria*, edited by Barbara Plankensteiner, 55–63. Ghent: Snoek, 2007.

Elgar, Frank, and Robert Maillard. *Picasso: A Study of His Work*. Translated by Francis Scarfe. New York: Thames and Hudson, 1956.

Eppihimer, Melissa. *Exemplars of Kingship: Art, Tradition, and the Legacy of the Akkadians*. New York: Oxford University Press, 2019.

Erll, Astrid, and Ansgar Nünning, eds. *A Companion to Cultural Memory Studies*. Berlin: Walter de Gruyter, 2010.

Ezra, Kate. *Royal Art of Benin: The Perls Collection in the Metropolitan Museum of Art*. New York: Metropolitan Museum of Art, 1992.

Fagg, William Buller. *Nigerian Images: The Splendor of African Sculpture*. New York: Praeger, 1963.

Fagg, William Buller. "Benin. The Sack That Never Was." In *Images of Power: Art of the Royal Court of Benin*, edited by Flora S. Kaplan, 20–21. New York: New York University, Grey Art Gallery & Study Center, 1981.

Faulkner, Raymond O. "The Battle of Kadesh." *Festschrift zum 80. Geburtstag von Professor Dr. Hermann Junker. Deutsches Archäologisches Institut, Abteilung Kairo* 16 (1958): 93–111.

Feldman, Marian H. "Darius I and the Heroes of Akkad: Affect and Agency in the Bisitun Relief." In *Ancient Near Eastern Art in Context: Studies in Honor of Irene J. Winter by Her Students*, edited by J. Cheng and M. Feldman, 265–93. Leiden: Brill, 2007.

Ferris, Iain. "The Hanged Men Dance: Barbarians in Trajanic Art." In *Roman Imperialism and Provincial Art*, edited by Sarah Scott and Jane Webster, 53–68. New York: Cambridge University Press, 2003.

Fetvaci, Emıne. *Picturing History at the Ottoman Court*. Bloomington: Indiana University Press, 2013.

Finnegan, Ruth. *Oral Literature in Africa*, rev. ed. Cambridge: Open Book Publishers, 2012.

Fleischer, Cornell. *Bureaucrat and Intellectual in the Ottoman Empire: The Historian Mustafa Âli*. Princeton, NJ: Princeton University Press, 1986.

Fleischer, Cornell. "The Lawgiver as Messiah: The Making of the Imperial Image in the Reign of Süleymān." In *Soliman le magnifique et son temps*, edited by Giles Veinstein, 159–77. Paris: Documentation Française, 1992.

Fleischer, Cornell. "Between the Lines: Realities of Scribal Life in the Sixteenth Century." In *Studies in Ottoman History in Honor of Professor V. L. Menage*, edited by Colin Imber and C. Heywood, 45–61. Istanbul: Isis Press, 1994.

Florescu, Florea Bobu. *Die Trajanssäule: Grundfragen und Tafeln*. Translated by Arnold Pancratz. Bonn: Rudolf Habelt Verlag GmbH, 1969.

Flower, Harriet I. "Alexander the Great and Panhellenism." In *Alexander the Great in Fact and Fiction*, edited by A. B. Bostworth and E. J. Baynham, 96–135. Oxford: Oxford University Press, 2000.

Fodor, Pál, ed. *The Battle for Central Europe: The Siege of Szigetvár and the Death of Süleyman the Magnificent and Nicholas Zrínyi (1566)*. Leiden: Brill, 2019.

Ford, Randolph. *Rome, China, and the Barbarians: Ethnographic Traditions and the Transformation of Empires*. New York: Cambridge University Press, 2020.

Foucault, Michel. "Subject and Power." In *Michel Foucault: Beyond Structuralism and Hermeneutics*, 2nd ed., edited by Hubert L. Dreyfus and Paul Rabinow, 208–28. Chicago: University of Chicago Press, 1982.

Foys, Martin K. "Pulling the Arrow Out: The Legend of Harold's Death and the Bayeux Tapestry." In *The Bayeux Tapestry: New Interpretations*, edited by Martin K. Foys, 158–75. Woodbridge, UK: Boydell and Brewer, 2009.

Frankfort, Henri. *The Art and Architecture of the Ancient Orient*, 4th rev. ed. Harmondsworth: Penguin Books, 1970.

Frassanito, William A. *Gettysburg: A Journey in Time*. New York: Charles Scribner's Sons, 1975.

Freed, Rita E. *Ramesses the Great, His Life and World*, an exhibition presented by the City of Memphis, Tennessee and the Egyptian Antiquities Organization in cooperation with Memphis

Brooks Museum of Art and the Institute of Egyptian Art and Archaeology, Memphis State University. Memphis: City of Memphis, 1987.
Freeman, Edward A. *The History of the Norman Conquest of England, its causes and results*, 6 vols. Oxford: Clarendon Press, 1867–1879.
Fryd, Vivien Green. "Rereading the Indian in Benjamin West's 'Death of General Wolfe.'" *American Art* 9, no. 1 (Spring 1995): 72–85.
Fuhrmann, Heinrich. *Philoxenos von Eretria: Archäologische Untersuchungen über zwei Alexandermosaike*. Göttingen: Kaestner, 1931.
Furtwängler, Adolf. *Das Tropaion von Adamkilssi und provinzialrömsiche Kunst*. München: Verlag der K. Akademie, 1903.
Gaballa, G. A. *Narrative in Egyptian Art. Deutsches Archaëologisches Institut, Abteilung Kairo*. Mainz am Rhein: von Zabern, 1976.
Galt, John. *The Life and Studies of Benjamin West, Esq. President of the Royal Academy of London, Composed from Materials Furnished by Himself*. London: Printed for T. Cadell and W. Davies, 1820.
Gameson, Richard. "The Origin, Art, and Message of the Bayeux Tapestry." In *The Study of the Bayeux Tapestry*, edited by Richard Gameson, 157–211. Woodbridge, UK: The Boydell Press, 1997.
Gardiner, Alan H. *The Kadesh Inscriptions of Ramesses II*. Oxford: Griffith Institute, 1960.
Gareau, Michel. *Charles Le Brun: First Painter to Louis XIV*. New York: Abrams, 1992.
Garrard, Timothy. "Benin Metal-Casting Technology." In *The Art of Power, The Power of Art: Studies in Benin Iconography*, edited by Paula Ben-Amos and Arnold Rubin, 17–20. Los Angeles: Museum of Cultural History, University of California, Los Angeles, 1983.
Gauer, W. *Untersuchungen zur Trajanssäule. Erster Teil Darstellungsprogramm und künstlerischer Entwurf. Monumenta Artis Romanae* 13. Berlin: Mann, 1977.
Geary, Patrick. "The Historical Material of Memory." In *Art, Memory, and Family in Renaissance Florence*, edited by Giovanni Ciappelli and Patricia Lee Rubin, 17–25. Cambridge: Cambridge University Press, 2000.
Gell, Alfred. *Art and Agency: An Anthropological Theory*. Oxford: Clarendon Press, 1998.
Gibson-Wood, Carol. *Jonathan Richardson: Art Theorist of the English Enlightenment*. London: Yale University Press, for the Paul Mellon Center for Studies in British Art, 2000.
Giglio, Giovanni Andrea. *Dialogue on the Errors and Abuses of Painters*. Edited by Michael Bury, Lucinda Byatt, and Carol M. Richardson, translated by Michael Bury and Lucinda Byatt. Los Angeles: Getty Publications, 2018.
Gombrich, Ernst H. *Art and Illusion. A Study in the Psychology of Pictorial Representation*. Princeton, NJ: Princeton University Press, 1960.
Gombrich, Ernst H. *Aby Warburg: An intellectual Biography*. Chicago: University of Chicago Press, 1986.
Grabar, Oleg. "Are Pictures Signs Yet?" *Semiotica* 25 (1979): 185–88.
Grafton, Anthony. "Historia and Istoria: Alberti's Terminology in Context." *I Tatti Studies in the Italian Renaissance* 8 (1999): 37–68.
Grape, Wolfgang. *The Bayeux Tapestry: Monument to a Norman Triumph*. Translated by David Britt. Munich: Prestel Publishing, 1994.
Green, David. "From History Painting to the History of Painting and Back Again: Reflections on the Work of Gerhard Richter." In *History Painting Reassessed. The Representation of History in Contemporary Art*, edited by David Green and Peter Seddon, 31–49. Manchester, UK: Manchester University Press, 2000.
Green, David, and Peter Seddon, eds. *History Painting Reassessed. The Representation of History in Contemporary Art*. Manchester, UK: Manchester University Press, 2000.
Griffiths, Gordon. "The Political Significance of Uccello's Battle of San Romano." *Journal of the Warburg and Courtauld Institutes* 41 (1978): 313–16.
Grilli, Elise. *Japanese Picture Scrolls*. London: Elek Books, 1959.
Groenewegen-Frankfort, Henriette Antonia. *Arrest and Movement: An Essay on Space and Time in the Representational Art of the Ancient Near East*. London: Faber and Faber, 1951.

Grossman, Loyd. *Bejamin West and the Struggle to be Modern*. New York: Merrell, 2015.

Gunsch, Kathryn Wysocki. *The Benin Plaques: A 16th-Centruy Imperial Monument*. London: Routledge, 2018.

Gunsch, Kathryn Wysocki. *Arts of Africa*. New York: Thames and Hudson, for the Museum of Fine Arts, Boston, 2019.

Habachi, Labib. *Features of the Deification of Ramesses II*. Glückstadt: J. J. Augustin, 1969.

Haeny, Gerhard. "New Kingdom 'Mortuary Temples' and 'Mansions of Millions of Years.'" In *Temples of Ancient Egypt*, edited by Byron E. Shafer, 86–126. Ithaca, NY: Cornell University Press, 1997.

Halbwachs, Maurice. *On Collective Memory*. Translated by Lewis A. Coser. Chicago: University of Chicago Press, 1992.

Hamberg, Per Gustaf. *Studies in Roman Imperial Art: with Special Reference to the State Reliefs of the Second Century*. Uppsala: Almqvist & Wiksells, 1945.

Hansen, D. P. "Art of the Akkadian Dynasty." In *Art of the First Cities: The Third Millennium B.C. from the Mediterranean to the Indus*, edited by Joan Aruz and Ronald Wallenfels, 189–209. New Haven, CT: Yale University Press, 2003.

Harper, Prudence O., and Pierre Amiet. "The Mesopotamian Presence: Mesopotamian Monuments Found at Susa." In *The Royal City of Susa: Ancient Near Eastern Treasures in the Louvre*, edited by Prudence O. Harper, Joan Aruz, and Françoise Tallon, 159–82. New York: Metropolitan Museum of Art 1992.

Harper, Prudence O., Joan Aruz, and Françoise Tallon, eds. *The Royal City of Susa: Ancient Near Eastern Treasures in the Louvre*. New York: Metropolitan Museum of Art, 1992.

Harrington, Peter. "Military History's Loss is Art History's Gain." *Quarterly Journal of Military History* 16, no. 1 (Autumn 2003): 44–49.

Harris, Enriqueta. *Velázquez*. Ithaca, NY: Cornell University Press, 1982.

Harth, Dietrich. "The Invention of Cultural Memory." In *A Companion to Cultural Memory Studies*, edited by Astrid Erll and Ansgar Nünning, 85–96. Berlin: Walter de Gruyter 2010.

Haskell, Francis. *Past and Present in Art and Taste. Selected Essays*. New Haven, CT: Yale University Press, 1987.

Haskell, Francis. *History and Its Images. Art and the Interpretation of the Past*. New Haven, CT: Yale University Press, 1993.

Healy, Mark. *Qadesh 1300 BC: Clash of the Warrior Kings*. Oxford: Osprey, 2001.

Heim, Suzanne. "Royal and Religious Structures and Their Decoration." In *The Royal City of Susa: Ancient Near Eastern Treasures in the Louvre*, edited by Prudence O. Harper, Joan Aruz, and Françoise Tallon, 123–27. New York: Metropolitan Museum of Art, 1992.

Hicks, Carola. *The Bayeux Tapestry: The Life Story of a Masterpiece*. London: Chatto & Windus, 2006.

Hicks, Dan. *The Brutish Museums. The Benin Bronzes, Colonial Violence and Cultural Restitution*. London: Pluto Press, 2020.

Hitt, Jack. "Atlanta's Famed Cyclorama Mural Will Tell the Truth About the Civil War Once Again." *Smithsonian Magazine* (December 2018): 64–75.

Hodgkin, Thomas, ed. *Nigerian Perspectives: An Historical Anthology*. Oxford: Oxford University Press, 1960.

Holliday, Peter J., ed. *Narrative and Event in Ancient Art*. Cambridge: Cambridge University Press, 1993.

Holliday, Peter J. *The Origins of Roman Historical Commemoration in the Visual Arts*. Cambridge: Cambridge University Press, 2002.

Holliday, Peter J. *American Arcadia: California and the Classical Tradition*. New York: Oxford University Press, 2016.

Hölscher, Tonio. *Griechische historienbilder des 5. Und 4. Jahrhunderts v. Cr*. Würzburg: Triltsch, 1973.

Hölscher, Tonio. *The Language of Images in Roman Art*. Translated by Anthony Snodgrass and Annemarie Künzl-Snodgrass, with a foreword by Jas Elsner. Cambridge: Cambridge University Press, 2004.

Holly, Michael Ann. *Panofsky and the Foundations of Art History*. Ithaca, NY: Cornell University Press, 1984.

Hoogstaten, Samuel van. *Samuel van Hoogstraten's Introduction to the Academy of Painting; or, the Visible World*. Edited by Celeste Brusati, translated by Jaap Jacobs. Los Angeles: Getty Research Institute, 2021.

Hudson, Hugh. *Paolo Uccello, Artist of the Florentine Renaissance Republic*. Saarbrücken, Germany: Verlag Dr. Muller Aktiengesellschaft & Co., 2008.

Hugo, Herman, S. J. *The Siege of Breda by the Armes of Phillip the Fourt vnder the gouernment of Isabella*. Translated by "CHG." Louanii: Ex officina Hastenii, 1627.

Hurwit, Jeffrey M. *The Acropolis in the Age of Pericles*. New York: Cambridge University Press, 2004.

Hurwit, Jeffrey M. "The Problem with Dexileos: Heroic and Other Nudities in Greek Art." *American Journal of Archaeology* 111 (January 2007): 35–60.

Ikeda, Shinobu. "The Image of Women in Battle Scenes: 'Sexually' Imprinted Bodies." In *Gender and Power in the Japanese Visual Field*, edited by Joshua S. Mostow, Norman Bryson, and Maribeth Graybill, 35–48. Honolulu: University of Hawaii Press, 2003.

Inalcik, Halil. "State, Sovereignty and Law during the Reign of Süleyman." In *Süleyman the Second and His Time*, edited by Halil Inalci and Cemal Kafadar, 229–48. Istanbul: Isis Press, 1993.

Inalcik, Halil, and Cemal Kafadar, eds. *Süleyman the Second and His Time*. Istanbul: Isis Press, 1993.

Inneh, Daniel. "The Guilds Working for the Palace." In *Benin Kings and Rituals: Court Arts from Nigeria*, edited by Barbara Plankensteiner, 103–17. Ghent: Snoek, 2007.

Ishii, Yukio. *Gunki monogatari ikusabito to kankyo: Shura no gunzo*. Tōkyō: Miyai Shoten, 2014.

Iwao, Seiichi, and Teizo Iyanaga. *Dictionnaire historique du Japon*. Maisonneuve et Larose, 2002.

Janney, Caroline E. *Remembering the Civil War: Reunion and the Limits of Reconciliation*. Chapel Hill: University of North Carolina Press, 2013.

Janouch, Gustav. *Conversations with Kafka*. Translated by Goronwy Rees. New York: Frederick A. Praeger, 1953.

Jobert, Barthélémy. *Delacroix*. New and expanded English ed. Princeton, NJ: Princeton University Press, 2018.

Johns, Catherine. "Art, Romanisation, and Competence." In *Roman Imperialism and Provincial Art*, edited by Sarah Scott and Jane Webster, 9–23. New York: Cambridge University Press, 2003.

Jones, Mark Wilson. "One Hundred Feet and a Spiral Stair: The Problem of Designing Trajan's Column." *Journal of Roman Archaeology* 6 (1993): 23–38.

Joubin, André. *Journal de Eugène Delacroix. Publiée d'après le manuscrit original avec une introduction et des notes par André Joubin*, 3 vols. Paris: Plon, 1932.

Judt, Daniel. "Cyclorama: An Atlanta Monument." *Southern Cultures* 23 (Summer 2017): 23–48.

Judt, Daniel. "Atlanta's Civil War Monument, Minus the Pro-Confederate Bunkum." *The Atlantic*, March 2019.

Justi, Carl. *Diego Velázquez and His Times*. Translated by A.H. Keane, and revised by the author. London: H. Grevel & Co., 1889.

Kafadar, Cemal. "The Myth of the Golden Age: Ottoman Historical Consciousness in the Post-Süleymanic Era." In *Süleyman the Second and His Time*, edited by Halil Inalci and Cemal Kafadar, 37–48. Istanbul: Isis Press, 1993.

Kafadar, Cemal. "A Rome of One's Own: Reflections on Cultural Geography and Identity in the Lands of Rum." *Muqarnas* 24 (2007): 7–25.

Kamensky, Jane. *A Revolution in Color. The World of John Singleton Copley*. New York: Norton, 2016.

Kemp, Martin. *Leonardo*. New York: Oxford University Press, 2004.

Kennedy, J. "The East." In *The Roman World*, edited by John Wacher, 266–308. Hoboken, NJ: Taylor and Francis, 2013.

Kessler, Herbert L., and Mary Shreve Simpson, eds. *Pictorial Narrative in Antiquity and the Middle Ages*. Washington, DC: National Gallery of Art, 1985.

Kleinfelder, Karen L. "Monstrous Oppositions." In *Picasso and the Mediterranean*, published in conjunction with an exhibition of the same name at the Louisiana Museum of Modern Art,

September 20, 1996–January 19, 1997. Humlebaek, Denmark: Louisiana Museum of Modern Art, 1996: 22–33.

Krstic, Tijana. "Conversion and Converts to Islam in Ottoman Historiography of the Fifteenth and Sixteenth Centuries." In *Writing History at the Ottoman Court: Editing the Past, Fashioning the Future*, edited by H. Erdem Çipa and Emıne Fetvaci, 58–79. Bloomington: Indiana University Press, 2013.

Lancaster, Lynne. "Building Trajan's Column." *American Journal of Archaeology* 103, no. 3 (1999): 419–39.

Lancelot, [Antoine]. "Suite de l'Explication d'un Monument de Guillaume le Conquérant" (May 9, 1730), *Memoires de littérature tirez des Registres de l'Académie Royale des Inscriptions et Belles-Lettres*, VIII. Paris 1733: 602–68.

Larrea, Juan. *Guernica*. Translated by Alexander H. Krappe and edited by Walter Pach, with an introduction by Alfred H. Barr. New York: C. Valentin, 1947.

Lawal, Babatunde. "The Present State of Art Historical Research in Nigeria: Problems and Possibilities." *Journal of African History* 18, no. 2 (1977): 193–216.

Layiwola, Adepeju. "The Benin Massacre: Memories and Experiences." In *Benin Kings and Rituals: Court Arts from Nigeria*, edited by Barbara Plankensteiner, 83–89. Ghent: Snoek, 2007.

Lee, Rensselaer W. "Ut pictura poesis: The Humanistic Theory of Painting." *Art Bulletin* 22, no. 4 (1940): 197–269.

Lehmann-Hartleben, Karl. *Die Trajanssäule. Ein römisches Kunstwerk zu Beginn der Spätantike*. Berlin and Leipzig: W. de Gruyter & Co., 1926.

Leick, Gwendolyn. *Mesopotamia: The Invention of the City*. New York: Penguin, 2003.

Lemagnen, Sylvette. "The Hidden Face of the Bayeux Tapestry." In *The Bayeux Tapestry. New Approaches: The Proceedings of a Conference at the British Museum*, edited by Michael John Lewis, Gale R. Owen-Crocker, and Dan Terkla, 37–43. Oxford: Oxbow Books, 2011.

Lendon, J. E. *Soldiers and Ghosts: A History of Battle in Classical Antiquity*. New Haven, CT: Yale University Press, 2006.

Levine, Robert S., ed. *The Norton Anthology of American Literature, Vol. A, Beginnings to 1820*, 9th ed. New York: Norton, 2017.

Lichtheim, Miriam. *Ancient Egyptian Literature, Vol. 2: The New Kingdom*. Berkeley: University of California Press, 1978.

Liverani, Paolo, Michael Pfanner, Stephanie Langer, and Frederike Fless. *Katalog der Skulpturen IV: Historische Reliefs*, Monumenta Artis Romanae 40. Wiesbaden: Dr. Ludwig Reichert Verlag, 2018.

Lloyd, Seton. *The Archaeology of Mesopotamia. From the Old Stone Age to the Persian Conquest*. London: Thames & Hudson, 1978.

Locquin, Jean. *La peinture d'histoire en France de 1747 à 1785: étude sur l'évolution des idées artistiques dans la seconde moitié du XVIIIe siècle*. Paris: H. Laurens, 1912.

López-Rey, José. *Velázquez' Work and World*. Greenwich, CT: New York Graphic Society, 1968.

Lowry, Joanna. "History, Allegory, Technologies of Vision." In *History Painting Reassessed. The Representation of History in Contemporary Art*, edited by David Green and Peter Seddon, 95–111. Manchester, UK: Manchester University Press, 2000.

Lubin, David M. *Grand Illusions: American Art and the First World War*. New York: Oxford University Press, 2016.

Lyttelton, George Lord. *The History of the Life of King Henry the Second, and of the Age in which he lived, in five books*, 3rd ed., 5 vols. London: printed for J. Dodsley, in Pall Mall,1769.

Machiavelli, Niccolò. *The Prince*. Translated with an introduction by George Bull. New York: Penguin, 1981.

Mackenzie, Alexander. *History of the Frasers of Lovat, with Genealogies of the Principal Families of the Name: to which is added those of Dunballoch and Phopachy*. Inverness: A&W Mackenzie, 1896.

MacNamidhe, Margaret. *Delacroix and his Forgotten World. The Origins of Romantic Painting*. London: I. B. Tauris and Co., 2015.

MacQuitty, William. *Abu Simbel*. New York: G. P. Putnam's Sons, 1965.

Mamassian, Pascal. "Ambiguities and Conventions in the Perception of Visual Art." *Vision Research* 48, no. 20 (September 2008): 2143–53.

Marin, Louis. "Toward and Theory of Reading in the Visual Arts: Poussin's *The Arcadian Shepherds*." In *The Reader in the Text*, edited by S. R. Suleiman and I. Crossman, 293–324. Princeton, NJ: Princeton University Press, 1980.

Martin, Russell. *Picasso's War*. London: Simon & Schuster, 2003.

Martin, Therese, ed. *Reassessing the Roles of Woman as "Makers" of Medieval Art and Architecture*, 2 vols. Leiden: Brill, 2013.

Martínez, Jusepe. *Practical Discourses on the Most Noble Art of Painting*. Translated by David McGrath and Zahira Véliz. Los Angeles: Getty Research Institute, 2017.

Mason, Penelope E. *A Reconstruction of the Hogen-Heiji Monogatari Emaki*. New York: Garland Publishing, 1977.

Mason, Penelope E., and Donald Dinwiddie. *History of Japanese Art*. Saddle River, NJ: Pearson Prentice Hall, 2005.

McCormick, Melissa. *The Tale of Genji: A Visual Commentary*. Princeton, NJ: Princeton University Press: 2018.

McNamara, Carol. *Benjamin West: General Wolfe and the Art of Empire*. Ann Arbor: University of Michigan Museum of Art, 2012.

Meiss, Millard. *Painting in Florence and Siena after the Black Death: The Arts, Religion, and Society in the Mid-Fourteenth Century*. Princeton, NJ: Princeton University Press, 1951.

Michel, Christian. *The Académie Royale de Peinture et de Sculpture: The Birth of the French School, 1648–1793*. Translated by Chris Miller. Los Angeles: Getty Research Institute, 2020.

Millen, Ronald, and Robert Erich Wolf. *Heroic Deeds and Mystic Figures: A New Reading of Rubens' Life of Maria de' Medici*. Princeton, NJ: Princeton University Press, 1989.

Mills, Cynthia, and Pamela Simpson. *Monuments to the Lost Cause: Women, Art, and the Landscape of Southern Memory*. Knoxville: University of Tennessee Press, 2003.

Minardi, Mauro. *Paolo Uccello*. Milan: 24 ore cultura, 2017.

Mitchell, Charles. "Benjamin West's *Death of General Wolfe* and the Popular History Piece." *Journal of Warburg and Courtauld Institutes* 7 (1944): 20–33.

Mitchell, William John Thomas. *Iconology: Image, Text, Ideology*. Chicago: University of Chicago Press, 1986.

Moffitt, John F. "Diego Velazquez, Andrea Alciati and *The Surrender of Breda*." *Artibus et Historiae* 3, no. 5 (1982): 75–90.

Monroe, J. C. "Power by Design: Architecture and Politics in Precolonial Dahomey." *Journal of Social Archaeology* 10 (2010): 477–507.

Montagna, Dennis. "Benjamin West's *The Death of General Wolfe*: A Nationalist Narrative." *American Art Journal* 13, no. 2 (1981): 72–88.

Montfaucon, Bernard de. *Les monumens de la Monarchie française, qui comprennent l'Histoire de France, avec figures de chaque regne, que l'injure des tems a epargnées*, 5 vols. Paris: Julien-Michel Gandouin et Pierre-François Giffart, 1729–1733.

Moscati, Sabatino. "Le origini della narrativa storica nell'arte del Vicino Oriente antico." *Memorie della Accademia Nazionale dei Lincei* Series VI 10 (1961): 4–100.

Murase, Miyeko. *L'Art du Japon*. Paris: Éditions LGF, Livre de Poche, 1996.

Murnane, William J. *The Road to Kadesh. A Historical Interpretation of the Battle Reliefs of King Seti I at Karnak*. Chicago: Oriental Institute of Chicago/University of Chicago, 1985.

Murphey, Rhoads. *Exploring Ottoman Sovereignty: Tradition, Image and Practice in the Ottoman Imperial Household, 1400–1800*. London: Continuum, 2008.

Musée national d'art modern France. *1937: Exposition Internationale des Arts et des Techniques*, catalogue of an exhibition held at the Centre Georges Pompidou 13 Juin-20 Août 1979. Paris: Centre Georges Pompidou, 1979. [Contains short essays by Le Corbusier, Léger, Aragon, Robert Delaunay, André Breton, and Amédée Ozenfant.]

Museum für Völkerkunde zu Leipzig. *Kunst aus Benin. Afrikanische Meisterwerke aus der Sammlung Hans Meyer*. Leipzig: Museum für Völkerkunde zu Leipzig: Grassimuseum, 1994.

Musset, Lucien. *The Bayeux Tapestry*. Translated by Richard Rex. Woodbridge, UK: The Boydell Press, 2005.

Nafziger, George F., and Mark W. Walton. *Islam at War: A History*. Westport, CT: Praeger, 2003.

Nagazumi, Yasuaki. *Gunki monogatari no sekai*. Tōkyō: Iwanami Shoten, 2002.

Necipoğlu, Gülru. *Architecture, Ceremonial, and Power: The Topkapi Palace in the Fifteenth and Sixteenth Centuries*. Cambridge, MA: Architectural History Foundation and the MIT Press, 1991.

Necipoğlu, Gülru. "A Kānūn for the State, A Canon for the Arts: Conceptualizing the Classical Synthesis of Ottoman Art and Architecture." In *Soliman le magnifique et son temps*, edited by Giles Veinstein, 159–77. Paris: Documentation Française, 1992.

Necipoğlu, Gülru. *The Age of Sinan: Architectural Culture in the Ottoman Empire*. Princeton, NJ: Princeton University Press, 2005.

Neff, Emily Ballew. "A 'Dreadful Apparatus': John Singleton Copley's *Watson and the Shark* and the Cultures of Natural History." In *Framing the Ocean, 1700 to the Present. Envisaging the Sea as Social Space*, edited by Tricia Cusack, 195–210. New York: Routledge, 2014.

Nevadomsky, Joseph. "Contemporary Art and Artists in Benin City." *African Arts* 30, no. 4 (1997): 54–63.

Nigro, Lorenzo. "The Two Steles of Sargon: Iconology and Visual Propaganda at the Beginning of Royal Akkadian Relief." *Iraq* 60 (1998): 85–102.

Nissen, Hans J. *The Early History of the Ancient Near East, 9000–2000 BC*. Translated by Elizabeth Lutzeier and Kenneth J. Northcott. Chicago: University of Chicago Press, 1988.

Ockinga, Boyo. "On the Interpretation of the Kadesh Record." *Chronique d'Égyptologie* 62 (1987): 38–48.

Orderic Vitalis. *The Ecclesiastical History of Orderic Vitalis*, 6 vols. Edited and translated by Marjorie Chibnall. Oxford: Clarendon Press, 1969–1980.

Okudaira, Hideo. *Narrative Picture Scrolls*. Translated by Elizabeth Ten Grotenhuis. Trumbull, CT: Weatherhill, 1973.

Oppler, Ellen C., ed. *Picasso's Guernica*. New York: Norton, 1988.

Owen-Crocker, Gale R. "Reading the Bayeux Tapestry through Canterbury Eyes." In *The Bayeux Tapestry: Collected Papers*, 243–65. Farnham, UK: Ashgate Variorum, 2012.

Packer, James E. *The Forum of Trajan in Rome: A Study of the Monuments*, 3 vols. Berkeley: University of California Press, 1997.

Palomino de Castro y Velasco, Antonio. *El Museo Pictorico y Escala Optica*. Madrid: Por L. A. de Bedmar, impressor del reyno, 1715–1724 [translated in Enriqueta Harris, *Velázquez*. Ithaca, NY: Cornell University Press, 1982].

Panofsky, Erwin. *Studies in Iconology: Humanistic Themes in the Art of the Renaissance*. New York: Oxford University Press, 1939.

Panofsky, Erwin, and Fritz Saxl. "Classical Mythology in Early Medieval Art." *Metropolitan Museum Studies* 4 (1932–1933): 228–80.

Parkman, Francis. *Montcalm and Wolfe*. Boston: Little, Brown and Company, 1884.

Pastan, Elizabeth Carson. "Imagined Patronage." In *The Bayeux Tapestry and Its Contexts: A Reassessment*, edited by Elizabeth Carson Pastan and Stephen D. White, 59–81. Woodbridge, UK: The Boydell Press, 2014a.

Pastan, Elizabeth Carson. "Representing Architecture." In *The Bayeux Tapestry and Its Contexts: A Reassessment*, edited by Elizabeth Carson Pastan and Stephen D. White, 183–209. Woodbridge, UK: The Boydell Press, 2014b.

Pastan, Elizabeth Carson, and Stephen D. White with Kate Gilbert. *The Bayeux Tapestry and Its Contexts: A Reassessment*. Woodbridge, UK: The Boydell Press, 2014.

Pedersen, Johannes. *The Arabic Book*. Translated by Geoffrey French, edited with an introduction by Robert Hillenbrand. Princeton, NJ: Princeton University Press, 1984.

Phillips, Mark Salber. "History Painting Redistanced. From Benjamin West to David Wilkie." In *What Was History Painting and What Is It Now?*, edited by Mark Salber Phillips and Jordan Bear, 67–85. Montreal: McGill-Queens Press, 2019.

Phillips, Mark Salber, and Jordan Bear, eds. *What Was History Painting and What Is It Now?* Montreal: McGill-Queens Press, 2019.

Plankensteiner, Barbara. "Benin-Kings and Rituals: Court Arts from Nigeria." *African Arts* 40, no. 4 (2007a): 74–87.

Plankensteiner, Barbara. "Introduction." In *Benin Kings and Rituals: Court Arts from Nigeria*, edited by Barbara Plankensteiner, 21–39. Ghent: Snoek, 2007b.

Plankensteiner, Barbara. *Benin: Visions of Africa*. Milano: 5 Continents, 2010.

Podlecki, Anthony J. "The Political Significance of the Athenian 'Tyrannicide-Cult.'" *Historia: Zeitschrift für Alte Geschichte* 15 (April 1966): 129–41.

Polastron, Lucien X. *Books on Fire: The Tumultuous Story of the World's Great Libraries*. London: Thames & Hudson, 2007.

Pollitt, J. J. *Art and Experience in Classical Greece*. Cambridge: Cambridge University Press, 1972.

Pollitt, J. J. *Art in the Hellenistic Age*. New York: Cambridge University Press, 1986.

Pollitt, J. J. *The Art of Ancient Greece: Sources and Documents*. New York: Cambridge University Press, 1990.

Pope-Hennessy, John. *Paolo Uccello*. New York and London: Phaidon, 1969.

Preston, Paul. "George Steer and *Guernica*." *History Today* 57, no. 5 (2007): 12–19.

Pritchard, James B. "The Asiatic Campaigning of Ramses II." In *Ancient Near Eastern Texts: Relating to the Old Testament*, 255–56. Princeton, NJ: Princeton University Press, 1969.

Proctor-Tiffany, Mariah. *Medieval Art in Motion: The Inventory and Gift Giving of Queen Clémence de Hongrie*. University Park, PA: The Pennsylvania State University Press, 2019.

Prown, Jules D. *John Singleton Copley*, 2 vols. Cambridge, MA: Harvard University Press, 1966.

Prown, Jules. *American Painting from Its Beginnings to the Armory Show*. Introduction by John Walker. Cleveland: World Publishing Company, 1969.

Prown, Jules D. "Benjamin West and the Use of Antiquity." *American Art* 10, no. 2 (1996): 28–49.

Ralby, Aaron. "Battle of Kadesh, c. 1274 BCE: Clash of Empires." In *Atlas of Military History: An Around-the-World Survey of Warfare through the Ages*, edited by Amanda Lomazoff and Aaron Ralby, 54–55. San Diego: Thunder Bay Press, 2013.

Rather, Susan. "Benjamin West, John Galt, and the Biography of 1816." *The Art Bulletin* 86, no. 2 (June 2004): 324–45.

Ray, Beverly. "Analyzing Political Art to Get at Historical Fact: *Guernica* and the Spanish Civil War." *The Social Studies* 97, no. 4 (2006): 168–71.

Read, C. H., and O. M. Dalton. *Antiquities of the City of Benin and from Other Parts of West Africa in the British Museum* London: William Clowes and Sons, Ltd., 1899.

Rebora, Carrie. "Copley and Art History: The Study of America's First Old Master." In *John Singleton Copley in America*, edited by Carrie Rebora, Paul Staiti, Erica E. Hirshler, Theodore E. Stebbins Jr., and Carol Troyen, 3–23. New York: Metropolitan Museum of Art, distributed by Harry N. Abrams, 1996.

Reed, Christopher. *Bachelor Japanists: Japanese Aesthetics and Western Masculinities*. New York: Columbia University Press, 2017.

Reilly, Lisa. *The Invention of Norman Visual Culture: Art, Politics, and Dynastic Ambition*. Cambridge: Cambridge University Press, 2020.

Reischauer, Edwin O., and Joseph K. Yamagiwa. *Translations from Early Japanese Literature*. Cambridge, MA: Published for the Harvard-Yenching Institute by the Harvard University Press, 1951.

Reynolds, Joshua. *Discourses on Art*. Edited by Robert R. Wark. San Marino, CA: Huntington Library, 1959.

Richardson, John. "A Different Guernica." *The New York Review of Books* 63, no. 8 (May 12, 2016): 4–6.

Richardson, Jonathan. *An Essay on the Theory of Painting*. London: W. Bowyer, for John Churchill, 1715.

Riding, Christine. "The Raft of the Medusa in Britain." In *Crossing the Channel: British and French Painting in the Age of Romanticism*, edited by Patrick Noon and Stephen Bann, 66–73. London: Tate Publishing, 2003.

Rieff, David. *In Praise of Forgetting. Historical Memory and Its Ironies* New Haven, CT: Yale University Press, 2016.

Robins, Gay. *The Art of Ancient Egypt*. London: British Museum Press, 1997.

Rockwell, Peter. "Preliminary Study of the Carving Techniques on the Column of Trajan." In *Marmi Antichi:problemi d'impiego, di restauro e d'identificazione*, edited by Patrizio Pensabene, 101–11. *Studi Miscellanei* 26. Roma: "L'Erma" di Bretshchneider, 1985.

Roman, Cynthia Ellen. "James Gillray's *The Death of the Great Wolfe* and the Satiric Alternative to History Painting." In *What Was History Painting and What Is It Now?*, edited by Mark Salber Phillips and Jordan Bear, 90–110. Montreal: McGill-Queens Press, 2019.

Rosellini, Ippolito. *I monumenti dell'Egitto e della Nubia disegnati dalla spedizione scientifico-letteraria toscana in Egitto*, 9 vols. Pisa: Presso N. Capurro e c., 1832–44.

Rosenheim, Jeff L. *Photography and the American Civil War*. New Haven, CT: Yale University Press, for the Metropolitan Museum of Art, 2013.

Rossi, Lino. *Trajan's Column and the Dacian Wars*. Translated and revised by J. M. C. Toynbee. Ithaca, NY: Cornell University Press, 1971.

Rossi, Lino. "A Historiographic Reassessment of the Metopes of the Tropaeum Traiani at Adamklissi." *Archaeological Journal* 129, no. 1 (1972): 56–68.

Roth, Henry Ling. *Great Benin: Its Customs, Art and Horrors*. New York: Barnes & Noble, 1968 [reprint of Halifax (England): F. King and Sons, 1903].

Rubin, James H. "Manet's Heroic Corpses and the Politics of Their Time." In *Perspectives on Manet*, edited by Therese Dolan, 119–38. Burlington, VT: Ashgate Publishing Company, 2012.

Rubin, Patricia Lee. "Art and the Imagery of Memory." In *Art, Memory, and Family in Renaissance Florence*, edited by Giovanni Ciappelli and Patricia Lee Rubin, 67–85. Cambridge: Cambridge University Press, 2000.

Rubin, Patricia Lee. *Images and Identity in Fifteenth-Century Florence*. New Haven, CT: Yale University Press, 2007.

Rubin, William, ed. *Pablo Picasso: A Retrospective*. New York and Boston: Museum of Modern Art and New York Graphic Society, 1980.

Rumpf, Andreas. "Zum Alexander-Mosaik." *Mitteilungen des Deutschen Archäologischen Instituts, Athenische Abteilung* 77 (1962): 229–41.

Ryder, Alan Frederick Charles. *Benin and the Europeans, 1485–1897*. Harlow: Longmans, 1969.

Said, Edward W. *Orientalism*. New York: Random House, 1978.

Said, Edward W. *Culture and Imperialism*. New York: Knopf, 1993.

Saint-Marc, Elsa. "Techniques de composition de l'espace dans l'*Ippen hijiri-e*." *Arts Asiatiques* 56, no. 1 (2001): 91–109.

Säve-Söderbergh, Torgny. *Temples and Tombs of Ancient Nubia. The International Rescue Campaign at Abu Simbel, Philae and Other Sites*. London: Thames and Hudson, for UNESCO, 1987.

Saward, Susan. *The Golden Age of Marie de' Medici*. Ann Arbor: UMI Research Press, 1982.

Saxl, Fritz. "Velázquez and Philip IV." In *Lectures* 1, 311–24. London: Warburg Institute, University of London, 1957.

Schama, Simon. *Dead Certainties: Unwarranted Speculations*. New York: Knopf, 1991.

Schama, Simon. *The Power of Art*. London, Bodley Head, 2009.

Schjeldahl, Peter. "The Reign in Spain: Velazquez and the King." *The New Yorker*, January 2, 2011.

Schmandt-Besserat, Denise. *Before Writing: From Counting to Cuneiform and How Writing Came About*. Austin: University of Texas Press, 1992.

Schmandt-Besserat, Denise. *When Writing Met Art: From Symbol to Story*. Austin: University of Texas Press, 2007.

Schulman, A. R. "Diplomatic Marriage in the Egyptian New Kingdom." *Journal of Near Eastern Studies* 38, no. 3 (1979): 177–93.

Scott, Sarah. "Provincial Art and Roman Imperialism: An Overview." In *Roman Imperialism and Provincial Art*, edited by Sarah Scott and Jane Webster, 1–7. New York: Cambridge University Press, 2003.

Scott, Sarah, and Jane Webster, eds. *Roman Imperialism and Provincial Art*. New York: Cambridge University Press, 2003.

Searle, John Rogers. "*Las Meninas* and the Paradoxes of Pictorial Representation." *Critical Inquiry* 6 (1980): 477–88.

Seckel, Dietrich, and Akihisa Hasé. *Emaki*. Translated by Armel. Gueme. Paris: Delpire, 1959.

Seige, Christine. "238. Relief Plaque: Battle Scene." In *Benin Kings and Rituals: Court Arts from Nigeria*, edited by Barbara Plankensteiner, 457. Ghent: Snoek, 2007.

Shapiro, H. Alan. *Personifications in Greek Art: The Representations of Abstract Concepts, 600–400 B.C.* Zurich: Akanthus, 1993.

Shear, Julia L. *Serving Athena: The Festival of the Panathenaia and the Construction of Athenian Identities*. Cambridge: Cambridge University Press, 2021.

Smith, A. Mark. "The Latin Source of the Fourteenth-Century Italian Translation of Alhacen's *De aspectibus* (Vat. Lat. 4595)." *Arabic Sciences and Philosophy* 11, no. 1 (2001): 27–43.

Solkin, David H. *Painting for Money: The Visual Arts and the Public Sphere in Eighteenth-Century England*. New Haven, CT: Yale University Press, for the Paul Mellon Centre for Studies in British Art, 1993.

Sontag, Susan. *On Photography*. New York: Farrar, Straus and Giroux, 1977.

Spalinger, Anthony J. *Icons of Power. A Strategy of Reinterpretation*. Prague: Charles University, Faculty of Arts, 2011.

Spencer, Diana. *The Roman Alexander: Reading a Cultural Myth*. Exeter: University of Exeter Press, 2002.

Stafford, Pauline. *Queen Emma and Queen Edith: Queenship and Women's Power in Eleventh-Century England*. Oxford: Blackwell Publishers, 1997.

Staley, Allen. *Benjamin West: American Painter at the English Court*, catalogue of an exhibition held at the Baltimore Museum of Art: June 4–August 20, 1989. Baltimore: Baltimore Museum of Art, 1989.

Starn, Randolph, and Loren Partridge. "Representing War in the Renaissance: The Shield of Paolo Uccello." *Representations* 5 (Winter 1984): 33–65.

Steinbock, Bernd. *Social Memory in Athenian Public Discourse: Uses and Meanings of the Past*. Ann Arbor: University of Michigan Press, 2013.

Stewart, Andrew. *Faces of Power. Alexander's Image and Hellenistic Politics*. Berkeley: University of California Press, 1993.

Stewart, Andrew. *Art, Desire, and the Body in Ancient Greece*. Cambridge: Cambridge University Press, 1997.

Stewart, Andrew. *Classical Greece and the Birth of Western Art*. New York: Cambridge University Press, 2008.

Stock, Ann-Kathrin, Hannah Gajsar, and Onur Güntürkün. "The Neuroscience of Memory." In *Memory in Ancient Rome and Early Christianity*, edited by Karl Galinsky, 369–91. Oxford: Oxford University Press, 2016.

Stoneman, Richard. *Alexander the Great: A Life in Legend*. New Haven, CT: Yale University Press, 2008.

Suzuki, Keizō. *Shoki Emakimono no Fūzoku Shiteki Kenkyū*. Tōkyō: Yoshikawa Kōbunkan, 1960.

Taylor, Michael W. *The Tyrant Slayers: The Heroic Image in Fifth Century B.C. Athenian Art and Politics*, 2nd ed. Salem, NH: Ayer, 1991.

Thomas, Hugh. *The Norman Conquest*. Lanham, MD: Rowman and Littlefield, 2008.

Thompson, Robert Farris. *African Art in Motion: Icon and Act*. Los Angeles: University of California Press, 1974.

Tóibín, Colm. "The Art of War." *The Guardian*, April 29, 2006.

Tomita, Kojiro. "The Burning of the Sanjô Palace (*Heiji Monogatari*): A Japanese Scroll of the Thirteenth Century." *Museum of Fine Arts Bulletin* 23 (October 1925): 49–55.

Triandafyllidou, Anna. "National Identity and the Other." *Ethnic and Racial Studies* 21, no. 4 (1998): 593–612.

Tyldesley, Joyce. *Ramesses II: Egypt's Greatest Pharaoh*. London: Viking, 2000.

Tyler, Elizabeth M. *England in Europe: English Royal Women and Literary Patronage, c. 1000–1150*. Toronto: University of Toronto Press, 2017.

Utley, Gertje R. "From Guernica to The Charnel House: The Political Radicalization of the Artist." In *Picasso and the War Years: 1937–1945*, edited by Steven A. Nash with Robert Rosenblum, 69–79. New York: Thames and Hudson, for the Fine Arts Museums of San Francisco and the Solomon R. Guggenheim Museum, 1999.

Van den Hout, Theo P. J. *The Elements of Hittite*. New York: Cambridge University Press, 2011.

Varley, Paul. *Warriors of Japan as Portrayed in the War Tales*. Honolulu: University of Hawaii Press, 1994.

Vasari, Giorgio. *The Lives of the Artists*. Translated with an introduction and notes by Julia Conaway Bondanella and Peter Bondanella. Oxford: Oxford University Press, 1991.

Veinstein, Giles, ed. *Soliman le magnifique et son temps*. Paris: Documentation Française, 1992.

Vijgen, Theo. *The Cultural Parameters of the Graeco-Roman War Discourse*. Turnhout: Brepols, 2020.

Walton, Jeremy F. "Sanitizing Szigetvár: On the Post-Imperial Fashioning of Nationalist Memory." *History and Anthropology* 30, no. 4 (2019): 434–47.

Weitzmann, Kurt. *Illustrations in Roll and Codex: A Study of the Origin and Method of Text Illustration*. Princeton, NJ: Princeton University Press, 1947.

Weitzmann, Kurt. *The Joshua Roll: A Work of the Macedonian Renaissance*. Princeton, NJ: Princeton University Press, 1948.

Westenholz, Joan Goodnick. *Legends of the Kings of Akkade: The Texts*. Winona Lake, IN: Eisenbrauns, 1997.

White, Hayden V. "The Burden of History." In *Tropics of Discourse: Essays in Cultural Criticism*, 27–50. Baltimore: Johns Hopkins University Press, 1978.

White, Hayden V. "The Narrativization of Real Events." In *On Narrative*, edited by W. J. T. Mitchell, 1–23. Chicago: University of Chicago Press, 1981.

White, Stephen D. "Is the Beaux Embroidery a Record of Events?" In *The Bayeux Tapestry and Its Contexts: A Reassessment*, edited by Elizabeth Carson Pastan and Stephen D. White, 32–58. Woodbridge, UK: The Boydell Press, 2014a.

White, Stephen D. "The Prosopography of the Bayeux Embroidery and the Community of St Augustine's, Canterbury." In *The Bayeux Tapestry and Its Contexts: A Reassessment*, edited by Elizabeth Carson Pastan and Stephen D. White, 82–104. Woodbridge, UK: The Boydell Press, 2014b.

Wickhoff, Franz. *Roman Art. Some of its Principles and their Application to Early Christian Painting*. Translated and edited by Mrs. S. Arthur Strong. New York: Macmillan Company, 1900.

Wilkinson, Richard H. *The Complete Temples of Ancient Egypt*. London: Thames and Hudson, 2000.

Willett, Frank. *African Art: An Introduction*. New York: Praeger, 1971.

Willett, Frank. "Benin." In *Afrika: Kunst und Kultur. Meisterwerke afrikanischer Kunst Museum für Völkerkunde Berlin*, edited by Hans- Joachim Koloss, 41–46, 199–202. Munich: Prestel, 1999.

Wilson-Bareau, Juliet, with essays by John House and Douglas Johnson. *Manet: The Execution of Maximilian, Painting, Politics, and Censorship*. London: National Gallery Publications, 1992.

Wind, Edgar. "The Revolution of History Painting." *Journal of the Warburg Institute* 2, no. 2 (1938–1939): 116–27.

Winter, Irene J. "After the Battle Is Over: The Stele of the Vultures and the Beginning of the Historical Narrative in the Art of the Ancient Near East." In *Pictorial Narrative in Antiquity and the Middle Ages*, edited by Herbert L. Kessler and Mary Shreve Simpson, 11–32. Washington, DC: National Gallery of Art, 1985.

Winter, Irene J. "Sex, Rhetoric, and the Public Monument. The Alluring Body of Naram-Sîn of Agade." In *Sexuality in Ancient Art. Near East, Egypt, Greece, and Italy*, edited by Natalie Boymel Kampen, 11–26. Cambridge: Cambridge University Press, 1996.

Wood, Jeremy. *Rubens: Copies and Adaptations from Renaissance and Later Artists*, 2 vols. London: Harvey Miller, 2011.

Woodhead, Christine. "An Experiment in Official Historiography: The Post of *Şehnāmeci* in the Ottoman Empire, c. 1555–1605." *Wiener Zeitschrift für die Kunde des Morgenlandes* 75 (1983): 157–82.

Yates, David C. *States of Memory: The Polis, Panhellenism, and the Persian War*. Oxford: Oxford University Press, 2019.

Young, James E. *The Texture of Memory: Holocaust Memorials and Meaning*. New Haven, CT: Yale University Press, 1993.

Zanker, Paul. *The Power of Images in the Age of Augustus*. Translated by Alan Shapiro. Ann Arbor: University of Michigan Press, 1988.

Index

For the benefit of digital users, indexed terms that span two pages (e.g., 52–53) may, on occasion, appear on only one of those pages.

Figures in this index are indicated by *f* following the page number